ZOO STUDIES

ZOO STUDIES
A New Humanities

Edited by
Tracy McDonald
and
Daniel Vandersommers

McGill-Queen's University Press
Montreal & Kingston • **London** • **Chicago**

ISBN 978-0-7735-5690-4 (cloth)
ISBN 978-0-7735-5691-1 (paper)
ISBN 978-0-7735-5815-1 (ePDF)
ISBN 978-0-7735-5816-8 (ePUB)

Legal deposit second quarter 2019
Bibliothèque nationale du Québec

Printed in Canada on acid-free paper that is 100% ancient forest free
(100% post-consumer recycled), processed chlorine free

We acknowledge the support of the Canada Council for the Arts, which
last year invested $153 million to bring the arts to Canadians throughout
the country.

Nous remercions le Conseil des arts du Canada de son soutien. L'an
dernier, le Conseil a investi 153 millions de dollars pour mettre de l'art
dans la vie des Canadiennes et des Canadiens de tout le pays.

Library and Archives Canada Cataloguing in Publication

Title: Zoo studies : a new humanities / edited by Tracy McDonald and
    Daniel Vandersommers.
Other titles: Zoo studies (2019)
Names: McDonald, Tracy, 1966– editor. | Vandersommers, Daniel,
    1984– editor.
Description: Includes bibliographical references and index.
Identifiers: Canadiana (print) 20190065044 | Canadiana (ebook)
    20190065052 | ISBN 9780773556904 (hardcover) | ISBN
    9780773556911 (softcover) | ISBN 9780773558151 (ePDF) | ISBN
    9780773558168 (ePUB)
Subjects: LCSH: Zoos—Philosophy. | LCSH: Zoos—Social aspects. | LCSH:
    Zoos—Moral and ethical aspects. | LCSH: Animals and civilization. |
    LCSH: Human-animal relationships. | LCSH: Humanities—Philosophy.
Classification: LCC QL76 .Z66 2019 | DDC 590.73—dc23

"The crickets might move with us, the branches and underbrush appear to be full of them, full of high Cs and Ds. They can reach as high as an F at the end of summer when they are laying eggs. Their cries seem to fall on you from above, don't they? It feels like an important night for them. Remember that. Your own story is just one, and perhaps not the important one. The self is not the principal thing."

– Michael Ondaatje, *Warlight*

CONTENTS

Figures | ix
Acknowledgments | xiii

Introduction | 3
Daniel Vandersommers and Tracy McDonald

1 Psychotic Humans, Psychotic Animals: The Zoo
and the Mental Hospital, 1656–1794 | 19
Matthew Senior

2 The Antelope Collectors | 45
Nigel Rothfels

3 Failed Zoo Experiments: Primatology, Aeronautics,
and the Animality of "Modern" Science, 1891–1903 | 65
Daniel Vandersommers

4 Sculpting Dinah with the Blunt Tools of the Historian | 93
Tracy McDonald

5 Stereoscopic Animals: Spectatorship, Kodiak Bears,
and the Keystone *Animal Set* | 119
Zeb Tortorici

6 "Try Telling That to the Polar Bears": Rationing and
Resistance at the Wartime Zoo | 145
John Kinder

7   Gust (ca 1952–1988), or a History from Below of the
       Changing Zoo | 167
       Violette Pouillard

8   Child Stars at the Zoo: The Rise and Fall of
       Polar Bear Knut | 191
       Guro Flinterud

9   Pandas and the Reproduction of Race and Heterosexuality·
       in the Zoo | 211
       Marianna Szczygielska

10 Flying Penguins in Japan's Northernmost Zoo | 237
       Takashi Ito

11 Al Gore, *Blackfish*, and Me: Eco-activist Progress
       and Prospects for the Future | 262
       Randy Malamud

12 Reorienting the Space of Containment, or from Zoosphere
       to Noösphere and Beyond | 276
       Ron Broglio

13 Zoomorphic Bodies: Moving and Being Moved
       by Animals | 294
       Jonathan Osborn

       Bibliography | 313
       Contributors | 333
       Index | 337

FIGURES

1.1 Pierre-Alexandre Aveline, *Veüe et perspective du Salon de la Ménagerie de Versailles*, 1689. (Bibliothèque Nationale de France, Cabinet des Estampes.) 25

1.2 Pieter Boel, engraving by G. Scotin, *Quartier des Demoiselles*, c. 1670. (Bibliothèque Nationale de France, Cabinet des Estampes.) 30

1.3 Pieter Boel, study of a civet and goose foot; study of a fox. (Musée du Louvre.) 32

1.4 The Salpêtrière in 1812. (*Plans des hôpitaux et hospices civils de la ville de Paris levés par ordre du Conseil général d'administration de ces établissements*, Paris, 1820.) 34

1.5 Plan for the Eglise Saint-Louis de la Salpêtrière by Louis Le Vau, 1669. (Vessier, *La Pitié-Salpêtrière.*) 37

1.6 Parishioners attending mass at Saint-Louis de la Salpêtrière, 1952. 37

1.7 Charles Bell, "Madness." (*The Anatomy and Philosophy of Expression as Connected with the Fine Arts*, 1806.) 40

2.1 *Hippotragus niger* (sable antelope) from *The Book of Antelopes*, 1894–1900. Lithograph by Joseph Smit from a watercolour by Joseph Wolf, under the direction of Sir Victor Brooke. (Courtesy of the Wildlife Conservation Society Archives.) 48

2.2 The Antelope Wall, National Collection of Heads and Horns, New York Zoological Park. (Courtesy of the Wildlife Conservation Society Archives.) 60

3.1 A model soaring bird sketch that Langley sent to Baker and Black-burne. (Smithsonian Institution Archives. Image SIA2018-110263.) 78

3.2 Sketch of a soaring John crow and a soaring seagull Langley sent to Ridgeway. (Smithsonian Institution Archives. Image SIA2018-110264.) 79

3.3 Langley's Great Aerodrome – Crashed on the Potomac, piloted by Charles Manly. (*Sueddeutsche Zeitung* photo. Almany Stock photo.) 85

5.1 "Kodiak Bears" Brookfield Zoo. Homemade stereoscope card, photographer unknown. Purchased by Zeb Tortorici in 2015 at an antique shop in North Carolina. 120

5.2 "Giant hippopotamus in the 'zoo,' Central Park, New York," sterograph, ca. 27 January 1904. (Retrieved from the Library of Congress, https://www.loc.gov/item/2015645136/.) 121

5.3 1894–95 advertisement for the "perfect stereoscope" in the Montgomery Ward & Co catalogue. (Courtesy of the UC Riverside California Museum of Photography.) 125

5.4 Keystone View Company *Animal Set* Stereographic Library, vols. 1 and 2, pictured with the stereoscope viewer and an elephant stereograph. (NYU Fales Library & Special Collections.) 129

5.5 Keystone stereoscope card, "A half mile of pork," stereograph, 1894. (Courtesy of the Keystone-Mast Collection at the UC Riverside California Museum of Photography.) 132

5.6 Keystone View Company, "83332K.U., box 119–21, 1926, Stocker and Feeder (Pens) Division of the Union Stock Yard & Transit Co, Chicago, Ill.," stereograph, 1926. (Courtesy of UC Riverside California Museum of Photography.) 134

5.7 Keystone View Company, "UX265 Splitting backbones and final inspection, hogs ready for cooler," stereograph, late nineteenth century. (Courtesy of UC Riverside California Museum of Photography.) 136

5.8 "Chimpanzees, most man-like of the apes," Bronx Park, New York, stereograph, 1904–14. 136

5.9 Cover of Cheyne-Stout's 1937 *At the Zoo: The Stereo-Book of Animals*, which includes a metal folding stereoscope attachment to view the images. 139

5.10 Stereoscopic images of African chimpanzees (Anna and Jiggs) and an orangutan from Borneo and Sumatra (Reddy), from Cheyne-Stout's *At the Zoo*. 142

7.1 Gust and keeper. (African Archives, Federal Public Service Foreign Affairs, Brussels, AGRI 187, 59 Ch. © Antwerp Zoo.) 168

7.2 Gust. (African Archives, Federal Public Service Foreign Affairs, Brussels, AGRI 187, 59 Ch. © Antwerp Zoo.) 169

9.1 Stephen and Laureen Harper with a panda cub. (The Canadian Press/Adrian Wyld.) 212

9.2 Illustration of Smokey Bear and family welcoming the pandas to the National Zoo, 1972. (Painted by Rudolph Wendelin, official artist of Smokey Bear, Smithsonian Institution Archives, record unit 365, SIA2012-6127.) 219

9.3 "The Mating Game" at the Giant Panda Experience Exhibition, Toronto Zoo. (Photo courtesy of Marianna Szczygielska.) 229

10.1 Annual attendance at Asahiyama Zoo, 1967–2014. ("Shiryō, Tōkei," Asahiyama Zoo, http://www.city.asahikawa.hokkaido.jp/asahiyamazoo/2200top/do52450_d/fil/nenbetu.pdf.) 242

10.2 Giraffes standing in the snow. (Photo courtesy of Takashi Ito, 30 March 2013.) 246

10.3 The front of the Penguin House. (Photo courtesy of Takashi Ito, 30 September 2016.) 249

10.4 The underwater tunnel of the Penguin Aquarium. (Photo courtesy of Takashi Ito, 30 September 2016.) 249

10.5 Mural painting of flying penguins in the Penguin House. (Photo courtesy of Takashi Ito, 30 September 2016.) 250

10.6 Mobiles of flying penguins in the Penguin House. (Photo courtesy of Takashi Ito, 30 September 2016.) 250

10.7 The penguin walk on the snow-covered promenade. (Photo courtesy of Takashi Ito, 30 March 2013.) 251

10.8 Panel at the entrance of the Seal Museum. (Photo courtesy of Takashi Ito, 30 September 2016.) 253

10.9 A spotted seal swimming in the Column Aquarium. (Photo courtesy of Takashi Ito, 30 September 2016.) 253

10.10 Snow globe of a flying penguin. (Photo courtesy of Takashi Ito, 2 August 2017.) 255

13.1 Map of the Toronto Zoo, 2018. 300

ACKNOWLEDGMENTS

This collection originated in a workshop held at the Design Annex of the Art Gallery of Hamilton on 2–3 December 2016. The editors would like to thank the Social Sciences and Humanities Research Council of Canada for a generous insight grant that funded the workshop. This grant also sponsored the post-doctoral fellowship in animal history at the Department of History at McMaster University, held by Daniel Vandersommers in 2016–17. The workshop received unsparing support from the Department of History, the Office of the Dean of Humanities, and the Wilson Institute for Canadian History at McMaster. We are grateful to the McMaster's Arts Research Board, which provided a scholarly publication grant to help acquire image rights and defray other costs. Vandersommers would like to thank the Consortium for History of Science, Technology and Medicine and the National Endowment for the Humanities for their financial support when he was a postdoctoral fellow in 2017–18.

Thank you to Debbie Lobban and Wendy Benedetti in the Department of History and to the stellar staff at the Design Annex for excellent organizational help and support. Much gratitude goes to Richard Ratzlaff for his long-time enthusiasm and encouragement for this collection. A special thank you to our insightful and engaged commentators at the workshop: David Clark, Sheri Crawford, Stefan Dolgert, Angela Fernandez, James Gillett, and Alice Kuzniar. We would also like to thank the workshop's additional participants and discussants: Ralph Acampora, Kathryn Denning, Jesse Donahue, Susan Nance, Judith Nicholson, and Erica Tom. We would like to recognize Sean Kinnear for editorial assistance. And we are thankful for the masterful copy-editing of Carolyn Yates, with McGill-Queen's University Press. Finally, we very much appreciate the helpful feedback from our two anonymous readers for MQUP.

ZOO STUDIES

TOWARDS A NEW HUMANITIES

Daniel Vandersommers and Tracy McDonald

It would make sense to begin this volume (in an all-too-human manner) by citing statistics and data that would underscore, beyond a shadow of a doubt, the centrality of zoos to contemporary society – the hundreds of millions of tickets sold every year, the tens of billions of dollars contributed to the global economy, the hundreds of thousands of workers employed, the total number of large cities that possess zoos, or the thousands of species and hundreds of thousands of animals housed within them. Through statistics, we could legitimate the zoo as a topic for scholarly analysis. Yet such rhetorical poetics, such amassing of numbers, would be entangled with the zoo itself or, more precisely, would share a common intellectual history with the zoological project, a history in which humans seek mastery of our world by counting, aggregating, and sorting, all for the purpose of display.

Alternatively, we could begin this volume by invoking the zoo experience. Instead of citing statistics, we could resurrect childhood memories of sights, sounds, and smells – the pelages, the scales, the plumages; the screeches, the roars, the grunts, the cries; the odors, the musk, the stench. We could take you, the reader, through the transference to yesteryear, to your fond and formative feelings established in the zoo, when you wanted to touch wild animals so that you could feel wild yourself. Yet these sensory poetics would still share origins with the zoological programme, one in which humans justify their mastery of the world by transforming nonhumans into playthings through which they could suppress, repress, work through, forget, or make right the realization that they have flattened the ecological terrain in which they have lived, and from which they are derived.

Instead, we begin this volume by simply asking you to pretend that you have never before stepped foot in a zoo. For a few of you this fantasy will not take much imagination. For the rest of you, the majority of you, set aside your memories and your grade school field trips. Set aside your stuffed animals – snuggly sloths and bears and poison dart frogs – from zoo gift stores. Set aside the giant panda soda cups with the curly-cue straws. Set aside your preconceived notions about zoos and conservation, education, science, and entertainment. Set aside your cultural training. Forget *The Zookeeper's Wife* (2017), *We Bought a Zoo* (2011), *Zookeeper* (2011), *Madagascar* (2005), and the television shows by Jack Hanna. And forget the headlines – zoo stars' births, birthdays, and euthanizations; tiger escapes; or the grand openings of new lairs, elephant crossings, gorilla forests, lion safaris, and panda canyons. Forget it all.

Zoos are so commonplace. Almost all of us have been to one. But few of us have done more than stroll upon their outermost surface. Few of us have ever really walked into a zoo. It is the institutions in our lives that we take for granted, that we experience as "normal," and that we see physically and most often to which we remain blind. As you turn the following pages, leave your assumptions at the gate. Zoos are complex institutions, and you deserve a tour that will take you behind the scenes. *But still, do not lean over the railing. And do not feed the animals.*

Based on a common dictionary definition, "humanity" can mean "human beings collectively," "the state of being human," "the quality of being humane; benevolence," or "learning concerned with human culture, especially literature, history, art, music, and philosophy." As this volume testifies, when the academic disciplines associated with the humanities foreground zoo animals as subjects worthy of scholarly analysis, a strange mirroring effect occurs; the interrogators see not only their supposed subjects – animal individuals – but also their own reflections. By thinking about zoos, the contributors to this volume rethink "humanity" and all four of its definitions. First, they examine zoos as institutions that conduct routine maintenance of "the human," as part of what Giorgio Agamben would call the "anthropological machine" that manufactures the human in the first place.[1] Second, in so doing, they raise questions about what it means to be human by considering what it might mean to be (zoo) animal. Third, they individually and collectively press us to look beneath endeavours we have deemed "humane" and benevolent, to examine these concepts and to see if they are indeed what we say they are. Finally, by rethinking the three definitions above, they interrogate the humanities by shining light upon its own, our own, blind spot: the "animal." The goal of this volume is to push us towards a new humanities fitting for an era that desperately needs a more capacious, empathetic vision, and to urge us towards a knowledge system that can be human-driven without being restricted to, and by, our own species. The goal is to inspire a humanities that is interdisciplinary, ecological, sustainable, and embracing – one that is self-reflective and outward-looking rather than obsessed with its own autopoiesis and narcissism. The goal is to help forge a humanities not centred on humans. Zoos help us consider every valence of "humanity" by pointing us not only towards the animals that live within us but also, more importantly, towards those that live alongside and despite of us.

In this volume, zoo animals are taken seriously as individuals. They possess their own subjectivities and tell their own stories. Over the last three decades or so, humanities scholarship concerning human-animal relations has leaned towards the human end of the relationship, and has explored what animals can say, and have said, about human society. In this way, animals have been extensively excavated as symbols of or in human cultures, as metonymic extensions of ourselves. Indeed, animals, like all symbols, serve as useful mirrors for their makers. They allow us, when we look closely, to see the features to which we are typically blind; they increase our introspection, our vision of ourselves. Frequently, though, as we come into view, as we gain clarity, the animals we are looking at blur into the background or into us. The reality is simple, if seemingly counterintuitive: when we look at animals, they all too frequently disappear. There is nowhere that this phenomenon is more apparent than in the zoo. We contend that animals must first be approached as individuals, with unique idiosyncrasies, personal wishes, personal desires, personal emotions, and personal biographies that matter. Like other subjects of scholarly analysis, animals deserve attention as beings shaped by complex matrices of cultural, environmental, evolutionary, and historical forces that overlap with, but also diverge from, the ones that structure our own lives as human individuals. Until we listen to what animals have to say themselves, the reflection we see upon their surfaces will always be marred by our own chimeras, in all of their meanings from fantasy to delusion to monster. As Ron Broglio, a contributor to this volume, states elsewhere:

> The animal surface is contrasted with and co-opted by the human who uses his own reflexive interiority (i.e., "thinking") to divide the animal surface into cuts of meat and then to project the schematic cuts onto the body of the beast. The cattle, now imagined as meat, have been turned inside out. Since these animals are not considered to have an interiority and since they do not speak in our language, their inside is symbolically made outside, a mere surface to be exposed for human use, even before this is done literally, in the process of slaughtering and consuming them ... Real animals do, of course, look back, and in this look the dominant schemas that order our world and regulate our relations with animals are upset.[2]

In this volume, as you stroll through zoos past and present, you will find animals looking back. The contributors herein, inspired by the latest work in animal, human-animal, and critical animal studies, listen, in different ways, to what zoo animals have to say.

Many social activists, since at least the end of the eighteenth century, have associated humanity with kindness, with the humane. Our search for a new humanities is a call to action, a summons to tear down walls, dissolve borders, and extend kindness both within and beyond our species. The notion of "the human" has almost always, at least by its enlightened Western definitions, excluded "the animal." A more honest humanities would acknowledge the beings that it has consumed and situated itself against, and would instead seek a more ecological "human," capable of acknowledging its dependence on and interconnection with animals.

Thinking about the zoo is one way to rethink our relations with our Others, to strive for, in the words of philosopher Timothy Morton, "solidarity with nonhuman people."[3] Re-evaluating the zoo is essential as we confront the Anthropocene. The zoo is an institution that gives form to some of the abstraction and globality of our age. By giving a face to biodiversity, ecological transformation, climate change, interspecies relations, and nonhuman personhood, the zoo very well may be a perfect place to think about and through some of the hyperobjects (and the lives encapsulated within them) that too frequently transcend our perception.[4] If we look closely at the zoo, we may be able to see the animals that we take for granted, even within the environmental discourses that surround the institution. Re-evaluating the zoo raises profound questions regarding the most salient topics of humanities scholarship: from power to rights, to race, gender, and sexuality, to capital, to conservation, to empathy, intimacy, and love, to name only a few.[5]

Since this volume brings together scholars from across the academy, this juncture is a fitting place for a brief look at what has been written about zoos to date. Historians were among the first to study zoological parks as institutions that could and should be analyzed as both artifacts of and windows into society. In 1987, in her classic of environmental history *The Animal Estate: The English and Other Creatures in the Victorian Age*, Harriet Ritvo laid the groundwork for a future zoo studies. She focused on the animal-related discourses of nineteenth-century England – discourses that surrounded topics as diverse as beef, pet keeping, compassion, rabies, and hunting – all of which shared the central theme of exploitation. In her fifth chapter, titled "Exotic Captives," Ritvo examined the Regent's Park Zoo (founded in 1828) and its animal inhabitants as symbols of British imperialism. Not only was this one of the first scholarly examinations to demonstrate that a zoo was far more than just a zoo, but it also established a new methodology for thinking about animals by encouraging historians to read zoo animals as living texts of human society.[6]

While other academic zoo histories preceded and followed Ritvo's classic, most zoo histories remained narrowly focused and institutionally subsidized.[7] In the 1990s, as several American zoos celebrated key anniversaries, the number of zoo histories expanded. Some of these works were sweeping narratives of zoological parks across time and space, while others were studies of individual zoos embedded in local histories. In general, this literature placed zoo history along the trajectory of progress, where zoos triumphed alongside civilization as the twentieth century unfolded.[8] Nonetheless, the sheer volume of popular zoo histories produced in the 1990s underscores the degree to which zoos were coming into view for both scholars and the public.

At the beginning of the millennium, several academic histories paved the way for further zoo history research. In 1998, Eric Baratay and Elisabeth Hardouin-Fugier published *Zoos: Histoire des jardins zoologiques en occident (XVIe–XXe siècle)*, which documented the transition of Renaissance menageries into recognizable contemporary zoos.[9] In his 2002 book, *Savages and Beasts: The Birth of the Modern Zoo*, Nigel Rothfels, a contributor to this volume, examined the German entrepreneur Carl Hagenbeck's animal collecting and zoo-building endeavors in the nineteenth century. Rothfels was one of the first to call attention to the complicated processes involved in establishing zoological parks. He traced the rise of international animal trading, described the Hagenbeck revolution that introduced naturalistic enclosures to zoos, and used both topics as windows into global business and German culture. That same year, Elizabeth Hanson published *Animal Attractions: Nature on Display in American Zoos*. Through research in several American zoo archives, she demonstrated the importance of zoological parks not only to cultural history, but also to environmental history and the history of science.[10] Zoo history was on the rise.

In 2009's *Modern Nature: The Rise of the Biological Perspective in Germany*, historian of science Lynn Nyhart furthered Rothfels's exploration of German zoological parks and extended Hanson's analysis of zoos as scientific and environmental institutions. Since then, in the last decade, zoo history has proliferated and diversified, and has addressed many of the most pressing twenty-first century concerns. This burgeoning historiography is cutting-edge and innovative, covering a wide-ranging geographic-temporal landscape as well as a diverse array of topics spread across environmental history, cultural history, and the history of science.[11] As this volume reaches publication, many other historically based zoo studies will soon join the growing literature on zoo history.

This growth, however, is only the beginning. While historians represent the first and the largest group of academics to explore zoological parks as a subject of inquiry for the humanities, they have, until recently, prioritized questions of society, culture, environment, and science.[12] All too often, they have overlooked zoos' most central components: the animals themselves. Of course, zoo inhabitants made appearances in historical narratives, yet too frequently these appearances were for the sake of anecdotes and examples in larger ventures of argumentation, about larger processes concerning human history. Rarely were animals – as subjects, as agents, as actors, as individuals – studied in their own right. We humans have found it virtually impossible to not see and use ourselves as the measure of all we survey, trapped as we are in an "epistemological anthropocentrism."[13]

In *Ciferae: A Bestiary in Five Fingers*, philosopher Tom Tyler seeks a "new, encompassing, more-than-human, 'we.'"[14] He eloquently demonstrates the ways in which theorists have used animals as ciphers, as "something that stands for nothing," loathing them for not fitting in but unable to leave them alone.[15] It has been the work of scholars outside of history that has truly transformed zoos into a topic worthy of a "studies," an inter- and multidisciplinary nexus where a complex topic can be truly examined in all of its richness and through all of its layers, contradictions, and significations. "Zoo studies," as such, has become possible only through the work of scholars who direct attention to valences of meaning that transcend, undercut, circumvent, or disrupt the very notion of the zoo.

Most important in this regard is the formative *Zoo Culture: The Book about Watching People Watch Animals*, published by Bob Mullan and Garry Marvin in 1987 (the same publication year as Ritvo's classic), and *Reading Zoos: Representations of Animals and Captivity*, published by this volume's Randy Malamud in 1998. In *Zoo Culture*, Mullan, a documentarian, and Marvin, an anthropologist, put forward two asseverations that would become central to subsequent work on zoos. The first was that zoos tell us as much about humans as about animals. The second was that animals do not need zoos; humans do. *Reading Zoos* passionately demonstrated the second claim. Through a powerful cultural and literary critique, Malamud depicted zoos as institutions that rip animals from their ecosystems in order to decontextualize them for the titillation of urban multitudes. This foundation, though, is not without shortcomings, for in the process of directing attention to zoos' silencing of animals these early critiques glossed over the institution's complexities and, more importantly, sometimes failed to see individual animals and hear their voices. In so doing, zoo animals in these early works still, too often, remained cultural artifacts in projects of cultural criticism and critique.

As Malamud was finishing *Reading Zoos*, others began to explore the institution using an array of methodological toolkits. In her 1997 *Spectacular Nature: Corporate Culture and the Sea World Experience*, ethnographer and folklorist Susan G. Davis demonstrated how sites of animal captivity could be read as spaces of entertainment, performance, industry, and commerce. In his 2001 *A Different Nature: The Paradoxical World of Zoos and Their Uncertain Future*, zoo director and architect David Hancocks used history, biology, ethics, and zoo planning to call attention to the inadequacies of most zoological parks. This classic pushed zoos to reinvent themselves by using exceptions like the Arizona-Sonora Desert Museum, the Bronx Zoo, the Emmen Zoo in Holland, Wildscreen in England, and Seattle's Woodland Park Zoo as templates for the future. That same year, in her *After the Ark? Environmental Policy Making and the Zoo*, sociologist and conservationist Nicole Mazur similarly looked into the future of zoo policy, and especially into advertising, corporate sponsorship, and other issues central to the business of the zoo. In the early 2000s, philosophers Ralph Acampora and Keekok Lee, following the pioneering work of Dale Jamieson, began to untangle zoos' complexities and contradictions with their respective "Zoos and Eyes: Contesting Captivity and Seeking Successor Practices" and *Zoos: A Philosophical Tour.*[16] Still, individual animals too frequently reside in the margins of works that excavate the zoo's architecture, contextualize the zoo's policies, and examine the philosophical and ontological lives of the zoo's animals.

Like zoo histories, the works on zoological parks from disciplines across the academy have increased in number and expanded in reach. Zoo studies has emerged at the intersection of law and ethnography;[17] in political science;[18] in science and technology studies;[19] in sociology;[20] in ethics;[21] at the crossroads of visual, cultural, and race studies;[22] at the nexus of the environmental humanities and continental philosophy;[23] and at the junction of ethics and photojournalism.[24] As in zoo history, more works are in progress, and as their approaches continue to become more interdisciplinary and more responsive to contemporary human-animal relationships, as well as to our current ethological knowledge, zoo animals can begin to tell us new stories.[25]

Scholars have finally realized the global significance of zoological parks past and present. They have realized that the zoo's business is big business, as well as a complicated and contradictory business. However, until recently most academic studies of zoological parks remained cordoned off in the disciplines from which they arose. Dialogue between and among zoo scholars has only just begun. *Zoo Studies: A New Humanities* marks an attempt to bring a diverse group of scholars thinking about zoos together in a single volume and hopes to spark a global dialogue about zoological parks – past, present, and future.

This collection complements three other edited volumes that examine zoos and their place in our world: *Metamorphoses of the Zoo: Animal Encounter after Noah* (2010), *Increasing Legal Rights for Zoo Animals: Justice on the Ark* (2017), and *The Ark and Beyond: The Evolution of Zoo and Aquarium Conservation* (2018).[26] Whereas these three collections mostly address the future of zoological parks, exploring their inadequacies and shortcomings and offering solutions that range from termination to reform, *Zoo Studies: A New Humanities* makes the past, present, and future the foci of attention and asks us to pause and take stock. Before we offer prescriptions for the future, we must first look closely at the zoos that surround us, and that have surrounded us since the Enlightenment. The chapters that follow establish a foundation upon which prescriptions can be built, and weave together case studies that concern real individuals.

This volume examines zoos past and present in nearly equal measure. All of the chapters embrace elements of both evidence-based thinking and also theoretical frameworks and analyses. Those that explicitly examine historical zoos indeed look to the future, and those that explicitly examine specific contemporary zoos indeed resonate with the past. What resides at the core of each and every chapter, however, is the very idea, the very notion, and the all-too-human concept of "zoo" itself. Yet at the heart of each and every chapter, individuals bleed out of their epicardia encasements, escaping the confines of "zoo" and animating the stories and arguments of this volume's contributors.

Zoo Studies: A New Humanities offers a unique blend of interdisciplinary approaches, yet one that also offers coherence. Though we agree with anthropologist Anna Tsing's belief that "organisms don't have to show their human equivalence (as conscious agents, intentional communicators, or ethical subjects) to count,"[27] we also believe that in order to take zoo animals, placed on display as single entities, seriously, we must first see them as individuals before we see them as either representatives of their species (how they are framed in zoos and by zoological and conservationist discourses) or as actors knotted into multispecies entanglements (how they could be theorized through multispecies ethnography or posthumanism).[28] With a wide variety of methodological approaches, and through a diverse array of theoretical tools, the contributors to this volume seek to locate individual animals, within specific zoos, in the past and present. Although they tell quite different stories, they collectively, through their engagement with animal studies, forge a new methodological toolkit by which scholars in the humanities can begin to take nonhuman animals, and their complex relationships with us, seriously.

Readers could pick up this book and peruse it from start to finish or choose the areas that interest them. The volume is organized chronologically and moves generally from less to more abstract considerations. It begins with the shared architectural world of insane asylums and menageries in seventeenth-century France and ends in speculative, alternative worlds that are theorized by interrogating the metaphysics of the zoo or generated, through artistic expression, by experiencing animals at the zoo. Between these endpoints, many diverse topics, wrapped up in the zoo, are explored: animal collecting, science and knowledge production, spectatorship, food studies, gender and sexuality, exhibition design and aesthetics, popular culture, and activism, to name a few. The volume also makes some of the first forays into the experimental world of animal biography, providing concrete and individual experiences of capture and captivity in the political and economic world of zoos.[29]

Contemplations of the nature of zoo business are present in every chapter. Zoos have felt pressure for decades to reconfigure themselves as conservation centres that make every attempt to more ethically accommodate animals in enclosures that alleviate boredom and provide what they, not we, need. Collectively, this volume provides a critical examination of the business of zoos. More important, each chapter, in vastly different ways, locates the individual voices, expressions, resistances, and agencies of animals. Rather than amalgamate their individualities here into a single summary or thesis, we challenge you to discern the polyphony as you work through the following pages.

In chapter 1, Matthew Senior examines the first modern zoo alongside the first modern mental hospital, both designed by French royal architect Louis Le Vau in the mid-seventeenth century. Using German philosopher Peter Sloterdijk as a starting point, Senior argues that both institutions were halfway houses of Being. By peering into the royal Ménagerie at Versailles; the Ménagerie's eventual evolution into the Jardin des Plantes; and two hospitals, La Salpêtrière and the Bicêtre, Senior looks into the nature of captivity, with all of its psychological traumas.

In chapter 2, Nigel Rothfels investigates an aspect of the history of modern zoos that is often overlooked. We associate zoos today with charismatic megafauna like elephants, gorillas, chimpanzees, lions, tigers, and bears. Yet in the early years of the New York Zoological Park, now the Bronx Zoo, director William Hornaday was preoccupied with collecting and housing antelopes. This interest in antelopes was linked to the fact that they were rare, beautiful, and being hunted relentlessly to the point that several species were already extinct. Antelopes became trophies both dead, represented by horns mounted on a wall, and alive, as exhibits in the zoo. And unlike other zoo stars, their value was expressed through the entirety of the collection, not by their individual grandeur.

In chapter 3, Daniel Vandersommers explores two experiments, one in primatology and the other in aeronautics, staged in the National Zoological Park at the end of the nineteenth century. Though on the surface they appear quite different, a closer look reveals a common structure. Vandersommers tells the stories of Richard Garner, Samuel Langley, and two "failed" experiments, and then contemplates the roles of humans, animals, and their respective agencies in the creation of scientific knowledge.

Moving from scientific experiments rooted in the zoo, in chapter 4 Tracy McDonald turns to an inhabitant of the zoo. This chapter is the volume's first foray into a new genre: animal biography. The protagonist is Dinah, a young gorilla. She was purchased in Gabon in August 1913, by the Richard Garner of chapter 3, at approximately eighteen months of age. She was then "acclimatized" and transported to the New York Zoological Park, where she lived until her death in August 1915. McDonald navigates the ways in which the humans who interacted with Dinah constantly projected their agendas, hopes, desires, fears, and prejudices onto her, using her as a convenient vehicle of expression, their own personal cipher. Using the skillset of the historian attempting to study one who has left no written or spoken record, McDonald restores some of Dinah's tracks on the pages of history.

In chapter 5, Zeb Tortorici looks at the representation of zoo animals, in the late nineteenth and early twentieth centuries, through the stereoscope. The stereoscope – an optical device and immensely popular form of home entertainment and pedagogy from the 1850s to the 1930s – allowed individuals to see phenomenally realistic three-dimensional static images by merging left-eye and right-eye views of the same scene. Tortorici looks at a series of stereoscopic images of zoo animals and argues that stereoscopic representations of nonhuman animals, in both captivity and death, serve to distance the viewer from the viewed.

The volume then moves from visual consumption to literal, as John Kinder examines the history of food rationing at American zoos during World War II in chapter 6. In the depths of war, zoos struggled to feed their inhabitants, and this chapter details the innovative strategies developed to address the universal crisis of food shortage. Kinder addresses both their successes and failures, showing that many zoo animals made the ultimate sacrifice. He not only shows how Americans transformed zoo animals (living and dead) into symbols, but also demonstrates how animals could assert a gastronomic resistance of their own. This chapter points us towards a larger cultural debate about the value of zoos and zoo animals in times of war. Kinder also asks us to think about a layer of the zoo that usually remains invisible to zoogoers: feeding the animals.

In chapter 7, Violette Pouillard provides another work of animal biography. She reconstructs the life of Gust, a Western gorilla who arrived as a baby to the Antwerp Zoo in 1953 and resided there until his death in 1988. Building on the work of historians who conducted "history from below" in order to reveal the voice and agency of the voiceless, Pouillard interweaves Gust's story with the story of the changing face of the modern zoo in the second-half of the twentieth century. She conveys the ways in which zoo narratives about Gust turned him into a symbol to "encourage human sympathy" that also denied the reality of his suffering under the constraints of captivity.

In chapter 8, Guro Flinterud looks at the changing narratives that surrounded the polar bear Knut, born at the Berlin Zoo in December 2006. She places her analysis of the heartrending life trajectory of the baby zoo star who inevitably grows into an adult in the context of the more familiar tale of the ill-fated human child star. Flinterud uncovers a shifting story, one that idealized the young cub because he appeared cute and cuddly yet demonized the adolescent Knut for being what he had always been: a polar bear.

In chapter 9, Marianna Szczygielska focuses on the recent giant panda exhibition in the Toronto Zoo. She analyzes the ways in which this animal display not only evokes reproductive hopes (with breeding being the focal point of the pandas' residency) and naturalizes heterosexuality as national, public, and precarious, but also racializes the nonhuman animals as powerful symbols of Canadian-Chinese friendship. She demonstrates how the public display of institutionalized panda intimacy in the zoo is deeply entangled with the symbolic economies of race, class, and gender, as well as with international diplomacy, global capitalism, and neoliberal politics. Szczygielska offers an innovative and timely reading of a single zoo exhibit, showing how it is embedded in today's world.

From Canada, the volume moves to Japan, where in chapter 10 Takashi Ito examines the revival of zoological parks in the late 1990s. He focuses on Japan's northernmost zoo, the Asahiyama Zoo on the island of Hokkaido. His study picks up where Ian Jared Miller's study of the zoo, as an example of "ecological modernity," leaves off by placing the Asahiyama Zoo in the context of "ecological postmodernity." He begins with the colonial history of the region and the early rise and fall of zoos in Japan before zooming in on two "animals-in-action" exhibits that feature seals and penguins respectively. He concludes by interrogating how the concepts of *kawaii* (cuteness) and *kawaiso* (pity) blur the boundary between human and nonhuman animals.

Chapter 11 stands out as a deliberately brash call to arms. Randy Malamud begins with two "radical" cinematic texts (Al Gore's *An Inconvenient Truth* and Gabriela Cowperthwaite's *Blackfish*) that have become accepted, mainstream, and popular because they were, he argues, so rhetorically clever and, more simply, true. He invites readers to position themselves as activists and ecological ethicists using his own brand of rhetoric to challenge, destabilize, and push us, hard, to react.

Moving into more abstract territory, in chapter 12 Ron Broglio looks at how nonhuman animals challenge human-built spaces like the zoo, with its Enlightenment bars and Linnaean demarcations. He argues that humans engage in a vertical striving to separate ourselves from "a nonhuman outside, an outside not on our terms," and then deem the resulting human verticality superior. With their untold ways of being, animals challenge our "metaphysical verticality" and suggest another future. Broglio traces glimpses of worlds in which human and nonhuman animals were more integrated, from the 32,000-year-old paintings in the Chauvet Cave in France to the transcendence of shamans to contemporary examples of zoo animals who challenge human striations and push us towards speculative futures.

Zoo Studies: A New Humanities concludes with a collaboration between choreographer Jonathan Osborn and interpreter Danielle Baskerville. In chapter 13, Osborn presents us with ARK, a choreographic performance work that imagines the Toronto Zoo as an anthropomorphically designed space for animals, a space where the human body has the potential to become zoomorphically affected through kinaesthetic exchange with living nonhuman bodies. Osborn outlines the work's domain, conceptualization, research process, and methodological practices and their resonant effects on choreographic structure and movement vocabulary. He then reflects on how an aesthetic practice grounded in movement, kinaesthetic empathy, and embodied memory can produce novel critical insights into the decentring of the humanist subject as well as alternative ways to think about relating to zoos and their inhabitants and the phenomenological relations between species. The film of Osborn and Baskerville's performance accompanies this volume and is meant to be watched alongside this final chapter.

Each chapter of this volume will invite you on an excursion, a foray, into the shared architecture of the zoo and the humanities. More important than the thirteen chapters that follow are the spaces between them. Reading, like zoogoing, should not be delimited by walkways, by the segmentation of chapters, or by the walls of disciplines. We the editors believe that this volume's greatest contribution resides in its own interstices, where the authors' voices may escape and meet your own, where ecologies of empathy, humility, and curiosity may point us towards a new humanities.

NOTES

1 Agamben, *The Open.*

2 Broglio, "Thinking with Surfaces," 242.

3 Morton, *Humankind.*

4 Morton, *Hyperobjects.*

5 The unifying theme of this collection is the zoo as an institution of animal captivity; however, we recognize that the zoo, throughout history, was also an institution of literal human captivity. While human zoos are not the explicit focus of this volume (though themes of race, ethnicity, imperialism, patriarchy, violence, postcolonialism, etc., are woven through its chapters), we would also like to acknowledge the growing literature on human zoos. For more, see Bruce, *Through the Lion Gate,* 44–96; Rothfels, *Savages and Beasts,* 81–142; Ames, *Carl Hagenbeck's Empire of Entertainments;* Newkirk, *Spectacle;* Blanchard, Boetsch, and Snoep, *Human Zoos;* Blanchard et al., *Human Zoos.*

6 Ritvo, *The Animal Estate,* 205–42. For another early academic history of

European zoos that similarly emphasizes issues of imperialism, see Jahn, "Zoologische Gärten."

7 For academic histories of zoos that preceded *The Animal Estate*, see Horowitz, "The National Zoological Park"; "Animal and Man in the New York Zoological Park"; "Seeing Ourselves through the Bars"; Stott, "The American Idea of a Zoological Park"; Stott, "The Historical Origins of the Zoological Park."

8 For histories of individual zoos, see Ehrlinger, *The Cincinnati Zoo and Botanical Garden*; Ross, *Let the Lions Roar!*; Carolyn and Don Etter, *The Denver Zoo*; Denisenko, *Ot zverintsev k zooparku*; Egorovoi, *Moskovskii zoologicheskii park*; Bridges, *Gathering of Animals*; Rosenthal, Tauber, and Uhlir, *The Ark in the Park*; Zoological Society of Philadelphia, *An Animal Garden in Fairmount Park*; Wegeforth and Morgan, *It Began with a Roar!*; Guillery, *The Buildings of the London Zoo*; Barrington-Johnson, *The Zoo*; Blau and Rothfels, *Elephant House*; Bierlein and HistoryLink, *Woodland*. For other histories of zoological parks, see Fisher, *Zoos of the World*; Hahn, *Animal Gardens*; Croke, *The Modern Ark*; Blunt, *The Ark in the Park: The Zoo in the Nineteenth Century*; Kiley-Worthington, *Animals in Circuses and Zoos*. See also Hyson, "Urban Jungles" and "Jungles of Eden." Finally, for an expansive and cataloguing survey of global zoo history, see Kisling, ed., *Zoo and Aquarium History*.

9 The book was translated into English and republished in 2002 as Baratay and Hardouin-Fugier, *Zoo: A History of Zoological Gardens in the West*.

10 Hanson, *Animal Attractions*. See also Mitman, "When Nature *Is* the Zoo."

11 Miller, *The Nature of the Beasts*; Ito, *London Zoo and the Victorians*; Guerrini, *The Courtiers' Anatomists*; Bender, *The Animal Game*; Bruce, *Through the Lion Gate*; Flack, *The Wild Within*.

12 The newly articulated field of animal history seeks to broaden the focus. See, e.g., Nance, ed., *The Historical Animal*; Few and Tortorici, eds., *Centering Animals in Latin American History*. Concerning animal history and zoos, see Vandersommers, "Narrating Animal History from the Crags."

13 Tyler, *Ciferae*, 3.

14 Ibid., 8.

15 Ibid., 3.

16 See also Jamieson, "Against Zoos" and "Against Zoos Revisited."

17 Braverman, *Zooland*. Also see Braverman, *Wild Life*.

18 Itoh, *Japanese Wartime Zoo Policy*; Donahue and Trump, *American Zoos during the Depression*. Also see Donahue and Trump, *Political Animals* and *The Politics of Zoos*. Concerning political theory, see Donaldson and Kymlicka, *Zoopolis*.

19 Friese, *Cloning Wild Life*.

20 Grazian, *American Zoo*.

21 Gruen, ed., *The Ethics of Captivity*. See also Gruen, *Entangled Empathy*, which resonates neatly with many of the contributions to this volume. A classic, though dated, study of zoos and animal ethics is Bostock, *Zoos and Animal Rights*.

22 Uddin, *Zoo Renewal*.

23 Chrulew, "Animals as Biopolitical Subjects." See also Chrulew, "An Art of Both Caring and Locking Up."

24 McArthur, *Captive*.

25 See, e.g., Morin, *Carceral Space, Prisoners and Animals*. See also Traisnel, *Capture*. Zoos are also discussed throughout Gruen, ed., *Critical Terms for Animal Studies*.

26 Acampora, ed., *Metamorphoses of the Zoo*; Donahue, ed., *Increasing Legal Rights for Zoo Animals*; Minteer, Maienschein, and Collins, eds., *The Ark and Beyond*. Another must-read collection, specifically focused on elephants (though not entirely on zoos), is Wemmer and Christen, *Elephants and Ethics*. See also these two foundational volumes: Norton, Hutchins, Stevens, and Maple, *Ethics on the Ark*; Hoage and Deiss, *New Worlds, New Animals*.

27 Tsing, *The Mushroom at the End of the World*, 158.

28 Of course, even this notion of zoo animals as "representatives" is not fixed, singular, or static. Zoo animals have many cultural lives as members of their species. For more along this line of thinking see Heise, *Imagining Extinction*.

29 See also, Roscher and Krebber, eds., *Animal Biography: Re-framing Animal Lives* (forthcoming).

CHAPTER ONE

PSYCHOTIC HUMANS, PSYCHOTIC ANIMALS: THE ZOO AND THE MENTAL HOSPITAL, 1656–1794

Matthew Senior

In his controversial 2001 essay "Rules for the Human Zoo," the German philosopher Peter Sloterdijk advances the thesis that Western humanism and statecraft have always been based on an exchange of ideas and letters between friends. With wry humour, Sloterdijk calls this long transferal of political and philosophical ideas "Greco-Roman mail." He continues: "We can trace the communitarian fantasy at the root of all humanisms back to the model of a literary society, in which participation through reading the canon reveals a common love of inspiring messages."[1] But alongside this polite, often superficial and facile humanism with its emphasis on the rational choices of educated subjects runs another political project in the West, a more radical, "pastoral" humanism, which Sloterdijk and Foucault trace back to Plato's *Statesman*. This form of humanism consists of breeding and raising a healthy, productive population overseen by a cadre of elite leaders with specialized knowledge who are themselves guided by a pastor-sovereign, who goads his flock towards ever higher and more impossible incarnations of the human species. The ultimate task of the pastoral leader, acting as a eugenicist, is to "weave together," through marriage, the desirable traits of the soldier and the philosopher and thereby to breed the ideal population. The humanistic state, in this more radical sense, is thus a kind of zoo or theme park.[2] Another way that Sloterdijk contrasts the traditional literary and linguistic project of humanism with the deeper eugenic pattern is to suggest that reading (*Lesen*) has always been tied to biological selection (*Auslesen*).[3]

A central idea that Sloterdijk derives from Plato is that the pastoral leader is ever mindful of humanity's underlying animality. The sovereign governs humans as a herd that evolves constantly over time. Describing the emergence of the human being from a prior animal state, Sloterdijk speaks of a traumatic "shattering" of animality, as the emergent human acquires a world and language, or in Heidegger's vocabulary a "house of Being." Sloterdijk observes, in an aside, that this transition would only produce "psychotic animals" were it not that humans were able to take refuge in the house of Being: "We could go so far as to suggest that man is the being in which being an animal is separate from remaining an animal. Because of his shattered animality, the indeterminate being falls out of the environment and manages to develop a world in an ontological sense. … Such an exodus would create only psychotic animals were it not that concurrent with the entrance into the World there is also an entrance from that world into what Heidegger terms the 'house of Being.'"[4]

Two of Sloterdijk's far-reaching, transhistorical ideas merit further attention in an enquiry into the nature of zoos: (1) that human societies can be understood as nature parks or zoos, making clear that the political, from the beginning, has always been the biopolitical, and (2) that human consciousness and cultural formations are structured around a fall from or a shattering of animality, which is attenuated and mitigated by language and houses of Being. Related to this second idea is Sloterdijk's remark that failure to transition from an animal to a human state can result in trauma and psychosis. In this chapter, I will explore two spaces of transition and contact between animality and humanity: the zoo, where animals are forced to leave their natural habitats and are traumatized and psychologically altered, and the mental hospital, where humans who experience psychological trauma are housed and treated like animals. My specific historical context for exploring these questions begins with the co-creation of the first modern mental hospital and the first modern zoo by the same royal architect, Louis Le Vau, who began work on the Salpêtrière in 1656 and submitted his design for the Ménagerie at Versailles in 1662. This period concludes in 1794, with the transfer of the last animals from the Ménagerie to the Jardin des Plantes, and the unchaining of the mad at Bicêtre and the Salpêtrière between 1797 and 1800. Before looking in more detail at these two institutions, however, it is necessary to examine the history of the idea of pastoral power in the West as first discussed by Plato in *Statesman* and later taken up by Christianity and raison d'état political theory during the seventeenth century.

The Magna Carta of Pastoral Power

At the beginning of *Statesman*, "the Magna Carta of a European pastoral philosophy" according to Sloterdijk,[5] the Stranger from Elea takes the lead role in the dialogue and proposes that the ruler or king is an artisan who shapes and controls tangible objects, and more specifically, living objects: "The royal science is not like that of a master-workman, a science presiding over lifeless objects; the king has a nobler function, which is the management and control of living beings."[6] In a manner that prefigures Derrida's refusal, in *The Animal That Therefore I Am*, to separate humans from other animals, the Stranger playfully points out the difficulty of establishing definitive differences between humans and other animals.[7] Having proven that the art of statecraft is the government of herd animals the Stranger cautions against separating humans too quickly from other animals, and points out how absurd it would be if another animal set itself apart from all others: "Suppose now that some wise and understanding creature, such as a crane is reputed to be, were, in imitation of you, to make a similar division, and set up cranes against all other animals to their own special glorification, at the same time jumbling together all the others, including man, under the appellation of brutes."[8]

After further narrowing down man as a "tame, walking, herding animal," the Stranger takes a perverse delight in declaring that man is a herd animal "without horns," and further is a "bipedal animal" like a bird.[9] The statesman is therefore similar in his herding function to a bird keeper: "The king is found running about with the herd and in close competition with the bird-catcher, who of all mankind is the most adept at the airy life."[10] Another pointedly animal dimension of governing humans revolves around the fact that the human herd is dedicated to propagating a single species or race:

Stranger: And of which has the Statesman charge, – of the mixed or of the unmixed race?
Young Socrates: Clearly of the unmixed.[11]

The pastoral leader is thus a breeder of a particular race of humans.[12] If he is like an actual shepherd of herd animals, he must have many skills and be able to meet all of his flock's needs. The ideal pastoral ruler is "a physician of his herd; he is also their match-maker and *accoucheur*, no one else knows that department of science. And he is their merry-maker and musician, as far as their nature is susceptible of such influences, and no one can console and soothe his own herd better than he can, either with the natural tones of his voice or with instruments. And the same may be said of tenders of animals in general."[13]

In his 1979 "Omnes et Singulatim: Towards a Criticism of 'Political Reason,'" Foucault reads *Statesman* as a foundational text in the history of pastoral power (an expression he coined).[14] In this tradition, which begins in the East with the idea of the ruler as a shepherd who watches over and cares for each individual member of the flock, the state must provide for and govern its citizens as both individuals (*singulatim*) and as a collective flock (*omnes*). Judaism and Christianity added to this heritage, with the ideal of God or God's representative on earth as a caring shepherd who rejoices more in finding one lost sheep than in looking after the whole herd. Christianity also contributed the monastic practice of spiritual direction to the pastoral tradition, with its emphasis on absolute obedience, the obligation to tell the truth about oneself, and close psychological ties between spiritual director and followers.

In his reading of *Statesman*, concerning the passage cited above, Foucault argues that the point at which the ruler is called "the physician of his herd" and the "match-maker and *accoucheur*" who soothes his herd "with the natural tones of his voice or with instruments" is the point at which the analogy between the herdsman and the political leader breaks down. The political herdsman has neither the diverse skills nor the time to meet the multiple needs of his human herd. Foucault argues that at this point the dialogue moves away from the metaphor of the ruler as a herdsman and towards the idea of the political leader as a supervisory "weaver" of society who delegates individuals' pastoral care to a series of specialists – the doctor, the carpenter, the farmer, etc. – while exercising true political power through the science of statecraft.

It must be said, however, that Plato tarries long and in detail with the animal nature of humans. If the shepherd of humans is an organizer and practitioner of the science of government, the fundamental task is still a zoological one. The essentially biological nature of statecraft emerges again in the seventeenth and eighteenth centuries in the treatises of raison d'état theorists such as Louis Turquet de Mayerne (1555–1618), Nicolas Delamare (1639–1723), and Johann Heinrich Gottlob von Justi (1717–1771). In commenting on these texts, Foucault observes that the modern state seeks to fortify itself by increasing its citizens' vitality, productivity, and happiness. Modern sovereigns realize that they are in a perpetual battle with other states and that human resources are the most important arms in this incessant struggle. In organizing this battle, the state pays attention to and gathers statistics on both individuals and groups or populations. It reaches out to touch the individual while at the same time marshalling individuals into groups for specific tasks. The bureaucracies charged with these biopolitical tasks in early modern societies were referred to collectively as "the police." This differs from the contemporary meaning of the police as concerned only with criminal matters. Instead, Foucault writes: "Life is the object of the police: the indispensable, the useful, and the superfluous. That people survive, live, and even do better than just that, is what the police has to ensure."[15] The police focus on both individuals and populations, defined as "a group of live individuals ... a group of beings living in a given area."[16]

The Age of Chronos

To return to *Statesman* and give a more complete account of the philosophy and mythology of the pastoral ruler, it is necessary to examine the myth of the golden age and the cyclical nature of time in the pastoral tradition. The Stranger recounts that during the age of Chronos, "God himself was the shepherd of mankind and ruled over men, just as man, who is by comparison a divine being, still rules over the lower animals." During this idyllic time, humans "dwelt naked, and mostly in the open air, for the temperature of their seasons was mild; and they had no beds, but lay on soft couches of grass, which grew plentifully out of the earth." There was no form of government; the earth brought forth food for maintaining life; humans had "boundless leisure ... and the power of holding intercourse, not only with men, but with the brute creation."[17] During the succeeding age of Zeus, the

gods abandoned direct pastoral care of the world and left humanity to govern themselves. In a cosmic, visionary passage, Plato describes the moment
of transition from the golden age to the iron age as God letting go of the
universe: "the pilot of the universe let the helm go, and retired to his place
of view."[18]

Abandoned by the gods, the universe drifted; harmony between humans
and animals broke down: "Deprived of the care of God, who had possessed
and tended them, humans were left helpless and defenseless, and were
torn in pieces by the beasts, who were naturally fierce and had now grown
wild."[19] Despite the strife of the ensuing iron age, however, the Stranger is
not sure that humans were happier during the perfectly harmonious golden
age, because there is no surviving evidence that they had the pleasure of
telling stories or any "love of knowledge and discussion."[20] There is no
record of the conversations humans then held with animals or gods. During
the present cycle of history, rulers look back nostalgically to a primordial
past when humans lived intimately with animals. From the point of view of
cyclical time, the golden age will return again; the future will restore the past.

The Ménagerie

To the extent that a monarch such as Louis XIV could manage a huge collection of wild animals and display them in orderly fashion, he would evoke
the memory of the golden age when humans were ruled by Olympian gods.
The Sun King was systematically celebrated as Apollo at Versailles, where
the rising sun struck the windows of his bedroom and the fountains and
waterworks behind his chateau represented the solar god driving his chariot
across the sky. To the extent that an absolute king could envision his people
as a flock of living beings, he would also be following in the footsteps of
Plato's *Statesman* and exercising an ancient form of power that was vital to
the emerging modern state.

When one looks at the Versailles Ménagerie from the perspective of Aveline's 1689 engraving (figure 1.1), one can see the zoological vision at the
heart of pastoral power that merges humans and animals. From the point
of view of the engraving, tiny humans and animals move about on a complex geometrical grid like pieces on a chessboard. Men and women in the

Figure 1.1 Pierre-Alexandre Aveline, *Veüe et perspective du Salon de la Ménagerie de Versailles*, 1689.

great courtyard are separate from animals and gaze at them in cages. From the perspective of the elevated viewer, however, humans themselves evolve within the space of the complete system that contains both humans and animals. The courtiers' movements and shapes are not that different from those of the animals they observe. The Stranger's joke about the similarity between humans and birds even seems to be true. Most of the animals the humans observe are birds. The dress and gestures of the courtiers seem to emulate those of the birds. The engraving is historically accurate: the Ménagerie was initially stocked with exotic and domestic birds; lions, tigers, elephants, and a rhinoceros were added later.[21] The early association between zoos and biopolitical power can also be seen in the fact that people from other countries were often exhibited in zoos, a practice that intensified during the nineteenth century.[22]

Historians of the Ménagerie offer various assessments of its originality and importance. Gustave Loisel, in his definitive work on the history of zoos, situates Louis XIV's menagerie in the long history of princely animal collections, beginning with the Persian *paradeisos*, a walled park containing multiple species of wild animals for hunting and display, indiscriminately housed together. A defining moment in zoo history occurred when Alexander the Great commissioned Aristotle to study animals he had confiscated during his military campaigns, and thereby founded a connection between zoos, war, and natural history. Louis XIV was celebrated as a second Alexander for his military victories, but also for offering the animals in his collections as specimens for the Académie des Sciences. The Académie functioned as a back door to the Ménagerie, with many animals ending up on its dissecting tables.[23] The illustrations found in the pages of the Académie's *Histoire des animaux* juxtapose precise engravings of dissections of lions, chameleons, monkeys, and birds with pleasurable images of the lives the animals led at Versailles.

Cruelty and Intimacy

Running through Loisel's history of zoos is an alternating current of cruelty and intimacy that binds sovereigns to their exotic beasts. Roman generals and consuls paraded wild animals through the streets to celebrate military victories and turned them loose in the Coliseum. In repeated and incomprehensibly cruel and senseless acts of slaughter, thousands of lions, tigers, and elephants were put to death. "Sylla, having received a number of lions from Bocchus, the king of Mauritania, had a great number of animals killed to celebrate his nomination as prefect: 100 male lions … Julius Caesar instituted the first bull fights in Rome; he had a giraffe and 400 lions sacrificed for the feast of his elevation to the forum."[24]

Romans enjoyed the spectacle of animals fighting in staged battles between elephants, tigers, lions, bears, and dogs. Human combatants, including emperors themselves, leapt into the arena on occasion and took part in killing exotic animals. Caligula had criminals thrown into the arena to be torn apart by lions; Christian martyrs faced a similar fate. The taste for animal combat was revived during the Renaissance and survived until the day of Louis XIV.

Alongside this delight in animal slaughter, Loisel describes wealthy Roman households populated with tame animals, especially cats and singing birds. Among patricians and emperors, pet lions and other show animals were common. Marc Antony appeared on occasion in the streets of Rome seated next to an actress in a chariot drawn by lions. Heliogabalus often walked the hills of the Vatican with four lions on a leash, or four deer.[25] Close intimacy to the point of partial identity with animals on the part of aristocrats reappeared during the Renaissance. Isabeau of Bavaria (1370–1435) was constantly accompanied by a small menagerie consisting of a pet leopard, a monkey dressed in a fur-lined coat with a gold chain around its neck, an owl, a porpoise, and dozens of song birds.[26] Marie d'Anjou (1404–1463) had a similar collection of rabbits, a porpoise, two bustards, deer, parrots, and starlings. Marie's son, Louis XI of France, kept a pet lioness.[27] The Bourbon kings, especially as children, displayed both devotion and incredible cruelty towards animals. Louis XIII loved birds, and as a child he enjoyed sending captured song birds into his pet hawks' waiting talons. Louis XVI had a tame deer he cherished as a child, but which he shot to death with a gun as his guardians looked on with apparent approval.[28]

Loisel describes the Ménagerie as "the most beautiful collection of living animals arranged in a single space since Antiquity," and notes that, unlike the king's other menagerie at Vincennes, it was not a space for animal combat.[29] The most original aspect of the Ménagerie was the way animals were displayed:

> The design Le Vau conceived was ingenious and entirely original. Until this moment, in all of the princely courts in France and abroad, the lodgings of wild animals kept in captivity were disseminated in different parts of the domain: in one place, "the house of ferocious beasts," in another place, "the aviary," here "the park for deer," there "the elephant stables" … At Versailles, Louis XIV wanted all of the animals to be grouped together, in the same space as plants and flowers; and thus in reality he created the first zoological garden … He wanted everything to be built in luxury and arranged to be seen from a single point of view (*d'un seul regard*).[30]

Foucault credits Le Vau with the invention of a new way of seeing that may have given rise to the Panopticon:

> Bentham does not say whether he was inspired, in his project, by Le Vaux's Ménagerie at Versailles: the first zoo in which the different

elements are not, as they traditionally were, distributed in a park ... one finds in the program of the Panopticon a similar concern with individualizing observation, with characterization and classification, with the analytical arrangement of space. The Panopticon is a royal menagerie; the animal is replaced by man, individual distribution by specific grouping and the king by the machinery of a furtive power.[31]

Foucault comments that the Panopticon can be used for different purposes – for surveillance, for punishment, for discipline, and also for pleasure: "It does not matter what motive animates him [the observer]: the curiosity of the indiscreet, the malice of a child, the thirst for knowledge of a philosopher who wishes to visit this museum of human nature, or the perversity of those who take pleasure in spying and punishing."[32] The connection between confining and viewing animals and subjecting humans to a similar classificatory gaze had already been established in seventeenth-century France. Le Vau was the royal architect for both the Ménagerie and the Salpêtrière, the work camp Louis XIV commissioned to imprison criminals, vagabonds, prostitutes, and the mentally ill.

Eric Baratay and Elizabeth Hardouin-Fugier analyze in detail the architectural precedents for the Ménagerie. The radiocentric design was used to landscape hunting parks in the forest of Compiègne for Francis I (1494–1547). Louis Savot's 1624 *L'architecture française des bâtiments particuliers* theorizes this design. The design was adopted by landscape architect André Le Nôire and can be seen throughout Versailles. The same *patte d'oie* (goose foot) structure also appears in the urban plans of Leon Battista Alberti and was probably derived from Vitruvius, whose works contain circular designs for cities with radiating streets as opposed to the standard quadrilateral plans of Roman cities. The intended effect of the Versailles design, according to Baratay and Hardouin-Fugier, was to create a theatre setting for viewing animals. Prior to the zoo's construction, perspectival stages had been erected in parks surrounding princely estates, incorporating landscape elements into the set design. This theatricalization of nature prepared the way for the Ménagerie, where cages and fences put animals on stage and subjected them to the classical unities of space, time, and plot. Gravel in the enclosure for ostriches and a large basin of water for aquatic birds function as stage props, creating a desert décor for the ostriches and a lake for the birds.

As an overall pattern and theme, Baratay and Hardouin-Fugier interpret Versailles as an imposition of culture on nature. Animals and landscapes are plotted and framed by geometric patterns and stage sets. Culture swallows up nature and submits it to the monarch. Aurelia Gaillard similarly focuses her interpretation of the animals at Versailles on the aesthetic frames through which they are seen, and argues that the presence of statues of human-animal figures derived from Ovid fills the spectacle with a mythical atmosphere. Gaillard also argues that animals appear to conform to the rituals and rules of the civilizing process, as defined by Norbert Elias.

Peter Sahlins takes a similar approach, interpreting the animals as models of *civilité*, but with the added dimension of *honnêteté*. Elias's model for court behaviour focuses on the courtiers' submission to a hierarchical etiquette defined by the monarch. From Elias's perspective, courtly behaviour reinforces social hierarches and obedience to the king. *Honnêteté*, by contrast, is a more egalitarian ideal; virtue and distinction are available to anyone, provided they distinguish themselves and show respect for others. There are thus two gazes to be considered in analyzing the Ménagerie: the monarch's panoptical gaze, which imposes hierarchy and commands submission, and the courtiers' more humble, admiring gaze, fixed on the animals as models of grace and virtue.

My own work on the Ménagerie, influenced by Foucault, has focused on "individualizing observation," "characterization and classification," and "the analytical arrangement of space."[33] As Foucault points out in his comments on the Panopticon, the visual *dispositif* could be used by many observers for many purposes. The Ménagerie was visited by kings, courtiers, foreign dignitaries, artists, poets, and anatomists who have left behind various records of their impressions. An engraving of Pieter Boel's *Quartier des Demoiselles* reveals many of the different lenses through which visitors saw the animals (see figure 1.2). The birds are, most immediately, objects of pleasure and display, their vitality set off against the architecture and statuary surrounding them. Human and hybrid figures from Ovid's *Metamorphosis* look down upon the birds, situating them in a mythical and enchanted past. The birds are certainly models of *civilité* and decorum, as Gaillard and Sahlins argue. But they are also sketched and engraved with exactitude and realism, named and numbered by Boel, who observed them closely and made countless *études* of the mammals, reptiles, and birds he

Figure 1.2 Pieter Boel, engraving by G. Scotin, *Quartier des Demoiselles*, c. 1670.
(1) Muscovy ducks, (2) demoiselle cranes, (3) black-crowned cranes, (4) Canada
geese, (5) Guinea fowl, (6) great bustards.

observed in the king's garden. This exactness in depicting and naming animals is in concert with the revolution in natural history that occurred during the seventeenth century.

In this chapter, I explore a new reading of the Ménagerie, as I suggest that
Louis XIV's zoo was a biopolitical demonstration, positioning the monarch
as a shepherd of animals and humans. To extend Baratay's observations, I
agree that animals appear on a classical stage to act out dramas and emotions
common to humans and animals and to hint at a return to the *paradeisos* or
the golden age, when humans lived and talked with animals. In addition to
being set décor, I wonder if the natural elements in the birds' cages – gravel
that evokes a desert or water that suggests a lake – do not create habitats or
biospheres, an ecosystem where select animal populations can thrive and reproduce. From this pastoral perspective, the successful acclimatization of exotic animals from Africa and India does not so much symbolize imperial
conquest as it does the monarch's miraculous capacity to create viable habitats for his animals.

Psychotic Animals

To return to Sloterdijk's observation that the taming and domestication of human and nonhuman animals is sometimes traumatic, and always psychotropic, one wonders if anyone at Versailles noticed that some animals did not adapt well to captivity. The first mention I find of this issue are Buffon's comments, a century later, that animals confined to zoos behave in an "altered and constrained manner, unworthy of the scrutiny of a philosopher, for whom the only beautiful nature is, if you will, nature that is free, independent, and wild."[34]

One can see anxiety and suffering on the faces and in the body language of some of Boel's animals. A civet sits in a tight crouch, looking warily outwards; a fox snarls defensively (see figure 1.3). A lion grimaces and raises its paw; a monkey tenses and gesticulates nervously. Who cannot see that these animals are violated in their natures and would instantly flee the zoo if given the chance?

Henri Ellenberger, among others (including contributors represented in this volume), has studied the phenomenon of specific psychoses suffered by zoo animals, and he has compared these pathologies to similar symptoms exhibited by mental patients confined in clinical settings. Ellenberger describes the trauma an animal suffers when taken from the wild: "In its native habitat the animal is narrowly integrated into a space-time system which includes its individual or collective 'territory' and its biorhythms. The animal is also part of a social system in which group relations are thoroughly regulated even to the smallest detail. The animal uprooted from these systems, as well as from his *Umwelt*, is completely disoriented."[35] An animal's reaction to this trauma may consist of "attacks of acute agitation often resulting in severe wounds or death," "prolonged stupor," or "a kind of hunger strike, which can result in the animal's death if it is not forcibly fed."[36] Zoo animals also exhibit "repetitive movements" as a response to the stress of captivity, as well as coprophagia. As almost every chapter of *Zoo Studies: A New Humanities* will demonstrate, the psychoses and pathologies of captivity are many, and they pervade the history of the zoological park. Ellenberger observes that mental patients suffer a similar "trauma of commitment" when institutionalized against their wills and suddenly torn from their normal environments. Like animals in zoos, humans suffer from the compression of

Figure 1.3 Pieter Boel, study of a civet and goose foot (*top*);
study of a fox (*bottom*).

their social worlds and the exaggerated effects of social ranking in captivity. In zoo environments, animal hierarchies are more brutally enforced, in part because lower ranking animals cannot flee and escape the physical abuse of alpha animals.

The Salpêtrière

It would seem that the mental suffering inflicted on animals at Versailles was unintended and went unnoticed – or was perhaps deliberately glossed over – except in some of the studies of animal painters. The animalization of madness in seventeenth-century mental hospitals was noticed; and it was, in some sense, intensified for therapeutic reasons. The mentally ill human was considered to have regressed to an animal state. It was fitting and beneficial to treat such a person like an animal and put her on display in a setting that bore a striking resemblance to the Versailles Ménagerie.

Idleness, Unreason, and Madness

The Salpêtrière's history as a place of human confinement begins in April 1656, with a royal edict that called for the arrest and confinement of beggars, indigents, prostitutes, and the mentally ill. Paris was inundated at this time with an infinite number of vagabonds and beggars who were leading openly licentious lives. To curb this libertine behaviour and, at the same time, to help them, the king issued written orders during the month of April, setting aside five different houses and calling them collectively the Hôpital Général. Louis XIV ordered that the poor of all ages and genders were to be confined there; the infirm and the old should also receive all manner of assistance; those unable to work should be employed at various tasks; and all should be instructed in the duties of piety.[37]

Following the wars of religion and the civil war of 1648 to 1652 known as the Fronde, the number of vagrants living in Paris had grown to nearly one-tenth of the population.[38] Prior to Louis XIV's creation of the Hôpital, this population had been subjected to straightforward repression. A 1606 decree of Parliament stipulated that beggars were to be "publicly beaten, branded on the shoulder and chased from the city." The new idea of the

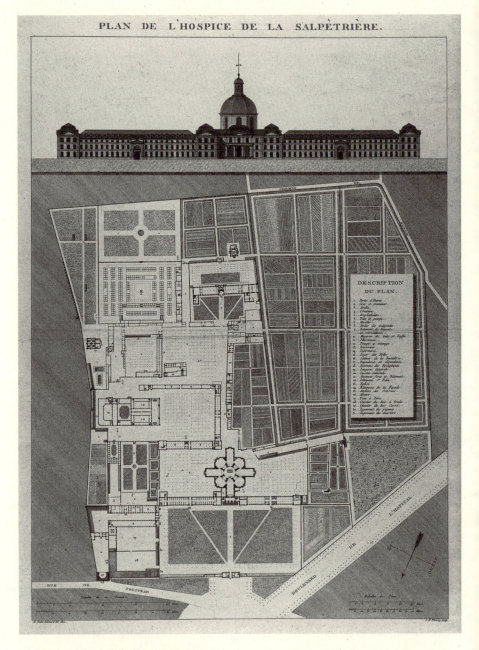

Figure 1.4 The Salpêtrière in 1812.

Salpêtrière was to confine this population and reeducate it. As the edict specifies, this took place in "five different buildings under the name of the Hôpital Général." Of these five houses, two received the greatest number of inmates: the Salpêtrière, which was for women and children, and Bicêtre, which was for men.

The word "hôpital" did not refer to a medical facility in the seventeenth century. The Salpêtrière was part of the Hôpital Général, a group of work camps for punishing and reeducating vagrants, prostitutes, criminals, and the mentally ill. The mass of unemployed and disabled were confined because they represented a threat to public order. The preamble to the 1656 document declares that Louis XIV created the Hôpital because "he believed it was his religious duty to provide assistance to the poor and to calm the disorders that this war [the Fronde] had caused."[39] The creators also argued that beggars ruined the economy because, by refusing to work, they deprived the market of an agricultural workforce, which drove up the cost of grain. Following the royal decree of 1656, the first arrests took place, and yielded about 800 women and a number of children for the Salpêtrière. At this time, there were already several buildings on the site, but more space was needed as thousands of indigents were rounded up. Le Vau was put in charge of plans to expand the Salpêtrière in 1656.

When Le Vau arrived, certain buildings, numbered in figure 1.4, already existed: storage facilities (2 and 3); le bâtiment de la Vierge (8); and le bâtiment St Jacques (9). Le Vau built le bâtiment St Joseph (10) and le bâtiment St Claire (13). The Salpêtrière could now house four thousand people. When this larger population called for the construction of a new church, Le Vau drew up a design and surveyed the site in 1670. Throughout the seventeenth and eighteenth centuries, a series of structures were added according to Le Vau's original plans: La Force (17), a prison for criminals, built in 1684; the basses loges (20), the infamous lock-up cells for the mentally ill, built sometime before 1754; and more loges (29), built between 1783 and 1786.

Documents from the period detail how different segments of the population were housed and treated differently in separate buildings. At any given time there were about six thousand detainees confined for economic reasons; these were what St Vincent de Paul called bons pauvres (the good poor). This group was divided into several categories and housed separately. About two thousand women performed manual labour and lived in crowded dormitories, usually four to a bed and two on the floor. The Catholic mass and frequent prayers were held at prescribed hours. The *filles-mères* consisted of unmarried women waiting to give birth. There was also a group of about 1,500 orphans. In addition to this population, there were another 1,700 individuals who were more forcefully restrained; women convicted of crimes and prostitutes were housed in four separate buildings. Finally, and subject to the worst treatment of all, were the seriously mentally ill who could not perform work and were confined to the *basses loges.*

I will have more to say about their treatment later, but first I want to comment on the architectural centrepiece that Le Vau designed for the Hôpital Général: L'Eglise Saint Louis de la Salpêtrière. The plan of this building shows that the Hôpital's overriding intention was to confine the unproductive and the unreasonable in one space, to segregate them into separate categories, and to subject them, symbolically, to a single point of reference and power (see figure 1.5).

The plan of the church consisted of a domed structure divided into eight separate chapels, where different groups could assist at mass without coming into contact with each other. The dome and the round plan were common at this time, inspired by the Roman Baroque. According to art historian Anthony Sutcliffe, "During the Counter-Reformation it was agreed that the faithful should be brought closer to the altar and the pulpit. The space under the dome helped meet this need. Natural lighting could be enhanced by windows in the drum of the dome."[40] Le Vau's church, however, does something absolutely structurally unique with these conventions. As Maximilien Vessier, the author of a history of the Salpêtrière, points out: "Four naves and four angled chapels, for a total of eight separate entryways and a single altar in the middle. Eight independent doors, which allow the different categories of detainees to participate in the religious services, cordoned off with their group, but also united with the assembly. [Following the service], they return to the asylum without ever encountering the other pensioners."[41] The chapel's radial plan, with sight lines that converge at a central point, is similar to the gardens of Le Nôtre and the Mènagerie at Versailles. The concentric, octagonal design was derived from the writings of Vitruvius, who mapped out an ideal city with the same layout. In the Salpêtrière, the priest at the central altar has a perspectival view of all the inmates, while each group can only see him and not the entire assembly (see figure 1.6).

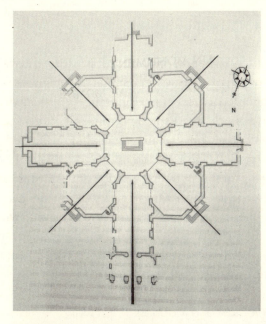

Figure 1.5 *Left*
Plan for the Eglise Saint-
Louis de la Salpêtrière, by
Louis Le Vau, 1669.

Figure 1.6 *Below*
Parishioners attending mass
at Saint-Louis de la
Salpêtrière, 1952.

Today, we might wonder why the poor, the disabled, prostitutes, criminals, and the insane were grouped together. One common denominator was idleness. Foucault calls the Hôpital a "city of pure morality" (*une cité de la moralité pure*) because to not work was a sin. Since the Fall, work was a form of penance. Bossuet, a Catholic theologian, argued that the harvest of agricultural crops was a continuous miracle, and that God could suspend this miracle at any time: "At any moment, the expectation of the harvest and the fruit of our work can escape us; we are at the mercy of the inconstant heavens that make it rain on the tender shoots of grain."[42] To refuse to work was a provocation, a second original sin. Bourdaloue, another theologian, wrote: "What is, essentially, the disorder of a slothful life? It is ... in reality, a second revolt of the creature against God."[43]

Unreason and Madness

In addition to idleness, the other common denominator of the Hôpital's inmates was unreason (*déraison*). The disparate mass of individuals confined to the hospital – beggars, criminals, prostitutes, etc. – were understood to be a group in revolt against reason, "an independent people who knew neither law, order, nor superior. Impiety, sensuality, and *libertinage* reigned supreme among them; most of the murders, thefts, and violence, committed during the day and at night, was the work of their hands."[44] Thus treatment for all internees sought to force them to conform to the norms of reason, even if the meaning – and in fact the hope for a cure – escaped some of them.

There is an important distinction between unreason (*déraison*) and madness (*folie*). All of the inmates were unreasonable, but only some were truly mad with an extreme, incurable form of unreason. Foucault draws an analogy with original sin: "What original sin can be considered in relation to diverse kinds of sin, that is what madness is in relation to other kinds of unreason: the principle, the original movement, the greatest guilt in its instantaneous contact with the greatest innocence, the ultimate model, continually repeated, of what must be forgotten in shame."[45]

There was a separate vocabulary and special treatment for the mad (see figure 1.7). Police registers categorized them as the insane (*des insensées*), the demented (*des hommes en démence*), the deranged (*des gens à l'esprit aliéné*), and the completely mad (*des personnes devenues tout à fait folles*).[46] Some of the *insensées* were confined with other internees, unless they were deemed *furieuse*, that is, if they were violent or totally incapable of work. The *furieuses* were kept in the *basses loges*.

A visitor to the Salpêtrière at the end of the eighteenth century describes the condition of the *furieuses*: "Mad women given to episodes of fury are chained up like dogs to the doors of their cells (*loges*), and separated from their guards and visitors by a long passageway covered with iron bars; the women's food is passed to them across these bars, as well as their straw, which they sleep on; rakes are used to clean away some of the filth surrounding them."[47] A human being who had lost her rationality was treated like an animal. As Foucault comments: "Those that are chained to the walls of the cells are not really men who have lost their reason, but rather beasts fallen prey to a natural rage, as if, at its extreme point, madness, separated from the less serious *moral* unreason with which it was confined, broke through and joined ranks with the immediate violence of animality. This model of animality is evident in the asylums and gives them feeling of cages and menageries."[48] In its purest form, madness, in the case of the *furieuses*, was distinguished from the other forms of *déraison* with which it was enclosed. It was identified with pure animal violence and liberty – the same pure animal liberty that classical reason most fears and constrains.

Treating the mad like animals was considered the only way to cure them, if a cure was at all possible. According to many accounts, the mad, like animals, were indifferent to extreme conditions. Pinel reports that a man at Bicêtre did not like to wear a wool shirt in the coldest months of winter and took great pleasure in applying snow and ice to his bare chest and letting it melt, "*avec une sorte de délectation.*" If there was any hope for healing the insane, it was by treating them like animals. A certain Gregory, a Scottish farmer, became famous for curing mania using such tactics. According to Pinel, "His method consists in making the alienated do the roughest farm chores and in using them as beasts of burden or lackeys; at the slightest sign of revolt, they are reduced to obedience with a volley of blows."[49] In this model, the insane are not ill; on the contrary, they are physically healthier and stronger than ordinary people.

In general, one of the key meanings of confinement was to hide scandalous behaviour and avoid the effects of contamination, but the spectacle of the insane chained up in their cells was an exception to this rule. It was considered

and the frowning eyebrow ; but this would only give the idea
of passion, not of madness. Or he mistakes melancholia for
madness. The theory upon which we are to proceed in attempting to convey this peculiar look of ferocity amidst the
utter wreck of the intellect, I conceive to be that the expression of mental energy should be avoided, and consequently

the action of all those muscles which indicate sentiment. I
believe this to be true to nature, because I have observed
(contrary to my expectation) that there was not that energy,
that knitting of the brows, that indignant brooding and
thoughtfulness in the face of madmen which is generally
imagined to characterise their expression, and which is so

Figure 1.7 Charles Bell, "Madness."

an edifying moral spectacle to observe the mentally ill in the Salpêtrière.[50] The
meaning of this spectacle was not to exalt and celebrate madness, as had been
done during the Renaissance, but to show it as entirely objectified and tamed.
According to Foucault: "During the classical period madness is on display,
but from the other side of the bars; if it is shown, it is from a distance, beneath
the gaze of a reason that no longer has any relationship with it and cannot
be compromised by any resemblance to it."[51]

Quoniam in furorem versus est

One final nuance about madness is revealed in the spectacle of insanity as animality. The insane person does not simply become an animal like any other, but reveals instead the underlying, core animality of the human being to which any human could revert but for the grace of God. The spectacle of the totally mad human-animal provoked a religious response in seventeenth-century society. Many religious orders, such as the Lazarists, were particularly concerned with the treatment of the mentally ill. St Vincent de Paul, the founder of the Lazarists, had a brother who was found to be mad and committed to Bicêtre. De Paul reacted as follows: "We must honor Our Lord in that condition He found Himself in when they sought to bind Him because He had become mad, *quoniam in furorem versus est*, in order to sanctify that state in those whom divine providence has kept there."[52] From a religious perspective, the insane person, although behaving and in need of being treated like an animal, was, according to seventeenth-century understandings of madness, still a human being distinct from the other animals in nature. Christ allowed himself to be taken for mad, thereby sanctifying this condition and inspiring Christians to imitate him. The Christian redemption and recuperation of the insane person as still human makes an ultimate distinction between confined humans and animals during the Classical Age and shows the underlying theological thought behind the Salpêtrière. Somehow, miraculously, in a shattered state, in a shattering that returned the human to the animal, an invisible distinction was preserved.

It may be that in the enclosures of the Ménagerie and the *basses loges* of the Salpêtrière, a failed domestication of Being takes place. The zoo and the mental hospital are halfway houses of Being where, however fleetingly and impossibly, wild and untamed beings resist and suffer.

NOTES

1 Sloterdijk, "Rules for the Human Zoo."

2 Ibid., 25.

3 Ibid., 23.

4 Ibid., 20, 21.

5 Ibid., 24.

6 Plato, *Statesman, The Dialogues of Plato.*
7 In *The Animal That Therefore I Am,* Derrida refuses the longstanding
   historical and philosophical opposition between "man" and the collective
   singular noun "the animal," which groups together all animals and oppos-
   es them to "man." In opposition to the collective singular, Derrida invents
   the neologism *animot,* a homonymic pun on *animaux,* the plural in French.
   Although Derrida makes it clear that he does not consider humans to be
   simply animals with no distinguishing traits and specific ethical responsibil-
   ities, the thrust of his essay is to seek his own hidden animal nature, most
   notably by standing naked before his domestic cat, transfixed by its
   inscrutable gaze.
8 Plato, *Statesman,* 459.
9 Ibid., 462.
10 Ibid., 463.
11 Ibid., 462.
12 Plato uses the word *genos* (race, stock, kin) to make a distinction between
   mixed or hybrid kinds of animals that cannot reproduce, such as the ass,
   and fertile, unmixed kinds of animals that can reproduce. For the various
   meanings of *genos,* see Liddell and Scott, *A Greek-English Lexicon,* con-
   sultable online at http://www.perseus.tufts.edu/hopper/text?doc=Perseus
   %3Atext%3A1999.04.0057%3Aentry%3Dge%2Fnos. Although the
   Greeks and Romans did not understand race in the modern sense of the
   word, as a genetically distinct group of people with physiologically determined cognitive and cultural traits, it is clear, throughout *Statesman* and
   other works, that Plato consistently pursued a eugenic project: that of
   breeding a superior population by ordaining marriages between mates
   possessing superior warrior or philosopher traits. See Kennedy, Roy, and
   Golman, *Race and Ethnicity in the Classical World,* which contains key
   texts and a rich bibliography on the subject of race in the ancient world.
13 Ibid., 465–6.
14 Foucault, "Omnes et Singulatim."
15 Ibid., 250.
16 Ibid., 252.
17 Plato, *Statesman,* 470.
18 Ibid., 471.
19 Ibid., 472.

20 Ibid., 471.

21 On the history of the Versailles Ménagerie, see Loisel, *Histoire des Ménageries de l'Antiquité à nos jours*; see also Franklin, *La Vie Privée d'autrefois*; Marie, *Naissance de Versailles*; Mabille, "La Ménagerie de Versailles"; Marie, *Versailles au temps de Louis XIV*; Berger, *In the Garden of the Sun King*; Mullen and Marvin, *Zoo Culture*; Ireye, "Le Vau's Ménagerie"; Hoage and Deiss, *New Worlds, New Animals*; Baratay and Hardouin-Fugier, *Zoos*; Robbins, *Elephant Slaves and Pampered Parrots*; Sahlins, "The Royal Menageries of Louis XIV."

22 See Boëtsch, Snoep, and Blanchard, *Human Zoos*.

23 See Guerrini, *The Courtiers' Anatomists*.

24 Loisel, *Histoire*, 1:92.

25 Ibid., 113.

26 Ibid., 174.

27 Loisel, *Histoire*, 2:256.

28 Ibid., 93, 135.

29 Ibid., 293.

30 Ibid., 104.

31 Foucault, *Discipline and Punish*, 203.

32 Ibid.

33 Senior, "Seeing the Versailles Ménagerie"; "The Ménagerie and the Labyrinthe"; "Introduction: The Animal Witness."

34 Quoted in Burkhardt, "Le comportement animal," 573.

35 Ellenberger, "The Mental Hospital and the Zoological Garden," 81.

36 Ibid.

37 "L'Hospital Général pour le Renfermement des Pauvres de Paris," quoted in Vessier, *La Pitié-Salpêtrière*, 57.

38 During the minority of Louis XIV, La Fronde was an uprising by the nobility against the queen mother and regent Anne of Austria and her minister Cardinal Mazarin.

39 Vessier, *La Pitié-Salpêtrière*, 61. See my "The Animal Witness," 14–17, for an earlier discussion of the Salpêtrière.

40 Sutcliffe, *Paris*, 37.

41 Vessier, *La Pitié-Salpêtrière*, 102.

42 Bossuet, quoted in Foucault, *Discipline and Punish*.

43 Bourdaloue, quoted in Foucault, *Discipline and Punish*, 84.

44 Quoted in Foucault, *Discipline and Punish*, 651.

45 Foucault, *Discipline and Punish*, 151.

46 Ibid., 262.

47 Quoted in Foucault, *Discipline and Punish*, 165.

48 Ibid.

49 Foucault, *Discipline and Punish*, 168.

50 "En France, la promenade à Bicêtre et le spectacle des grands insensé, demeure jusqu'a la Révolution une des distractions dominicales des bourgeois de la rive gauche." Two plays written in seventeenth-century France take up the theme of paying an entrance fee to visit the mad in asylums as a form of entertainment: *L'Hôpital des fous* (1630) and *Les Illustres Fous* (1650) by Charles Bys. This also occurred at Bedlam, in England.

51 Foucault, *Discipline and Punish*, 163.

52 Quoted in Foucault, *Discipline and Punish*, 172.

CHAPTER TWO

THE ANTELOPE COLLECTORS

Nigel Rothfels

Here I again sat, and with a longing heart and watched the movements of these loveliest of Africa's lovely antelopes. I was struck with admiration at the magnificence of the noble old black buck, and I vowed in my heart to slay him, although I should follow him for a twelvemonth.
– Roualeyn Gordon Cumming

In his 1919 biography of Frederick Courtenay Selous, John Guille Millais notes that the big-game hunter was inspired to pursue his trade in Africa after reading hunting memoirs in his youth. "There are few of us," Millais writes, "whose early aspirations and subsequent acts are not influenced by literature. Some book comes just at the time of our life when we are most impressionable and seems exactly to fit in with our ideas and temperment."[1] Pointing to "landmarks in the literature of African sport and travel, each book being more or less cumulative in its effect,"[2] Millais singles out the texts of Roualeyn Gordon Cumming, William John Burchell, Francis Galton, William Cornwallis Harris, Karl Johan Andersson, and William Cotton Oswell, arguing that these and others "could hardly have failed to make their impress on the minds of young men of the right kind."[3] For most of their readers today, and for many in the nineteenth and early twentieth centuries, these hunting memoirs can seem like little more than what James Emerson Tennent in 1861 bemoaned as the "monotonous recurrence of scenes of

blood and suffering."[4] Still, for those interested in ideas about animals, nature, and the "wild" in the nineteenth century, these books provided, as they
do now, a wealth of information.

Reading these memoirs carefully often leads to unexpected realizations.
If Cumming's name is recognized at all today, for example, it is likely as that
of an obsessive lion and elephant hunter prone to lengthy and often bloody
descriptions; perhaps because Cumming's descriptions of those hunts are
some of his most dramatic, or perhaps because his readers over the last century have simply been more and more interested in lions and elephants.
Whatever the case, thinking of Cumming as simply a lion and elephant
hunter can mean that we can lose track of his much broader agenda. Page
after page of his two-volume work is filled with accounts of hunting, and
only a small number feature lions or elephants. Cumming actually repeatedly
put his wider interests directly before his readers. Refering at one point to a
conversation with a farmer, for example, he writes, "This Boer informed me
that I could get all the rarer animals, which I wished to shoot, in his vicinity,
namely, sable antelope, roan antelope, eland, waterbuck, koodoo, pallah,
elephant, black and white rhinoceros, hippopotamus, giraffe, buffalo, lion,
&c."[5] For most readers today, the surprising thing about this list is not the
presence of elephants, rhinoceroses, hippos, giraffes, buffalos, and lions (a
group that remains at the core of both safari and zoo marketing); instead,
what stands out is that the first six species are varieties of antelope that most
nonspecialists would have difficulty identifying. Cumming's list points to a
story about antelopes, a story which illuminates a part of the modern history
of zoos that is usually neglected.

In Pursuit of the Rare and the Beautiful

Near the beginning of the second volume of his 1850 *Five Years of a Hunter's
Life in South Africa*, Cumming describes the first time he saw a sable antelope, a creature he unreservedly calls "the rarest and most beautiful animal
in Africa."[6] Describing the animals as "large and powerful," with backs and
sides "a glossy black, beautifully contrasting with the belly, which is white
as driven snow," Cumming devotes special attention to the horns, which are
"upward of three feet in length, and bend strongly back with a bold sweep,

reaching nearly to the haunches."[7] The hunter makes clear that he had long wanted to pursue sables, which he also calls "potaquaines" (borrowing from the local Tswane language), and the first one he tells us he saw was unsurprisingly impressive. He writes: "The one which was now before me was the first I had seen, and I shall never forget the sensation I experienced on beholding a sight so thrilling to the sportsman's eye."[8] Alas, with a tired horse and "dogs that had lost their spirit in the sun" this sable escaped, but a sleepless night followed as "the image of the antelope was still before me."[9] Hunting sables became a recurring theme for the rest of the memoir. In one of his several long accounts of stalking, chasing, and shooting animals, for example, Cumming characteristically describes his feelings upon killing a "noble" buck: "I was transported with delight when I came up and saw the surpassing beauty and magnificence of the invaluable trophy I had won. This potaquaine was very old, and his horns were enormous, fair set, perfect, and exquisitely beautiful. I cut off his head, and, leaving men to convey the flesh to camp, held thither in advance, escorting my hard-won trophy."[10] Thoughts about the size and perfection of the horns, the beauty of the animal's form, the impressiveness of the trophy, and the inherent nobility of the prey preoccupied both Cumming and those who followed him. He uses "noble" regularly in his memoir, but only for a small set of animals and natural phenomena: mountains, old trees, and deep forests could be noble, and so could elephants and lions, sable antelopes, and, occasionally, a few other animals in specific contexts, such as a fearless buffalo or an old waterbuck.

In the sense suggested by Millais that each notable work of hunting lore builds both from earlier accounts and towards a cumulative effect, the roots of Cumming's raptures about potaquaines can be traced to an earlier story by William Cornwallis Harris, who collected the first sable in 1836. In his 1838 *Narrative of an Expedition into Southern Africa during the Years 1836 and 1837*, Harris relates a story of hunting elephants in the Cashan Mountains when "a herd of unusually dark looking Antelopes attracted observation in an adjacent valley."[11] After spotting them in a pocket telescope, Harris improbably recalls, "I at once exclaimed that they were perfectly new to science; and having announced my determination of pursuing them, if requisite, to the world's end, I dashed down the slope, followed by the derision of the Hottentots, for my unsportsmanlike attention to an 'ugly buck,' *one* specimen of which, however, I assured them, I would rather possess

The Sable Antelope
HIPPOTRAGUS NIGER

Figure 2.1 *Hippotragus niger* (sable antelope) from *The Book of Antelopes*, 1894–1900. Lithograph by Joseph Smit from a watercolour by Joseph Wolf, under the direction of Sir Victor Brooke.

than all the Elephants in Africa!"[12] After three days filled with frustration as he followed the herd, Harris was finally "rewarded by the gratifying sight of ... two bucks grazing by themselves, unconscious of our approach in a stony valley."[13] He fired. The "hind leg of the handsomer of the two was dangling in an instant, and in another he was sprawling on the earth. Quickly recovering himself, however, he led me more than a mile over the sharp stones ere he was brought to bay, when, twice charging gallantly [Harris' hunting dogs], he was at length overthrown and slain."[14] The hunt over, Harris writes:

> It were vain to attempt a description of the sensations I experienced, when thus, after three days of toilsome tracking, and feverish anxiety unalleviated by any incident that could inspire the smallest hope of ultimate success, I at length found myself in actual possession of so brilliant an addition to the riches of Natural History … The horns, which were flat, and upwards of three feet in length, swept gracefully over the back in the form of a crescent. A bushy black mane extended from the lively chestnut coloured ears to the middle of the back; the tail was long and tufted; and the glossy jet black hue of the greater portion of the body, contrasted beautifully with a snow-white face and belly. I thought I could never have looked at or admired it sufficiently.[15]

In the 1839 revised version of his memoir, *The Wild Sports of Southern Africa*, Harris concludes this section by writing that at this moment his companion observed "the Sable Antelope would doubtless become the admiration of the world."[16] Harris completed a drawing and description of the animal on the spot, and then the skin was carefully removed and taken to Cape Town, where the French collector Jules Verreaux completed the specimen's taxidermy. The mount was then shipped to England, officially presented and described at a meeting of the Zoological Society of London on 9 January 1838, and stands today as the type specimen for *Hippotragus niger* in London's Natural History Museum.[17]

Cumming echoes Harris's earlier depiction of the sables' dramatic colouration, using "glossy black" where Harris uses "glossy jet black," and "white as driven snow" where Harris uses "snow white." Similarly, while Harris relates that the horns "were flat, and upwards of three feet in length, [and that they] swept gracefully over the back in the form of a crescent," Cumming writes that his buck's horns are "upward of three feet in length, and bend strongly back with a bold sweep." The echoes do not stop there. Both hunters claim that they saw something inherently courageous in the sables, something that caused the animals to fight to the end. Where Harris, then, writes about following a wounded animal for days and then watching it charge his hounds repeatedly, Cumming relates in another account that

after following a bloody spoor he found "the ever-wary, the scarce, the lovely, long-sought sable antelope, and a most noble specimen – perhaps the
finest buck in all the district" resting "on the side of his native rugged mountain." Rather than shooting the animal then and there, Cumming called for
his dogs so that the sable could die fighting.[18] For Harris and Cumming, the
ideas of "nobility," "beauty," and "rarity" seem to have complemented and
reinforced each other. Just as it was unlikely that an "ugly" animal could be
seen as noble and a "common" animal could be seen as beautiful, it seems
that the sable's appearance, rarity, and purported courage immediately made
it one of the animals most sought by nineteenth-century hunters. Once Harris and Cumming established its reputation, most who followed did little
more than agree. In his 1899 *A Breath from the Veldt*, Millais, for example,
simply reaffirmed his forerunners: "In general appearance and sporting qualities the Sable Antelope (*Hippotragus niger*) yields the palm to none of its
kind. There is about the whole animal that indescribable charm that is so intensely African and so characteristic of the wild life … Apart from its satin-
like hide, sweeping horns, erect mane, and great strength, the sable antelope
presents an appearance of fearlessness and nobility that is very striking, to
say the least of it."[19] Returning to Cumming's hopes for "sable antelope,
roan antelope, eland, waterbuck, koodoo, pallah, elephant, black and white
rhinoceros, hippopotamus, giraffe, buffalo, lion, &c," it makes sense that
the list begins with the sable antelope. The interest in antelopes in this period,
however, went far beyond the sable and indeed far beyond the roan antelope,
the eland, the waterbuck, the koodoo, and the pallah.

A Collection of Antelopes

In a 1909 issue of the *Bulletin* of the New York Zoological Society, William
T. Hornaday, the director of the New York Zoological Park in the Bronx,
provided a brief history of the park's first ten years. Reviewing the improvements to the grounds, the buildings, and the collections, and noting financial
contributions of close to five hundred thousand dollars from the members
of the society in addition to more than two million dollars from the city of
New York, Hornaday introduced the still relatively new park to the public.
He writes, "The imperial City of New York presents to the world her Zoo-

logical Park, and invites mankind to behold in it a huge living assemblage of beasts, birds and reptiles, gathered from every region of the globe, kept together in comfortable captivity, and skillfully fed and tended, in order that millions of people may know and appreciate the marvels of the Animal Kingdom." Building something worthy of the animals and the city, he writes, "has been a gigantic task; but the people of New York have proven equal to it."[20]

The collection of animals in the park that summer included 246 species of mammals (with 743 specimens), 644 species of birds (with 2,816 specimens), and 256 species of reptiles (with 1,969 specimens), for a total of 1,146 species and 5,528 specimens. These numbers make clear that the zoo grew very quickly in its first decade. Compared to today's Bronx Zoo, arguably still the flagship zoological garden of the United States where, in 2015, there were 162 species of mammals (with 1,466 specimens), 281 species of birds (with 1,748 specimens), and 149 species of reptiles (with 646 specimens) for a total of 592 species and 3,860 specimens, the 1909 collection had almost 80 per cent more species and over 43 per cent more specimens of mammals, birds, and reptiles.[21] Even considering that many of the "species" on display in 1909 would not be considered such today, the decline in the number of both species and specimens over the last century tells an important story about the changing identity of zoological gardens. While the nineteenth-century zoo's ideal was two (or even just one) of every kind, today's zoos focus on larger habitats, fewer species, and encouraging "natural" behaviours. When twenty-first-century zoo directors want to tout the cutting-edge qualities of their institutions, they talk about millions of dollars poured into gigantic exhibits that take visitors to other worlds; Hornaday's task in 1909 was different and was largely one of listing numbers of species and buildings.

He begins by noting the "African hoofed animals," among which he includes "Mountain Zebra and Grant Zebra, two species of Elephants, a pair of Black Rhinoceroses, a Hippopotamus, a pair of Giraffes, a Sable Antelope, a Kudu, a Bakers Roan Antelope, an Addax, two species of Gnu, a Beisa, a breeding pair of Leucoryx Antelope, an Eland, a Waterbuck and a Wart-Hog."[22] He then lists over twenty species of deer and seventeen species of bears, "represented by 37 specimens, including four species of the gigantic Alaskan Brown Bear group, represented by seven specimens."[23] "The collections of apes, baboons and monkeys, and small mammals and large cats," he continues, "are quite as rich as those mentioned above."[24] Among the birds he notes the single California condor; a variety of eagles, swans, cranes, falcons, flightless birds, pelicans, macaws, and cockatoos; and "a hundred smaller varieties." Among the reptiles he lists rattlesnakes, cobras, adders, "Crocodilians liberally represented, and Pythons, Boas, Anacondas, small Serpents, Lizards, Iguanas, Turtles, Tortoises, Terrapins, and Amphibians in great variety."[25] The buildings for housing the animals included twelve described by Hornaday as of the "first rank," made of brick and stone; another thirteen of "secondary importance," including various barns and houses for deer, camels, buffalos, llamas, and wild horses; and another fourteen "open-air installations" ("several very elaborate and costly") for housing wolves, wild sheep, sea lions, alligators, wild fowl, etc.[26] Among the most important buildings in place after the first ten years of operation were the Elephant House, Lion House, Reptile House, Primate House, Large Bird House, and the Antelope House. That Hornaday's article appeared in the special "Hudson-Fulton" issue of the *Bulletin*, an issue dedicated to celebrating the three hundredth anniversary of the discovery of the Hudson River and the one hundredth anniversary of the first commercial steamboat on the river, makes clear that long lists of animals and buildings were part and parcel of making the case that New York had become one of the most important cities in the world.

The story of the Antelope House goes back to the park's very beginning. As Elwin R. Sanborn put it in a feature article for the *Bulletin* in January 1904, "Ever since the opening day of the Park, the temptation to secure some of the interesting antelopes now becoming so rare, has been difficult to resist."[27] In fact, the park had acquired a few smaller antelopes over these years, but the animals had not lived long and the problem, Hornaday was convinced, was inadequate housing. He wanted a building designed specifically for antelopes and, until it was in place, he rarely succumbed to the temptation to acquire any. Then, in 1902, the time seemed right to progress. In June, the parks department contracted with architects to design "a large and finely appointed building for tropical hoofed animals, such as giraffes, African antelopes of every description, zebras and wild horses, and wild cattle of the equatorial zone."[28] The eventual elliptical building, which opened in November 1903, was 142 feet long and 78 feet wide, in "buff brick, gray limestone and terra cotta" with twenty-four stalls for animals inside, each with a separate, radiating outside yard, shaded by trees.[29] Eland heads, carved in limestone by one of the leading animal sculptors of the day, Alexander Phimister Proctor, decorated the pediments above the building entrances. The construction budget was set at fifty-five thousand dollars with the fencing, gates, wrought iron, and wire (including 1,392 feet of perimeter fencing) alone expected to cost close to nine thousand dollars. Concrete flooring, which sloped down to catch basins in front of the exhibits, was used for the stalls, while macadam, for which the park acquired a new steamroller, was used for the yards. An article in the July 1903 *Bulletin* noted that, for several months, the "society has been seeking far and wide for the species of hoofed and horned animals specially desired for the Antelope House collection." Some had arrived, others awaited shipment in Europe, and still others were "on the way from the interior of Africa." The initial collection of animals was expected to cost around fifteen thousand dollars and Hornaday urged patience because, "in the procuring of such rare species as the Eland, Sable Antelope, Roan Antelope and a few others, time is a factor that cannot be ignored, and the best we can do is to procure them as soon as the difficulties in each case will permit."[30]

Throughout 1903, Hornaday was occupied with both completing the building's construction and acquiring the collection to fill it. As he had done in the past, he relied almost entirely upon the expertise and connections of German animal dealer Carl Hagenbeck for obtaining animals.[31] While Hagenbeck and Hornaday had corresponded for years, questions about how to acquire sufficient antelopes, and which kinds to acquire, became a focus in over sixty letters and cables sent back and forth in the months that led up to the opening of the building. As Hagenbeck eventually admitted in a letter of 28 August, "I must tell you, it is the hardest job to collect antelopes."[32] Hornaday knew what he wanted and, at least early in the year, knew he would have to be patient. As he wrote to Hagenbeck on 20 February, "Our new Antelope House is going to require a large lot of expensive animals, and some of them will be of such rarity that they are not to be picked up every day."[33] As summer approached, though, he became increasingly concerned about Hagenbeck's struggles to acquire certain species, but he was still adamant about what needed to be in the collection. On 19 June, for example, he wrote to Hagenbeck:

Now, with regard to animals for the Antelope House. I am getting very nervous about this matter, because there are so few animals in the market. I send you enclosed an order for species that we wish, if it is possible to get them. I had hoped that by this time you would have a number of animals on hand; but I think you will have to see what you can do about getting some from the Duke of Bedford, the London Zoological Garden, and other Zoological Gardens. We should have at least hartebeest, one black antelope, (Hippotragus niger), and a bunch of Antelope cervicapra. If any Saiga antelopes are to be had, we would like two.

Now, it will not do for us to be caught empty-handed in the filling of the Antelope House. We have now the pair of gnus which we have ordered of you, and the one waterbuck from Frankfort, with a female waterbuck to come from Antwerp. That is all; and the Antelope House contains twenty-two compartments! I am going to send you an order for a male of each of the species I have mentioned, and if you can get a female also, so much the better; but a male we must have, provided they can be procured without too great a sacrifice in the matter of price.[34]

Hagenbeck began to push the idea of giraffes, two of which he had ready to go. Hornaday was reluctant, though, because of the price. At $5,500 for the pair, the two animals would take more than a third of the entire budget for the building's collection. On 28 August, Hornaday writes, "Regarding the giraffes, it is still impossible for us to put so much money into one species. It would be quite out of the question for us to find any member of the Society who would give us a sufficient sum to buy the pair you mention. Of course, we would be extremely glad to have the animals; but we have already called upon our members for so much money, the ones who give the large sums have grown tired, and we cannot press them farther at this time."[35] On the same day, Hagenbeck wrote to Hornaday saying that he had received word that within two weeks a "Beatrix Antelope" would arrive. Hagenbeck writes, "The Beatrix Antelope comes from Central Arabia, & in all my life I have only seen one alive in the Zoological Gardens in London."[36]

Soon, more encouraging news from Hagenbeck arrived. Letters related the successful acquisition of addax, a pair of nilgai, several blackbuck, redunca antelopes, Isabella gazelles, another pair of gnus, a roan antelope, and a blesbok; then came the big news. On 14 September, Hagenbeck writes: "I am pleased to tell you, that I am in hopes to get the large bull Eland of which

I wrote you two months ago. I inspected the animal last week at Woburn Park. It is the finest, I ever saw. It was born in June 1897 in the Duke's Park. The animal has got splendid large horns, & I don't think, that it weighs much less than about 2000 weight. His Grace only lets me have the animal as a favour to me, as I helped him to bring the animals for him from different directions by my own people to his Park." The opportunity to get an eland for $1,250 and for it to have come from the Duke of Bedford's collection, one of the most famous in the world, was accepted instantly by Hornaday, who then cabled a follow-up accepting the two giraffes as well.

On 16 October, twenty-four crates from Hagenbeck arrived in New York, and the animals were quarantined at the zoological park. On 5 November, the animals cleared quarantine with congratulations from the Department of Agriculture on such a remarkable shipment. Several of the animals were in less than optimal shape, however. The eland's crate had fallen off the wagon on the way to the Antelope House and the animal had some abrasions. In a letter to Hagenbeck from 9 November, Hornaday also noted that a horn of one of the gnus was barely hanging on and that a female blackbuck was increasingly lame in her hind legs and appeared "partially paralyzed" as she "goes around sliding her hind feet over the floor." She was removed from exhibit "because she makes such a lame appearance," but the gnu, despite its horn, was retained. On 26 November, the Antelope House opened to the public and an announcement in the *New York Times* the next day argued that "the building, with its collection, constitutes one of the finest features in the park."[37] On opening day, every stall was occupied. One of the two larger stalls was occupied by the giraffes; the other housed Duke, the eland from Woburn standing six feet at the withers. There were a pair each of two species of gnus – the white-tailed gnu (now called the black wildebeest) and white-bearded gnu (now called the blue or brindled wildebeest) – along with an addax, an Isabella gazelle, a blesbok, an Arabian oryx, a nilgai, four blackbuck, a roan antelope, a waterbuck, two reedbucks, a duiker, and two dorcas gazelles.[38] On opening day, the building also housed a Steller's sea lion, two ostriches, four zebras, and two "equine deer" (i.e., Malayan sambar deer).

After the opening, Hagenbeck continued to offer additional antelopes, but Hornaday was only interested in a few key species; he did not want to add more unless they were particularly important to the collection. Responding to only the latest in a series of offers from Hagenbeck, Hornaday wrote on 1 October 1904, almost a year after the building opened: "Our Antelope House is now so well filled that it will not be wise for us to purchase any more small antelopes. We have got to resolutely save space for such fine, large species as the Sable Antelope, Kudu, female Eland, and one or two others that are specially large and showy."[39] Throughout this correspondence, Hornaday makes clear that he wanted the large, the showy, and the male, preferably with large, perfect horns. The fact that his tastes aligned so closely with those of the big-game hunters was no coincidence.

The Book of Antelopes

The fascination with antelopes in the nineteenth century was rooted in their beauty, rarity, and variety, but also in the belief that they were disappearing quickly before the guns of pot and sport hunters. Part of the awareness of rarity can undoubtedly be traced back to the fact that the first-known extinction of a large African mammal in modern times was that of an antelope: the South African bluebuck or blaubok (*Hippotragus leucophaeus*), which disappeared forever around 1800. This extinction was followed by that of the quagga in the second half of the nineteenth century. With the disappearance of these large African mammals and the almost-complete destruction of the bison in the United States, concerns over the future of large game became increasingly prominent among both big-game hunters and zoo proponents. Importantly, these hunters and zoo advocates were often one and the same people. Hornaday, himself, for example, was a hunter, director of the New York Zoological Park, and author of such critically important books about the need for conservation as *The Extermination of the American Bison* (1887) and *Our Vanishing Wildlife: Its Extermination and Preservation* (1913). During the early decades of the New York Zoological Park, moreover, many of its executive committee, officers, and key financial supporters were also big-game hunters, and the zoo's extraordinary early commitment to saving the American bison was driven by the concerns of these affluent hunting men.

The connections between the sport-hunting and conservation movements have long been highlighted; less well known are the connections between the sport-hunting and zoo movements. Few people today, for example, think of Hornaday as a hunter because, over the last half-century especially, zoo directors have been seen more as people trying to save, rather than shoot, wildlife. In the nineteenth and early twentieth centuries, however, the lines between hunters and zoo proponents are less easy to draw. Some of Hornaday's letters, for example, make clear that even he was aware of the difficulties of disentangling his various interests. In a letter from 12 January 1904, he responded to a photograph he had received detailing the results of a recent hunting excursion in German East Africa. He writes, "I am much interested in your hunting trip and your collection of horns. As I make it out, you killed three white-bearded gnu, three white-tailed gnu, eleven hartebeests, two elands, four gazelles, two small antelopes I cannot name, and four Grant's gazelles. I cannot name the horns of the small gazelles in the front row. My conscience troubles me somewhat about your <u>six</u> gnu and <u>eleven hartebeest</u>! From all I hear, gnu are becoming so scarce that the white-tailed species is in great danger of becoming extinct within the next ten or fifteen years, and the other species will follow it in due course of time."[40] Hornaday was "troubled," but also acknowledged that the hunter "undoubtedly had a fine trip" and now had "a fine collection of horns," a collection he should endeavour to retain at all costs. He writes: "I have given away so many trophies that I have become wise, and warn you against the dangers of giving things away that ought to be kept."[41]

Hunters and zoo proponents of the period were members of a larger circle of those interested in natural history. The supporters of the new zoos in Paris, London, Berlin, New York, and elsewhere were thus usually connected to efforts to build large natural history museums. They were also often keen hunters and, significantly, readers of hunting memoirs and natural histories. All of these interests overlapped, and it is not surprising that the aspirations of hunters and zoos to acquire antelopes were echoed in a singularly remarkable work of natural history, *The Book of Antelopes*, serially published and collected in four volumes between 1896 and 1900. In a letter to Hornaday of 28 August 1903, proposing the purchase of the Beatrix antelope, Hagenbeck wrote, "You can see a fine picture of it in the 'Book of Antelopes' by Sclater & Thomas, Vol. IV."[42] Already in January 1903 – at the beginning of the antelope year – Hornaday had purchased his own copy of *The Book of Antelopes* from a London dealer, and it appears that he referred to it regularly.[43] In the increasing globalization of the animal business at the end of the nineteenth century, it makes sense that a German animal dealer based in Hamburg and a zoo director in New York City would both check their facts against a book written by the secretary of the Zoological Society of London and a taxonomist at the Natural History Museum.

The beginnings of *The Book of Antelopes* apparently stretch back to an 1870 conversation between Sir Victor Brooke and Philip Lutley Sclater, who was secretary of the Zoological Society of London from 1860 to 1902. Sclater described Brooke as "an ardent sportsman, much attached to Natural History," who had attended comparative anatomist Sir William Flowers's lectures at the College of Surgeons and who wanted to "commence serious work in Natural History."[44] Because of his interests as a sportsman, Sclater recommended that he focus on ruminants, and Brooke evidently threw himself into the task, presenting papers to the Zoological Society four times between 1871 and 1878. During these years, Brooke also travelled extensively to important museums; collected his own antelopes; and oversaw a commissioned series of watercolours by Joseph Wolf, which were then put on stone by the Dutch artist Joseph Smit, who had been brought to London by Sclater to work on a variety of projects. Unfortunately, Brooke was then taken away from his research and died in 1891 at the age of forty-eight, "leaving his great work still unfinished, and represented mainly by a series of over a hundred lithographic plates."[45] In the interest of completing the project, Brooke's family put all the materials at the disposal of Sclater, who, recognizing especially the beauty and value of the images, "undertook to prepare the letterpress of an entirely new work on the Antelopes" with the help of Oldfield Thomas of the Natural History Museum, who agreed to prepare the taxonomy, scientific description, and synonymy of the over 130 species described.

Each of the entries in *The Book of Antelopes* has a similar structure. A full-page colour lithograph is followed by Thomas's scientific description of the species, after which comes Sclater's much lengthier text describing the animals' distribution and natural history using extended excerpts taken largely from hunting memoirs. Each entry concludes with a brief description of the lithograph that indicates its source material. In Sclater's text, the entries repeatedly document the antelopes' demise over the course of the nineteenth century. To be sure, only one antelope presented in the text was then extinct – *Hippotragus leucophaeus* – but the general story of, as Richard

Lydekker described in a 1901 review of the work in *Nature*, "dying species" that must be watched "with the utmost anxiety by all naturalists" was a persistent theme throughout the four volumes.[46] As Sclater makes clear, the whole project of *The Book of Antelopes* was driven by the realization that Wolf's illustrations were unusually important. The full-page illustration of the sable antelope by Wolf (figure 2.1), an image that was also embossed in gold on the covers of the four volumes, shows why Sclater and others admired these illustrations so much. It is not that Wolf's work accurately represents the sable's physical qualities (in fact, the muzzle seems too narrow, the shoulders too massive, and the feet and hindquarters too delicate); but that the work is more about the nobility of the vigilant buck, an animal that seems, like the rest of the herd, aware of but unintimidated by the hunter. One can almost hear the stamping hoof and snort of the impatient animal. The portrait captures the moment just before the shot and thus captures much of the fantasy of antelopes in the period. In many ways, it seems, the attractions of *The Book of Antelopes* were the same as those of the Antelope House and even of Cumming's memoir. When Lydekker described the volumes as a work "the like of which has never before been seen, and which will remain a monument alike of the ability and industry of its authors and of a group of lovely animals which are only too rapidly and too surely disappearing forever before the advance of an all-devouring civilization,"[47] he could have easily been reviewing the Antelope House in New York or a mid-nineteenth-century hunting memoir set in Africa.

When, in 1910, Madison Grant, secretary of the New York Zoological Society, pompously declared "as big-game sportsmen, we are the last of our race," he extended an argument that was clear in *The Book of Antelopes*. For Grant, Hornaday, and Sclater, the facts were obvious: "the inexorable disappearance of the grand game animals of the world" was simply indisputable. The resulting obligation was also clear: "the imperative necessity of gathering now the collections that will adequately represent [the animals] hereafter when remnants of the wild species of to-day will exist only in protected game preserves, – or not at all."[48] Grant was speaking on the occasion of a luncheon for benefactors of the park intended to raise awareness and resources for a growing collection not of living animals, but of trophies: what Grant and Hornaday called the National Collection of Heads and Horns, then housed in the administration building of the Bronx Park. As Hornaday

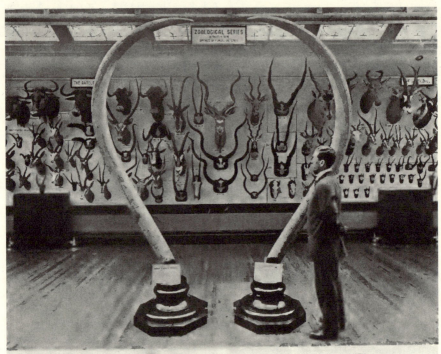

AFRICAN ELEPHANT TUSKS, PRESENTED BY THE LATE CHARLES T. BARNEY.
Some of the heads and horns from the Barber Collection may be seen on the wall.

Figure 2.2 The Antelope Wall, National Collection of Heads and Horns,
New York Zoological Park.

put it, "It is indeed time for the men of to-day who care for the interests of
the men of to-morrow, to be up and doing in the forming of collections that
a hundred years hence will justly and adequately represent the vanishing wild
life of the world."[49] In the end, the "antelope wall" in the National Collection of Heads and Horns, with over one hundred specimens (figure 2.2),
should be seen as an almost inevitable artifact of the disappearance, beauty,
and variety of antelope species. In the cases of such animals as rhinos, elephants, lions, tigers, and bears, trophies were usually measured in inches and
pounds; with antelopes, the trophy was, as much, the collection itself. In a
way, antelopes are a quadruped version of such other obsessions of nineteenth-century natural history collecting as shells, butterflies, beetles, and
birds. Antelopes were collected in hunting memoirs, in a four-volume ency-

clopedia, in an antelope house, and on a wall for the same reasons. They were arranged in these collections according to the same principles Hornaday suggested: the large, the showy, and the male, preferably with perfect horns. Cumming's ordered list of six species of antelope he wanted to hunt and kill – sable antelope, roan antelope, eland, waterbuck, koodoo, and pallah – could just has easily have served Sclater, Hornaday, and Grant.

The history of zoos has usually been written, especially by the zoological gardens themselves, as a story of science, education, conservation, and, sometimes, recreation. In these histories, the zoo emerges as a destination for those who want to learn about and protect the animals of the world, and a way for city workers and their families to spend a nice day in a civilized park. In all of these, too, there is an embedded story of progress – the zoo of today is always better than the zoo of the past, and the zoo of the future will always be better than the zoo of the present. There are many other histories to tell, though. With Hagenbeck, for example, there is the story of an extraordinary commercial venture – zoos, in this account, should be seen as part of an economic history of empire, a way to exploit raw materials (animals) from colonized countries. Zoos, of course, are also part of Western efforts to impose order on the rest of the world, a way to present the natural landscapes, different cultures, and histories of the world in highly controlled ways to domestic audiences. The late nineteenth- and early twentieth-century obsession with antelopes, however, points to a very different but important story about the connections between the origins of zoos and big-game hunting, a story that helps us understand why, even today, zoos continue to present animals as trophies.

NOTES

1 Millais, *Life of Frederick Courtenay Selous*, 65.
2 Ibid.
3 Ibid., 67.
4 Tennent, *Sketches of the Natural History of Ceylon*, 142.
5 Roualeyn, *Five Years of a Hunters Life*, 82.
6 Gordon Cumming, *Five Years of a Hunters Life*, vol. 2, 13.
7 Ibid.
8 Ibid.

9   Ibid., 14.

10 Ibid., 222.

11 Harris, *Narrative of an Expedition into Southern* Africa, 257.

12 Ibid.

13 Ibid., 258.

14 Ibid.

15 Ibid., 259–60.

16 Harris, *The Wild Sports of Southern Africa*, 255.

17 Harris, "On a New Species of Antelope," *Proceedings of the Zoological Society of London*, part 6 (9 January 1838): 1–3.

18 Gordon Cumming, *Five Years of a Hunters Life*, vol. 2, 214.

19 Millais, *Life of Frederick Courtenay Selous*, 199.

20 Hornaday, "The Zoological Park of Our Day," *Zoological Society Bulletin* 35 (September 1909): 543.

21 The 1909 figures do not list amphibians separately. The 2015 figures come from the Wildlife Conservation Society's Annual Report, http://fscdn.wcs.org/2016/03/18/6sdq21m3co_WCS_AnnualReport15.pdf. The 2015 list also includes forty-seven species of amphibians with 3,149 specimens, thirty-four species of invertebrates with 2,180 specimens, and sixty-eight species of fish with 1,491 specimens.

22 Hornaday, "Zoological Park," 547. The name "Leucoryx Antelope" can be confusing. The animal being referenced, called the leucoryx antelope at the time, is now called the scimitar-horned oryx, or *Oryx dammah*; the *Oryx leucoryx* of today was known at the beginning of the twentieth century as the Beatrix antelope, or *Oryx beatrix*.

23 Ibid. Many of the "species" in this collection are now considered sub-species. Current bear taxonomy recognizes only eight species: *Ailuropoda melanoleuca* (giant panda), *Remarctos ornatus* (spectacled bear), *Melursus ursinus* (sloth bear), *Helarctos malayanus* (sun bear), *Ursus thibetanus* (Asian black bear), *Ursus americanus* (American black bear), *Ursus arctos* (brown bear), and *Ursus maritimus* (polar bear).

24 Ibid.

25 Ibid.

26 Ibid., 544.

27 Sanborn, "The Antelope House," *Zoological Society Bulletin* 12 (Antelope

House Number) (January 1904): 126–7. Sanborn's article was based on thorough notes provided to him by Hornaday. Hornaday also provided similar notes to reporters for the major newspapers.

28 "The Antelope House," *Zoological Society Bulletin* 8 (January 1903): 65.

29 Ibid.

30 "The Antelope House," *Zoological Society Bulletin* 10 (July 1903): 101.

31 For more on Hagenbeck, see Rothfels, *Savages and Beasts*.

32 Carl Hagenbeck to William T. Hornaday, 28 August 1903, New York Zoological Park, Office of Director, William T. Hornaday and W. Reid Blair Incoming Correspondence and Subject Files 1895–1940. The wavy underline appears to be in Hornaday's hand.

33 William T. Hornaday to Carl Hagenbeck, 20 February 1903, New York Zoological Park, Office of Director, William T. Hornaday and W. Reid Blair Outgoing Correspondence 1895–1939.

34 William T. Hornaday to Carl Hagenbeck, 19 June 1903, New York Zoological Park, Office of Director, William T. Hornaday and W. Reid Blair Outgoing Correspondence 1895–1939.

35 William T. Hornaday to Carl Hagenbeck, 28 August 1903, New York Zoological Park, Office of Director, William T. Hornaday and W. Reid Blair Outgoing Correspondence 1895–1939.

36 Carl Hagenbeck to William T. Hornaday, 28 August 1903, New York Zoological Park, Office of Director, William T. Hornaday and W. Reid Blair Incoming Correspondence and Subject Files 1895–1940. The double underline appears to be in Hornaday's hand, as is a marginal notation: "Oryx Beatrix. 3.5" high. Horns 2 ft. long. Persia and Arabia."

37 "New Antelope House: An Attractive Addition to the Bronx Zoological Park," *New York Times*, 27 November 1903, 8.

38 Sanborn, "The Antelope House," 130.

39 William T. Hornaday to Carl Hagenbeck, 1 October 1904, New York Zoological Park, Office of Director, William T. Hornaday and W. Reid Blair Outgoing Correspondence 1895–1939.

40 William T. Hornaday to Mr Mitchell, 12 January 1904, New York Zoological Park, Office of Director, William T. Hornaday and W. Reid Blair Outgoing Correspondence 1895–1939. Emphasis original.

41 Ibid.

42 Carl Hagenbeck to William T. Hornaday, 28 August 1903, New York Zoological Park, Office of Director, William T. Hornaday and W. Reid Blair Incoming Correspondence and Subject Files 1895–1940.

43 If Hagenbeck used the books to give Hornaday a sense of what the animals looked like, Hornaday appears to have used them to add details to Hagenbeck's descriptions, adding marginalia to Hagenbeck's letters. The books may also have been used to prepare the labels for the exhibits, which listed range countries, etc. Hornaday was so pleased with the purchase of *The Book of Antelopes* that he immediately ordered a second set for Fairfield Osborn, chairman of the Executive Committee of the Zoological Society and curator of Vertebrate Paleontology at the American Museum of Natural History. See William T. Hornaday to Mr Spencer C. Blackett, Mgr, Kegan Paul, Trench, Trubner & Co, Ltd, 19 January 1903, New York Zoological Park, Office of Director, William T. Hornaday and W. Reid Blair Outgoing Correspondence 1895–1939.

44 Sclater, "Preface," v.

45 Ibid., vii.

46 R.L., "Review of *The Book of Antelopes*, by Sclater and Thomas," 510. R,L. appears to be Richard Lydekker, who also wrote the entry for antelopes in the eleventh edition of the *Encyclopedia Britannica*. There are several points of alignment in the organization and text of the *Britannica* entry and the *Nature* review by R.L. Lydekker was an acknowledged expert on antelopes and deer and was very familiar with the backstory behind *The Book of Antelopes*. See *Encyclopedia Britannica*, 11th ed., vol. 2, *Andros to Austria* (Cambridge: Cambridge University Press, 1910), 89–92. There is one bibliographic reference for the *Britannica* article: *The Book of Antelopes*.

47 Ibid., 509.

48 William T. Hornaday, "National Collection of Heads and Horns," *Zoological Society Bulletin* 40 (July 1910): 667.

49 Ibid., 668.

CHAPTER THREE

FAILED ZOO EXPERIMENTS: PRIMATOLOGY, AERONAUTICS, AND THE ANIMALITY OF "MODERN" SCIENCE, 1891–1903

Daniel Vandersommers

Between 1890 and 1910, to gain support for the public zoo movement, zoo boosters praised zoological parks as institutions that would advance knowledge by supporting both scientific research and education. Zoos around the world, therefore, staged countless experiments. In this chapter, I will tell the story of two of these experiments, conducted in the National Zoological Park (NZP) around the turn of the twentieth century. Though from a contemporary perspective both experiments appear to be failures, they successfully demonstrate the wild natures and unpredictable animalities hidden beneath the anthropocentrism of modern science.

On the surface, the two experiments of this chapter seem to have been staged in, and for, quite different realms of scientific thought: primatology and aeronautics. Yet a close look at them, and at their embeddedness in the zoological park, reveals a common structure. It should be no surprise that primatology and aeronautics were scientific endeavours born in the public sphere, for science and society have always been closely intertwined. It should also be no surprise that these experiments were built upon animals, real and symbolic. Late-nineteenth-century humanism still needed to subjugate and conquer its Other, "the animal," in order to define humanity, empire, and civilization. However, the shared structure I reveal in this chapter goes much deeper. I show that science was indeed built upon animals with, and in, the public, but it also calls attention to a meta-rhetorical project of capital-S Science regarding humans, animals, and agency. Modern science used real animals in order to conquer "the animal" – primate language, avian flight, and other endeavours attributed to nonhumans. And when "real an-imals" inevitably ran away from human expectations, Science was born and was turned into a narrative by rewriting human failures and glossing over animal resistances. In this chapter, I thus tell two stories that lay the struc-ture of science bare. As Bruno Latour once said, description is explanation, and describing, rather than explaining, may allow us to finally hear nonhu-man voices.[1]

Richard L. Garner: Zoo Experiments and the Birth of Primatology

In 1891, shortly after the National Zoological Park's grand opening, Richard L. Garner, a local anthropologist in Roanoke, Virginia, carried speculations about gorillas to the nation's capital. He suggested that the new zoo, spon-sored by the Smithsonian, could serve as a laboratory for groundbreaking anthropological research.[2] Garner postulated, in the words of a Washington journalist, that monkeys possessed "articulate speech like that of human beings and differing from the latter only in development." Garner sup-ported such claims with a series of experiments done with a graphophone, a recent improvement on Thomas Edison's phonograph. As the *Washington Star* explained:

> He has been experimenting of late with the graphophone in this connection, securing a "record" of squeaks and gibberings by one monkey and subsequently grinding them out through a trumpet for the benefit of another monkey, in order to observe what remarks were elicited from the second monkey in response. In this way he has hoped to gradually make up a lexicon of the monkey language, which would probably not be very voluminous, inasmuch as the simian vocabulary does not appear to contain more than forty words. The doctor thinks he has already secured five of them.[3]

Word of Garner's experiments spread quickly.

As Garner continued this experiment, he eventually reached out for the support of Frank Baker, fellow anthropologist and acting manager of the NZP. Baker remained dubious of Garner's claims, but he admitted, according to the *Star*, that "there was something in the idea – inasmuch as in the case there was an illustration to be found of evolution backward from the language of man to the speech of the monkeys." This was a fitting response from an anthropologist who had just published "The Ascent of Man," which advanced Lamarckian evolutionary theory by comparing human and anthropoid limbs. Baker recognized some merit in Garner's line of research.[4] If evolution explained man's body, surely it could explain man's language. Garner argued that the language of a monkey appeared analogous to that of a human infant – mostly composed of vowel sounds. He suggested, though, that the human child possessed an advantage not given to monkeys, namely "education for" and "hereditary experience of the use of" vocal organs. In this way, Garner compared the language of monkeys and human children. While their language proved structurally similar, human children, according to Garner, inherited greater future possibilities due to a mix of culture (education) and evolution (drawing from the Lamarckian concepts of "heredity" and "use"), or, that is, both nurture and nature. Baker would have surely been familiar with Garner's version of recapitulation theory. However, Baker doubted Garner's claims that he had deciphered the monkey's "monosyllabic" words for "pain," "satisfaction," "fear," and "menace."[5] Through the medium of the *Washington Star*, the public received an education concerning Garner's simian theory and Baker's reaction to it, and this episode proved to be only the beginning of a scientific saga that would capture headlines over the course of the year.

Later in 1891, another article, written by Garner himself, hit the headlines. In this feature, Garner summarized the origin story of his notion of simian speech, rooting it in a zoo experience. He informed his readers that the ideas were born seven years earlier in the Cincinnati Zoological Garden, where, Garner explained, he "was deeply impressed by the conduct of a number of monkeys caged with a savage rib nosed mandrill, which they seemed to fear very much." After studying this primate enclosure, which was divided into several compartments, Garner noticed that "every movement of the mandrill seemed to be closely watched by the monkeys that could see him and instantly reported to those" who were out of sight. This behaviour of the monkeys, caged together, "confirmed" and "inspired" Garner's belief in monkey speech. To gather data, he then studied monkeys aboard ships, in travelling menageries and museums, employed as hand-organists, and kept as pets. More importantly, though, Garner conducted further research in the zoos of New York, Philadelphia, Cincinnati, and Chicago. Eventually, he arrived on the NZP's doorstep.[6]

In a letter written to Samuel Langley, the secretary of the Smithsonian Institution, Baker worried about Garner's prior use of professionally trained primates for his experiments. He called Garner's scientific credentials into question, and told Langley that Garner "was first a peddler of trees and nursery stock afterwards a real-estate drummer. Do not understand that I consider that these occupations in any direct way detract from his merits as a citizen or diminish his general worth. I merely think that they are not exactly those that enable one to 'catch the eel of science by the tail.'"[7] Garner fell short of the standards that Baker believed should characterize a man of science. Nonetheless, he (with Langley's recommendation) gave Garner access to the zoo, a place where any tax-paying American should be able to put science into action. Indeed, Baker explained to Johns Hopkins zoologist William Keith Brooks that since the "National Zoological Park is a public institution, I have thought it proper as Manager to give investigators as wide a liberty as is compatible with the health and comfort of the animals."[8] Since Baker foresaw no harm in allowing Garner to talk to monkeys, he had no reason to censor his research. Even though Garner's previous experiments may not have passed a peer review by professional anthropologists, and even though Baker found them "illusory and of no real value," in the world of popular science and public zoos, Garner's peers approved – Americans were enamored with the thought of talking with monkeys.

Garner went to work in Washington. First, he separated two monkeys (female and male) that had lived together in the same cage. Second, using the graphophone, Garner recorded the female's sounds. He then replayed them for the male: "The surprise and perplexity of the male were evident. He traced the sounds to the horn from which they came, and failing to find his mate he thrust his hand and arm into the horn quite up to his shoulder, withdrew it, and peeped into the horn again and again. He would then retreat and again cautiously approach the horn, which he examined with evident interest." Garner reversed the procedure, recording the male and playing his utterances for the female, which prompted similar reactions. He concluded, unperceptive both to the obvious lack of a control group and to his anthropomorphizations, that the sounds emitted represented a verbal language. Garner replicated this experiment in the Chicago and Cincinnati zoos, but it was in the NZP that "the simian tongue was reduced to record" for "the first time in the history of philology."[9] Using the zoo as a laboratory, Garner sought to bring human and nonhuman primates closer together.

In Chicago, Cincinnati, and Washington, DC, Garner studied his recordings, seeking patterns that could break their code. Eventually, he claimed that he had deciphered sounds that translated to milk-water-drink-thirst, eat-hunger-food, pain-sick, and menace-cry-of-alarm. Garner not only strove to discover monkey vocabulary, but also tried to speak monkey himself. He admitted that this endeavour was still in its infancy, but drew several conclusions – all of which he believed true for capuchins, the species to which he mostly limited his studies. According to Garner, the capuchin marked the "Caucasian of the monkey race," for it was "less vicious and more willing to treat one civilly." It also seemed to possess more refined language capabilities.[10] These claims sparked interest (and encouraged racism) in both the nation and its capital. In 1892, much of the literate public sphere had heard of Garner's recently published *The Speech of Monkeys*.[11]

Garner forged his experimental methodology and expanded the public profile of his research within the NZP. Using the zoo as a home base, and with Smithsonian financial support, he planned an expedition to the Gabon River to continue recording – this time with wild gorillas. For these outdoor experiments, he intended to bring "phonographs, telephones, photographic apparatus, an electric telegraph, and a complete taxidermist's outfit" with him. He also prepared to take two cages – one to protect him while he conducted experiments and one to hold a living gorilla in case he captured one alive. By attracting wild gorillas to his cage, Garner planned to replicate his zoo experiments outdoors in equatorial forests, recording the sounds of gorillas that approached and then replaying those recordings for others. By comparing gorillas' responses over time, he hoped "to get an inkling of the meanings intended." An expedition of this design simply represented an expanded, larger-scale zoo experiment. Garner even hoped to "secure desirable specimens alive for the National Zoological Park." These specimens were to include not only gorillas, but other "strange beasts as yet unfamiliar to science."[12] By providing the NZP with new exotic-animal capital at a moment when most of its collection hailed from North America, Garner could reimburse the zoo for its support. He could also supply himself with non-capuchin primates for future experiments.

Garner's experiments fascinated Americans far beyond Washington, Cincinnati, and Chicago. Sometimes, the story of his relationship with the NZP even developed fanciful and comedic valences. On 13 December 1891, the *Buffalo Daily Courier*, for example, published "Talking with Gorillas," which not only informed its readership that Garner planned to capture a living gorilla for the NZP, but also that "the idea is to place the animal in an official position directly under Prof. S.P. Langley, head of the Smithsonian Institution, by which means it is absolutely certain any gorilla would be swearing in seven languages within six months – in case he could survive that long in such a position."[13] Between 1891 and 1892, magazines and newspapers across America publicized Garner. *Current Literature* published "Phonographing the Language of the Apes."[14] The *Youth's Companion* published "Monkey Talk."[15] The *Cosmopolitan* published "Simian Speech and Simian Thought," authored by Garner.[16] The *Daily Picayune*, in New Orleans, published "Monkeys Can Count: They Can Also Call for Peanuts in Their Language."[17] The Salt Lake City *Weekly Tribune* published "Richard L. Garner: Now in Africa Making Investigations in the Monkey Language."[18] And the *Wheeling Sunday Register* referenced Garner's research in an article about a lovesick monkey.[19] The experiments Garner created in the NZP, as he attempted to replicate them along the Gabon, aroused the scientific sensibilities of a nation.

They also raised the ire of established men of science. Baker, in a letter to Brooks, admitted his true feelings:

His scheme for going to Africa appears to me very wild and fantastic. As stated to me he proposes to take a cage weighing seven hundred pounds with a large quantity of electric and other apparatus (with which by the way he appears to be imperfectly acquainted) through a trackless jungle into the heart of gorilla country. In this cage he will establish himself, enticing to him those shy and wary animals by means of lures and then get them to speak into his phonograph so that he may record their language. This sounds more like Jules Verne than it does like a proper scientific experiment.[20]

Despite its callow immaturity in the eyes of one scientist, Garner drew attention to the NZP. Surely, Baker was aware that Garner's shortcomings could at least serve as a publicity stunt of sorts at a very important moment in the life of the zoo. Garner interested Americans so much that correspondence meant for him occasionally ended up on Baker's desk.[21] The public associated Garner with the NZP, for in many respects it functioned as Garner's storehouse, booster, advertiser, marketplace, publisher, and laboratory.

Garner's expedition was in many ways deemed a success. He embarked for Liverpool in July 1892 to gather supplies and continue his advertising. In December, he left for the Great Lakes of Africa (the region in the Great Rift Valley that surrounds Lake Victoria and Lake Tanganyika) to gather information about the area's human and animal inhabitants. Eventually, he placed his cage near Lake Fernan Vaz, along the Gabon River. When describing this outdoor laboratory, Garner emphasized the rugged masculinity that enabled him to tame the perilous, equatorial wild, and especially highlighted the need for self-protection. Along with food and equipment, Garner stored "two revolvers, one magazine rifle, one air gun and hollow arrows filled with prussic acid, which [he] discharged with a blowgun." He also fashioned makeshift ammonia bombs that could suffocate a gorilla from ten feet away, in case the above firepower was not enough to stop an angry ape.[22]

However, Garner's expedition proved successful as more than a display of imperialistic chauvinism. He did see, in his words, "a great many gorillas," as he informed the press after his return to America: "My position was such that gorillas would come very close and I could sit silently and study every detail of movement and expression." Garner also reported that he learned "six or eight words of the chimpanzee language," yet, conveniently, he could not explain what they were because they were "not amenable to any known etymology or orthography." He also concluded that, while far from completely deciphered, the language of monkeys contained forty or fifty "utterances." Finally, Garner's expedition to the French Congo enabled him to discover that "many things ... in magazine articles and natural history about the gorilla are fiction." He returned to the United States in 1894.[23]

Clearly, Garner could not discern simian language. Clearly, he could not reduce the complex behaviours of nonhuman primates to the signs of the English language. Yet his experiments drew public attention to the possibility that monkeys and humans shared a closer affinity than previously imagined. By travelling to Africa, Garner travelled, in the eyes of the white American public, to Eden, to a land before time, where the origins of humanity still lived in wild jungles. Donna Haraway, in her *Primate Visions*, emphasizes the Edenic dimensions of early primatology and calls attention to notions of race and gender entwined with the images of primates throughout the twentieth century.[24] Even though this examination of Garner pushes back Haraway's intellectual history of primatology to the early 1890s, it does not change her primary thesis that primates, as boundary dwellers, functioned as perfect tabula rasas onto which "White Capitalist Patriarchy" could inscribe its own pretensions and insecurities, a process that brought about the emerging and specialized field of primatology in the first place.[25] Garner also underscores an important corollary evident in Haraway's classic (and a major contention in the "science studies" movement in which she is a major figure), namely, that "the boundary between technical and popular discourse is very fragile and permeable."[26]

Garner, using the NZP, popularized the primate-centred life and human sciences. He, and the science-culture hybrid he embodied, helps to explain not only the emergence of the new twentieth-century primatology, but also the growing public interest in previously erudite scientific issues. Baker, in his own research, asked similar questions, both implicitly and explicitly, of primates as Garner. How did human cultures arise from primate cultures? What can humans learn about themselves by looking at their primate ancestors? What can humans learn about primates through this quest for human knowledge? How do close examinations of primates solidify American-male-white-scientific supremacy? Whereas Baker encoded these questions in the language of Lamarckian evolutionary theory and the morphological concerns of anatomy and anthropology, Garner packaged them in rhetoric and narratives that lay audiences could easily understand.

When Garner returned to America, his name again filled headlines for several years. In Charlotte, newspaper audiences read "He Knows Six Gorilla Words."[27] In Knoxville, "Talks to Gorillas."[28] In Topeka, Bismarck, and Trenton, "The New Philology."[29] Even in Prescott, Arizona, newspaper-toting miners received updates about Garner's expedition to Africa.[30] An entire nation read about his zoo experiments.

For Garner, the years between 1891 and 1894 marked only the beginning of a long career dedicated to the speech of monkeys, and throughout the 1890s he returned to the French Congo numerous times. In 1900, he published *Apes and Monkeys*, which detailed his research on "simian speech" after his first return from Africa.[31] He never lost sight of the general public; in the opening pages, he perfectly expresses the intentions that undergirded his science, and states, "A careful aim to avoid all technical terms and scientific phraseology has been studiously adhered to, and the subject is treated in the simplest style consistent with its dignity." Furthermore, Garner in the third person admitted early in the book, reaffirming one of Baker's original concerns, that "most of the acts related are those of his own pets. A few of them are of apes in a wild state. The author has carefully refrained from abstruse theories or rash deductions, but has sought to place the animals here treated of in the light to which their own conduct entitles them, allowing the reader to draw his own conclusions."[32]

In 1905, five years after the publication of *Apes and Monkeys*, Garner built a house on the shores of Lake Fernan Vaz. Between 1916 and 1919, with the full sponsorship of the Smithsonian Institution, he made his last expedition to the French Congo in search of more missing links between human and monkey languages and cultures. Shortly after he returned to the United States from Africa for the last time, he died in Chattanooga, Tennessee.[33] Although many of Garner's grand claims about being able to discern and translate simian language proved at best naively overstated and at worst purposefully deceptive, and although his experiments proved at best unprofessional and at worst pure profiteering, his larger project addressed questions that fascinated both scientists and laypeople alike. How similar were humans and monkeys? What could monkeys teach us about our own natural history? Have we had language and culture from the beginning? Salient questions like these made Darwin and Lamarck palpable to Americans at the turn of the century, and Garner, by foregrounding these questions in high-profile zoo experiments, enhanced their popularity and relevance in the public sphere. As American zoo-goers came increasingly into contact with their living ancestors, held captive in monkey houses, some grew curious about the implications of this encounter. Garner's research on language created a narrative that, at least in some ways, lessened the gap between human and nonhuman primates by exploring the long-held "fantasy" of cross-species exchange. In addition, Garner created a discursive space for other counternarratives concerning the affinities between human and nonhuman primates, which would become the central concern of the new science of primatology.

By "communicating" with monkeys, Garner experimented at the fringe of humanity, in a realm Haraway labels "science fiction," "where possible worlds are constantly reinvented in the contest for very real, present worlds."[34] For American zoo-goers in the 1890s, primates represented exotic new worlds, and language functioned as a mechanism through which to order the order of *primata*. Despite Baker's professional opinion, Garner's research eventually proved important to early primatology, and was verified (posthumously) by comparative psychologist, ethologist, and primatologist Robert Mearns Yerkes in the mid-1920s.[35] Yerkes, hired as a psychobiologist at Yale University in 1924, founded the Yale University Laboratories of Primate Biology in New Haven, Connecticut, and the Anthropoid Breeding and Experiment Station in Orange Park, Florida, where the primate language Yerkish was first developed and where the field of primatology was partially legitimated.[36] The history of language and primatology is a complex one that needs to be told. Garner, though, shows that this history may indeed find one origin in the birth of the NZP, where primates were, for the first time, showcased before a nation, and where a tree-peddler-turned-scientist first staged his famous phonograph experiments.

Samuel Langley: Zoo Experiments and the Birth of Aviation

Langley served as the third secretary of the Smithsonian Institution from 1887 to 1906. As secretary, Langley devoted significant time to his own scientific interests. Before he entered the Smithsonian, he pursued an academic life at Harvard Observatory, the Naval Academy, Western University of Pennsylvania, and the Allegheny Observatory. Shortly after his arrival in Washington, though, Langley pursued a new line of research for which he would be remembered – aeronautics. On 6 May 1896, he successfully flew the Aerodrome No. 5, an aircraft equipped with a one-horsepower steam engine, three-fourths of a mile, exceeding any distance reached by previous experimental aircrafts. After this flight, and with the support of the United States Army, Langley developed the Great Aerodrome (also known as Aerodrome A). Piloted by Charles M. Manly, this flying machine failed to actually fly, and crashed into the Potomac River on 7 October and again on 8 December 1903. Nine days after this second failed flight attempt, the Wright Brothers famously completed their four successful flights near Kitty Hawk, North Carolina. Despite his failed experiments, Langley was a major figure in the history of aeronautics, and his Great Aerodrome, despite its crash landings, marked an important, high-profile flight attempt. In addition to his Aerodrome experiments, Langley also published articles on aerodynamics.[37]

On the surface, Langley's involvement in science seemed far removed from the life sciences. Aeronautics, the scientific study of flight through the atmosphere, joined the sciences of physics, meteorology, and aerodynamics with engineering. Nonetheless, Langley rooted many of his aeronautic experiments in zoology, taking advantage of the opportunities offered by the NZP. On 14 March 1901, Langley informed Baker that he wanted to measure the wings of six different birds – the condor (*Sarcroramphus gryphus*), the golden eagle (*Aquila chrysaetos*), the Egyptian crane (*Grus cineara*), the Jamaica buzzard (*Cathartes aura*), the albatross (*Diomedea exulans*), and the frigate bird (*Fregata aquila*). He hoped Baker would "prepare a table giving in each case, in addition to the names as above, a column to be filled in later with the weight of the bird; the wing surface, divided by weight, showing how much goes to the pound; [and] the distance from tip to tip of the wings as extended in flight." He also hoped Baker would procure any of the above species not currently held in the NZP, suggesting that the frigate bird could be found in Santiago's harbour, the albatross "in the neighborhood of New Zealand" or "on the Island Laysan, one of the Hawaiian group," and the buzzard (also known as a "John crow") in Jamaica. In addition, the Smithsonian secretary added that he was "particularly interested in getting the largest specimens," and he emphasized that he wanted all the above measurements taken on living, not dead, birds.[38] In response, Baker informed Langley that the zoo only possessed the golden eagle, but all the other desired birds could probably be purchased from Carl Hagenbeck, the famous Hamburg animal dealer. Regarding the John crow, Baker suggested that a Turkey buzzard might suffice since it belonged to the same species.[39]

Within five weeks, Baker had acquired a condor and a Jamaican buzzard (although presumably not from Hagenbeck, since it would take longer than five weeks to make a transatlantic animal purchase), and he immediately sent the measurements of the three soaring birds then in the zoo, taken by head keeper William H. Blackburne, to Langley. The condor weighed eighteen pounds and eight ounces, with a nine-foot, two-and-a-half-inch wing span. The golden eagle weighed twelve pounds, with a six-foot, ten-inch wing span. The John crow weighed three pounds and twelve ounces, with a four-foot, nine-inch wing span. In addition, Baker informed Langley that he had sent a letter to Hagenbeck, to the commanding office in Santiago, to a prominent animal dealer who previously sent the NZP a pair of flamingoes, and to the Fisheries Commissioner of the New Zealand government concerning the frigate bird and albatross.[40] The NZP functioned as a storehouse and purchasing centre for living animals, and when Langley instructed Baker to acquire these additions, he used this zoo-as-storehouse for his own purposes.

The NZP acquired the animals Langley needed and provided him with personal assistants. Quickly – in the above letter listing the condor, eagle, and buzzard's sizes – Baker mentioned that Blackburne did not "attempt the calculation of wing surface to weight on account of the considerable variation in the shape of the wing."[41] After receiving this letter, Langley responded with a four-page instruction manual on how to properly calculate wing surface, also showcasing his reputation as a micromanager. First, he described the basic method that Blackburne should employ:

The determination of wing surface, however, may be made far more accurately by placing the bird, alive or dead, on a sheet of coarse white or brown paper wide enough to receive the shadow of the body and tail of the bird and at least one of the wings. Let the shadow be taken near noon, when a pencil can readily be run around it and a correct outline traced. The wing should be supported by the tip so as to be a trifle turned up as during flight, when the shadow is taken. Afterward the sheet of paper may be ruled up roughly into inch squares and the number of whole squares may be taken and also the number of broken squares (which may generally be averaged a half a square each). Hence we get the area of the wing and thence of the two wings.[42]

This process seemed quite rudimentary. Stand a large bird on a piece of paper at high noon. Spread its wings to their fullest extent. Trace its shadow. Fold paper into squares. Repeat. After outlining this methodology, Langley elaborated on how to assess wing curvature. "The curvature," he explained, "should be referred to a plane parallel to that of the level sheet of paper the bird is standing on." He continued to give an example:

> Suppose, for instance, the bird were facing the south, and were consequently under the sun at noon when it is highest; then we may suppose two north and south sections to be made through the wing, one quite close to the body (1), the other at some point near the middle of the wing (2). In many specimens the section nearest the body will have the chord of its arc pointing slightly downward, as in this illustration, (C) while the chord near the middle of the wing may be pointing horizontally or a little upward, (D). This may be not always so.[43]

This process of calculating wing surface area and curvature proved quite mechanical. The living birds in the above description failed to prove living at all – they were placed on paper, manipulated, and reduced to mere pencil sketches. Langley's interest lay not in the birds themselves, but in their outlines, which were riddled with bisections. The "soaring birds" that captivated Langley were not the same ones that captivated zoo-goers. The animal images looked similar to those produced by a taxidermist – pinned and opened for study – and possessed no hint that they were derived from anything but dead bodies (see figure 3.1).[44]

Blackburne and Baker knew otherwise, for they were the ones chosen to pose living birds of prey on a single sheet of paper, with wings extended and presumably flapping, long enough to get an accurate tracing that would appease the secretary. While no record exists on how this task was accomplished, it is clear that the condor gave Blackburne a difficult time because Langley concluded his letter, "I am very sorry to hear of the annoyance that I have been to the condor in these measurements, but I hope that useful bird will feel persuaded that it is all in the cause of science."[45] Whether Langley's concern about the condor was genuine, or whether he was using "condor" as a euphemism for "Blackburne," remains unclear; however, no matter

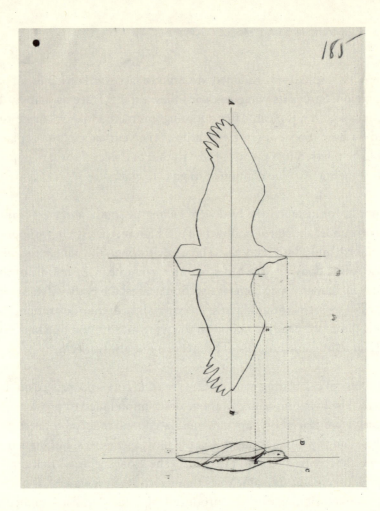

Langley's feelings, the condor must have acted out in some way, refusing to adhere to the script it was asked to follow for the sake of science.[46]

These measurements of living zoo birds advanced Langley's research on flight. To accompany the letter, Langley also sent Baker and Blackburne a copy of a missive he had sent a year earlier to Robert Ridgeway, curator of birds at the United States National Museum, which revealed Langley's true purpose for his study. Langley informed Baker and Blackburne, "I may mention that the line AB in the drawing enclosed with the letter to which this is a postscript, is supposed to be drawn to represent the trace of a plane passing through the centre of gravity of the bird when its wings are extended in the attitude of flight" (see figure 3.2). While these drawings, Langley admitted, would be difficult to obtain from a living bird, he wanted Blackburne to

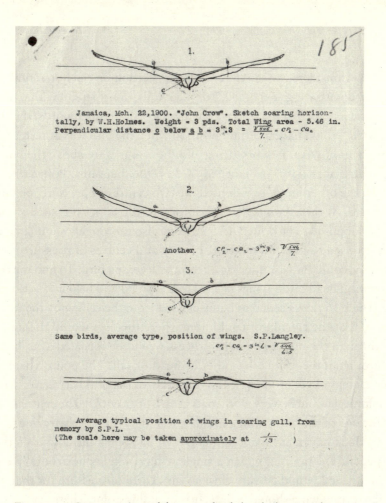

Figure 3.1 *Opposite* A model soaring bird sketch that Langley sent to Baker and Blackburne.

Figure 3.2 *Above* Sketch of a soaring John crow and a soaring seagull Langley sent to Ridgeway.

"familiarize himself" with them.[47] More important, the images Langley sent to Ridgeway, of a soaring John crow, reveal how the NZP's birds could be helpful to a scientist interested in aeronautics, aerodynamics, and the engineering of flying machines.[48]

The Ridgeway letter demonstrates that, in studying these living birds, Langley was most interested in their centre of gravity and centres of pressure. As Langley explained, all birds possess one centre of gravity, but this centre could be "considered with reference to its position on the horizontal plane of the bird with wings extended," or it could be considered "with reference to a vertical plane" of the bird with wings closed. In other words, the centre of gravity "would have a certain position when the bird was at rest, and another position when it was soaring and the wings were above the body."[49] This centre of gravity was labelled "C" on the diagrams. Points "A" and "B," on the other hand, represented the two centres of pressure, one under each wing. At these points, "all the efforts of the upper pressure of the air may be supposed to be centered."[50] Langley also thoroughly summarized the methods used to find the centre of gravity and centres of pressure, which, ironically, could only be done on a recently deceased bird. To find the centre of gravity, a dead bird's wings needed to be spread and held in position with wire. The bird then needed to be suspended from the ceiling by the tip of its wing so that the calculator could note where this line would theoretically pass through the body. The same process would be repeated after hanging the bird, from the ceiling, by either its head or tail. The point where these two imaginary lines crossed, within the body of the bird between its breasts and mantle, should be very close to its centre of gravity.[51] The centre of pressure for one of the bird's wings could be found by accurately tracing its outline on thick paper, cutting it out, and then balancing the cutout on the tip of a pencil. The point at which a single wing could lay horizontally on the end of a pencil would be very close to the centre of pressure for that wing, and the second wing should have a corresponding point. These centres could be corroborated by cutting the wings from the dead body and balancing these as well.[52]

The purpose of explaining, in such detail, Langley's methodology in analyzing bird anatomy is to underscore four important points about the avian foundations of his aeronautical experiments. First, it is clear that Langley thought about birds as machines that achieved flight by neutralizing the opposing forces of downward gravitational pull and upward air pressure. By doing so, he hoped to replicate their physical structure in his designs for flying machines, thus rooting his aeronautical technology in the evolutionary "technology" exemplified within any given bird of flight. Second, in order to properly assess this evolutionary technology, Langley needed both dead and living birds. From living birds, Langley could find weight (something that could not be calculated from a dead bird once fluids were lost and decomposition set in); wing surface, divided by weight, creating a surface-per-pound ratio; and distance of actual wingspan as a living bird spread its wings in life, not as humans spread them in death. Modelling living birds enabled Langley to verify many of the figures determined from dead birds. Third, comparing how Langley thought about birds with how he thought about flying machines inevitably brings parallels to light, and shows the life sciences' influence on a branch of science (aeronautics) usually considered distinct from those sciences focused on organisms. Fourth, Langley's conflation of birds with flying machines, and vice versa, shows how deeply Cartesian perspectives on animal automata had infused the mentalité of science over the preceding three centuries.

Langley's Avian-Aeronautic Foundations

While Langley's interests in the NZP's birds materialized in 1901, he had thought about birds before. According to his memoirs, Langley "often stated that even as a boy he was interested in watching the motions of hawks and buzzards, and he wondered by what mysterious power birds so much heavier than the air could maintain themselves in space and could move about at will without apparent movements of their wings." In 1886, listening to a paper delivered at the American Association for the Advancement of Science, this formative curiosity developed into a professional interest when "it seemed to him that prevailing theories as to how birds fly were not based on sound facts, and he resolved, as a fundamental problem, to ascertain by scientific observation and experiment what mechanical power was required to sustain a weight in air and make it move at a given speed."[53] From the beginning, then, birds sparked and shaped Langley's interest in human flight.

In 1891, in *Experiments in Aerodynamics*, Langley first announced that "mechanical flight is possible with engines we now possess."[54] While this is not the place to detail Langley's physics, mathematical computations, or proposals concerning the actual engineering of engine-powered flying machines, it is worth noting the bird references perched in this foundational text. In his third chapter, "The Suspended Plane," Langley challenged what he saw as a widely held misconception about the physics of avian flight, namely, that "the energy expended [by flying birds] increases with the velocity attained."[55]

This assumption, first forged by the French engineer and physicist Claude-Louis Navier in 1832 while studying the flight of a swallow, wrongly likened avian motion to pedalistic animal motion and advanced the view that "there exists the same ratio between the efforts necessary for simple suspension and for rapid flight as exists for terrestrial animals between the effort required for standing upright and that required for running."[56] After "proving" this mathematically, Navier's assertion led to the longstanding opinion in the scientific community that "mechanical flight is practically impossible."[57] However, in *Experiments*, Langley blamed Navier for faulty differential equations, figuring wrong constants, and assuming that the physics of flight for all birds (from swallows to eagles) could be computed in exactly the same way.[58] Essentially, Langley accused Navier of generalizing about birds, ignoring their differences, and imposing mathematical formulas used for calculating terrestrial animal work and motion on the ground on analysis of a bird's work and motion through the air. The class of animals labelled "birds" should not be thought about monolithically. By challenging Navier's conclusions, Langley opened a previously closed space regarding the possibility of human flight. It is fitting, then, that in *Experiments*, Langley used "bird" and "flying machine" interchangeably when he argued the opposite of the Navier thesis – that "effort ... of a bird or flying machine in the air is greatest when it is at rest relatively to the air, and diminishes with the horizontal speed which it attains."[59] While Langley's direct discussion of birds in *Experiments* received limited page-space within the book, birds lay at the core of his work's central thesis that human flight may indeed be possible. Langley's revision of aeronautical physics depended upon viewing birds differently – as distinct both from each other and from land-based animals – and flight differently – as distinct from land-based locomotion. Unsurprisingly, *Experiments* led Langley to experiments with birds themselves.

Two years after he posited that human flight was possible, Langley published "The Internal Work of the Wind," which examined directly the flying behaviours of birds. In fact, he opened with the following remark: "It has long been observed that certain species of birds maintain themselves indefinitely in the air by 'soaring,' without any flapping of the wing, or any motion other than a slight rocking of the body; and this, although the body in question is many hundred times denser than the air in which it seems to float with an undulating movement, as on the waves of an invisible stream."[60] In this paper, Langley offered an explanation for soaring, which challenged Navier's claims resulting from an overemphasis on flapping. Langley concluded that wind was inherently "irregular" and that, in the concise words of Charles Walcott, "these irregularities might be a source of power and might to a considerable degree account for the ability of certain birds to soar with outstretched, unflapping wings."[61] This important conclusion set the precedent of taking soaring birds seriously in the study of aeronautics, for if the wind gave these birds "invisible support," then it could conceivably do the same for a "future aerodrome."[62] Langley focused on birds, recognizing that a successful flying machine would need a "mechanical brain" that replicated the birds' abilities to "see the wind" and to constantly exploit its ever-changing irregularities.[63]

As Langley wrote these two classics of aeronautics, he was simultaneously at work on designs for his future aerodrome. Between 1891 and 1895, he built four model aerodromes. In 1896, his fifth model became the world's first successful motorized flying machine, achieving a distance of 3,000 feet.[64] While quite the accomplishment, Langley knew that such a feat was far from the daily successes of the albatross, seagull, and buzzard. Langley's aeronautic research, since the publication of *Experiments*, relied on the idea of birds; however, to further his research, he needed to take his work one step further. He decided that he should not depend upon the idea of these soaring birds, but should study the living, breathing birds themselves. Enter NZP.

Langley's Zoo-Aeronautic Laboratory

Langley's examination of zoo birds did not end with the measuring instructions he sent to Baker and Blackburne. Between 1901 and 1903, he again asked them for a favour, this time requesting photographs of buzzards in flight.[65] Since captive buzzards could not "soar" within their cages, Baker decided to attract "wild" buzzards from outside the zoo to the park's rock face promontory by exposing carrion. After "extensive but fruitless trials," Baker realized that there was no need to set bait at all because buzzards were "quite frequently seen flying about over" the bird cages within the zoo, eyeing the smaller captive birds as potential (yet unattainable) prey. The entire zoo itself, in this case, functioned as bait, operating as a peculiar, liminal medium between the encaged and the wild. Baker immediately had grand towers constructed for the sole purpose of capturing soaring, wild buzzards on film.[66] The zoological park not only functioned as a storehouse and purchasing centre for Langley's experiments, but also as a malleable laboratory that could alter its infrastructure according to their needs.[67]

To conduct these photographic experiments, Baker hired a local photographer to assist the Smithsonian photographer.[68] He had electrical lines routed to the towers for the powering of a helio-photographic apparatus; had the western tower fitted with a chronograph; and immediately ordered a chronometer, two Anastigmatic photographic objectives, and all the parts needed for a fully functional camera.[69] Baker and Blackburne were building not simply makeshift towers, but a well-equipped photographic laboratory.

From atop these towers, Langley studied birds in flight. In the words of Rene Bache, who wrote a paper about these experiments: "These soaring birds point their heads against the wind, spread their wings in a certain way and are lifted by the wind straight up into the air without any exertion on their part. They can progress against the wind by falling forward and slightly downward. When they go with the wind it holds them up by catching in the hollows beneath their wings. To an observer on the ground these birds appear to sail through the air for miles without moving a wing."[70] Surely seeing and photographing majestic birds navigating the currents above inspired Langley. Nature's greatest fliers expended almost no energy in flight. Why should Man not be able to do the same? A buzzard "is sustained by the wind in just the same manner as a boy's kite is upheld in the air."[71] While watching the buzzards soar, Langley specifically focused on the angles of their wings in relation to the wind, for he had long realized, since "The Internal Work of the Wind," that the question of flight is one of mechanics.[72]

As Langley pursued his buzzard research within the NZP, he worked on building his Great Aerodrome (see figure 3.3). The birds studied from the towers shaped Langley's engineering priorities, for during the construction of the Great Aerodrome he was most concerned with "how air currents act in supporting plane surfaces."[73] He hoped to design artificial surfaces that could replicate buzzards' natural planes; however, balancing artificial wings proved to be one of the most difficult tasks.[74] The caged condors next to the towers gave Langley another insight. Since these condors were enclosed and lacked the space for a running start, they would simply drop from the top of

Figure 3.3 Langley's Great Aerodrome – Crashed on the Potomac,
piloted by Charles Manly.

their cage and soar to the bottom. If the Great Aerodrome could not produce
the force needed to push into the air, it may be able to create enough force
to fly after being released from a height.[75] In this way, Langley designed his
Great Aerodrome with lessons learned from both wild and caged birds, both
within the NZP.

For Langley, the zoo offered a place to think through aviation by examining
those individuals who had been flying since the Eocene. In so doing, Langley
infused aeronautics, aerodynamics, physics, and meteorology with life science, and with life itself. Even though this important point may often be
forgotten, Langley knew that life existed at the core of all sciences, no matter
how mathematical, theoretical, and anthropocentric. Beneath all equations
lay a swallow's fluttering wings. Once a man of science realized this humbling
fact, suddenly human capabilities could reach out to the heavens.

The Animality of "Modern" Zoo Science

But, then again, Langley's Great Aerodrome, the one inspired by zoo birds,
reached nowhere, especially not the heavens. It crashed into the Potomac.
Twice.

Garner failed, too. Both his scientific method and critical thinking were flawed. He was clearly more of an entertainer than a scientist, and his time in Africa was driven more by the male imperialistic project than by the pursuit of knowledge. Worse than that, he failed to accomplish his task – to discern a nonhuman primate language.

Yet failed zoo experiments can speak volumes about animals commodified. Through failed experiments, the animals usually silenced by science can be heard chirping through the fissures of triumphalist façades. Failed experiments can reveal the animality of science usually made invisible. Of course, as historians and philosophers of science are well aware, scientific failures have always been important to knowledge production. The failures and successes of an experiment are constructed by the politics of the laboratory, the structure of the experiment's apparatus, and the prejudices of the society outside that laboratory. I could conclude by forging an apologetics of sorts, showing how the failures of Garner and Langley were both pre-conditioned as well as important chapters in both the history and social construction of primatology and aeronautics, respectively. In a different way, though, I could conclude by emphasizing that Garner and Langley should both be seen as liminal figures, boundary dwellers, scientists existing at a historical nexus where an outmoded Enlightenment Cartesianism met an emerging twentieth-century zoology in a sphere both public and professional. I would rather consider, though, what the failures above might say about zoos and their animals.

Through *The Nature of the Beasts*, Ian Jared Miller presents a study of Tokyo's Ueno Park Imperial Zoological Garden, the first modern zoo in Japan, founded in 1882. Miller argues that "when the Ueno Zoo made caged animals into representatives of pristine 'nature' it instituted a separation between people and the natural world, introducing a break between humanity and animality that recast Japanese – together with Westerners – as the rational masters of a new natural history based on Linnaean nomenclature and the tenets of evolutionary theory."[76] He assigns the label of "ecological modernity" to this "doubled process of intellectual separation and social transformation."[77] Similarly, the "beasts" of the NZP – capuchins, gorillas, condors, golden eagles, Egyptian cranes, Jamaican buzzards, albatross, frigate birds, and turkey buzzards – that were forced to participate in Garner and Langley's experiments embodied Americans' removal from nature. Indeed, they embodied the same "modern" doubled process of separation and transformation. Both Garner and Langley sought to extract knowledge from primates and avians, respectively, in order to further the ends of an imperialistic America. Seen together, their equation was simple: Conquer animal language and flight. Then employ both for human triumphalism.

Both Garner and Langley tried to force their animals to play along in their master narratives. Garner shoved graphophones into the faces of capuchins and gorillas. Langley forced condors to hold still on paper so that they could be traced. Yet, zoo animals often ran away from expectations. The zoological park was a place filled with surprises. Bruno Latour famously exclaimed that "we have never been modern," and the animals of the supposedly modern zoo give evidence to this proposition and point us towards modernity's deception.[78]

The primate and avian individuals above were surely used by Garner and Langley as symbols of modernity and human sovereignty. Most of these animals were, after all, stolen from faraway ecosystems and held prisoner in Washington, DC. They also lived multiple lives and possessed multiple ontologies. If these captive animals, collectively, marked the rise of a dark modernity and a separation from nature, they also signified the beginnings of an intellectual transformation in humanistic thought that would eventually counteract modern forces.

Garner and Langley looked towards "the animal" to advance science and to become modern, but in so doing they saw more complexity in their subjects than had scientists of previous generations. Garner recognized that primates possessed language. Langley recognized that birds housed tremendous diversity – and he wished to "see the wind," too. Both Garner and Langley, despite their commitment to their problematic projects, recognized that animals had agency. It was this very agency that they desired to co-opt. Garner and Langley realized that animals had faces, even if they could not discern their features. Yet they failed in their experiments because "real" animals resisted imperialism. At the dawn of the twentieth century, animals were coming into view but were still not seen.

Zoo animals, then, should be read as embodied texts that symbolize the modernity from which their literal bodies ran. As these animals became subjects in and through the diverse experiments done within the zoo, they prepared zoo-goers to think about animals in new ways. By not living up to expectations, by refusing to follow modern scripts, by being more successful than human scientists, by becoming elusive, by becoming more-than-zoo-animals, the inhabitants within the zoo directed attention to the fault lines that undergirded an outmoded humanistic tradition. Though the experiments above were built upon zoo animals, they ultimately direct attention to the enclosed nature of modern science and the wild nature of animality at the turn of the century.

NOTES

1 Latour, *Reassembling the Social,* 137. In addition to all of the participants in the Hamilton workshop, I would like to thank Daniel Watkins for his thoughts on an early version of this chapter.

2 For more on Garner, see Rich, *Missing Links.*

3 "Do Monkeys Talk?," *Washington Star,* 1891, "Scrapbook, 1887–1902," Smithsonian Institution Archives (SIA), record unit 74, box 285 (hereafter cited as "Scrapbook").

4 Baker, "The Ascent of Man."

5 "Do Monkeys Talk?"

6 Garner, "Do Monkeys Express Themselves in Words?," unknown newspaper, 8 June 1891, "Scrapbook"; John P. Harrington, "He Spoke: Biography and Scientific Work of Richard Lynch Garner" (Washington, DC: Government Printing Office, 1941), 10, Richard Lynch Garner Papers, box 5, folder entitled "Biographer's Papers," National Anthropological Archives. The implications of the experiments described in this section for the history of twentieth-century biology can be found in Radick, "Primate Language and the Playback Experiment."

7 Baker to Langley, 3 May 1892, SIA, record unit 365, box 12, folder 25.

8 Baker to Brooks, 22 April 1892, SIA, record unit 365, box 12, folder 25.

9 Garner, "Do Monkeys Express."

10 Ibid.

11 Garner, *The Speech of Monkeys.*

12 "To Talk with Gorillas," unknown newspaper, 1891, "Scrapbook."

13 "Talking with Gorillas," *Buffalo Courier,* 13 December 1891, "Scrapbook."

14 "Phonographing the Language of the Apes," *Current Literature* 10, 2 (June 1892): 207.

15 "Monkey Talk," *Youth's Companion*, 6 June 1901, 296.

16 "Simian Speech and Simian Thought," *Cosmopolitan*, May 1892, 72.

17 "Monkeys Can Count," *Daily Picayune*, 29 May 1892, 16.

18 "Richard L. Garner," *Salt Lake Weekly Tribune*, 11 August 1892, 7.

19 "A Love-Sick Monkey," *Wheeling Sunday Register*, 22 May 1892, 9.

20 Baker to Brooks, 22 April 1892, SIA, record unit 365, box 12, folder 25.

21 Baker to Ruffin, 12 April 1892, SIA, record unit 365, box 12, folder 25.

22 "Monkey Talk," *Bismarck Daily Tribune*, 27 March 1894, 1.

23 Ibid.

24 Haraway, *Primate Visions*. In a similar vein, see Haraway, "Primatology Is Politics by Other Means." For more on the history of primatology, see Montgomery, "Place, Practice and Primatology"; Rees, "Reflections on the Field."

25 Haraway, *Primate Visions*, 13.

26 Ibid., 14.

27 "He Knows Six Gorilla Words," *Daily Charlotte Observer*, 1 April 1894, 4.

28 "Talks to Gorillas," *Knoxville Journal*, 15 July 1895, 8.

29 "The New Philology," *Kansas Weekly Capital and Farm Journal*, 7 June 1894, 10; "The New Philology," *Trenton Times*, 6 April 1894, 6; "The New Philology," *Bismarck Daily Tribune*, 18 April 1894, 4.

30 Untitled blurb about Garner, *Arizona Weekly Journal-Miner*, 22 January 1896, 4.

31 Garner, *Apes and Monkeys*.

32 Ibid., iii–iv.

33 Register to the Papers of Richard Lynch Garner, "Introduction" and "Chronology," National Anthropological Archives, Smithsonian Institution.

34 Haraway, *Primate Visions*, 5.

35 Register to the Papers of Richard Lynch Garner, National Anthropological Archives. For more on Yerkes and primatology, see Haraway's fourth chapter in *Primate Visions*, "A Pilot Plant for Human Engineering: Robert Yerkes and the Yale Laboratories of Primate Biology, 1924–42."

36 Yerkish was a language developed by humans for primates, and it required primates to use a keyboard with keys of lexigrams, symbols that represent larger concepts, instead of letters.

37 "Historical Note," Samuel P. Langley Collection, National Air and Space Archives, Accession no. xxxx–0494; Walcott, *Biographical Memoir of*

Samuel Pierpont Langley, 1834–1906, 252–4. For more on Langley and other experimenters preceding the Wright Brothers, see Anderson, *Inventing Flight*; Crouch, *A Dream of Wings*; Hallions, *Taking Flight*; Tobin, *To Conquer the Air.*

38 Langley to Baker, 14 March 1901, SIA, record unit 74, box 99, folder 7. Unless otherwise noted, this archival information applies to all letters below until note 65.

39 Baker to Langley, 15 March 1901.

40 Baker to Langley, 30 April 1901; Baker to Hagenbeck, 25 March 1901; Baker to Hatfield, 30 April 1901; Baker to Ayson, 30 April 1901; Baker to Whitside, 30 April 1901.

41 Baker to Langley, 30 April 1901.

42 Langley to Baker, 14 May 1901.

43 Ibid.

44 Soaring bird sketch, SIA, record unit 74, box 99, folder 7.

45 Langley to Baker, 14 May 1901.

46 Ibid.

47 Ibid.

48 Sketches attached to S.P. Langley to Mr Robert Ridgeway, 29 March 1900, SIA, record unit 74, box 99, folder 7. Birds #1 and #2 ("John crows") were done by Holmes (?) with the assistance of photographs and sketches taken by both himself and Langley. Bird #3 ("John crow") and Bird #4 (gull) was sketched by Langley. Langley had communicated with Ridgeway about "soaring" and "hovering" birds prior to his interest in studying flight in the National Zoo. A few of these letters are contained in "Notes on Bird Flight – Langley," Samuel P. Langley Collection, Accession #xxxx–0494, box 44, National Air and Space Museum, Air and Space Archives. In this collection, there is data (compiled by either Langley or Ridgeway) concerning American bald eagles, American white pelicans, common turkey buzzards, South American condors, humming birds, English kestrels, and frigate birds.

49 Langley to Ridgeway, 29 March 1900.

50 Ibid.

51 Ibid.

52 Ibid.

53 Walcott, *Biographical Memoir*, 2512.

54 Langley, *Experiments in Aerodynamics* (Washington, DC: The Smithsonian Institution, 1891), 107.

55 Ibid., 12.

56 Ibid. Navier was responsible for these calculations, and the results were published in Gay-Lussac, Flourens, and Navier, *Rapport sur un Mémoire de M. Chabrier concernant les moyens de voyager dans l'air et de s'y diriger, contenent une nouvelle théorie des mouvements progressifs* (Paris: Mém. Acad. Sci. XI, 1832), 61–118.

57 Langley, *Experiments*, 4.

58 Ibid., 12.

59 Ibid., 34.

60 Langley, "The Internal Work of the Wind" (Washington, DC: The Smithsonian Institution, 1893), 1.

61 Walcott, *Biographical Memoir*, 253.

62 Langley, "Internal," 22.

63 Ibid., 22. Langley borrows the nautical term "see the wind" from Louis Pierre Mouillard, who experimented with gliders prior to Langley's research career in aeronautics. See his *L'empire De L'air*.

64 Walcott, *Biographical Memoir*, 253–4.

65 Rathbun to Baker, 8 October 1901; Baker to Blackburne, 9 October 1901, SIA, record unit 74, box 99, folder 8. Unless otherwise noted, this archival information applies to all letters below. Only the folder numbers will change.

66 Baker to Langley, 9 October 1901, folder 8.

67 Note on costs of scaffolding, 6 November 1901, folder 8.

68 A.B. Baker to Dr Frank Baker, 26 November 1901, folder 8; Langley to Hodge, 13 December 1901, folder 9. The National Museum, as a part of the Smithsonian, was institutionally linked to the zoo.

69 Note, 29 April 1902, folder 9; Langley to Smillie, 8 February 1902, folder 8; Langley to Baker, 12 February 1902, folder 8; Langley to Bausch and Lomb Optical Company, 29 April 1902, folder 9; Langley to Bausch and Lomb Optical Company, 7 May 1902, folder 9; Langley to the Rochester Optical and Camera Company, 5 June 1902, folder 9.

70 Bache, "Photographing Wild Birds on the Wing to Find out How to Make a Flying Machine for Man," 19 June 1902, "Scrapbook, 1896–1907," SIA, record unit 74, box 286, folder 3, 2.

71 Ibid., 2–3.

72 Ibid., 3.

73 Ibid.

74 Ibid., 4.

75 Ibid., 5.

76 Miller, *The Nature of the Beasts*, 2–3.

77 Ibid., 3.

78 Latour, *We Have Never Been Modern*.

CHAPTER FOUR

SCULPTING DINAH WITH THE BLUNT TOOLS
OF THE HISTORIAN

Tracy McDonald

In her article "Nonhuman Animal Testimonies: A Natural History in the First Person," Concepción Cortés Zulueta presents the history of Michael (1973–2000), a gorilla orphaned after poachers in Cameroon killed his mother.[1] Michael learned a variant of American Sign Language, and Zulueta tries to use Michael's own words to tell his story. Inspired by this rare attempt to record an animal's story, rather than to reflect on what thinking about animals can tell us about ourselves, I will write part of the story of Dinah, a young gorilla who arrived on the grounds of the New York Zoological Park on 24 August 1914. Unlike Michael, Dinah did not learn American Sign Language, and so the historian must rely on the sources generated by the humans who encountered her. Historians have only just begun to work in the realm of animal biography.[2]

Why attempt a biography of a three-year-old gorilla? First, Dinah and the traces she left behind have value in and of themselves. Second, we dragged her, violently, into our history when we captured her, named her,[3] caged her, "acclimatized" her, transported her, monitored her, examined her, treated her, exhibited her, consumed her, commodified her, photographed her, filmed her, and sculpted her. To remember and to acknowledge her story and her life is part of an appeal to a "fundamental compassion"[4] from which our own conception of humanity has excluded other sentient beings. Finally, I hope that writing about Dinah may help to address the visceral "empathy gap" in her story and in so many of our dealings with nonhuman animals. As Donna Haraway writes about the relationships between the women who ran centres in parts of Africa that attempted to integrate captive chimps into the wild in the 1970s: "The narratives tell of profound loss and also of major achievements – by people and by animals. The people and the animals in these stories are *actors* enmeshed in history, not simply objects of knowledge, observers, and victims."[5]

Dinah is one such actor embedded in the tissues of history as we experience, write, and understand it. Jacques Derrida considers the danger of making the animal "speak" in the ways that we speak, of assigning it our words; but he also makes a plea to not abandon our attempts to understand in the face of this linguistic hurdle. "But in forbidding myself thus to assign, interpret or project, must I for all that give in to the other violence or *asinanity* [bêtise], that which would consist in suspending one's compassion and in depriving the animal of every power of manifestation, of the desire to manifest to me anything at all?"[6] So the historian attempts to walk the line between assigning thoughts and words to Dinah, as so many people did, and letting her, or at least what we know of her life, speak. Indeed, her historical silence is but one form of the violence that we impose on animals.

In April 1911, William Temple Hornaday, director of the New York Zoological Society, contracted Richard Lynch Garner, self-declared primate expert, to capture live gorillas in West Africa. Garner arrived in Cape Lopez on 12 May, and returned to New York on 22 September with one young gorilla. The infant died on 5 October. Just over a year later, the society contracted Garner a second time. Beginning on 15 November 1912, Garner agreed to return to West Africa for twelve to twenty months to secure several live gorillas. He was to maintain the "specimens" for several months "in his personal care in order to enable them to become thoroughly accustomed to captivity and educated in food habits that will be calculated to promote their successful maintenance in captivity away from their natural supply of food."[7] In terms of ascribing thought and motive to the gorillas, the correspondence maintained that the gorillas selected their diet out of ignorance and obstinance; they simply needed to be shown the error of their ways and learn to appreciate milk, lamb, sausages, ham, chicken, bread, potatoes, gravy, and *all* of the banana, rather than the piece that captured their fancy on a given day. After the gorillas had been acclimatized, Garner was to take a steamer directly to New York, avoiding any "transshipment." He was offered $2,000 for his troubles, as well as a monthly stipend of $50 starting on

15 November 1912, and an additional $500 for each of the first three gorillas to land in New York in good condition and $200 for each gorilla thereafter.[8]

Dinah's story begins with Garner's second trip to the "contiguous gorilla countries"[9] in what was then the French Congo. Dinah may have been born around the same time that Garner arrived in the region, or up to two years earlier.[10] We know none of the details of her capture specifically, but we do know something of the ways in which young gorillas were typically obtained. In a letter of 7 May 1913, Garner appealed to Hornaday to push the New York Zoological Society to "take some steps to protect the lives of the anthropoid apes, by inducing the French Societies to appeal to the colonial authorities to arrest the reckless and murderous traffic in these animals. I have already given you some rough statistics of the vast numbers of these creatures that are annually sacrificed to the greed of mercenaries. Besides the ruthless slaughter of mothers and the wounding of young, the untold suffering to which most of the surviving captives are subjected is worse than brutal."[11] Garner did not acknowledge that he himself contributed to this "murderous traffic" in gorillas. Both the primary and secondary literature is replete with references to the ways in which young gorillas were secured for zoos; capturing babies almost always required killing protective adults. In fact, Garner related a tale of the capture of two gorillas later in the trip. Apparently, one of his hunters came upon a group of four (a mother, father, and two little ones), chased them, and captured the two infants. He had "one in each hand when both adults, hearing the cries of their young, turned on him and made battle." The hunter dropped the larger of the two, and its mother recovered it. The male retreated after the hunter dropped the second baby, but the hunter recovered it and handed it over to Garner.[12] That baby gorilla, who would be named Don, would later be Dinah's companion for the time he remained alive in captivity.[13]

By 12 January 1913, Garner was writing to Hornaday from Gabon. He then travelled inland and settled on an island in Lake Ngovi in early May.[14] Garner did not write again until August. In a lengthy postscript to a 15 August 1913 letter, Garner "celebrated" his "purchase of a fine, young, male gorilla, which I estimate roughly at 7 or 8 months of age. He is in good condition at present and seems to have his Sunday appetite with him. He is a perfect little demon, however, and don't make up to anybody, so far." Even tracking Dinah in Garner's letters is a tricky proposition. It is not until his letter of 29 September 1913 that we discover that the "male" he purchased on 15 August 1913 was actually a female whom, we only learn in October, he christened Dinah.[15]

Correcting the gender pronouns in Garner's account, we can begin to sculpt Dinah's life from the moment she entered the written record. According to Garner, he "had an awful frolic" building a cage for her as he lacked most of the necessary supplies; he was so afraid of the little ape escaping that he moved her into the dining room of his home. Garner began Dinah's food training immediately, giving her less plantain than she wanted and offering her bread and bananas – food items more readily available in New York – instead. At 9:30 p.m. on the first night of her new life with Garner, Dinah began to cry and he gave her a slice of bread. She lay down on her side in her bed, "eating it for all the world like a human child."[16]

Garner moved to Ngofu, on Lake Ngovi, where he knew he could acquire the necessary permission to occupy a site. The local administrator suggested that, rather than build from scratch, it would be cheaper and faster if Garner occupied and repaired a vacant trading station. It was here that Dinah experienced her first months of captivity:

This is a fine old place, located on a jutting point of land where the lake breeze has a fair sweep of several miles. The house has six rooms, including the old store room and a small room for kerosene etc. It has a fine veranda all around it and the front section is large enough for a ballroom – It is about 16½ × 33 feet. There are many bearing fruit trees, such as mangoes, avocadoes, cocoanuts, soursop, Batanga cherries, etc. and hundreds of fine pineapples now, just maturing. The grounds are well laid out and in fine condition and the house is now quite comfortable ... In many respects it is an ideal place to nurse gorillas as I have an abundance of space to spare them.[17]

Dinah was very quiet until the afternoon of 17 August, when she "woke up and cut some funny capers." According to Garner, she "beat a tattoo" on the floor of her cage and "sung out, 'Just come inside if you want to get busy, you pale-faced giant. I'll chew that wooden leg of yours until you will forget that it was ever broken.'"[18]

Thus began the process that followed Dinah to her grave: the humans who interacted with her could not resist articulating thoughts for her. All the while, Dinah was "grating" her teeth so loudly that "you could have heard them twenty yards away." Garner goes on to claim that "after surveying me and the cook's mate and the boy that I had cleaning up the veranda," Dinah winked at him and said, "Just pass a couple of those niggers in here to me. I want to examine them." It would not be the last time that Garner enthusiastically ascribed his own racist worldview to Dinah. She refused bread on August 17 and ate nothing beyond a few plantains and a local sour fruit. Garner noted that he needed a proper cage and that only then would he be able to "handle" her, as she was "a regular fury."[19]

In these first two weeks of her captivity, Garner reported that Dinah was "thriving" and "learning to eat bread and sweet bananas." There were also times when she refused both and Garner deemed it wise to "indulge it in a bit of its native food of wild fruits, buds, and leaves of several kinds." He worried that changing and restricting her diet too quickly would have a negative impact on her health, so he assigned a young man to attend to her every need, although he was never allowed to feed her or go into her cage. Only Garner went into the cage with her and offered her food, in an effort to accustom her to his presence. In other words, Dinah's first weeks consisted of being offered bread and bananas, and occasionally food that she actually wanted, from Garner himself who came and went with her bedding. In this same letter of 31 August, Garner wondered aloud if the hunters from whom he had bought the gorilla had determined the sex of the little being correctly, for he was beginning to think that "he" was indeed a "she" but could not get close enough to confirm his suspicions.[20]

Garner seemed extremely taken with Dinah, whom he noted that he found "more humanlike" than any gorilla he had interacted with before. A typical day consisted of Dinah accepting or rejecting food. When Garner gave Dinah food she did not want, she would take it from him and throw it to the back of her cage. Often, she waited until he walked away to retrieve the offending food item and then pushed it out through the bars. At other times, she would hide the food in the straw that made up her bed; her bedding was changed at least once per day, so the rejected food made its way out of the cage quickly enough. As Garner raked up the straw, bits

of banana peel, and pieces of ntondo (a relative of ginger), Dinah, beside
him, picked up the remnants of her cache. She took the clean straw and
grass and arranged her own bed "in a very systematic manner, drawing the
loose ends of the grass toward the centre and tramping them securely in
place."[21] If someone Dinah did not know came too close to the cage, she
would beat her chest rapidly with both hands. She slowly grew accustomed
to Garner and would search his pockets for food when he was in range or
grasp his coat as he walked by. Increasingly, she did not want him to leave
her. Garner wrote, "When I am not in sight and it wants something it calls
me with a peculiar little whining voice that you would not expect in an animal of its kind."[22] Still in these early days, only two weeks into captivity,
she would allow "no undue familiarity" and, according to Garner, made a
"grand assault at me the other day because I threw away from its cage a
box containing a lot of ntondo buds and if it had been out of the cage I am
sure we would have had a fight."[23] He did not consider the possibility that
he had seized her carefully stored food supply.

Garner maintained that the "little knave" seemed "inclined to be funny
sometimes."[24] In this same letter of 31 August, Garner included a detailed
account of a disturbing incident that he connected to Dinah's sense of
humour, as he ascribed it to her. The incident is worth recording in full as
it conveys, yet again, how Garner projected his own racist and sexist world-
views onto Dinah. Moreover, the story may reflect the influence of those
thoughts and views on her behaviour, if, on this occasion, her behaviour
was aggressive rather than playful.

I keep a native boy to help me in the care for the gorilla and for some
reason the latter had conceived an inordinate aversion to the boy,
whom I call "la bonne d'Ujina" – "chambermaid to the gorilla" – Ujina
being the native name of gorilla. This afternoon the boy came to carry
away the waste which I had drawn from the cage and as he stooped to
pick up the sheet of tin used as a tray, he got a bit too near the cage and
quick as lightning the gorilla thrust his arms out and seized the boy by
a lock of his kinks and suddenly drew him nearer to the cage. Almost
simultaneously he reached the other arm through another opening and
seized another lock of natural curls. He jerked the boy's head against

the slats and made an attempt to bite him: but the opening was too narrow. Fortunately, I was near and relieved the boy with the loss of a few raven ringlets to which the gorilla clung with tenacity. As the frightened boy jumped back from the cage, the gorilla held up both hands, each with a bunch of black wool in it and looked at me with the most quizzical expression and with apparent pride as if to say – "What do you think of that for a scrap?" I have never seen an expression on the face of any other gorilla that came so near to a laugh and in this case it was, at least, a sneer.[25]

Garner concluded his narrative by wondering why the gorilla would so dislike the boy since he had never had the chance to tease her; he never considered that his own contempt for the child may have affected the way that Dinah treated him. This account is disturbing on a host of levels. Garner's blatantly condescending, imperialist, and racist attitude towards the child is palpable, ascribing to Dinah his own constant "sneer." He considers it frightfully clever to dub the young man a "chambermaid to the gorilla," thus denying his masculinity and emphasizing his demeaned and servile role. It was not enough for him to be a young African male – Garner had to fashion him as a sexualized, servile female in the form of the chambermaid, and in French no less. Finally, his willingness to project his own attitudes onto Dinah and see their manifestations as funny and superior illustrates the ways in which he placed her above the region's native population.[26]

By the end of September 1913, Garner had stepped up Dinah's intake of "civilized" food. She now ate bread, boiled or dried buffalo, and sweet bananas, though Garner still included the local buds, flowers, leaves, and roots that Dinah loved. And he now knew for certain that she was female. She was also growing "much attached" to him and would begin to cry as soon as he was out of her sight. She consumed a lot of water, which Garner had locals canoe in from a great distance as the closest supply was "brackish."[27] Dinah lived in a bit of a construction zone as Garner and the men he hired worked to repair the house and build the cages.[28]

In late October, Dinah was joined by another young (supposedly) female gorilla. The new arrival was small and timid. According to Garner, Dinah took to the little one right away. Dinah's bowels "were in very bad condition for a few days: but meanwhile she ate like a trooper and appeared as cheerful as usual." [29] She had a sore on her nose that she refused to leave alone. She had grown more than an inch since her arrival in August, and had put on five or six pounds. Around this time, Garner informed Hornaday that he had sent "seven natives" to Fernan Vaz to pick up the wire grating that Hornaday had sent to him for the cages. Garner further complained that he could go nowhere himself as his gorilla is a "'fouled anchor.' I would no more risk it in the care of any native than I would risk leaving my watch over night on a park bench in Madison Square. Now that I have two gorillas to look after, of course the bondage is only made the more secure." [30]

On 10 November 1913, Garner wrote to say that he was now in possession of ten panels of wire grating, a box of hinges, and locks. He told Hornaday that Dinah was "growing like a weed and asks me to say that she will be along in a few more months to stir things up at the zoo park and she adds that she will then be about three years old." [31] Garner assured Hornaday that the sores on her face and nose were healing and had not left any scars. The new arrival had been dubbed Tootsy, and Garner had been reduced to taking "some chances on her by a system of starvation" to get her to eat bread and bananas; she all but refused to drink water. Hornaday was understandably worried about receiving the gorillas alive in New York and Garner assured him that he was like a "foster-mother" to his charges and that he would bring them back safely. Thus, Dinah challenged gender identities across the board. Garner had found it difficult to imagine that so rambunctious a young being could be female. He also indulged in a demasculinization of the young man in his employ through his care of Dinah. At the same time, Garner's role as nursemaid to his captives challenged his own masculinity as Dinah began to treat him more and more like a gorilla mother.

Almost three months into her captivity, Dinah was now comfortable climbing on Garner, sitting in his lap, and searching through his pockets. She had taken to insisting that he break up her food and put it directly into her mouth in small pieces, refusing to take it into her own hands. Garner defended himself against the charge of "spoiling her," writing, "I think all such little indulgences are beneficial in the fact that they please and tranquilize the animal." She was a little calmer than she had been before her new gorilla companion arrived, but she still refused to let Garner out of her sight. If he left her "alone for an hour during the day she would scream herself hoarse." [32]

These observations are worth considering carefully. Dinah was increasingly and profoundly attached to and dependent upon Garner. Gorillas experience anxiety when separated from a mother or surrogate, and maintaining this attachment was very likely the key to her survival with Garner.[33] The loss of her connection with Garner upon arrival in New York may go a long way to explain her decline within a few weeks of entering the park.

In a letter of 27 November 1913, Garner wrote that he had discovered that Tootsy was also, in fact, male, and renamed him Don, after Don Quixote, because he was constantly "charging at windmills."[34] Again, gendered tropes played a role in the original pronouncement of Don's sex. Dinah was large, lively, and active; therefore, she must be male. Don was small, frail, and timid; therefore, obviously, he must be female. Even once his sex was accurately determined, the decision to name him Don Quixote, with that character's feminine qualities of impracticality and idealism, embraces his traditionally unmasculine personality. He was not like Dinah at all. Don was reticent and shy while Dinah was playful, ticklish, "laugh[ed] like a child," and was growing rapidly and putting on weight. Both gorillas were fed roast, dried and boiled buffalo, antelope, bush pig, chicken, and sweet bananas. "They still crave certain wild fruits, plants, leaves, and bark and I indulge them in some of their choice bush diet."[35] On New Year's Day 1914, Garner wrote an upbeat, closely written, seven-page letter to Hornaday. He reported that Dinah was eating well, growing, and appeared happy and lively, prompting Garner to describe her as a "regular tomboy." Since the arrival of a gorilla companion, Dinah filled her days playing with Don like a "boisterous" older sister. She revelled in running past him, knocking him over, and then, when he protested, embracing and comforting him.

In early February, Dinah continued to appear healthy and playful. Garner wrote, "Dinah is the finest I ever saw. She is as playful as a kitten and as rough as a bear. She is fat and hardy."[36] However, Garner faced another housing crisis. After all the work that he and his local workforce had done to repair the old trading station – making it mosquito proof, building a chicken house, adding a kitchen – he was informed that the property had been ceded to another company and that he would have to vacate. He fought hard to delay the move to the next dry season.

March 1914 brought significant loss and distress to both Dinah and Garner. In a letter of 27 March, Garner reported that Don had died: "As a specimen of the gorilla race he was not of great value perhaps, as he had always been so frail and morose: but as a companion for Dinah he is a great loss. Since his death she has not been playful or even gentle as she had been before and while she has a big open cage eight by nine feet to play in and the best food that I can procure for her, she continually demands my personal companionship. She is in fine physical condition and has a good appetite: but is lonely and morose."[37] Ever a practical man, Henry Fairfield Osborn, eugenicist and then-head of the New York Zoological Society, heard of little Don's death and wrote immediately to Hornaday to make sure that Garner was instructed to save his skin and skeleton.[38] Garner continued to reassure Hornaday that he was doing his utmost to acquire more gorillas. Ten days after Don's death, Dinah was still "morose, sad, and often sullen." Her stomach was constantly upset.[39] By the end of the month her physical symptoms seemed to have resolved, but she remained visibly distressed in her solitude. She had not played at all since Don's death and had lost between six and eight pounds.[40]

In late January 1914, Hornaday wrote his first letter to Garner about an illness that was affecting the primates at the New York Zoological Park.[41] In a letter of 15 April 1914, he informed Garner that all of the park's primates had died from the disease. He sent Garner another one thousand dollars and asked him to acquire three or four more chimps along with "all the showy West African monkeys that you can conveniently take care of."[42] Garner quickly obtained a chimp. In a 6 June letter, Garner wrote that losing Susie (a chimpanzee who had travelled with Garner on the lecture circuit and whom he had left in Hornaday's care), Baldy (the park's most famous chimpanzee), and all the other New York primates, together with Don, had given him the "blues." In addition, his captives had come under attack.

> About the time that I was receiving all these knock-out blows from some unseen foe; and I had the greatest anxiety about Dinah, some son of Ham tried to injure her, as I found abundant evidence and the same criminal (as I suspect) tried to kill the chimp and came within an ace of succeeding. He has now recovered and appears to be all right. Some brute drove a knife or a bamboo picket into him and for about two weeks I seriously thought I should have to kill him to relieve his suffer-

ing. During twelve days he did not eat a morsel and for eight days didn't taste water.[43]

The attack on the chimp and Dinah were, in all likelihood, attacks directed at Garner given the infinite care he showed them and the utter contempt he had for the local population; hurting them would hurt Garner more than any other action in terms of both sentiment and pocket.

By mid-June, Garner's optimism for capturing any more chimps, much less gorillas, had begun to fade. He wrote Hornaday to explain that the timber industry was the main culprit. First of all, the money the industry promised locals for timber meant that potential hunters were occupied felling trees. Moreover, the "vast spread of the industry drives the apes from all sections contiguous with the waterways." But Dinah was becoming playful again and was increasingly difficult for Garner to recapture when he let her out of her cage. Luckily for him, he discovered that she was desperately afraid of umbrellas and so one became his tool of choice to drive her back inside.[44]

On 27 June 1914, Garner informed Hornaday that he had "bought a motor and especially fitted out a small craft" that he "sent in charge of a competent white man to make a complete tour of the lakes and rivers within a hundred miles or so of this place in search of gorillas, chimpanzees, or rare monkeys but I have not much hope of finding anything worthwhile and certainly not monkeys that you would care for."[45] Garner had finally given up. He notified Hornaday that he would be taking an English steamer leaving sometime between 5 and 12 July and due to land in New York in the middle of August. He reported that Dinah was again in "excellent condition." He claimed that she now seemed to have forgotten Don and that she happily wrestled and boxed with him and engaged in a "pitch-battle with hay – all this ended with a climbing race up a mango tree and at this Dinah always wins and is conscious of it."[46]

Here, the up-close and intimate portraits of Dinah end. The last direct mentions of her when she was still in Garner's care took the form of strangely coded cablegrams in which gorillas were "cabinets."[47] A telegram of 23 August asked Hornaday to meet him with two small transfer cages.[48] In his *Confessions of a Scientist*, Raymond Ditmars, head of the reptile and later mammal collections of the New York Zoological Park, claimed that while

Garner had booked a cabin for himself and a tool house on the ship's deck for Dinah for the return trip, the actual sleeping arrangements for the voyage became reversed; Dinah slept in the cabin and Garner bunked in the tool house. While amusing, this story may or may not represent some apocryphal myth-making surrounding Garner and Dinah's relationship.[49]

It was clear that Garner wanted to hear how Dinah was doing after they were separated. In November 1914, he sent Hornaday a postcard with his mailing address.[50] On 28 December 1914, Garner sent an angry letter to Hornaday, complaining that he had not received the promised photographs and lantern slides of Dinah and ended his letter with a demand for news about her.[51] He ended a short note of 28 January 1915, in all capital letters, with "PLEASE TELL ME HOW DINAH IS COMING ON."[52]

The *Bulletin of the New York Zoological Society* published a short notice in September on Dinah's arrival that included photographs from the first of two extended photo sessions. We know that Dinah had her picture taken a great deal in the first months. In the *Bulletin*, she was described as three years old and in perfect health, "thanks to Mr Garner's careful development of her habits and temperament. She is cheerful and affectionate, very lively, and full of playfulness, and her appetite is everything that could be desired." The notice did not fail to point out these characteristics were "well-nigh the direct opposite of nearly every gorilla that ever came out of Africa."[53]

Dinah attracted celebrity visitors. One of the first was Djuna Barnes, the modernist journalist and author of prose and poetry. Barnes is best known for her 1936 work *Nightwood*, which is one of the earliest novels to portray lesbian relationships. In October 1914, Barnes published "The Girl and the Gorilla" in *New York World Magazine*, in which she embraced many of the contradictions, myths, and perceptions that Dinah embodied. Garner was present for the introductions and assured Barnes that, even though she was the first woman to "come within caressing or battling distance" of Dinah, the young primate would not reject her. Barnes's opening paragraph established Dinah's role for Barnes who had come "to study her." "A new species has come to town! We thought we have a line on all the different kinds of femininity in the world, their fads, their fancies and fashions, their virtues and indiscretions – when suddenly enters Dinah the bush girl." Barnes claimed that from the "public's side of the bars" – thereby emphasizing her special access – Dinah appeared to be "only a vague, grey thing with a head sunk between shoulders – a bundle of unfathomable apprehensions." But up close, she was a challenge to the gender norms and conventional beliefs of the early-twentieth century. Barnes reported that she crawled around after Dinah for twenty minutes until she asked herself whether the "advantages of civilization" would enable her to "dominate this rather unique situation." Barnes did so by asking Dinah to hold forth on the United States, and so put a critique of her time and place into Dinah's mouth. In the article, Dinah criticized traditional views of femininity, society's disapprobation towards feminism, high taxi fares in New York City, and the trickery of the city's electric light. Barnes concluded her piece with a supposed challenge from Dinah to her male keeper, Fred Engelholm. Barnes claimed that Dinah growled at Engelholm and lunged at him, forcing him to catch her in mid-air. As in Guro Flinterud's discussion of Knut the polar bear's behaviour in chapter 8 of this volume, it is unclear whether Dinah was being playful or aggressive. Nonetheless, it worked for Barnes's analysis to portray her as challenging Engelholm rather than as recognizing him as a trusted playmate.

The last lines of Barnes's article are a nod to one of imperialism's native sons: "It had just been borne in upon him that even here Kipling's remark about the female of the species rings true."[54] In Barnes's article, Dinah became a symbol and a vessel for the historical moment of challenge to and confusion around traditional conceptions of gender and the meaning of civilization in early-twentieth-century New York City.[55]

The park spared no expense in celebrating its acquisition of a live gorilla. A member of the board of directors commissioned the renowned sculptor Eli Harvey to create a life-sized bronze of Dinah.[56] By his own account, Harvey, in order to create detailed studies for his work, "had the good fortune to see much of Dinah up to a period within four days of her death."[57] She clearly made an impression on Harvey and he wrote a piece on her for *Art World* magazine in 1917. Beginning with a short history of attempts to capture gorillas, he described the months that Garner spent with Dinah and Don in Gabon as a time "to accustom them to their white captor as companion, and teach them to eat more civilized food than the acrid food of their native jungles." The thoughts and feelings that Harvey imposed on Dinah are worth quoting at length because, like Barnes, he used Dinah and his interaction with her to articulate his views and concerns about the modern world. First, he revealed that he has no idea how gorillas were typically captured, and imagines that Dinah's parents had left her unattended while they searched for food. As a conservative Quaker who hated modernist art with a passion, Harvey regularly admired the purity and simplicity of his animal subjects revelling in what he saw as strong pronatal and maternal values. Thus, his social agenda is the antithesis of Barnes's, and the two figures nicely capture the tensions of the day regarding issues of femininity and motherhood.[58] Harvey wrote:

> Dinah always inspired me with a feeling of sympathy, as her large deep-brown eyes gazed dreamily into mine, her head lowered until the chin rested upon the chest, as it is wont to do owing to the short thick neck and long spinal processes in that region; this depression of the head, with reluctant glances from beneath the very protruding orbital ridges gave Dinah an air of diffidence. The slow and limited rotary movement of the head from side to side necessitates a supple mental turning of the eyes to focus upon a desired object. All movements of body or limb, if compared with the chimpanzee, are slow; and except under great stress or excitement of emotion, silence reigns: no chattering, not even a grunt to break the mystery!

With this bond of sympathy between the gorilla-model and the sculptor, imagination easily became reality, and hence the following soliloquy:

> Alone! Alone! I know not where – things are so strange, passing strange – so cold, the sun's rays come aslant and cheerless. The inhabitants have bleached into spectres; they give me food so tasteless, they tell me I am in exile the only one of my race snatched from the bosom of my family and brought across wide oceans to live and die in captivity. For what? A holiday? No, not that! Then why was I so ruthlessly snatched from my happy abode in the trees while my parents were away seeking dainty morsels of food for me? I was happy in a mother's love, whose warmth equalled the equatorial sun bathed in the humid atmosphere of the deep, dark, and hospitable jungles, – and yet they seized upon me! Why?
>
> But the real pathos of it all is that these manlike apes do not even know that they are martyrs to the cause of science. Dinah, however, was

of such amiable and obliging disposition, I am constrained to believe she would have been a willing martyr to the cause, had one been able to explain it to her.[59]

For Harvey, Dinah's real tragedy was not so much that she was taken from her home, fed unfamiliar food, and exhibited in an alien environment, but rather that she was unable to grasp the value she held for science, civilization, and men. The sculptor soothed his concerns by believing that even after all of her suffering, had Dinah been able to consent, she would have done so.[60]

Another sculptor, Eugenie Shonnard, also spent a good deal of time with Dinah over the course of several months on repeated visits to the park. Her recollections provide a glimpse of Dinah that more closely match those gleaned from Garner's correspondence. According to Shonnard's recollections, Dinah was playful and energetic. The first time she entered her enclosure, Shonnard was nervous and found herself humming and singing. On every subsequent visit, Dinah would insist that Shonnard sing to her: "every day when I would go she would demand that I would sing to her before I could handle her. She would stand on her hind legs, stand up straight. She was about like this and thump, lick, *umphhh* ... that means come on and sing. And we did, before we did any work." Shonnard reminisced that in order to prompt Dinah to cooperate, she had to ask her to do the exact opposite of what the artist required. "To get her to sit on a chair where I could see her, I had to forbid her getting on it 'Dinah, don't you go near that chair.' Up she would go and sit on the chair. Then, if I saw she was going to get off the chair, I'd tell her, 'Get right off that chair!' She thought, 'I'll stay here.'" Dinah was curious about the clay and the work in progress, and she was keen to play with the cloths that covered the clay to keep it moist. In one session, Dinah poked Shonnard in the ribs and stole her rag. She promptly swallowed it; just the end was sticking out of her mouth. Zoo staff had warned the artist that the young primate was fond of playing with water. They were convinced getting wet put her at risk of illness and begged Shonnard to keep all water out of reach. But Shonnard was desperate: "So I grabbed the water, the forbidden water, and put it on the floor because I knew she would go for the water. She went for the water, starting throwing it all over herself and I pulled the rag out of her mouth like this! I called the keeper and told him what had happened. I said I can't help it, I had to get the water to save the rag – to get the rag out of her. So, he came right over with alcohol and bathed her with alcohol and she didn't catch cold. But she was a very, very intelligent creature."[61] Later in the summer, Shonnard returned to the park to show Hornaday the bust of Dinah. On that day, the artist lamented that she did not have time to visit Dinah; she was only able to wave at her from a distance. Shonnard felt that this unintentional snub had significant repercussions on her relationship with her model. Shonnard recalled that when she returned to work with Dinah a month later, "She never allowed me to see her face again. She was so hurt. She put her arms around her face. I never saw her again, and she died about two months after."[62] It is clear that Dinah made very deep and lasting impressions on Shonnard and Harvey, and they both expressed mixed feelings about her captivity. Harvey comforted himself, as Hornaday did, by falling back on the young primate's value to science. Shonnard was more ambivalent and critical of herself. She felt that she had personally betrayed Dinah. Perhaps that sense of personal betrayal is representative of a much larger one.

Once Dinah arrived in New York City, there was no papa Garner, as he had referred to himself in the postcards he wrote to Susie, reporting on her day-to-day progress. The historian is forced to look elsewhere for the tracks she left behind to continue the narrative of her life. The first newspaper article to mention Dinah was published before she left Lake Ngovi. The headline is striking: "Captive Gorilla Is Happy." The article reported that Garner had captured "the finest specimen of the race ever seen," and in contrast to "most gorillas, who are morose and sullen, she is lively and possessed of a happy disposition."[63] The headline points to the fact that it was important for many who encountered Dinah to believe that she was happy. Yet, according to William Bridges, editor and curator of publications of the New York Zoological Society from 1935 to 1966, Dinah was losing interest in food by mid-November.[64]

Her story was not picked up by the press again until December 1914, when she had fallen ill. Moreover, Dinah was not only New York's only gorilla – she was the last gorilla who could be captured until the end of the war. The headline "Jungle Baby Lolls in Invalid Luxury" captures the tensions and contradictions surrounding perceptions of Dinah. On the one hand, there was the obvious discomfort with investing so much time and resources into a "mere animal." On the other hand, there was affection and curiosity towards her. Dinah was initially diagnosed with "infantile paralysis," but

after testing her spinal fluid the diagnosis was switched to "locomotor atax-
ia."[65] The experts prescribed fresh air. Dinah, "dressed like a French doll,
with a lace cap and tucked in a fur rug," could be seen daily on the zoo
grounds in a pram pushed by Engelholm. This maternal role did not always
sit well with her caregiver, who blamed Garner for creating a "spoilt infant."
He accused Garner of indulging Dinah's every whim when they were in
Gabon and of petting "her all the way from Africa to New York" serving as
her "cook and valet"[66] – roles that now fell to Engleholm. Without Garner,
Dinah was adrift.

There was talk in January 1915 of taking Dinah to Palm Beach. The ar-
ticles that covered the story showed a similar disquiet regarding the fuss over
an animal.[67] Ultimately, Dinah remained in the Bronx until her death. She
appeared on the cover of the January 1915 edition of the *Bulletin of the New
York Zoological Society*. In a spread, containing numerous photographs of
Dinah, Hornaday wrote a piece on what was so far known about gorillas.
He covered the usual imperialist ground: Gorillas were discovered by Paul
B. Du Chaillu, who received high praise for his problematic, to say the least,
Adventures in Equatorial Africa (1861). Hornaday summarized his experience of gorillas in captivity, until Dinah: "The objectionable features of the
gorilla are its much too savage habits, and its aversion to food and life in captivity. It is not an animal of philosophic mind, nor is it given to intelligent
reasoning from cause to effect. It reminds one of children who refuse to taste
a new kind of food because they know in advance that they won't like it! And
what can we do with a wild animal that is not amenable to the pangs of
hunger, and would rather die than yield?"[68] But Dinah was different. She
was, by most reports, friendly and lively. Hornaday's 1915 piece is full of
ambivalence and contradictions. The zoo director was wary of gorillas. They
had failed him before. In the 1907 *Guide to the New York Zoological Park*,
Hornaday counselled zoo-goers that if a gorilla ever arrived at the park they
should visit as soon as possible, before it "dies of sullenness, lack of exercise,
and indigestion."[69] But Dinah was not sullen; she was friendly and engaged.
So perhaps Hornaday hoped she would be different. His ambivalence turned
to a conviction that she foolishly chose to "rather die than yield" to reason
and rational care.

In his 1915 write-up, Hornaday offered a sense of Dinah's daily life at the
zoo. "Throngs" of people came every day to see her. She seemed to have won

the hearts of visitors, photographers, and reporters alike. Like Harvey, Hornaday emphasized the exalted position that educated, civilized society had bestowed upon Dinah: "She posed for scores of pictures, moving and fixed, and in every way strove to fill the high position in the zoological world to which nature and the Zoological Society had elected her."[70] And like Harvey, Hornaday underlined the importance of Dinah's role in his scientific world. Hornaday professed to be the first observer to note the "humanlike" quality of the gorilla's eyes, and went on to describe her "mannish hands and feet," her fur's texture and colouring, her gait, and her diet. Hornaday also admitted that by November 1914, Dinah's appetite was faltering and the muscles in her legs and arms were presenting signs of paralysis. According to the director, there was "no excuse whatsoever" for her symptoms. Her therapy consisted of massage and "electrical treatment." Hornaday concluded with his firm conviction that an adult gorilla would never be exhibited in a zoological garden.[71]

In February, another animal was introduced into Dinah's life. There is strangely no consensus on the origins, nature, sex, or breed of this animal. According to the *Richmond Times-Dispatch*, Dinah's "attending physicians" thought she would survive because she had "found a sweetheart." Her hoped-for saviour was first reported as a mongrel who had strayed onto the zoo grounds. The article claims his name was Little Nemo and that Dinah wept every time he left her cage.[72] The *New York Tribune* claimed that he was a fox terrier who belonged to one of the park's keepers.[73] The *Bulletin of the New York Zoological Society* said the dog was a "small bull terrier."[74] He disappeared from the records as abruptly as he arrived.

A month before her death, Washington, DC's *Evening Star* devoted half a page to Dinah's story. The headline "She Was Caught Young" led an upbeat article that focused on Dinah's excellent care at the zoo. The article emphasizes that due to the size and strength of full-grown gorillas, only baby ones "like 'Dinah' can be secured and civilized." It details her features: "A striking point in her appearance is her nose, with its half human elevation. Her whole face is jet-black, shiny, and smooth as polished ebony, and her large liquid brown eyes make a distinct appeal to the observer."[75] It also describes her as cheerful and affectionate, lively and playful, and in possession of a fine appetite. To conclude, it catalogues Dinah's diet: A raw egg at 8 a.m.; seasonal fruit at 10:30; bread or crackers and water at 11:30; "hot roast beef, broiled chicken, or lamb with gravy, mashed potatoes and bread" at 1:30 p.m.; more fruit and bread at 3:00; more milk and a raw egg at 5:30; and a drink of plain milk at 8:30.[76] Dinner came from the Rocking Stone Restaurant on the park grounds. "Civilized food" had won out and there was no trace of anything Dinah would have eaten in the wild.

We are able to piece together rather a lot about Dinah's eleven months at the zoo. Scores of people converged on her cage to look at her. Ditmars, Elwin R. Sanborn (the park's official photographer), and a cameraman from *Pathe's Weekly* filmed her. Sanborn did at least two major photo sessions with her. Barnes visited, and Dinah put her head on her knees.[77] Shonnard visited a number of times and, according to Shonnard, she bonded with her and felt betrayed when the artist abandoned her. Harvey had her model for him, although he maintained a much greater physical distance than had the two women. We know what Dinah ate. We know about the cage that she occupied. We know she was attached to Engelholm, but perhaps not enough to keep her alive. We know she had a brief attachment to a small dog. And we know that, once she fell ill, she was pushed around the park daily in a pram.

On 2 August 1915, the press announced Dinah's death. The most detailed and voluble article was published in the *New York Tribune*: "Dinah the sad-eyed little gorilla, the only one of her kind in captivity, died from starvation yesterday at the Bronx Zoo. John [*sic*] Engelholm, her keeper and the only one she cared for, this side of the Congo, was with her when she breathed her last." The real cause of death, according to the article, was homesickness. Despite his best efforts, Engelholm simply could not replace "a gorilla mother who carries you close to her big hairy chest and shields you from all harm":

Dinah was one very small gorilla, alone in a strange cold world. The memory of the hot, damp Africa days took away her appetite in this colorless hostile world. Day by day the arms with which she clung to Engelholm when especially lonely grew thinner and thinner. They took her from her cage, and her keeper bought her a baby carriage in which he wheeled her around the grounds, heavily wrapped, with her ugly little face peering out on the unfamiliar scenes ... Probably by now she is disporting in the tall, tall palms and devouring the wondrous cocoanuts that grow in that land where good monkeys go.[78]

The *Tribune* article's author, too, could not resist channelling thoughts and feelings into Dinah, even after her death. Men did not good surrogate mothers make, but good monkeys, like good humans, find their reward in heaven.[79]

A *New York Tribune* article of 19 January 1916 reported that Dinah died from "exhaustion and starvation, malnutrition and rickets. During the last two weeks of her life she was offered at least twenty different kinds of food, but ate practically nothing save oranges and a little oatmeal."[80] These claims were taken from the 1915 annual report of the New York Zoological Society. The article took a distinctly anti-zoo tone, adding that in 1915 the zoo lost 251 specimens and showed a decline in visitor attendance.

A few years later, any sympathy that Dinah may have cultivated in Hornaday had soured into gendered contempt. In his 1922 *The Minds and Manners of Wild Animals*, he wrote of Dinah, "Her mind was dull and hopelessly unresponsive. She learned next to nothing and she did nothing really interesting."[81] He continued to note that, in terms of intellect, chimpanzees and orangutans are vastly superior to gorillas: "Our own Dinah was no exception to the rule. Personally she was a stupid little thing, even when in excellent health. Her most pronounced and exasperating stupidities were shown in her refusal to eat, or to taste, strange food, even when very hungry. Any ape that does not know enough to eat a fine, ripe banana, and will only mince away at the inner lining of the banana skin, is an unmitigated numskull, and hardly fit to live. Dinah was all that, and more."[82] Thus, Hornaday suggests that Dinah deserved to die. Her death was not the fault of the zoo or any of her caretakers. Her failure to thrive was brought on by a thick-headedness unique to her. Yet, the chapter is rife with contradiction, and Hornaday revealed that he understood full well the environment required for a gorilla to survive in captivity. He remarked, "It seems that an exhibition cage, in a zoological park or garden thronged with visitors, actually tends to the suppression, or even the complete extinguishment, of true gorilla character."[83]

As evidence of Dinah's inadequacies, he pointed to the life and death of another captive gorilla who to his mind was most unlike her. In the September 1921 issue of the New York Zoological Society's *Bulletin*, Alyse Cunningham wrote about her relationship with a young gorilla, John Daniel. John was purchased by Major Rupert Penny from a department store in London in 1918, where the young ape had been part of the shop's Christmas display. John was underweight, experiencing cold symptoms, and "rickety."[84] Care for the sickly primate fell to Cunningham, a young relative of Penny's who was living in his London home. Within a few months, John had full run of the house. He refused stale food and loved lemon jelly, as long as it had been made that day. He liked visitors, whom he would take by the hand and lead around the room. He made up endless games to amuse himself, and he loved to be chased. The problem that Penny and Cunningham faced was that they could not leave John alone, nor could they leave him with anyone else. If they were out of his sight, for even a moment, he would scream. When they wanted to discipline him, their only recourse was "to tell him he was very naughty, and push him away. He would drop to the floor and cry and be very repentant, holding one's ankles and putting his head on our feet."[85] In January 1921, they decided that they had to part with him. They contacted an animal trader who assured them that John Daniel was going to a wealthy collector in Florida. Once in possession of the young primate, the trader handed him over to the Ringling Brothers. He died on 17 April 1921.[86]

I include this short synopsis of John Daniel's life because Hornaday retold his story and asserted that John Daniel was the only intelligent gorilla that he had ever encountered. Hornaday placed the blame for Dinah's death onto Dinah herself, rooted in her own stubborn ignorance. He threw in a gendered dismissal of her as a "stupid little thing" and contrasted her alleged lack of intelligence to John Daniel's brilliance. In this way, Hornaday skillfully shifted the blame for her death away from the New York Zoological Park's decisions and actions and placed them on Dinah herself, and on Garner, even though he knew full-well that Dinah under Garner's care was very much like John Daniel under Cunningham's. In fact, some years earlier on 6 October 1914, Hornaday had written to Carl Hagenbeck's son about Dinah: "The Gorilla he brought is a very great prize. It is about three years old and good natured. It exercises as much as any chimpanzee, and it eats like a pig. I see no reason why it should not live here at least six or more years. I never heard of another Gorilla that was so good-natured and lively as this one."[87] Hornaday denounced Dinah after her death to protect his own reputation and that of his staff and zoo.

In *The Animal That Therefore I Am*, Derrida shows how Descartes, Kant, Heidegger, Lacan, and Levinas turned the "animal" into something "seen and not seeing," and, in so doing, "denied it as much as misunderstood it." And Derrida's treatise circles "round and round this immense *disavowal*, whose logic traverses the whole history of humanity."[88] Hornaday disavowed Dinah just like the behavioural psychologist Herbert Terrace repudiated Nim.[89] They used their own purported scholarly devotion to science to disavow animals that they had imprisoned in its name. Hornaday's last words on Dinah was that she was "a stupid little thing" who "learned next to nothing" and "did nothing really interesting." In much the same way, Terrace publicly denied that Nim had learned language. It is this abjuration and perpetual exploitation – the denial of will, choice, past, desire, agency, and a future other than the one we provide – that create the contours of the violence within our relationship with nonhuman animals. Perhaps the attempt to reclaim one of those lives for history is a small start towards righting the centuries of wrongs in our relations with and treatment of them.

NOTES

1 I would like to thank the Social Sciences and Research Council of Canada for generous financial support; Jonathan Bone for help with the worst of Garner's handwriting; Leilani Dawson and Madeleine Thompson for archival assistance; and Mayhill Fowler, Anne Keary, Sean Kinnear, Violette Pouillard, Jen Squibb, Dan Vandersommers, and the participants in the Zoo Studies: Toward a New Humanities Workshop (2–3 December 2016) for their advice and insights.

2 As we see in Violette Pouillard's contribution to this volume, this task is not an utterly foreign one for the historian. Since the 1960s, historians have attempted to write history "from below," a history of those individuals who leave no written record of their own but appear in the records of the state, the court, and the writings of others. Pouillard discusses the ways in which animal biography follows the now established methodologies of microhis-

tory, social history, history from below, and subaltern history. She also renders an impressive reconstruction of a typical life in the wild for young gorillas, and of their experiences immediately after capture, which is useful for imagining Dinah's early life. Moreover, in March 2016, Mieke Roscher and Andre Krebber hosted an international conference, titled Animal Biographies – Recovering Animal Selfhood through Interdisciplinary Narration? This led to Krebber and Roscher, eds., *Animal Biography: Re-framing Animal Lives.*

3 See Derrida, *The Animal That Therefore I Am*, 19–20, on the importance of naming.
4 Ibid., 26–7.
5 Haraway, *Primate Visions*, 129 (emphasis original).
6 Derrida, *The Animal That Therefore I Am*, 18.
7 Manuscript Agreement, 1912, WCSA 1001.
8 Handwritten and typed contracts November 1912, WCSA 1001.
9 R.L. Garner to W.T. Hornaday, 7 May 1913, WCSA 1001.
10 If his initial estimation of her age in August is correct. R.L. Garner to W.T. Hornaday, 15 August 1913, WCSA 1001. However, in a letter of 10 November 1913, Garner put her age at well over two years. R.L. Garner to W.T. Hornaday, 10 November 1913, WCSA 1001. The latter is most likely the most accurate estimate.
11 R.L. Garner to W.T. Hornaday, 31 May 1913, WCSA 1001. See also Noah Cincinnati, "Too Sullen for Survival," 169; Gott and Weir, *Gorilla*, 73–4. Gott and Weir mention a *Life* article from November 1951 that reported that six adults were killed to secure two infant gorillas for American zoos.
12 R.L. Garner to W.T. Hornaday, 29 October 1913, WCSA 1001.
13 R.L. Garner to W.T. Hornaday, 29 September 1913, WCSA 1001.
14 R.L. Garner to W.T. Hornaday, 7 May 1913, WCSA 1001.
15 R.L. Garner to W.T. Hornaday, 29 September and 29 October 1913, WCSA 1001.
16 R.L. Garner to W.T. Hornaday, 15 August 1913, WCSA 1001.
17 R.L. Garner to W.T. Hornaday, 7 October 1913, WCSA 1001.
18 R.L. Garner to W.T Hornaday, 17 August 1913, WCSA 1001
19 R.L. Garner to W.T. Hornaday, 15 August 1913, WCSA 1001.
20 R.L. Garner to W.T. Hornaday, 31 August 1913, WCSA 1001.
21 Ibid.

22 Ibid.

23 Ibid.

24 Ibid.

25 Ibid.

26 Rich, *Missing Links* focuses on Garner's attitudes towards black people in Africa and the United States.

27 R.L. Garner to W.T. Hornaday, 29 September 1913, WCSA 1001.

28 Ibid.

29 R.L. Garner to W.T. Hornaday, 29 October 1913, WCSA 1001. In a contribution to the *Bulletin of the New York Zoological Society*, Garner strenuously objected to the notion that gorillas were vegetarians thus the amount of meat in Dinah's diet which may explain her stomach issues. He also noted in the same article that in the wild gorillas only ate bitter, "even acrid" fruit and vegetables. R.L. Garner, "Gorillas in Their Own Jungle," 62, 3 (May 1914): 1104.

30 R.L. Garner to W.T. Hornaday, 29 October 1913, WCSA 1001.

31 R.L. Garner to W.T. Hornaday, 10 November 1913, WCSA 1001.

32 Ibid.

33 See the brief discussion based on the work of zoologist George Schaller in Cincinnati, "Too Sullen," 176–7.

34 R.L. Garner to W.T. Hornaday, 1 January 1914, WCSA 1001.

35 R.L. Garner to W.T. Hornaday, 27 November 1913, WCSA 1001.

36 R.L. Garner to W.T. Hornaday, 9 February 1914, WCSA 1001.

37 R.L. Garner to W.T. Hornaday, 27 March 1914, WCSA 1001.

38 Henry Fairfield Osborn to W.T. Hornaday, 14 May 1914, WCSA 1001.

39 R.L. Garner to W.T. Hornaday, 7 April 1914, WCSA 1001.

40 R.L. Garner to W.T. Hornaday, 28 April 1914, WCSA 1001.

41 W.T. Hornaday to R.L. Garner, 28 January 1914, WCSA 1001.

42 W.T. Hornaday to R.L. Garner, 14 April 1914, WCSA 1001.

43 R.L. Garner to W.T. Hornaday 6 June 1914, WCSA 1001.

44 R.L. Garner to W.T. Hornaday 17 June 1914, WCSA 1001.

45 R.L. Garner to W.T. Hornaday, 27 June 1914, WCSA 1001.

46 Ibid.

47 Cablegram from R.L. Garner to W.T. Hornaday, 20 July 1914, WCSA 1001. See also Bridges, *Gathering of Animals*, 347.

48 Telegram from R.L. Garner to W.T. Hornaday, 23 August 1914, WCSA 1001.

49 Rich, *Missing Links*, 57, quoting Ditmars, *Confessions of a Scientist*.

50 Postcard from R.L. Garner to W.T. Hornaday, 14 November 1914, WCSA 1001.

51 R.L. Garner to W.T. Hornaday, 28 December 1914, WCSA 1001.

52 R.L. Garner to W.T. Hornaday, 28 January 1914, WCSA 1001.

53 "The Zoological Park Gets a Gorilla," *Bulletin of the New York Zoological Society* 62, 5 (September 1914): 1150.

54 Djuna Chappell-Barnes, "The Girl and the Gorilla," *New York World Magazine*, October 1914.
    This whimsical projection is the last line of Barnes's article. The "remark" Barnes refers to is from the Rudyard Kipling poem "The Female of the Species," and is the last line of six of the poem's thirteen verses: "the female of the species is more deadly than the male." As Jeremy Rich notes, Dinah represented the kind of alternate femininity that Barnes saw in herself, "a proud individual unbound by social graces." *Missing Links*, 162.

55 Rich, *Missing Links*, 161–2, argues that Barnes and Shonnard challenged traditional views of femininity with and through Dinah.

56 Bridges, *Gathering of Animals*, 350. The cost was $880.25.

57 Eli Harvey, "Little Miss Dinah of Africa," *Art World*, July 1917, 341.

58 See Harvey, *The Autobiography of Eli Harvey*, esp. 33 on modernism and 53 on animals and pronatalism.

59 Harvey, "Little Miss Dinah," 341–2.

60 Thank you to Sean Kinnear for drawing attention to this point.

61 Oral history interview with Eugenie Shonnard, 27 February to 9 April 1964, Archives of American Art, Smithsonian Institution.

62 Harvey, "Little Miss Dinah," 341–2.

63 "Captive Gorilla Is Happy," *Washington Post*, 10 June 1914.

64 Bridges, *Gathering of Animals*, 350.

65 Gott and Weir, *Gorilla*, 104.

66 "Jungle Baby Lolls in Invalid's Luxury," *New York Times*, 21 December 1914.

67 "New York's Gorilla May Spend Winter in Florida Resort," *Washington Post*, 10 January 1915. See the crack in the *Battleboro Daily Reformer* on "aping society," 15 February 1915.

68 Willam T. Hornaday, "Gorillas Past and Present," *Bulletin of the New York Zoological Society* 18, 1 (January 1915): 1182.

69 Hornaday quoted in Cincinnatti, "Too Sullen for Survival," 174.

70 Hornaday, "Gorillas Past and Present," 1183.

71 Ibid., 1184–5.

72 "Dog Sweetheart Gives Invalid Gorilla Chance after Physicians Fail," *Washington Post*, 21 February 1915; "'Dinah' has a Sweetheart," *Richmond Times-Dispatch*, 21 February 1915.

73 "Dinah, Heartsick Baby Gorilla Dies from Starvation in Zoo," *New York Tribune*, 2 August 1915.

74 "Items of Interest: The Gorilla," *Bulletin of the New York Zoological Society* 63, 4 (July 1915): 1254–5.

75 This description is lifted word for word from William T. Hornaday, "Gorillas Past and Present," *Bulletin of the New York Zoological Society* 18, 1 (January 1915): 1183.

76 "She Was Caught Young," *Evening Star* (Washington, DC), 11 July 1915. Also lifted from Hornaday, "Gorillas Past and Present," 1183.

77 Barnes, "The Girl and the Gorilla."

78 "Dinah, Heartsick Baby Gorilla Dies from Starvation in Zoo," *New York Tribune*, 2 August 1915. Engelholm's first name is Fred, not John.

79 Rich, *Missing Links*, 158–9 provides more examples of similar articles.

80 "Dinah 'Zoo' Pet, Starved to Death," *New York Tribune*, 19 January 1916.

81 Hornaday, *The Minds and Manners of Wild Animals*, 93.

82 Ibid., 94.

83 Ibid., 93.

84 Ibid., 94–5; Alyse Cunningham, "A Gorilla's Life in Civilization," *Bulletin of the New York Zoological Society*," 24, 5 (September 1921): 118.

85 Cunningham, "A Gorilla's Life," 123.

86 Ibid.; Gott and Weir, *Gorilla*, 104–6.

87 Letter from W.T. Hornaday to Lorenz Hagenbeck, 6 October 1914, WCSA 1001.

88 Derrida, *The Animal*, 14 (emphasis mine).

89 See *Project Nim*, directed by James March (New York: Red Box Films, Passion Films, BBC Films, 2011), DVD.

CHAPTER FIVE

STEREOSCOPIC ANIMALS: SPECTATORSHIP, KODIAK BEARS, AND THE KEYSTONE *ANIMAL SET*

Zeb Tortorici

I begin with a deceptively simple question: How, and why, have humans rendered nonhuman animals visible through the optical device known as the stereoscope?[1] The image titled "'Kodiak Bears' Brookfield Zoo" (figure 5.1) seems to visually convey the vexed relationship between zoo spectatorship, techniques of observation, and the institution of captivity. It is a photograph that I took of a homemade stereoscopic card – popularly known as a stereograph or a stereoview – that I purchased in an antique store in Asheville, North Carolina, in 2015. There is no other identifying information on the stereograph itself, and it was the only one I saw in that particular shop that was not professionally produced.

Among the hundreds of stereographs that I looked at in numerous antique shops, there was something about this particular image and its accompanying typewritten words that stood out to me. Perhaps it was the bear's sad and vacant stare, the bars behind which it is held captive, or the way its claws are almost parallel with the iron rods' vertical shadows. I took the card home and examined it through my own stereoscopic viewer, and what stood out to me most was the way in which the bear's body has a certain depth, particularly through the shapes of (and the almost geometric shadows produced by) the bars. Initially, I did not even notice a second Kodiak bear – in the back, under the right side of the rocks – because its black-and-white body blended in with its surroundings.

This stereograph, the homemade creation of an unknown amateur who visited and photographed the Kodiak bears at Chicago's Brookfield Zoo in

Figure 5.1 "Kodiak Bears" Brookfield Zoo. Homemade stereoscope card,
photographer unknown. Purchased by Zeb Tortorici in 2015 at an antique shop
in North Carolina.

the mid-twentieth century, contrasted sharply with the others I have seen
since – in libraries, in archives, in antique shops, and on the Internet – many
of which depict people, animals, landscapes, places, or monuments. The photographs of the bears that compose the stereograph are likely from the
1950s, when the stereo camera, which uses two or more lenses and a film
frame for each lens to mimic human binocular vision, became widely commercially available. The bears are the likely descendants of Brookfield Zoo's
first three Kodiak bears who, at seven months old, were taken from Kodiak
Bear Island (the islands of the Kodiak Archipelago in southwest Alaska) one
year before the Chicago Zoological Society opened Brookfield's gates to the
public in 1934.[2]

What also caught my attention that day in the antique store was my own
speculation about the amateur photographer's impulse to document this
caged Kodiak bear as it seems to stare back at its human spectators. This
captured image provides the viewer with a moment of archival abjection –
one bear's archived abjection, in which we are implicated through our act
of witnessing a historical image of zoo captivity. Similar photographs of

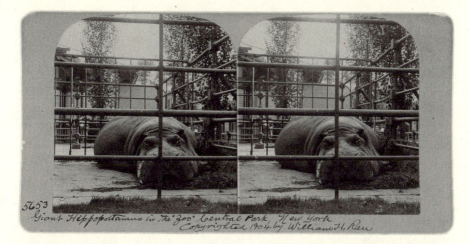

Figure 5.2 "Giant hippopotamus in the 'zoo,' Central Park, New York," stereograph, ca. 27 January 1904.

these particular Kodiak bears – and of their progenitors and descendants – were certainly captured by thousands of zoogoers over the course of the twentieth century. Yet this stereograph is unique; and the more closely I looked, the more distorted and illegible it became, in part because of the photos' poor focus and the stereograph's low production quality (one of the photographs even fell off of the card as I held it!), but also because the animals as stereoscopic subjects are doubled, constantly and unpredictably coming in and out of focus for human viewers.

Stereographs – to be looked at through a stereoscope viewer, which enabled people to see a phenomenally realistic three-dimensional image by merging left- and right-eye views of the same scene – were an immensely popular form of home entertainment from the 1850s to the 1930s. The amateur "Kodiak Bears" stereograph contrasts with professional stereographs such as those made and marketed by companies like the Pennsylvania-based Keystone View Company and the New York-based Underwood & Underwood for entertainment and, increasingly, education. Figure 5.2 is one such professional image that was meant to entertain and edify viewers with a captive "Giant Hippopotamus" at the Central Park Zoo, one of the oldest municipal zoos in the United States. The photographs were taken in early 1904 by William H. Raw, a well-known photographer for the Keystone View Company, and the stereoscopic image was eventually incorporated into the company's *Animal Set*, which I analyze later in this chapter. This particular stereograph is located in the Library of Congress Stereographs Collection, which is made up of approximately 52,000 individual pieces, about 10 per cent of which are currently available online.³

The paired photographs in each of these two respective stereographs are nearly identical to one another, but a closer look reveals that they were shot at slightly different angles, which visually multiplies the photographic subject in question. Both depict unnamed zoo animals in captivity – Kodiak bears in Brookfield Zoo and a lone hippopotamus in Central Park Zoo – separated by space and several decades of the twentieth century. Yet one is homemade and has been neither disseminated nor granted archival status, while the other is professionally produced and has been archived in several institutional collections worldwide. But the most radical difference is in the illusion of depth visible through the stereoscope viewer. The hippopotamus (and its bars) jump out vividly, while the Kodiak bears do not. The hippo appears closer to the viewer than do the bears – an optical illusion produced by the visual staging of the harsh reality of zoo captivity. The image, perhaps by avoiding the sleeping hippo's vacant stare, seems to want to seduce us into believing that this particular creature leads a peaceful, carefree life. This, I argue, is what art critic Jonathan Crary calls "a compulsory and seductive vision of the 'real,'" made all the more seductive by the politics and staging of the photographs.⁴ The question of relief in each is a calculated one, and depends primarily on the photographer's position relative to the animals, cages, shadows, and "nature" (fake rocks in the case of the Kodiak bears and unattainable trees in the case of the hippopotamus). Perhaps what stands out more than anything else in these images, when viewed through the stereoscope, are the enclosure's unyielding bars.

These stereoscopic animals raise more questions than they can answer. By what circuitous route, for example, did an undated amateur stereograph taken at Chicago's Brookfield Zoo end up in an antique shop in North Carolina? What motivated the photographer to capture those particular bears? How many other homemade stereographs of zoo animals did that amateur photographer make, and how many of them (or others like them) have survived? How did professional zoo stereographs, such as that taken by William Raw in 1904, circulate, to what ends did they do so, and how were they viewed? Finally, what did those who looked at the whole series of animal images – and at species difference – through the stereoscope experience?

In this chapter, I focus on one central paradox in the visual representation of stereoscopic animals, with two main goals. First, through a diverse archival assemblage, I aim to introduce readers to the vast and largely unexplored world of stereoscopic animals, in hopes that others will conduct more sustained research on the topic, especially with an eye towards what this volume's Randy Malamud terms "imperial animal-looking."[5] I begin with the basic premise that all of the stereoscopic animals I examine here – captured, displaced, rendered captive or bred into zoo or slaughterhouse captivity, and at times dismembered – come to us through exactly the type of imperial looking and thinking about other animals that Malamud describes. Second, I explore how the stereoscope alters the relationship between the viewer and the viewed, especially when the viewed is an animal portrayed in commercialized captivity and death. I argue, in part, that we can only begin to make sense of stereoscopic zoo animals by contextualizing them alongside the increasing industrialization and commodification of animals (and animal parts) that took place in slaughterhouses and stockyards in the late nineteenth and early twentieth centuries. By looking at how stereoscopic images of animals were historically visualized, collected, and disseminated, we gain a better understanding of how human-animal ontological distancing was absolutely central to stereoscopic spectatorship in the United States in the first half of the twentieth century.

In the United States, zoos became popular at precisely the same time that slaughterhouses became industrial in the final decades of the nineteenth century and the early decades of the twentieth. This is no mere coincidence. The stereoscopic representations of living animals in zoos and dismembered animals in stockyards and slaughterhouses both stage a particular politics of visibility – and captivity – through the increased institutionalization of animal bodies. In photographing and viewing animals through the medium of the stereograph, whether amateur or professional, the viewer sought to attain greater proximity – a highly affective and almost tactile experience – to the animal in question, and to its body. As I will show, however, the stereoscopic exposure and observation of animals in captivity and death paradoxically distances the human viewer, both visually and ontologically, from the animal that is being viewed. In essence, nonhuman animals may be further away than they appear. This central paradox frames all of the stereoscopic animals that I discuss and analyze here.

First, I look at theories of stereoscopic visuality and highlight the ways in which nonhuman animals as stereoscopic subjects figure into the writings of Sir David Brewster, a Scottish mathematician, physicist, naturalist, astronomer, and inventor whose book *The Stereoscope: Its History, Theory, and Construction* (1856) made significant contributions to the field of optics. Brewster is also widely recognized for developing an improved version of the stereoscope, which was later made more compact by Oliver Wendell Holmes. Next, through an analysis of several professionally produced stereographs, I examine the presumed pedagogical and entertainment value of stereoscopic animals in late nineteenth- and early twentieth-century images of zoos, stockyards, and slaughterhouses to speculate as to the use and potential circulation of the images. Finally, I analyze the affective contexts within which the zoo and slaughterhouse stereographs were produced, marketed, and experienced. I conclude with a brief reading of Captain Ronald Cheyne-Stout's 1937 *At the Zoo: The Stereo-Book of Animals*, a patented book that came with its own folding stereoscopic attachment and that hailed itself as "the very first book of its kind – a book with deep pictures, pictures that seem almost alive."[6] Stereography in all its historical forms, as I will show, promises and produces the illusion of depth and proximity through pictures that are "almost alive," yet when institutionalized and commodified animals become its visual subjects, the fictive nature of that visual sleight of hand – that lifelike proximity – becomes all the more real. Not unlike contemporary theories of visuality, later stereoscopic representations of animals in captivity – such as *At the Zoo* – produced a visual fiction about animals, but one that persisted in part because it was so alluring. In essence, the closer human viewers thought they were getting to the stereoscopic animal in question, the further removed from the real animal they became.

Visualizing Animals

To understand the viewing impulse behind the images I examine in this chapter, I trace stereoscopic spectatorship back to the invention of the stereoscope (and to its earliest conceptual and scientific origins). In London in 1856, Brewster published *The Stereoscope*. Prior to the book's publication, Brewster had made major improvements to the earliest model of the stereoscope,

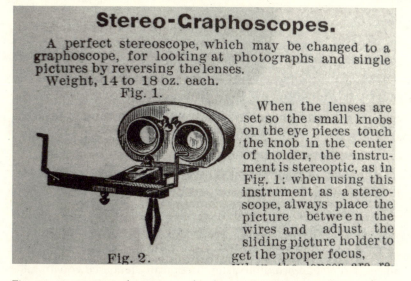

Stereo-Graphoscopes.

A perfect stereoscope, which may be changed to a graphoscope, for looking at photographs and single pictures by reversing the lenses. Weight, 14 to 18 oz. each.

Fig. 1.

When the lenses are set so the small knobs on the eye pieces touch the knob in the center of holder, the instrument is stereoptic, as in Fig. 1: when using this instrument as a stereoscope, always place the picture between the wires and adjust the sliding picture holder to get the proper focus,

Fig. 2.

Figure 5.3 1894–95 advertisement for the "perfect stereoscope" in the Montgomery Ward & Co catalogue.

which used mirrors to demonstrate binocular depth perception. Sir Charles Wheatstone, an English scientist, invented what came to be known as the mirror stereoscope in 1838, which used a pair of mirrors angled at forty-five degrees to show how the human brain would fuse two identical images into one, even when, through the use of mirrors that directed one eye to the left and the other to the right, the images were not actually in the same location. In his writings, Brewster went to some lengths to prove that years before his rival Wheatstone had invented the mirror stereoscope, he had in fact invented the "simple stereoscope," which was "without lenses or mirrors, [and] consisted of a wooden box 18 inches long, 7 broad, and 41 deep, and at the bottom of it, or rather its farther end, was placed a slide containing two dissimilar pictures of a landscape as seen by each eye."[7] Brewster's most significant improvement to the Wheatstone mirror stereoscope, which according to Brewster possessed several defects and "was ill fitted for general use, both from its size and its price," was the introduction of lenses instead of mirrors.[8] He called this the "lenticular stereoscope."

In 1861, Holmes improved upon Brewster's model and invented what was to become by far the most popular and marketable stereoscope viewer, illustrated in an advertisement published in the 1894–95 *Fall & Winter Montgomery Ward & Co. Catalogue and Buyers Guide* (figure 5.3). Holmes's model was both more compact and more economical than those created by

Wheatstone and Brewster, and it contained a viewing hood and an adjustable cardholder. Individuals with standard binocular depth perception would insert a stereograph (with two nearly identical images such as those reproduced in figure 5.2) into the cardholder, look through the lenses, and witness the two images almost magically fuse into one three-dimensional image. For Holmes, the stereoscope's visual effect was hyperreal: "The first effect of looking at a good photograph through the stereoscope is a surprise such as no painting ever produced. The mind feels its way into the very depths of the picture. The scraggy branches of a tree in the foreground run out at us as if they would scratch our eyes out. The elbow of a figure stands forth so as to make us almost uncomfortable."[9] Far from producing any sense of discomfort or unease from such proximity, stereoscopically rendered zoo animals would likely have been seen as an almost natural extension of human visual technology – and imperial ambitions.

According to Brewster's earlier formulation, the perceived three-dimensional depth and relief was not merely because the images were combined or superimposed, but rather because "superposition is effected by turning each eye upon the object, but the relief is given by the play of the optic axes in uniting, in rapid succession, similar points of the two pictures, and placing them, for the moment, at the distance from the observer of the point to which the axes converge."[10] For Brewster, the image as seen through his lenticular stereoscope has such realistic depth that "no portrait ever painted, and no statue ever carved, approximate in the slightest degree to the living reality now before us."[11] The stereoscopic image is thus said to supersede reality. But how does this living reality translate to humans' interactions with other species when they view those species through the stereoscope? Far too often, it translates into deathly reality for the animals involved, that is, the social death of the zoo and the bodily death of the slaughterhouse. According to Brewster, the pictures designed for the stereoscope fall into four classes: (1) representations of geometric solids; (2) "portraits, or groups of portraits, taken from living persons or animals"; (3) landscapes, buildings, machines, and instruments; and (4) solids, which may be the product of either nature or art.[12] In some ways, for Brewster, an encounter with a stereoscopic image was even better than an encounter with the real thing, for "a score of persons might, in the course of an hour, see more of Rome, and see it better, than if they had visited it in person."[13] Yet, in the case of institutionalized and commodified animals, who encounter human gazes justified by imperial thinking, the very notion of encountering a "real" or "authentic" animal is problematized by the fact that human exploitation strips stereoscopic zoo and slaughterhouse animals of their own animality.

Given that Brewster was a naturalist and scientist, it is no surprise that he would dedicate some of his book to the history and applications of the stereoscope to the natural world, and to the visualization of the animals within it. Brewster, for example, titled chapter 12 "Application of the Stereoscope to Natural History," and, though it encompasses only four pages out of 235, his own perception of the ways that animals and their "natural" worlds could be visualized and experienced through the stereoscope foreshadows many of the device's uses in entertainment and education in the decades to come. Brewster writes: "When we reflect upon the vast number of species which have been described by zoologists, the noble forms of animated nature, whether wild or domesticated, and the valuable services which many of them perform as the slaves of man, we can hardly attach too much importance to the advantage of having them accurately delineated and raised into stereoscopic relief."[14] Nonhuman animals may embody "noble forms of animated nature" but are nonetheless "slaves of man" that provide "valuable services." To continue, Brewster says that the "animal painters of the present day" primarily depicted animals with which they were familiar – dogs, horses, deer, cows, and a few others – because they were the "specimens of which were in their reach."[15]

On the other hand, Brewster continues, in order to create "accurate representations" of exotic animals such as giraffes and hyenas and "the rarer animals which are found alive only in zoological gardens and travelling caravans," artists necessarily turned to two-dimensional photography. Brewster, however, believed that the inability to see animals in three dimensions led to inferior artistic representations.[16] Technological developments in cameras and photography – along with the fact that, for Brewster, every photograph conveyed some essential truth – meant that animals in the jungles or on the plains could be photographed at increasing distances; to do so was to take them "captive in their finest attitudes and in their most restless moods."[17] Although Brewster is talking about visually capturing wild animals by pulling the "trigger" of a portable camera, his language of seizure and weaponry speaks to the violence that often lurks behind the desire to capture an animal through an image. While Brewster speaks metaphorically about exotic animals being taken captive through the stereoscopic image, literal animal captivity was crucial to the rise and evolution of stereoscopic spectatorship as mediated by Malamud's "imperial animal-looking."

If a photograph captured with a standard camera could grant visual access to the "vast number of specimens described by zoologists" in the nineteenth and twentieth centuries, Brewster argues that an image captured with a binocular camera and brought into relief through the stereoscope could be of even more value to naturalists, painters, and even poets "whose lyrics may require an introduction to the brutes that perish."[18] While he is speaking here of species extinction, visualizing animals in relation to their own deaths and disappearances became, for Brewster, one of the stereograph's most valuable applications to natural history. For him, "the repose of [animal] death" can be intimately viewed by students, artists, and scientists alike, but always in contrast to the "divine lineaments and delicate forms" of man. Finally, in Brewster's brief reflection on the stereoscope's applications to the many fields of natural history, he emphasizes ichthyology, ornithology, conchology, and entomology – fields of knowledge that relied entirely on the human collection and documentation of dead animals through (imperial) scientific expeditions. These are some of the many theories of visuality that frame the stereoscope and the nonhuman animals that could be viewed through it. Yet, most of the stereoscopic animals that I have encountered in my own research emphasize not natural history, but rather the productive potential (for the benefit of humans) in rural and domestic settings, exotic foreign locales, and institutions like the zoological garden and the slaughterhouse.

Collecting Animals

The sense of visual modernity that Brewster and others laid out in stereoscopy's early theories is dramatically enhanced in its later history, especially in the final decades of the nineteenth century and the early decades of the twentieth, when the modern institutions and technologies of the zoo and the slaughterhouse were increasingly viewed through the stereoscope. Stereoscopic images of live animals – in zoos, pastures, farms, parks, and "nature" – were often arranged and marketed in box sets like the two-volume Key-

Figure 5.4 Keystone View Company *Animal Set* Stereographic Library, vols. 1 and 2, pictured with the stereoscope viewer and an elephant stereograph.

stone View Company *Animal Set* (figure 5.4), which is comprised of well over one hundred stereoscopic images. This particular set was acquired, at my request, by New York University's Fales Library and Special Collections from Pasadena Antiques on Etsy in mid-2017, to further my research into stereoscopic animals.[19] As film and media studies scholar Pauline Stakelon notes, organizing stereographs into such collections "grants them an additional meaning beyond what is represented in each singular view, as a collection implies a certain sense of completeness."[20] The Keystone *Animal Set* mimics a "zoological collection" in that it represents a geographically diverse compilation of the entire animal kingdom, arranged visually for all – or at least those who had access to the stereographs and to a stereoscope viewer – to see. Yet, for the producers of these particular stereographs, when did an animal cease to be an "animal" for the purposes of its inclusion in the set?

Indeed, what led me to this particular animal set on Etsy was a concurrent listing on eBay from a seller in Burlington, Iowa, titled with the globalized discourse of captivity: "94 Animal Keystone Stereograph Cards – Worldwide Exotic, Caged, & Farm Animals."²¹

The many stereoscopic animals of the set itself include such specimens as "Langurs from India, with Projecting Eyebrows and Chin Tufts"; "A Texas Rattlesnake about Four Years Old"; "The American Red Fox Whose Wits Alone Save Him from Extinction"; "African Porcupine (*Hystrix cristata*), Angry and in an Attitude of Defense"; "Carabao, or Water Buffalo, Taking a Bath, Guam"; "Pretty Specimens of Coral and Shells"; "Llamas, the Pack Animals of the Highland Dwellers of South America," and so on. These animals were all presumably photographed in nature and not necessarily in captivity, though at times it is difficult to tell.

Captivity, and not necessarily zoo captivity, is a defining characteristic of both the images within the Keystone *Animal Set* and the ways that their stereographic descriptions naturalize a captive state. There are, for example, instances of oft-exotic petkeeping (as in "The Marmoset, a Much Prized Household Pet"; "Princess Gray Paws, a Persian Kitten"; "Jack and Fred Building a House for Their Pet Rabbits"; and "Felipe of Old Mexico with His Pet Baby Burro") and animal labour (as in "At His Daily Toil, Elephant in Lumber Yard, Burma"; "Out in the Pasture with the Sheep, Lambs and Colts"; "Jersey Cows in a Shaded Pasture Lane on a New York State Farm"; "An Eskimo Dog Team and Sledge, World's Fair, St Louis"; and "Honey Bees at Work"), all of which reify the commodification of nonhuman animals in a visually realistic, and almost haptic, way.

Zoo captivity is, however, positioned front and centre in the Keystone *Animal Set*: "Wild Cats in Lincoln Park Zoological Gardens, Chicago, Ill."; "A Live Badger Captured Near Lind, Washington"; "Atlantic Walrus, a Type of True or Hair Seal, 'At Home' in Bronx Park, N.Y."; "Yak or Grunring Ox (*Paephagus grunnieus*), from [unreadable] Zoo, Lincoln Park, Chicago, Ill."; "Rocky Mountain Sheep (*Ovis Montana*) – the Only Specimen Known to Be in Captivity"; "Pair of Nubian (Three-Horned) Giraffes, Native to [unreadable] Africa. Bronx Park, New York, N.Y."; "Wart Hog, a Weird Form of Wild Pig Common in Some Parts of Africa, Bronx Park, N.Y."; "Bactrian Camel (Central Asia) in the Zoo, Lincoln Park, Chicago, Ill."; "The Blue-Eyed White Alpaca from the Andean Foothills of South

America, Bronx Park, New York, N.Y."; "Hunianacoo, a Species of *Auchenia Vicunna*, Zoological Gardens, Melbourne, Australia"; "A Rare Specimen of a Rare Animal – Wonderful Lanain Rhinoceres in Bronx Park, New York, N.Y."; and "Bob and Betty's Barnyard Zoo," among others. While each of these stereoscopic images and their accompanying text are ripe for analysis, here I want to emphasize how the Keystone *Animal Set* is, as a whole, a type of zoo, in that it collects, assembles, and arranges a menagerie of animals from around the globe for presumed spectators in the United States. It invites its potential spectators into its highly constrained and fabricated world of animal existence, even when the animals are photographed in the wild. Given the structure and constitution of the *Animal Set*, the animals here are represented in "nature" only insofar as they can be possessed visually (if not physically), just like at the zoo. The set thus naturalizes the zoo's very concept, idea, and place in US culture and history through its images, descriptions, and arrangement.

Dividing Animals

Conspicuously absent from the Keystone *Animal Set* are dead animals or commodified animal bodies or parts, though these photographic subjects, as seen in slaughterhouse images, are both living and dead. Here, I argue that one flipside to the set of "Exotic, Caged, and Farm Animals" are those animals – cows, pigs, horses, and the like – that were destined for slaughter. To understand the viewing impulses behind the *Animal Set*, as well as the set's pedagogical and entertainment motives, we need to frame the late nineteenth- and early twentieth-century institution of zoo captivity alongside other forms of institutionalized animal captivity such as stockyards and slaughterhouses. For the animals in the stereographs are, in a sense, separated from their animality through their processing into meat. Nonetheless, the notion of collecting animals and animal parts – in real life and in stereographic library box sets – is central to the very constitution and configuration of stereoscopic animals, alive or dead. And, as I will show, in both the slaughterhouse and zoo stereographs, animals and animal bodies are socially and physically divided. Stockyard animals are divided by species, held within pens and enclosures, and physically dismembered. Zoo animals are divided

Figure 5.5 Keystone stereoscope card, "A half mile of pork," stereograph, 1894.

from most of their species, placed into cages and enclosures, some more natural looking than others, and their families and social bonds are carved up
and reinvented.

The stereograph in figure 5.5 (not included in the Keystone *Animal Set*),
one copy of which is located in the Keystone-Mast Collection, California
Museum of Photography, University of California, Riverside, is one of
dozens of Chicago stockyard images in a series produced by the Keystone
View Company, with the following classification (pencilled, likely by a Keystone secretary, on the back of the stereograph): "V18449/X5773 A Half
Mile of pork in Armour's Great packing house, Chicago, Ill."[22] The two
"Half Mile of Pork" photographs were taken in 1894 and disseminated
throughout the early decades of the twentieth century to present the viewing
public with (graphic yet hygienic) images of industrialized animal slaughter
and meatpacking at the Chicago's Union Stock Yards and Slaughterhouses.

While the image is unnerving, macabre, and fascinating, the first time I
looked at it through the stereoscope at New York University's Fales Library
and Special Collections (sometime in 2015), I was visually astounded. The
dangling pig carcasses appeared to be permanently suspended before my eyes
with more dimension and depth than any three-dimensionsal movie I had

seen in recent years, visual effects that are partly the result of the slaughter-house's obsessive mechanization. For as the cultural theorist Nicole Shukin reminds us, the assembly lines of automobile production directly inspired meat production, and vice versa: "Under the rafters of the vertical abattoir there rolled a moving line that not only served as a technological prototype for automotive and other mass modes of production but also excited new modes of visual consumption."[23] This singular viewing experience was the impetus to embark on my current research project on the topic of stereoscopic animals – in life and death, captivity and commodification – in the early twentieth-century United States. Such stereographs had a pedagogical value, especially when viewed in conjunction with accompanying text on the back of the card, as in figures 5.6 and 5.7.

On the back of the Keystone View Company stereograph of stocker and feeder pens that I purchased on eBay in 2015 (figure 5.6), produced as part of the same series as "A Half Mile of Pork," the card offers highly detailed information about the processes of animal assemblage in the Union Stock Yards and the everyday labour of animal transportation, slaughter, bleeding, skinning, and dressing in order to produce, distribute, and market meat. The stereograph reads:

140 – (20250), SELECTION OF THE UNION STOCK YARDS, CHICAGO ILLINOIS. *Lat. 42° N.; Long. 88° W.*

Here you have an excellent view of the thousands of cattle as they appear in the pens of the Union Stock Yards in Chicago. The cattle here shown are from the Kansas plains and have recently been unloaded from freight cars. All hours of the day trains take their load of living freight into the yards and unload their cattle, hogs, and sheep into the acres and acres of pens in the southern part of the city.

The great industry of the meat packing has come about largely because of the invention of the refrigerator (rē-fr ĭj' ēr-āt' ēr) cars and the refrigerator boats. Before it was learned how to ship fresh meats long distances, live stock had to be carried to the edge of the city where the meat was to be sold. In the case of the eastern cities this meant that the cattle of the plains had to be taken all the way across the Allegheny Mountains. Now this is changed. Meat-packing plants have sprung up

Figure 5.6 Keystone View Company, "83332K.U., box 119–21, 1926. Stocker and Feeder (Pens) Division of the Union Stock Yard & Transit Co, Chicago, Ill.," stereograph, 1926.

in the cities that are in the center of the stock-raising areas. Meats are packed in refrigerator cars and are readily shipped any distance. The meat of far-away New Zealand and Australia is kept fresh all the way to Liverpool and London by means of refrigerator ships.

The meat-packing center of the world is about the Union Stock Yards here seen. This plant was begun in 1865. It now covers 500 acres of ground and has several thousand stock pens. The yards are able to house at one time 75,000 cattle, 50,000 sheep, and 3,000 hogs.

Cattle are taken from the yards and are marched single file into the slaughtering gangways. The various processes of bleeding, skinning, and dressing take place in rapid order. Every process is inspected by Federal Meat Inspectors so that the meat is clean and fresh.

The sense of awe here that cattle – so-called living freight – can, after being shackled, killed, and processed, be shipped great distances locally or globally, with the technology of refrigeration is palpable. Equally remarkable is the almost-obsessive focus on the visibility of the stereoscopically rendered creatures: "Here you have an excellent view of the thousands of cattle as they appear in the pens of the Union Stock Yards in Chicago." This card also informs viewers that Chicago's Union Stock Yards, which began operations in 1865, is purportedly the world's premier meat-packing centre, where stereographs rendered the modernity of industrialized slaughter visible to national (and international) audiences. In fact, every stage of meat processing was photographed again and again between 1873 and 1925 in the Chicago Union Stock Yards and other nearby stockyards and slaughterhouses.

Comparing the stockyard stereographs to the zoo stereographs produced around the same time reveals how profoundly transformed the lives and social existences of animals are by human economic activity and manmade enclosures. The stereoscope renders the bars of such enclosures in three dimensions, even as the vertical bars of the zoo cage stand out visually much more than do the horizontal bars of the slaughterhouse stocker and feeder pens.

Zoo stereographs and slaughterhouse stereographs position the human subject from the animal object in radically different visual and affective ways. Zoo animals are typically pictured individually whereas slaughterhouse animals are pictured collectively. Slaughterhouse animals have no names, no identities, and no physical proximity to humans beyond that necessary for killing, processing, and inspection, as in the stereograph "Splitting backbones and final inspection of hogs before placing them in refrigerator rooms" (figure 5.7). These animals, unlike zoo animals, are granted no affective status. This contrast is perhaps most evident in the Keystone stereograph titled "Chimpanzees, most man-like of the apes," taken in the Bronx Park menagerie in the early decades of the twentieth century (figure 5.8), where we find important similarities and differences in terms of how the animals are described and rendered visible. The back of this stereograph reads:

V21213, CHIMPANZEES, MOST MANLIKE OF THE APES

The chimpanzee is believed to rank higher in intelligence than any other animal unless it be the elephant. These young ones will grow much larger, reaching a height of five feet. They will never lose the big ears and the sober look which they now have. We may laugh at monkey ways, but when a chimpanzee stops swinging in his trapeze, and looks at the crowd gathered around it with its sad, far-away expression, we wonder just what the animal is thinking about, and how much it really does think.

Figure 5.7 *Top* Keystone View Company, "UX265 Splitting backbones and final inspection, hogs ready for cooler," stereograph, late nineteenth century.

Figure 5.8 *Bottom* "Chimpanzees, most man-like of the apes," Bronx Park, New York, stereograph, 1904–14.

Perhaps it is longing for its native African forest, where it and its black cousin, the gorilla, can make good use of their long arms in swinging from the branches. It is a curious fact that the black chimpanzee lives in the home of the black man while the brown or reddish orangoutang is a native of the brown Malay's home in Bornea and Sumatra.

A baby chimpanzee and a human baby are much alike. Both have long arms, inward-turning legs and soles, and toes easily moved. When full grown the long black hair with which they are covered turns grey. They make fine pets, and can be taught many things which the average child of three or four years would learn. They readily learn to sit at the table, to eat with a knife, fork, and spoon, and to count in small numbers.

The chimpanzee is short-lived in captivity. It is believed to mate for life, and if one dies the other is apt to mourn itself to death. They live in small bands, feed on fruit, where the mothers stay with their young at night. The males remain on the ground below the nest. They often shift feeding on the ground, and their shrill cries are heard at any hour, day or night.

Whereas there is an expected affective disregard for the slaughterhouse an-imals (largely cattle, sheep, and hogs) in the stereographs above, here the anonymously authored text about the two unidentified Bronx Zoo chim-panzees is more emotionally complex and ambivalent. It emphasizes the chimpanzees' intelligence, the "somber look which they now have" in the zoo, and one chimpanzee's "sad, far-away expression" as it longs for its "na-tive African forest." Yet, at the same time, it anthropomorphically renders the chimp an anthropocentric prop: "They make fine pets, and can be taught many things," such as eating with utensils, swinging on the trapeze, and counting small numbers. The stereographs thus render the animals in ways that are particularly useful and productive for humans: in death, they sustain us; in life, they entertain us.

As radically different as these zoo and slaughterhouse stereographs are, they both propose a heightened visual, tactile, and affective experience with regard to the animals in question. This stereoscopic – as opposed to a pho-tographic – viewing experience plunges the viewer firsthand into these nearly tangible scenes of recently unloaded animal freight, of hanging pig carcasses, of caged bears and hippopotami, and of human-like chimpanzees. Yet in doing so, they visually divorce us from the very animals they depict, for as film studies scholar Meredith Bak notes, "stereo views threatened to decontextualize or even erase the subjects depicted."[24] Whereas the zoo animal stereographs seem to claim obsessively to represent animals in their truest, most natural states, the stereoscopic images themselves put forth, and to a certain extent reify, that the "true" state of these animals is to be commodified, to be perennially used for the purposes of human entertainment, edification, consumption, and viewing pleasure. And, while the zoo and slaughterhouse stereographs differ significantly, they share much in common in the ways that they visually render these and other animals as consumable creatures – no longer living beings, but once-living objects and things that have been visually frozen in time and three-dimensional space.

Disseminating Animals

In 1937, decades after the first animal stereographs were produced and marketed by companies like the Keystone View Company and Underwood & Underwood, Captain Ronald Cheyne-Stout – New York City's director of menageries from 1934 to 1939 – published his *At the Zoo: The Stereo-Book of Animals* (figure 5.9), which was the first collection of its kind.[25] It came with its own patented metal "folding stereoscope attachment, which for the first time makes available book illustrations in three dimensions." The folding stereoscope attachment – the invention of a certain Mr Van Dyke Hill who worked for the American Stereograph Corporation in New York City – was touted as being less unwieldy than the previous wooden stereoscopic invented by Brewster and Holmes (see figures 5.3 and 5.4). The photographs themselves were taken by Herbert C. McKay, a renowned photographer who published widely on photography theory and practice. The book claims that it "is different from any book you have ever seen. The pictures appear so lifelike, so real, that it is interesting to know something of the background that makes such an amazing book possible."[26] I have, throughout this chapter, explored so much of that particular historical background (much more so than does Cheyne-Stout), especially in terms of optical technology, animal institutionalization, and human-animal relations in the United States. While a more sus-

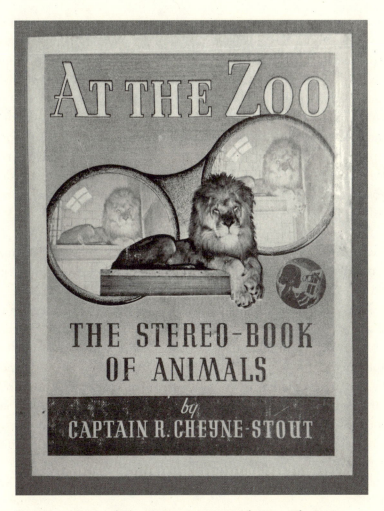

Figure 5.9 Cover of Cheyne-Stout's 1937 *At the Zoo: The Stereo-Book of Animals*, which includes a metal folding stereoscope attachment to view the images.

tained analysis of this book and its images must be left for a later date, I want to conclude with a brief exploration of how this book represents exactly the type of human-animal ontological distancing that I have been discussing.

Cheyne-Stout aims to convince his readers that these particular photographs of captive animals depict them in "nearly their natural state" and suggest that exotic animals in captivity are happier, healthier, and more comfortable, and ultimately better off than they would be in their natural environments.[27] Herein lies the crux of the problem: the images are optic (and haptic) untruths. They are simultaneously real and fabricated; they are based on human ideas about nonhuman animals that rely on the very negation of that (natural state of) animality to convey their sense of truth to human spectators. Put another way: the images present neither real nor natural animals, but rather mainstream human ideas of what particular animals might look like as commodities. This is the harsh reality that underlies stereoscopic animals. In his foreword, Cheyne-Stout unabashedly assures his readers of the following:

> The zoos in which these pictures were taken have been properly named Picture Book Zoos. The areas in which they are located are not large, and the exhibits have been so designed as to show as many species as possible with but a few numbers of each species. In photographing these animals we have attempted to show them to you in as nearly their natural state as possible and at the same time to convince you that in captivity they are happier and more comfortable and better off generally than they would be in the wild state. Their diet is maintained regularly, and doctors are available at all times in case of sickness. Their food is of the best and they have the companionship of their own kind at all times, which companionship is necessary to their happiness. The struggle for existence has been eliminated: they need not hunt, but neither are they hunted.[28]

Thus, zoogoers, amateur zoo photographers, and stereoscopic spectators can perhaps more easily convince themselves and others that the enhanced visual reality of the stereoscope represents animals in captivity in a hyper-real state of well-being – a fact that we know from the critical scholarship of menageries and zoos (as demonstrated in this volume), and even from the text and images of Cheyne-Stout's own book, was anything but the case.

This is merely the beginning of the several overlapping layers of (animal) distortion and abstraction that must take place in order to render zoo or slaughterhouse animals stereoscopically. Perhaps the most egregious example of human-animal ontological distancing in Cheyne-Stout's *At the Zoo* is that of "Anna and Jiggs," two Central Park chimpanzees that McKay photographed "in nearly their natural state" (figure 5.10). Cheyne-Stout describes the real animals in question:

> There is always a crowd watching Anna and Jiggs, particularly during the warm weather, when they are taken from their cage and give performances for the public. Anna, two and a half years old, was presented to the zoo at the age of six months by a woman who had brought her up from babyhood. Jiggs was bought by the zoo from an animal dealer who had imported him from Africa. He is three and a half years old. Both chimpanzees have been trained to use roller skates and to ride bicycles. They eat at the table, using knives, forks, and spoons; they sleep in real beds. In general they behave much like human beings. Anna is particularly lovable. She is tremendously fond of her trainer and obeys his orders to the letter. Jiggs is not always so well behaved; at times he may even bite and scratch and be difficult to handle.[29]

Cages, animal dealers, "importation" from Africa, roller skates, bicycles, knives, forks, spoons, and beds – all of which point to the enhanced visual reality of animal existence in zoos – demonstrate the unnatural nature of zoo "nature." For this is the visual reality that is enhanced, both visually and ontologically, by the optical technology of the stereoscope. Perhaps most importantly, such a reality can be traced genealogically from Brewster's stereoscopic viewing of "natural history" to the zoo and slaughterhouse stereographs and beyond, into the modern era.

Brenton J. Malin, in a recent book on the history of media technology, asserts that "the power of stereoscopic technology, the argument went, came directly from its capacity to transmit not only images but *feelings*."[30] The stereoscopic images in this chapter indeed sought to convey anthropocentric superiority, nationalism, and even civic pride by and through the highly efficient and modernized forms of institutionalized animal bodies – in zoos and slaughterhouses – for which the United States came to be known both nationally and globally. Seeing these and similar images in three dimensions had – and perhaps still has – the potential to radically influence the relationship between the viewer and the viewed, especially when refracted through the lens of species.

Figure 5.10 Stereoscopic images of African chimpanzees (Anna and Jiggs, *top*) and an orangutan from Borneo and Sumatra (Reddy, *below*), from Cheyne-Stout's *At the Zoo*.

In comparison to the two-dimensional photograph, a three-dimensional stereoscopic set of photographs tempted viewers with a sense of proximity, realism, and depth. Industrialized zoo captivity (and its intimately related images of animal slaughter) came to be naturalized in a way that previously could only be seen in a two-dimensional photograph or by visiting a zoo or slaughterhouse in person. Exposing animals through the stereoscope enabled new ways of relating to visual archives of animals, and to their collected, divided, dismembered, and disseminated bodies and body parts, in the past, especially for the intended audiences and spectators – primarily students in primary and secondary education, but also amateur photographers like the individual who shot the images of Brookfield Zoo's Kodiak bears sometime in the mid-twentieth century. If we return to the voyeuristic impulse of that photographer who shot and created a homemade stereograph of the "'Kodiak Bears' Brookfield Zoo," we find that this particular image cannot be understood or interpreted in isolation. It points to a much larger history of stereoscopic spectatorship – and of the production of stereoscopic animals – whose historical genealogy has only begun to be excavated.

NOTES

1 I am especially grateful to Daniel Vandersommers and Tracy McDonald for their critical feedback and help on this chapter, as well as to the participants of the "Zoo Studies and the New Humanities" workshop. I also thank Leigh Gleason, curator of collections at the California Museum of Photography, University of California, Riverside, for her help identifying sources and gaining access to the collections. Earlier iterations of ideas presented here on slaughterhouses and the stereoscope appeared previously in "Visualizing Animal Death," *Antennae: The Journal of Nature in Visual Culture* 40 (Summer 2017): 77–87. I thank Giovanni Aloi for his comments on those sections. For some recent scholarship on the stereoscope, see Thomas L. Hankins and Robert J. Silverman, *Instruments and the Imagination*; Sheenagh Pietrobruno, "The Stereoscope and the Miniature"; West, "Fantasy, Photography, and the Marketplace"; Bantjes, "Reading Stereoviews"; Malin, "Looking White and Middle-Class"; Fowles, "Stereography and the Standardization of Vision."

2 Deuchler and Owens, *Brookfield Zoo*, 46.

3 Library of Congress, "Stereograph Cards," http://www.loc.gov/pictures/collection/stereo/.

4 Crary, *Techniques of the Observer*, 132.

5 Malamud, *An Introduction to Animals and Visual Culture*, 53.

6 Cheyne-Stout, *At the Zoo*, "About this Book."

7 Brewster, *The Stereoscope*, 19.

8 Ibid., 64.

9 Oliver Wendell Holmes, "The Stereoscope and the Stereograph," *Atlantic Monthly*, June 1859.

10 Brewster, *The Stereoscope*, 53.

11 Ibid., 67.

12 Ibid., 135.

13 Ibid., 164.

14 Ibid., 189.

15 Ibid.

16 Ibid., 190.

17 Ibid., 191.

18 Ibid.

19 I am grateful to Marvin J. Taylor, director of the Fales Library & Special Collections, for purchasing the Keystone View Company *Animal Set* at my request.

20 Stakelon, "Travel through the Stereoscope," 415.

21 magsandpics, "94 Animal Keystone Stereograph Cards – Worldwide Exotic, Caged, & Farm Animals," eBay listing, http://www.ebay.com/itm/112458 748839?ul_noapp=true.

22 UCR-CMP, box 601-06-2.

23 Shukin, *Animal Capital*, 92.

24 Bak, "Democracy and Discipline," 53.

25 Leilani Dawson, "The Captain's Menageries: Ronald Cheyne-Stout and the Central Park and Prospect Park Zoos," *Wild Things*, 10 March 2015, http://www.wcsarchivesblog.org/the-captains-menageries-ronald-cheyne-stout-and-the-central-park-and-prospect-park-zoos/.

26 Cheyne-Stout, *At the Zoo*, "About this Book."

27 Ibid., "Foreword."

28 Ibid., 1.

29 Ibid., 42.

30 Malin, *Feeling Mediated*, 24. (Emphasis original.)

CHAPTER SIX

"TRY TELLING THAT TO THE POLAR BEARS": RATIONING AND RESISTANCE AT THE WARTIME ZOO

John Kinder

In the fall of 1942, Leo Blondin, the circus-performer-turned-superintendent of the Oklahoma City Zoo, had a problem. Wartime rationing and travel restrictions had curtailed the zoo's access to fresh food, and some of the animals were getting restless. There was no shortage of meat, since with the closing of local dog food factories sinewy horseflesh could be purchased for about one cent a pound. But fruits, vegetables, and exotic animal protein – such as whale blubber – were difficult to come by.[1] As the conflict dragged on, measures became increasingly desperate: the zoo's brown bears were "forced to eat corn pone," while its prized collection of monkeys subsisted on a diet of rotten bananas, which they often refused outright. By early 1943, the man whom newspapers genially dubbed "Uncle Leo" remained publicly optimistic that the zoo would survive the "beastial tragedy." Still, he conceded that some things were simply inedible, even to the hungriest of zoo animals. "Man may reconcile himself to a rationed diet on the basis of patriotism," he told a local journalist, "but try telling that to the polar bears."[2]

Blondin was by no means the first zoo professional to draw distinctions between "patriotic" animals – those who ate their rationed diets without complaint – and more politically suspect creatures. In 1918, *Stars and Stripes* magazine reported that nearly all of the animals at the Bronx Zoo were "patriotic, with the exception of the East Indian python, which [was] still an unreformed alien and insist[ed] on its suckling pig as usual."[3] While it would be easy to dismiss such caricatures as little more than colourful humor or crude jingoism, they hint at something far more profound: the limitations of zoos' control over the animals in their charge. Spurred on by fear, hunger, boredom, or sheer intransigence, zoo animals have a long history of frustrating their captors' whims. During World War II, however, zoo animals' gastronomic resistance – their unwillingness or inability to eat their prescribed rations – took on exaggerated significance. At a time when Americans of all species were expected to "do their bit" to ensure US victory, the spectacle of skeletal polar bears and abstemious pythons threatened to undercut zoos' efforts to brand themselves as essential wartime institutions.[4]

In this chapter, I will examine the history of food shortage at major American zoos during World War II. Rationing has been an important part of the popular memory of the "Good War" since its inception. Alongside Rosie the Riveter and G.I. Joe, home gardeners and other dietary patriots have come to epitomize the selflessness and "we-can-do-it" spirit of what Tom Brokaw nostalgically dubbed the "Greatest Generation."[5] Over the past few decades, scholars have challenged our rosy views of American dietary sacrifice, drawing attention to the ways in which ordinary citizens struggled to reconcile their patriotic ideals and their individual tastes.[6] Although often missing from such accounts, the history of wartime American zoos reveals similar tensions. From New York to San Diego, zoo administrators and volunteers adopted a range of strategies to make ends meet, from butchering animals on-site to collecting food scraps from visitors. At a time when "every meal served was a political act,"[7] zoos used their food-saving campaigns not only to cut costs but also to demonstrate their willingness to swallow hard – sometimes literally – on behalf of the war effort.

Unlike the kitchens of American suburbia, however, zoo galleys could not rely upon nationalistic appeals to tempt the hungry mouths in their charge. During World War II, many zoo animals failed to embrace "patriotic diets," their sick, emaciated, and sometimes dead bodies a symbolic and material affront to notions of collective sacrifice. In tracing zoos' various strategies to manage home front food shortages, I will examine a broader cultural debate about the value of zoos – and zoo animals – in times of military conflict. To zoo critics, animals' inability to live without red meat and other food commodities was just further proof of the need to close wartime zoos altogether. Zoo staff, on the other hand, frequently used humour to recast the animals' behaviour as an object lesson in Americanism, touting their individualism and perceived self-determination. More than an important chapter in the history of wartime animal keeping, the experience of American zoos in World War II reminds us of the struggle inherent in even the best zoological institutions: the desire to balance public expectations with animal welfare and health. At the same time, it suggests the need to consider zoo history not from the perspective of the captors but from the largely unwritten history of the caged.

Feeding the Wartime Zoo

Even in the best of times, most zoos endure a precarious existence. An outbreak of disease, a well-publicized escape, or a change in local government might be all that it takes to send a seemingly healthy zoo into a spiral towards disaster. Such threats are compounded in wartime, when resource priorities frequently shift towards the military and national defense. World War II was no exception. As a growing cohort of scholars has shown, World War II devastated the global zoo industry.[8] Although American zoos were spared the violence that reduced some of their European and Asian counterparts to rubble, the US involvement in World War II nonetheless presented zoos with a host of new challenges. One was a sudden loss of manpower. After the bombing of Pearl Harbor in December 1941, large numbers of zoo workers traded their khaki uniforms for Uncle Sam's olive drab. By 1944, more than sixty employees of the Bronx Zoo alone were serving – or had served – in the armed forces.[9] Decimated (sometimes quite literally) by conscription, a number of zoos hired their first women animal keepers, and many others took on women in greater numbers than ever before.[10] Despite such measures, many American zoos remained understaffed until the war's end.

The loss of keeper personnel was just the first in a long list of wartime problems. Shipping restrictions made it nearly impossible to acquire the charismatic megafauna – lions, elephants, giraffes – upon which zoos' livelihoods depended. Dwindling capital investment meant that many zoos were forced to shelve much-needed building projects, and shortages of gasoline and rubber (both heavily rationed by the federal government) threatened to deter car-driving visitors.[11] Adding to zoos' burden was a vast government bureaucracy whose wartime authority – to withhold resources and demand paperwork – seeped into all aspects of American life. Against this backdrop, even trivial matters assumed an air of complexity. Writing in 1946, Gus Knudson, director of the Woodland Park Zoo in Seattle, recalled that acquiring a single monkey took weeks of negotiation with agencies up and down the federal hierarchy.[12] Meanwhile, major zoos were inundated with a steady stream of animal gifts, few of which they desired and even fewer of which they could afford to keep. While some came from as far away as Australia and the Soviet Union – donations from foreign dignitaries or amateur animal collectors now in uniform – the bulk originated closer to home. Between 1941 and 1945, US zoo-goers dropped off guinea pigs, cats and dogs, cattle, beavers, songbirds, aquarium fish, and even the occasional goat.[13]

Yet no problem posed a greater threat to American zoos in World War II than food shortages. In order to survive, all zoos must acquire fresh food supplies every day, rain or shine – even under the threat of aerial bombardment. Writing in *Popular Mechanics* in April 1943, Wayne Whittaker observed, "A blueprint for feeding a zoo full of mammals, reptiles, and birds from every corner and climate in the world is as intricate as plans for an ocean liner." The menu of the Brookfield Zoo in Chicago, he reported, listed "more than a hundred separate items," from coffee and fruit for the gorillas to "blue clay" for the kangaroos (it prevented a fatal jaw disease). While some animals were easy to feed – bears, it seems, would consume just about anything put in front of their snouts – others required highly specialized diets. Brookfield's lone anteater forsook his namesake prey in favour of "porridge of milk, green bone paste, bananas, defibrillated blood, sweet potatoes, eggs, [and] cod liver oil." The zoo's famed pandas were equally picky, as was its 3,200-pound elephant seal, which ate one hundred pounds of mackerel – not any fish, mackerel – every day. Indeed, besides large shipments of red meat and fowl, Brookfield's yearly shopping list included a large assortment of (recently) living animal delicacies: "405 skinks (small lizards), 214 chameleons, 1,285 frogs … five quarts of worms, seven thousand mice, [and] fifteen pounds of ant eggs."[14]

How did American zoos manage to acquire such vast menus? The short answer is: they didn't – at least, not all of them. When it came to managing food supplies, World War II-era American zoos faced a twofold problem. The first was a lack of access to the foods themselves. While some zoo staples (grass, local fruits, vegetables) could be grown stateside, others had to be imported from overseas, including from America's enemies. For instance, with the outbreak of war, Allied zoos were cut off from Germany's world-renowned mealworms (the crunchy, yellowish beetle larvae popular with captive lizards and small mammals).[15] The second was a lack of transportation. No less distressing, American ships were increasingly reluctant to spare precious cargo space for nonessential goods such as children's toys, refrigerators, and exotic foods earmarked for zoos.

Consider the fate of the common banana, a favourite among zoo primates and zoo visitors alike. Banana supplies plummeted after the United States entered World War II. Though bananas' primary growing range was relatively close to the US mainland (most came from Central America), transporting them to American markets proved difficult. According to historian Virginia Scott Jenkins, "German submarine activity, requisitioning of ships by the US Navy, and the absorption of labor by the military reduced banana imports from an average of fifty-five million stems per year in the 1930s to a low of twenty-four million in 1943."[16] Of the relatively few bananas that reached American shores, some were sold on the black market, others were reserved for celiac patients, and still others were appropriated for military consumption. For nearly four years, zoo animals had to make do with what was left – fruit too old or bruised for human consumption – or they had make do with nothing at all. Only at the war's end did US banana shipments return to their prewar levels.[17]

Beyond the lack of access to certain foods, American zoos confronted a wartime rationing culture that equated individual sacrifice with patriotic citizenship. At its core, rationing was built upon a simple idea: when times are tough, scarce resources should be allocated to those who need them most. During World War II, that meant the military – the people whose bodies would be fed by rationed meats, whose jeeps would be fuelled by rationed gasoline, and whose exploits would be chronicled on rationed typewriters. In 1942, Franklin D. Roosevelt called rationing a "democratic, equitable solution" to a difficult problem, and most Americans agreed – in theory, if not always in practice.[18] Indeed, one government pamphlet declared that rationing "had a greater impact on civilian consciousness than any other measure during the war" outside of the draft.[19]

Under the auspices of the Office of Price Administration, the government rationed civilian consumption of a range of "essential" items, including tires, leather, gasoline, sugar, coffee, processed foods, fish, red meats, and fats. In addition, government-funded groups like the Committee on Food Habits sought to transform the nation's ideas about what to eat and why. Instead of thick beefsteaks, Americans were encouraged to "consume – and like – soybeans and organ meats"; instead of refined sugar, molasses and sorghum.[20] Above all else, government rationing programs conditioned Americans to view the dinner table (or, in zoos' case, the feed trough) as a key battleground in the fight to defeat the Axis.

War Sacrifices

Against this backdrop, World War II–era American zoos adopted three broad strategies to deal with the food-shortage crisis. The first involved eliminating the perceived source of the problem – the dietary needs of the animals themselves – by selling off animal stock or by killing them outright.

This approach is not as radical as it might appear. All zoos ascribe to what sociologists Arnold Arluke and Clinton Sanders call the "sociozoologic scale" of animal value: the belief that some animals are more important than others, and that no animals are as important as humans.[21] For this reason, even a modest-sized zoo will often kill hundreds, if not thousands, of animals in an effort to preserve the lives of its select few. The bulk of the dead are fish, insects, and skinned mammals specifically designated as "food." Processed into indiscriminate pellets, freeze-dried and vacuum-sealed for easy storage, and renamed "poultry" or "meat" or "animal protein," many food animals are barely recognizable as animals at all.[22] Zoos routinely attempt to minimize the spectacle of animals eating other animals – if only to ease the minds of empathetic, and perhaps willfully naïve, zoogoers. As Bob Mullan and Garry Marvin point out, "In some zoos live crickets might be fed to monkeys on public exhibition, and occasionally one might see mice running around a tank containing snakes ... but one never finds lions being fed live goats or antelopes."[23]

Zoos' slaughter is not limited to food animals. They also kill animal "pests" that threaten to harm the zoo environment or tarnish the experience of paying visitors. Throughout World War II, American zoos captured, destroyed, and – in some cases – meatified untold numbers of "destructive animals," mostly escaped pets and local fauna that made the tragic mistake of wandering too close to their grounds. In 1944, the native death toll at the Woodland Park Zoo alone included 2,309 rats, 785 mice, 121 moles, 5 hawks, and 31 mountain beavers. (The zoo sent 37 dogs and 10 cats to the pound.)[24] Moreover, wartime American zoos continued the long-held practice of killing animals whose detriments (disease, old age, etc.) or commercial value (as "meat on the hoof") rendered them no longer worth keeping. In March 1940, Ernest Untermann, director of the Washington Park Zoo, incurred the wrath of Milwaukee residents after he shot three of the zoo's fallow bucks. Untermann defended his actions on pragmatic grounds, and told a local paper: "We have enough deer, but there are lots of other animals we need but don't have."[25] Most zoos downplayed such practices to avoid bad publicity. If nothing else, the intentional killing of unneeded or surplus animals threatened to puncture two of the modern zoo's founding myths: that zoo animals are caged for their own protection, and that certain animals are worth seeing, even in the most unnatural of environments.

Outside the United States, World War II-era zoos cited an additional reason to sell or destroy the animals in their charge: to prevent their escape following an aerial attack. In September 1939, the London Zoo drained its aquarium and preemptively destroyed its entire collection of poisonous snakes and arachnids, a decision that would be debated (and, in some cases, copied) at zoos across the United States.[26] Other zoos quickly followed suit. At the Kursaal Zoo, located near the southeast tip of England, zoo staff killed seven lions, along with several bears, wolves, monkeys, hawks, eagles, and a tiger, as a precaution against air raids. The zoo closed for good shortly thereafter.[27]

Beginning in 1941, many American zoos created emergency plans in case of aerial attack. Although the Bronx Zoo decided against preemptively slaughtering its animals (its leaders reasoned that any escaped snakes and poisonous spiders would die from cold weather), it nonetheless armed keepers with rifles and instituted a twenty-four-hour watch.[28] The San Diego Zoo implemented similar measures. As Belle Benchley, the zoo's executive secretary, reassured the local press, the glass snake house was fitted with protective shutters, and each man on the twenty-five-member zoo staff was "equipped with a high-powered gun, which he will use if it becomes necessary to prevent danger to the public through possible escape of dangerous animals."[29]

Given such fears – and the fact that killing excess, pest, food, and otherwise "disposable" animals is an essential part of zoo culture – it is easier to understand why some American zoos chose to destroy their animal collections in response to wartime food shortages. In April 1942, Fred McDuff, an oil field equipment dealer from Seminole County, Oklahoma, donated the bulk of his private menagerie to the zoo in nearby Oklahoma City because he decided that his energies would be better spent raising chickens and collecting metal scrap for the war effort.[30] Writing to a colleague a few months later, Benchley expressed similar misgivings about adding to her own animal collection. Faced with food and staff shortages, she believed it was "foolhardy to bring in rare and valuable animals" only to "have them destroyed" shortly thereafter.[31] In October 1942, a zookeeper from Cedar Rapids, Iowa, shot his entire animal stock, telling the *Associated Press*, "We don't feel that we can conscientiously keep on buying meat for animals when human beings are limited to a certain amount a week."[32] That same year, keepers at the nearby Omaha Zoo killed several lions because of a lack of edible meat.[33]

Among the most publicized zoo casualties of World War II was the Hershey Zoo in Pennsylvania, which shuttered its doors on 20 December 1942. Explaining the decision in *Parks and Recreation Magazine*, zoo director Ward R. Walker pointed to the lack of personnel, the inability to import new specimens, and the declining attendance rates because of tire and gasoline rationing. But looming over everything else was a shortage of food. "We cannot, after all these years, resort to the feeding of such foods as moldy bread, soggy sweet rolls, tainted meat, and vegetable cuttings swept off the floor or removed from garbage cans," he explained. The animals would be sold off to other zoos with the hopes of repurchasing them in peacetime, though Walker noted that those with "meat value" – including bison, deer, and elk – would be set aside in case of an "extreme meat shortage" in the community.[34] Indeed, across the nation, zoos frequently came to the grim conclusion that some animals were better off dead: to be sold for profit; butchered for human consumption; or fed to lions, tigers, and other charismatic carnivores.

Zoo Gardening for Victory

Zoos' second course of action for surviving the food-shortage crisis was to grow food on-site, usually on unused green spaces or in empty animal exhibits. This strategy made sense not only on material grounds but also in terms of public relations. Throughout World War II, the federal government promoted stateside food production as the "first line of defense" on the home front. Across the country, Americans young and old grew vegetables, fruits, and grains – sometimes in plots no larger than a window box. According to historian Amy Bentley, at the peak of the gardening campaign in 1943, "three-fifths of the population produced more than eight million tons of food, some forty per cent of fresh produce consumed that year."[35] Home front victory gardens served several functions beyond supplementing wartime diets. They fostered community involvement, stimulated good health, and allowed more commercial food to be shipped overseas. Just as important, victory gardens provided ordinary Americans with a venue for publicly enacting their wartime patriotism.[36] In this context, American zoos embraced on-site food production for two reasons: as a means of feeding their animals and as a chance to display their commitment to the Allied victory.

The idea of gardening at the zoo did not begin during World War II. In 1917, the Bronx Zoo converted every spare quarter-acre of land into gardens for "war crops." Zoo staff planted beets, turnips, potatoes, sunflowers, carrots, and lettuce, saving $2,500 in food expenses.[37] Such practices re-emerged with even greater urgency during the Great Depression, when slashed budgets left zoos scrambling to stay open. As the political scientists Jesse Donahue and Erik Trump show, zoos in Chicago, Seattle, Detroit, and elsewhere set aside land for farming fresh vegetables. In Tulsa, Oklahoma, zoo staff went a step further and scoured local markets for "spoiled vegetables, picking up road-kill, and harvesting park grass and trees to feed their thirty-five animals."[38]

During World War II, the combination of food shortages and patriotic fervor pushed zoo gardening to new levels of productivity. Zoos dug up ornamental gardens and turned parking lots into fields of edible plants. At the San Diego Zoo, staff planted victory gardens of carrots, corn, alfalfa, peanuts, chard, and sweet potatoes.[39] In January 1946, Stanley Field, chairman of the Brookfield Zoo's building committee, reported that the zoo had cultivated more than nineteen acres of land and had harvested seventy-eight tons of green grass, four-and-one-half tons of alfalfa, twelve tons of soybeans, 124 tons of green soybean hay, and five hundred pounds of pumpkins in the previous year alone.[40] Some zoos even let staff grow their own food. Employees at the National Zoological Park in Washington, DC, for example, tilled small plots of land for personal use (off the clock and without zoo-owned tools). The scheme was justified on two grounds. Workers were expected to donate all unused roughage as fodder for the animals; in addition, zoo leaders believed that "anybody who contributes something to eat is doing the country a service."[41]

Beyond fruits and vegetables, zoos also produced ample baked goods. In 1942, the Oklahoma Zoo built its own bakery after local stale bread supplies ran short. (At the time, its animals ate about three thousand pounds of bread per month.)[42] The Washington Park Zoo set up similar facilities, as did the National Zoological Park, which developed its own "bear bread" of flour, yeast, and bran. As of May 1945, the zoo produced more than 360 pounds of the bread per day, along with other forms of animal feed.[43] US zoos were quick to publicize their self-sufficiency, if only to dispel the perception that zoos – and their animals – were drains on the public coffer. However, raising crops and baking bread only addressed part of the food shortage. For this reason, wartime American zoos turned to a third practice: substituting animals' normal fare with patriotic diets.

Patriotic Diets

Even in peacetime, zoo animals' diets rarely match those of their "wild" counterparts. According to Philip T. Robinson, a former veterinarian at the San Diego Zoo, "Feeding practices often vary widely from zoo to zoo, based on tradition and pragmatism as much as anything to do with science."[44] During World War II, zoos weighed a number of factors, including public opinion, in determining the diets of the animals in their charge. In the Bronx, zoo officials relaxed the ban on visitors feeding certain animals (elephants, llamas, deer, and mountain sheep), and allowed patrons to purchase small bags of "specially prepared food" from vending machines scattered around the park.[45] Other zoos encouraged visitors to bring food from home, even if it contained little nutritional value.

From the start of the war, American zoos embraced patriotic diets – a term taken from wartime propaganda – for two reasons. The first was pragmatic: cut off from overseas imports and unable (or unwilling) to purchase commercially processed foods, zoos were desperate to find anything to feed the animals in their care. At the same time, they hoped to score political points by demonstrating their commitment to government rationing campaigns. Thus, instead of tropical fruits, Brookfield Zoo monkeys ate homegrown apricots, peaches, raisins, and stewed prunes; instead of fresh shrimp imported from abroad, Chicago's flock of pink flamingos subsisted on native crustaceans dried in New Orleans.[46] In San Diego, zoo cooks used condemned macaroni products instead of wheat flour and substituted ant eggs from Germany with dried insects shipped north from Mexico.[47] Elsewhere, zoos replaced Japanese ants – "favorite food of many a zoo bird," according to *Time* magazine – with native water bugs from New Mexico.[48] Whenever possible, zoos tried to replicate the taste or appearance of animals' standard fare. Zoo kitchens added green bone paste and brewer's yeast to ground beef in order to stretch meat rations. They swapped sweet potatoes – which were cheap and plentiful – for bananas, papayas, and other exotic delicacies. Overseas, zoos resorted to even more desperate measures, often with ill effect. At the London Zoo, penguins were fed slivers of horse or cat meat dipped in cod liver oil instead of fish, while at the famed Tierpark Hagenbeck just outside of Hamburg, Germany, the carnivores ate "offal" instead of their usual "juicy quarters of meat."[49]

Of all the substitute foods used in wartime zoos, none attracted more public interest than meat. This focus makes sense given Americans' obsession with eating mammal flesh.[50] During World War II, the Office of Price Administration categorized meat as "the essential fighting food," as important to Allied victory as "tanks, planes, and bullets."[51] The choicest cuts were sent to military training camps and to troops stationed overseas, while those on the home front were advised to reduce their weekly intake of beef, pork, and lamb. The federal government urged Americans to "Share the Meat" and pushed organ meats and plant-based proteins as healthy (and patriotic) alternatives to prime cuts. Even so, few on the home front lost their hunger for

T-bones and pot roasts, particularly now that – after a decade of economic depression – they finally had the money to pay for them.[52]

As it turns out, most American zoos had little difficulty obtaining adequate supplies of meat of one kind or another. The top choice of wartime zoo menus was horseflesh, which was not only cheap but also abundant. At the Oklahoma City Zoo, tigers, lions, and bears consumed about two horses per week, often from eighteen- to twenty-year-old nags.[53] At the Woodland Park Zoo, butchers slaughtered horses on-site; the meat was fed to the animals, while the hides went to a leather shop to be cured and eventually sold.[54] Some zoos established business relations with local slaughterhouses, which would send them thousands of pounds of horsemeat at minimal prices. In 1942, the Brookfield Zoo purchased much of its horsemeat from Hill Packing Company in Topeka, Kansas, which slaughtered the horses, deboned the flesh and packed it in cartons, and then shipped it to Chicago in refrigerated freight cars.[55]

Horse-heavy diets were not unique to the 1940s. During World War I, the Oklahoma City Zoo saved twelve cents per pound by feeding their lion and bobcats horsemeat instead of beef.[56] In the 1930s, when the entire nation struggled to eat, horses – along with road kill and shelter animals – were staples in zoo carnivores' "Depression Diets."[57] The Brookfield Zoo turned to a horse-heavy meat menu as early as 1935, and Charles Schroeder, founder of the San Diego Zoo, boasted of his skill at acquiring cheap horsemeat south of the border: "I'd go to Mexico, buy old horses from Mexican skinners, dip and spray them, and bring them across the border. Then we used to stand the horse up, shoot him in the head, skin him, split the carcass, then the keepers would come in with their own knives and cut meat off the carcass for their animals."[58]

Throughout World War II, smaller zoos relied upon larger institutions as they planned their emergency menus. At Chicago's Brookfield Zoo, director Ed Bean, one of the nation's most prominent zoo leaders, received letters from zoos across the country asking advice about food substitutions. In February 1942, Dan Harkins, the curator of the Franklin Park Zoo in Boston, sent Bean a lengthy list of questions about wartime feeding practices:

> Please tell me how much green bone paste, brewer's yeast and cod liver oil do you add to each one hundred lbs. of ground meat?

Are you feeding fish to Polar bears? ...

What is your diet for baboons and monkeys, such as macaques, guenons, ringtails? The same every day?

What grain mixture do you feed your antelopes?

The same for your deer?

Any vegetable matter? Beet pulp, etc. ...

What are you feeding your elephants daily? Kind of hay? Quantity? To an adult? Vegetable matter? Grain?[59]

Similar requests arrived at Bean's desk from as far away as Detroit and San Antonio.[60] In his responses, he offered detailed advice about the Brookfield Zoo's wartime food substitutions.

Bean and his son Robert, who served as the zoo's curator of mammals, also counselled their fellow zoo professionals not to test the public's patience by complaining about food shortages. Writing to Benchley in June 1943, Robert stressed the importance of minimizing the zoo's wartime hardships, especially where food was concerned. Although Brookfield was allowed twenty-five pounds of brown sugar, animal keepers used corn syrup and other nonrationed sweeteners instead. Robert was especially critical of one fellow zoo director who "had his dear picture taken in front of a ration board wicket, pleading for canned peaches for his gorilla." In his eyes, "that is nothing but waving the red flag in the face of every person in the country – absolutely stupid." By complaining about food shortages, zoos risked losing public support at a time when all patriotic institutions were expected to sacrifice for the good of the nation. Instead, Bean argued, zoos should embrace substitute foods, silence their grumbling, and ride out the war as best they could.[61]

Not surprisingly, zoo directors went to great lengths to cast their animals' substitute diets in a positive light. In an internal report, Ed Bean insisted that recent changes in animal feeding had presented "no difficulties whatsoever."[62] Harry F. Nimphius, chief veterinarian of the Central Park Zoo, conveyed a similar message in a *New York Times* interview in January 1943. The zoo's monkeys, he jovially announced, had become "reconciled to the sweet potato as an ersatz banana." Although the zoo had cut the big cats' daily portion of horsemeat by more than half (for "patriotic reasons"), Nimphius joked that the animals could afford to shed a few pounds. "They're all fat," he said. "They'll be a little leaner, but they'll undoubtedly feel better. Just like the rest of us, a little cutting down won't hurt them."[63] When speaking to the press in particular, zoo publicists frequently used humour to defend "war diets" – and, by implication, zoos themselves – against critics. Asked about the ethics of feeding zoo animals in a time of mass privation, Leo Blondin of the Oklahoma Zoo retorted: "If they could only see the horses" the zoo had recently purchased. "Most of the poor animals can hardly stand when we buy them as food for the lions and tigers."[64]

On 12 May 1945, William Mann sent an equally reassuring message when he appeared on *Consumer Time*, a fifteen-minute radio show that aired on NBC. Launched in 1935, *Consumer Time* was produced by the US Department of Agriculture as a means of helping listeners become "more intelligent economic citizens."[65] The 12 May episode focused on alternatives to commercial pet food, which was difficult to obtain because of wartime rationing. Instead of canned dog food, Mann recommended dried kibble or small pieces of "government-inspected horse-meat." For dogs, he also suggested experimenting with cooked cereals, vegetables, and bone meal. Throughout the program, Mann emphasized the zoo's success in converting its animals to new diets. More than that, he touted the animals' willingness to accept ersatz foods as a model of wartime accommodation. At a time when millions of Americans scoured black markets in search of rationed items, he explained lightheartedly, monkeys "don't get nearly as excited as people do about wartime substitutes for their favorite foods!"[66]

Despite such assurances, not all zoo denizens embraced their patriotic diets. Across the United States, zoo directors hinted at many animals' reluctance to curb their appetites in the face of wartime shortages. In Milwaukee, the Washington Park Zoo's collection of chimpanzees rebuffed the zoos' efforts to substitute baked sweet potatoes for their prewar bananas. Though director Henry M. Kennon was confident that the chimps would eventually "come around," he admitted that they were right to complain: bananas were, after all, the "more ideal diet."[67] Animals that had eaten voraciously now hesitated, picked at their food, or – in some cases – refused to eat altogether.[68] For the most part, zoo officials downplayed problems with wartime diets, particularly when human food supplies were stretched especially thin. After the war, however, even Mann admitted that zoo animals were not the uncomplaining consumers he had led radio listeners to believe they were.

"There is no stage or screen star as temperamental as a lady lion when you first try to slip her horsemeat as a substitute for her customary slab of beef," Mann joked. "Nor are monkeys fooled when you try to serve potatoes masked in honey and palmed off as bananas."[69]

Of course, it would be a mistake to think – as zoo directors facetiously insisted – that animals' dietary decisions reflected their patriotic fervor (or lack thereof). Although World War II–era zoos often made it a point to depict their residents as exemplary wartime citizens, animals were by no means aware of the broader significance of their actions.[70] From the perspective of a caged polar bear or monkey, World War II existed only in the sense that it altered what sociologist Eileen Crist calls the animal's "lifeworld," its "everyday world of experience of activity and leisure, pleasure and pain, abundance and hardship, exhilaration and fear, rivalry and affection."[71] Some animals' wartime lifeworlds were marked by changes in smell or sound; others by reductions in food or living space; still others by new feelings of hunger or cold. Such changes were not necessarily traumatic in the long run: as zoologist Donald Griffin shows, animals can adapt to even radical changes in the environment.[72] However, during World War II, at least some zoo animals proved remarkably reluctant to adapt to their new circumstances – even at the risk of their health.

In an interview from 1943, Robert Bean of the Brookfield Zoo described two such renegades: a pair of recently acquired pythons that refused to eat. "We tried everything we could think of," Bean told a reporter, "choice fat rabbits, chickens, ducks, and other poultry – but the pythons just pushed back their plates." Eventually he discovered that the snakes had been "holding out" for White Leghorns, the breed of chicken they had eaten prior to their arrival at Brookfield.[73] From Bean's perspective, the pythons' gastronomic resistance – their outright refusal to bend to the zoo's dietary dictates – represented both a financial burden and a waste of precious resources. The snakes, however, had a different set of concerns. At some fundamental level, they understood that their food had changed, and – for whatever reason – they were unwilling to adapt to it. And so, rather than let the snakes die, the Brookfield cafeteria adapted to them.

Perhaps the best measure of the effects of American zoos' food shortages and substitute diets is the number of animals that died at them during World War II. Mortality rates at major zoos frequently topped 20 per cent per annum, and it was common for exhibit cages to be left empty for years on end.[74] Between 1942 and 1946, the Bronx Zoo lost 579 mammals, an average of about 116 per year.[75] Although zoo animals die of "natural causes" on a regular basis, the wartime environment proved especially deadly, even when zoos were thousands of miles from the front lines. Over the course of the war, the total animal population at Seattle's Woodland Park Zoo dropped from 1,347 in 1940 to 882 in 1945. Much of this decline can be attributed to the zoo's inability to replace lost stock. However, its 1945 annual report singled out food issues – namely, food of poor quality – as the explanation for the high rate of animal fatalities.[76]

Conclusions

At the end of World War II, few American zoos spent much time in reflection on their recent hardships. Despite lingering shortages of materials and feed, zoo directors proudly touted their wartime records. At a time when all Americans were expected to tighten their belts, zoos had publicly embraced wartime rationing regimes. Indeed, their prominent approaches to the food crisis – cutting food need, planting on-site gardens, and adopting ersatz war diets – closely mirrored the propaganda messages espoused by government food agencies.

However, zoos' handling of food shortages should not be solely attributed to the patriotic climate of the wartime home front. Food shortage was – and remains – a perennial issue for zoological institutions in the United States and around the globe. The structure of the modern zoo – with its large numbers of diverse animals on specific diets – virtually ensures that all zoos will face a food crisis at some time or another. In this instance, World War II only magnified – and publicized – a problem zoos had faced for more than a decade of economic depression.

For scholars of zoos and the humanities, the dietary history of American zoos during World War II suggests several lessons. First, it reminds us that all zoos are political, despite their frequent protests to the contrary.[77] While they often portrayed themselves as urban oases set apart from global politics, American zoos in World War II willingly echoed the nationalistic (and frequently martial) rhetoric of the wartime state. Moreover, this history demonstrates how zoos are bound up in what legal scholars Nancy Ehrenreich and Beth Lyon call a "global politics of food." In our global food system, they write, "inequalities of power and privilege across the globe affect who has access to food and who does not, who controls its production and who is harmed by that product, how consumptive choices are constructed and constrained, and whether eating is seen as a complex, biosocial activity or as nothing more than instrumental body maintenance."[78] During World War II, zoos struggled not only to locate adequate nutritious food but also to justify spending that food on nonhuman animals – living creatures whose nutritional needs ranked near the bottom of Americans' hierarchy of essential appetites (below overseas soldiers, home front workers, "food" animals, and even pets).

In this sense, the story of wartime rationing speaks to the precarious place of zoo animals – indeed, all animal life – in World War II–era American society. Although zoos often went to heroic lengths to remain open throughout the war years, all zoo animals existed on a spectrum of expendability. Unwanted zoo animals were shot, sold at auction, and – in a few cases – subjected to military experimentation.[79] They were even reduced to "meat," emergency rations for both human and nonhuman populations unwilling to adopt their own patriotic diets. To this day, zoo animals (and nonhuman animals in general) are among the earliest victims of food shortage and economic downturn. In July 2016, journalist Ben Morgan reported that more than fifty animals at the Caricuao Zoo in Caracas, Venezuela, had starved to death in the preceding six months, victims of a national crisis brought on by plummeting oil prices. Marlene Sifontes, a local union leader, characterized the starving animals' plight as a "metaphor for Venezuelan suffering."[80] But it is also further proof – as if more were needed – of zoo animals' secondary value, particularly when compared to humans. If American zoos during World War II sent any message, it is that some lives matter more than others, and that human lives (and appetites and desires and comfort and entitlement) matter most of all.

Finally, it is incumbent upon us to situate zoo animals' refusal to eat their wartime rations within a larger – and, thus far, largely unwritten – history of animal resistance. In his 2010 book *Fear of the Animal Planet: The Hidden History of Animal Resistance*, Jason Hribal writes, "Every captive animal knows, through learned response and direct experience, which behaviors

are rewarded and which ones are punished. These animals understand that
there will be consequences for incorrect actions ... Captive animals know all
of this and yet they still carry out such actions – often with a profound determination."[81] Deeming zoo animals' behaviour "resistance" is not to suggest that they understood the political dimensions of their actions or that
their eating practices were fuelled by anything more than distaste for substitute rations. Rather, it is to recognize their unwillingness to cede ultimate authority to their human captors. During World War II, zoos could cage
animals, starve them, slaughter them for food, and dictate nearly every aspect of their bodily existence. But – in some cases at least – zoos could not
make the animals eat. In this light, zoo leaders' joking pronouncements
about unhappy polar bears and finicky "lady" lions betray a deeper set of
anxieties – shared by many within the zoo community – about the possible
agency of the animals themselves.

NOTES

1 "Meat Ration Means Little to the Zoo," *Oklahoman*, 18 September 1942,
   13.
2 "Uncle Leo Bakes for His Pets as Rationing Comes to Zoo," *Oklahoman*,
   5 February 1943, 4.
3 "Bronx Zoo on War Diet," *Stars and Stripes*, 29 March 1918, 7.
4 On US zoos' efforts to justify themselves during World War II, see Kinder,
   "Militarizing the Menagerie."
5 Brokaw, *The Greatest Generation*.
6 Bentley, *Eating for Victory*; Collingham, *The Taste of War*.
7 Bentley, *Eating for Victory*, 31.
8 See Miller, *The Nature of the Beasts*; Itoh, *Japanese Wartime Zoo Policy*;
   Malamud, *Reading Zoos*; Litten, "Adieu Hippo."
9 New York Zoological Society, *49th Annual Report for the Year 1944* (New
   York: 1945), 62.
10 On women in World War II-era zoos, see Bender, *The Animal Game*, 240–2;
   Itoh, *Japanese Wartime Zoo Policy*, 154, 159; Rosenthal, Tauber, and Uhler,
   The Ark in the Park, 81.
11 Donahue and Trump, *American Zoos during the Depression*, 177.
12 Gus Knudson to the Board of Commissioners, 11 December 1946, folder

2/9, box 2, record group 8601, Woodland Park Zoological Gardens, Seattle, Washington (hereafter WPZG).

13 Gus Knudson, daily log, 1942, box 4, record group 8601, WPZG.

14 Wayne Whittaker, "Soup's on at the Zoo," *Popular Mechanics*, April 1943, 82–7.

15 "London Zoo to Breed Own Food," *Northern Star* (Lismore, NSW), 19 March 1940, 11.

16 Jenkins, *Bananas*, 29.

17 Ibid., 95–6.

18 Bentley, *Eating for Victory*, 14.

19 US Office of Price Administration, *Rationing in World War II* (Washington: GPO, 1946), 2.

20 Ibid., 25.

21 DeMello, *Animals and Society*, 50–4.

22 For a classic discussion of how animals are transformed into "food" – especially "meat" – see Adams, *The Sexual Politics of Meat*.

23 Mullan and Marvin, *Zoo Culture*, 5.

24 Woodland Park Zoological Gardens, *Annual Report 1945*, copy in folder 8, box 7, record group 5801-01, WPZG.

25 "A Bas Untermann, He Shot Sick Deer," 8 March 1940, clipping folder: 1940s, box 18, SHSW M89-188, Milwaukee County Historical Society, Milwaukee, Wisconsin.

26 "London Kills Zoo Snakes Lest Air Raid Free Them," *New York Times*, 3 September 1939, 14; *Reports of the Council and Auditors of the Zoological Society of London for the Year 1939* (Bungay: Richard Clay and Company, Ltd, 1940), 6; "Wardens for Wild Animals," *Daily Herald*, 8 April 1940.

27 "Animals at Zoo Shot," *Manchester Daily Herald*, 9 September 1939; clipping found in Newscuttings, vol. 36, July 1939–March 1940, London Zoological Society.

28 "Bronx Zoo Ready for Air Raid in City," *New York Times*, 18 December 1941, 35.

29 "S.D. Zoo Ready for Emergency," *San Diego Union*, 14 December 1941, B 2:2; see also Harry Milton Wegeforth and Neil Morgan, *It Began with a Roar: The Story of San Diego's World-Famed Zoo* (San Diego: Pioneer Printers, 1953), 161.

30 "Private Zoo at Seminole to Join City's," *Oklahoman*, 10 April 1942, 3.

31 Belle Benchley to Robert Bean, 15 July 1942, folder: San Diego, box 14, General Correspondence 1941–1942 (S–T), Chicago Zoological Society (hereafter czs).

32 "Zoo Animals Are Helpless Victims of Meat Rations," *Oklahoman*, 7 October 1942, 13.

33 Donahue and Trump, *American Zoos during the Depression*, 176.

34 Ward R. Walker, "Hershey Zoo Closes," *Parks and Recreation*, January–February 1943, 133, 134.

35 Bentley, *Eating for Victory*, 114.

36 Ibid., 114–29.

37 New York Zoological Society, *22nd Annual Report of the New York Zoological Society* (New York: 1918), 71.

38 Donahue and Trump, *American Zoos during the Depression*, 14, 12.

39 Wegeforth and Morgan, *It Began with a Roar*, 166, 170.

40 Stanley Field, "Report of the Chairman of the Building Committee," 5 January 1946, 1; copy available library of the czs.

41 "Victory Gardens Meeting March 29, 1943 at 4 p.m., Reptile House," record unit 365, box 197, folder 5, Smithsonian Archives, Washington, DC.

42 "War Is Pushing City into the Bakery Business," *Oklahoman*, 12 May 1942, 15.

43 "When the Cupboard Is Bare...," *Consumer Time*, aired on NBC on 12 May 1945.

44 Robinson, *Life at the Zoo*, 171.

45 "Bronx Zoo Relaxes Ban on Feeding of Animals," *New York Times*, 29 September 1940, 40.

46 R.H. Friedrich to Edward H. Bean, 17 March 1943, file 2:13, box 20, czs; Edward Bean to John T. Millen, 24 August 1942, file 1:3, box 112, Chicago Zoological Society, Office of the Director of the Brookfield Zoo, Edward H. Bean, Correspondence (1942), czs.

47 William Mann, "A Brief History of the Zoo," *Scientific Monthly* 63, no. 5 (November 1946): 357.

48 "Zoos for Morale," *Time*, 17 May 1943.

49 "Zoo's Penguins Have Catsmeat Menu Now," *Daily Express*, 11 October 1943; Hagenbeck, *Animals Are My Life*, 214.

50 See Ogle, *In Meat We Trust*.

51 Bentley, *Eating for Victory*, 95, 85.

52 Ibid., 92–3, 99.

53 "Meat Ration Means Little to the Zoo," 13.

54 Daily Logs, folder 4/4, box 4, record group 11 December 1946, folder 2/9, box 2, record group 8601, WPZG.

55 Ed Bean to J.A. Lacy, 27 March 1942, copy in 3:3, CZS.

56 "Horse Flesh Being Eating in this City," *Oklahoman*, 15 April 1918, 12.

57 Donahue and Trump, *American Zoos during the Depression*, 11.

58 Chicago Zoological Society, *Report of the Chairman of the Building Committee*, 20 July 1944, 3, CZS; Myers, with Stephenson, *Mister Zoo*, 26.

59 Dan Harkins to Edward H. Bean, 23 February 1942, file 1:3, box 112, Chicago Zoological Society, Office of the Director of the Brookfield Zoo, Edward H. Bean, Correspondence (1942), CZS.

60 Edward Bean to John T. Millen, CZS; R.H. Friedrich to Edward H. Bean, CZS.

61 Robert Bean to Belle Benchley, 15 June 1943, CZS.

62 Chicago Zoological Society, *Report of the Chairman of the Building Committee*, 20 July 1944, 3.

63 "War Streamlines Tigers at Zoo, But Monkeys Thrive of Ersatz," *New York Times*, 10 January 1943, 44.

64 "Uncle Leo Bakes for His Pets as Rationing Comes to Zoo," 4.

65 Donald E. Montgomery, quoted Newman, *Radio Active*, 146.

66 "When the Cupboard Is Bare...," *Consumer Time*, 12 July 1945, transcript available at https://archive.org/stream/CAT31324049/CAT31324049_djvu.txt.

67 "Yes, We Have No Bananas: War Diet Irks the Monkeys," *Milwaukee Journal*, n.d., clipping at WPZG.

68 Zoos had faced similar problems during World War I. At that time, they used humor to deflect attention away from the failures of their substitute diets – a practice that continued in World War II. As William Bridges, author of a popular history of the Bronx Zoo, recounts, "The United States went to war on April 6, 1917, and the Zoo went with it – all except the animals. Unpatriotically they declined to do their bit by eating less." Bridges, *Gathering of Animals*, 368.

69 Quoted in Robert MacMillan, "War Left Zoos in Pretty Fair Shape – Spectators Happy," *Chicago Daily News*, Sunday News, 10 March 1946, 60–1.

70 On efforts to portray World War II–era zoo animals as patriotic citizens, see Kinder, "Zoo Animals and Modern War," in *Animals and War*, 60–5.

71 Crist, *Images of Animals*, 142.

72 Griffin, *Animal Minds*.

73 Wayne Whittaker, "Soup's on at the Zoo," 83, 84.

74 Chicago Zoological Society, Stanley Field, "Report of the Chairman of the Building Committee," 20 July 1944, CZS.

75 New York Zoological Society, *51st Annual Report for the Year 1946* (New York: 1947), 25.

76 Gus Knudson, *Inventory and Yearly Report of Woodland Park Zoological Gardens, 1940*, WPZG; Woodland Park Zoological Gardens, *Annual Report 1945*, WPZG.

77 Fairfield Osborn Jr, "The World at the Zoo," *Animal Kingdom* (June 1958); William G. Conway, quoted in "Symposium: What's New at the Zoo?" *Rotarian* 130 (January 1977): 18.

78 Ehrenreich and Lyon, "The Global Politics of Food," 1–2.

79 See Kinder, "Zoo Animals and Modern War."

80 Ben Morgan, "At Least 50 Zoo Animals Fall Victim to Food Shortages in Venezuela," *Evening Standard*, 28 July 2016, 22. For similar stories of starvation in twenty-first-century zoos, see Fred Nathan, "Ukraine Crisis Leaves Animals in Kharkiv Zoo Fighting for Life," *Telegraph*, 9 April 2014; Natasha Daly, "War-Torn Yemen in Letting Its Zoo Animals Starve to Death," *National Geographic*, December 2016, http://news.nationalgeographic.com/2016/12/wildlife-watch-taiz-zoo-animals-starving-leopard-war/; "Starving Mosul Zoo Animals Receive First Food in a Month," *Reuters*, 2 February 2017, http://www.reuters.com/article/us-mideast-crisis-iraq-mosul-zoo-idUSKBN15H2MP.

81 Hribal, *Fear of the Animal Planet*, 25–6.

CHAPTER SEVEN

GUST (CA 1952–1988), OR A HISTORY FROM BELOW OF THE CHANGING ZOO

Violette Pouillard

Although the lower classes are no longer ignored by historians, they seem condemned, nevertheless, to remain "silent." But if the sources offer us the possibility of reconstructing not only indistinct masses but also individual personalities, it would be absurd to ignore it.
– Carlo Ginzburg[1]

We must account for nonhumans as living beings – not merely representations – in order to find the fullest possible explanation of history and to avoid simply engaging in self-flattery or self-deception.
– Susan Nance[2]

My starting point in this chapter is the juxtaposition of two photographs preserved at the colonial archives in Brussels, both taken at Antwerp Zoo in May 1953.[3] The first (figure 7.1), which depicts the close intimacy between a young gorilla who had arrived at the zoo a few days before and his keeper, has become a part of the Belgian collective imaginary around zoological gardens. Due, at least in part, to this picture, the young gorilla would become a celebrity under the name of Gust, a diminutive of Gustaaf.[4] The second photograph (figure 7.2) is far less iconic and, to my knowledge, has not previously been published. It also bears the date of 22 May and was probably taken a few hours before, as it shows the same gorilla curled up on himself.

Figure 7.1 *Above* Gust and keeper.

Figure 7.2 *Opposite* Gust.

Collective representations, books, and films on the history of Antwerp Zoo mainly depict Gust either as the young gorilla of the first photograph, still fragile but already saved by his symbiotic relationship with his keeper, or as a full-grown, impressive-but-gentle silverback and star of the zoo.[5] This reductionism reflects the gradual transformation of Gust's body and personality into a symbol of both the growing mastery over the (post)colonial African territories and the allegedly rationalized management of African fauna, under the authority of the Western centres of power, desired by the imperial powers and by the zoo itself.[6] It can also be linked with the "new opinion of zoos," at its height during the 1930s to 1950s, which perceived these institutions as places of encounter and, sometimes, friendship with animals,[7] even with apes who had long been depicted as fierce and untameable.[8]

However, the history of Gust is also that of the lost animal in the second picture, an animal who has gradually disappeared behind these symbols. In this chapter, I aim to reconstitute his life by analyzing both of the above images. This reconstruction is a way to understand why the decades-long life of one of Europe's most famous captive gorillas has remained obscure (despite being evoked in the form of short biographies in most histories of Antwerp Zoo), as well as what this silence tells us about the history of human-animal relationships at the zoo. This perspective relies on developments in the field of animal history that move beyond cultural representations to focus instead on animals as real beings and actors within dynamic relationships with humans.[9]

Addressing the history of zoo animals can rely on several approaches, from quantitative analyses to animal biographies.[10] In his study of the intellectual, cultural, and spiritual universe of Menocchio, a literate miller born in 1532 and executed around 1600 for his heretical opinions, Carlo Ginzburg reminds us that "even a limited case (and Menocchio certainly is this) can be representative." It ultimately appears that Menocchio's questioning, being partly a reflection of an oral tradition "deeply rooted in the European countryside," "isn't an exceptional case."[11] From this perspective, the history of certain animal individuals for whom we do possess a significant number of sources appears to be a way both to shed light on their experiences and to highlight the fate of the numerous animals that posterity has forgotten by taking into account "different, unexpected, multiplied aspects of the collective experience."[12] In so doing, this perspective shares close ties with history from below, which draws upon life experiences to highlight the history of subalterns – the poor, the working classes, the slaves – while avoiding both their victimization (the perception of them as passive beings) and, following the well-known Thompsonian formula, "the enormous condescension of posterity."[13] Finally, regarding zoo studies specifically, Gust's history contributes to the growing corpus of research[14] that rejects both the teleological historical works written by zoo managers,[15] which define the history of animal captivity as a succession of steps from the recreative old regime menageries to the current conservation centres, and the assertions made by zoo opponents since their foundation in the early nineteenth century, often dismissed for being sentimental.

The time in which Gust lived appears particularly propitious to teleological readings and interpretations. The second half of the twentieth century saw the rebuilding of many European zoos, among them the Antwerp Zoo, which was heavily bombed during World War II; the development of sanitary and hygienist tools, such as antibiotics, anaesthetics, and standardized food;

an unprecedented rise in criticism of the captivity and commodification of wildlife, especially regarding postcolonial species; and, in response to these critics, a significant decrease in the numbers of mammals caught in the wild, with an increase in captive breeding, itself requiring significant management shifts.[16] Gust's life allows us to view these changes (frequently depicted as leading to the apex of zoo history in the beginning of the twenty-first century) from below.

From the Equatorial Forest to Antwerp Zoo

Gust was a Western gorilla (*Gorilla gorilla*), a species whose geographic range encompassed territories that were part of the Belgian, Portuguese, Spanish, British, and French empires. Obtaining this species was therefore easier than was the case for the Eastern gorilla (*Gorilla beringei*), whose distribution was almost entirely restricted to the Belgian territories. Although all gorillas had been subject to protective measures since the late nineteenth and early twentieth centuries, it was possible to obtain capture permits, particularly by asking different colonial authorities. It was furthermore possible to illegally pass gorillas between colonial entities since different laws governed the cession of licences.[17]

Like hundreds of other gorillas during the late nineteenth and twentieth century, the young ape who would be named Gust was extracted from the equatorial forest and transported to the West to satisfy a fascination for exotic wildlife. In the case of great apes, this interest was reinforced by the scientific debates regarding the "origin of man" and by the discourse of racial anthropology.[18] Gust was captured in late 1952 or early 1953, likely in the "Portuguese Congo," also known as the Cabinda Enclave.[19] The capture and sale of gorillas by both African and European hunters was then widespread, and Cabinda, surrounded by both the Belgian and French Congo, was a well-known place to illegally sell, buy, and export gorillas.[20]

When Gust arrived at Antwerp Zoo in 1953, weighing around six kilograms, he was estimated to be approximately eight months old.[21] Ethological fieldwork on the subspecies *Gorilla beringei beringei*, completed with information about Western gorillas, enables us to partially overcome the sources' silence and to grasp some of what his life was like before capture. He would have been born into a group likely composed of several adult females, one or more adult males, and perhaps other infants as well as juveniles and subadults.[22] Like all young gorillas, he surely spent most of his time resting, travelling, playing, suckling, and exploring while his mother carried him. He likely interacted with other gorillas of his group, and if he was already occasionally venturing away from his mother, he would have always stayed within a few feet of her.[23] It is more than likely that hunters deliberately targeted Gust during a capture operation, since it was standard practice to seize young gorillas, who were more manageable and tameable. Typically, the capture of the baby involved slaughtering the mother and other members of the group defending their kin.[24] Gust's extraction signalled for him the end of any further contact with his mother and conspecifics and marked a radical change in feeding (particularly as he was still suckling) and in his environment. The effects of this sudden change may be partly understood by examining the destiny of orphaned gorillas, such as Simba II, a three-year-old female Mountain gorilla studied by Fossey: "Immediately following her mother's death, the infant … ceased her play activities with others, reduced her feeding, and spent much time simply sitting alone in a dejected manner." Subsequently, the silverback of her group took her under wing.[25] For his part, Gust underwent new environmental changes when he was sent to Leopoldville, in the Belgian Congo, several hundreds kilometres east of Cabinda. In May 1953 he was held at the local zoo of the Congolese Botanical and Zoological Society where, due to his young age, personality, and the plasticity of apes in human environments,[26] he apparently adjusted quickly; the vice president of the society, who described him as "delightful," "very kind," and in possession of a "mild and nostalgic gaze," petted him "often."[27]

The survival of recently captured gorillas was jeopardized by the environmental and social changes they experienced throughout the extraction process. Deprived of any social interaction with their group, and often separated from their mothers before weaning, they were exposed to a variety of anthroponotic diseases[28] and parasitic infestations, which often become unmanageable after the shock of capture and captivity.[29] High mortality among young captive gorillas may have contributed to the decision to send Gust rapidly by air to Antwerp Zoo. Like dozens of protected animals before him, he was an official gift from the Belgian Congo government, as the Congolese wildlife was used as a propaganda tool via its exhibition in the metropolis. He arrived on 18 May 1953 and was, at first, thought to be a female.[30]

An Infancy at the Zoo: 1953 to 1958[31]

When Gust arrived at Antwerp Zoo, he struggled to cope with the challenges of captivity and transport, and with adjustments in his social relationships with humans and in his captive environment (this time encompassing a radical change in biome type and climate), all while burdened by the fatigue of travel. The aforementioned photograph (figure 7.2) captures this moment, which sources describe more precisely. The gorilla, rapidly placed in the zoo's quarantine section, was in poor physical condition: "completely dehydrated," he "obstinately refused all food and drink and was suffering from a continual and seemingly severe diarrhoea."[32] He fought with humans still unknown to him: the staff in charge noted that he had a tendency to bite.[33]

Owing to the rarity of captive gorillas at the time – he was only the third or fourth gorilla to arrive alive at Antwerp Zoo since the end of the nineteenth century – and to their special status due to their taxonomic proximity to humans, the zoo described Gust as a "guest of honour." This special status was demonstrated, among other things, by a keeper's continual presence near his cage, and Gust rapidly benefitted from the staff's close care and attention.[34] Furthermore, in line with the hygiene and sanitary turn then prevailing in Western zoos, a paediatrician was consulted the day after his arrival. In the following days, he was given numerous medical examinations and medicines as well as various drinks and foodstuffs. While, three days after his arrival, zoo staff noted that his general condition had improved,[35] Gust struggled with difficulties for weeks, so much so that they waited for a month to inform the press of his arrival, wanting to be certain that he would recover and so to avoid any "disobliging comment."[36] After ten days, he lost weight and, like most gorillas captured in the wild, experienced several symptoms of illness.[37] He was also "absolutely indifferent" even when the staff, who made "every effort in order to distract him, to interest him in life," provided him with the company of a young chimpanzee.[38] However, in the beginning of July, he seemed to have adapted to his new situation:

his physical condition improved, he gained weight, and, on 11 July, the staff noted that he was playing a lot and was full of life.[39]

The fact that Gust, like the majority of gorillas who arrived alive in zoos from 1945 to 1954, survived his first months in captivity[40] must be related, beyond hygienic improvements, to idiosyncratic factors such as the special relationship he developed with his keeper Aloïs Samson. Figure 7.1 shows Gust grasping Samson's uniform in a manner very similar to that observed in free-living young gorillas "tightly clutching [their mother's] hair with [their] fingers."[41] Several photographs and short movies shot at the zoo in 1953 and 1954 show that, in addition to providing Gust with a sanitary routine and treatments, Samson gave him some of the physical contact that he would normally have received from his mother. In pleasant weather, he would regularly take Gust for a walk on the lawns of the zoo, where he could carry out activities crucial to the behavioural development of young gorillas, such as the manipulation of vegetation and tree climbing. Attention to, and awareness of, his needs for distraction, play-based learning, and social contact also took the form of toys[42] and long-lasting opportunities for interactions with other animals. There was a failed attempt to provide him with the company of conspecifics, when a female Western gorilla imported in 1955, Iosephine, died after three months.[43] The zoo managers subsequently encouraged extraspecific relationships, following a centuries-old tradition in menageries that aimed to counteract the social deprivation that many exotic animals suffered and that was felt to threaten their very survival. Gust's captive companions included two lion cubs during the winter of 1953–4, and a female chimpanzee with whom he got on well.[44] This awareness of the gorilla's needs reflected an acute degree of human-ape communication that was forged independently from scientific studies. Though a few works concerning wild gorillas had been published,[45] gorillas still appeared as new ethological territory.

This empirical understanding was, however, constrained by the zoo's framework, and especially by the encyclopaedic paradigm that characterized it. In zoos as well as in natural history museums, European scientific and colonial elites submitted the irreducible abundance and chaos of the natural world by appropriating, classifying, and exhibiting series of specimens. In 1955–6, the Antwerp Zoo held 5,737 animals, among them 570 mammals of 181 different species.[46] For the animals, this profusion implied restrictions in space, infrastructures, and occupations. From night until 8:30 a.m., Gust was confined in a small, latticed wooden cage in his temporary quarters inside the quarantine area, which he proved reluctant to enter since confinement and isolation is contrary to the nocturnal behaviours of free-living infant gorillas, who "continu[e] to night-nest with [their] mother and may continue to do so until the age of 5 years."[47] It is probably there that he developed the habit of "gnawing the ... paint from the ironwork in his cage."[48] Any outside access was restricted by the keeper's availability to accompany him and by the weather. From the visitors' point of view, Gust "disappeared" from the end of the summer until the end of spring, which reflected the confinement to which he was subjected.[49] In early 1956, almost three years after his arrival, Gust was still in quarantine, emphasizing a common story in the history of zoos whose financial, spatial, and administrative constraints frequently delayed the development of new buildings.[50]

The zoo industrial environment proved to be deleterious to Gust's health. Along with several episodes of illness (colds, angina, pharyngitis),[51] his weight gain began to slow in mid-1954,[52] and in February 1956 he suffered from paralysis of the hand and foot muscles.[53] After several examinations, he was diagnosed with acute lead poisoning from ingesting lead paint, provoked by his habit of gnawing the ironwork or by the flooring of his quarters, which was redone "with white paint to obtain a better background for pictures,"[54] testifying to captive animals' scenographic purpose. Saturnism, which affected dozens of captive animals including several gorillas,[55] was treated with high doses of vitamins and calcium.[56] The radiologist who examined Gust remembered his visit decades later: the gorilla, living in his quarter in the quarantine section, appeared "relatively isolated, but amused himself with the comings and goings of people passing in front of his cage. Although he sometimes seemed sad, a bit solitary, and lacking in idealism ... he had however a little distraction due to the numerous passers-by; he even followed them, snuffling under the door [of his cage]."[57] The poisoning episode likely forced the zoo to transfer Gust, indirectly alleviating his boredom: along with a chimpanzee, Jenny, he was relocated to a new building behind the birds of prey aviary, later described as a "large enclosure," where he was provided with gym equipment.[58]

During his first four years at the zoo, Gust adapted to a completely new environment and to his social isolation, and built relationships with humans, lion cubs, and at least two chimpanzees. Save for a plausible brief encounter with Iosephine, he never met any conspecifics. In 1957, the zoo bought a female Western gorilla, Kora, who was approximately two years old, from French Equatorial Africa's game department.[59] Gust was probably united with her as early as 1957,[60] but there is little information about their socialization process and their following years at the zoo. A new building was in the pipeline, the first at Antwerp Zoo specifically dedicated to apes, and the staff was looking towards the future. Gust, now a juvenile, was probably no longer the malleable infant he used to be.

In the Ape House (1959 to 1988)

In 1959, Gust was transferred to the brand-new ape house, built after the completion of a study of infrastructure and management practices in other zoos. He lived in a day cage of 4.5 by 4.5 metres in size. On one side, he faced visitors through a thick glass. On the opposite side, there were several doors, including one that separated him from the service corridor and, above it, another that gave him access to an "ante-chamber," through which he could theoretically access either a terrace exposed to the sun or his sleeping cage. Yet his movements between these areas were regulated by keepers via an arsenal of doors, metal grilles, and levers.[61] In particular, access to the outside terraces, which were separated from the public by water-filled moats, was heavily restricted in ways that illuminate Gust's life beyond the popular image of a zoo celebrity roaming his terrace.

First, the structure of the building displayed seven cages, and one reserve, connected to only three terraces due to "lack of space and funds."[62] Second, weather conditions once again limited outside access. In 1958–60, the animals could hypothetically go outside "during the warm weather."[63] Keepers attempted to "allow the apes out during the winter by leaving the communicating doors open," but stopped for a period because, according to director Walter Van den Bergh, "the Gorillas ... allow themselves to get cold and do not have the sense to return indoors to the warmth."[64] Van den Bergh was, at least partly, wrong.[65] Third, and indicating the priority given to the zoo's theatricality, "it was important that the grass should be well-rooted by the summer," and so the managers "renewed the grass and kept the apes indoors."[66] In the early 1970s, it does seem that apes had outside access on a regular basis.[67] But there was a fourth, prevailing limitation. The zoo had installed water-filled moats without substantial knowledge of the effects of bodies of water on apes, who cannot swim.[68] In free-living chimpanzees, those effects differ between individuals and groups, reflecting idiosyncratic, cultural, and geographical divergences; likewise, in zoos, some captive apes played with water, some entered the moats, and some drowned.[69] At Antwerp Zoo, on 19 July 1958, the orangutan Kobus fell into the water, was rescued with a pole, used the pole to escape, and was killed the moment he threatened to leave the garden.[70] A chimpanzee drowned around 1959 and two "very ... young Gorillas," likely the Eastern gorillas Kaisi and Kisubi, were saved from drowning by "a wire mesh barrier" that had been subsequently installed.[71] These accidents led the zoo managers to place one of the keepers "permanently outside" during the summer, especially in order to "[keep] an eye on the animals" and "intervene in case of need."[72]

When authorized to pace the terrace for the first time, Gust and Kora entered the water "up to their knees" and Kora tried to escape.[73] Gust was disciplined for his behaviour, as Van den Bergh explained in 1960: "During the warm weather all ... species [of apes] are allowed out on to outdoor terraces. The one exception is Gust ... who is only familiar with one keeper which would mean that should an emergency arise, the other keepers would not be able to intervene effectively."[74] Indeed, as the curator would explain decades later, "Gust was so attached to ... 'Samson' that the other keepers no longer had any influence over him." Restrictions on Gust's terrace use persisted throughout his lifetime for, after this test, managers "put a definitive end to trials of allowing [Gust and Kora] to go outside,"[75] with only a few exceptions.[76] The numerous zoo-goers who remember Gust pacing on his terrace have confused him with the Eastern gorilla Kaisi, who was allowed to go out, most of the time alone;[77] Gust gradually disappeared behind the zoo icon he had become. Reconstructing the puzzle of a typical day in his life is one way to reclaim him from behind this image.

In his day cage, Gust benefited from daylight passing through the glass ceiling protected by an iron trellis, as well as from keeper-regulated heating, ventilation, and humidity.[78] If his basic physical needs were catered to, his movements were restricted to the day and perhaps also the night cages,[79] which could explain why his toenails reached four to five centimetres long in August 1980.[80] His activities were drastically limited, as notions of hygiene then went hand in hand with sterile and bare enclosures. In 1960, the cages in the ape building looked "like empty rooms" with walls of enameled concrete and tiled floors. Environmental enrichment came in the form of the "tubular equipment for exercise and play" available in "most" cages, and the only equipment explicitly mentioned in Gust's cage was "a weighing machine in the shape of a mushroom" upon which he used to jump.[81]

Interactions with Kora must have formed Gust's most important activity. Contrary to their specific social structure, they were forced to live as a couple,[82] like many zoo gorillas in the 1960s and 1970s. Since the first birth of a Western gorilla in captivity at Columbus Zoo in 1956, and as gorillas' status among protected animals increased, captive breeding of these simians had become a priority in the zoo world,[83] and Antwerp Zoo staff wanted Gust and Kora to "start a family."[84] But they suspected Gust was sterile from at least the middle of the 1970s,[85] and later "assume[d] that the [lead] intoxication rendered [him] sterile as he [never showed] any sexual behavior."[86] It seems that Gust and Kora were only separated for short periods of time, including once for around two months in 1961 when Kora underwent a surgical operation to have her big toes amputated. She had suffered "from incurable abscesses, which had attacked her bones" and, after the surgery, she "continually dirtied the open sores with her fingers." This episode is most likely related to the conditions of her captivity, including her interactions with Gust, as the veterinarians noted: "she appeared to have anxiety issues and large, deep wounds had appeared at various places on her body."[87] There is little direct information about Gust and Kora's relationship, apart from a few instances of aggression,[88] which their captivity probably exacerbated; they had few opportunities to escape each other's company, and there were signals that the gorillas in the building "saw too much of each other."[89] Their social history could also have played a role, as ethological studies have revealed that hand-reared gorillas show more aggression than their mother-raised counterparts, and that "an infant ... dependent on one person" – as was the case with Gust – "may have extreme difficulties in adjusting ... to conspecifics later."[90] The fact that the staff continued to house Gust and Kora together, however, seems to indicate that they found a sort of modus vivendi.

Food constituted another occupation. In the 1970s Gust was, along with the other gorillas, fed twice a day. His ration was composed of fruits and vegetables, which made up 80 per cent of his diet in 1975; standardized food (oilcake made of pressed seeds and nuts); and bread. He was also given "extras" such as sunflower seeds or twigs with bark and leaves.[91] These proportions indicate that staff opted to compromise between standardized animal feeding (introduced in Philadelphia Zoo in the 1930s and imported into Europe after World War II), which aimed to prevent food deficiencies, and pleasurable feeding, made apparent by the provision of plant materials.[92]

There was one last important component of Gust's everyday life: his relationships with humans. Even if his bond with Samson gradually loosened, Gust remained "a great friend" of his keeper,[93] and this familiar presence certainly continued to reassure him. Furthermore, Gust stood every day in front of large numbers of visitors who, fond of gorillas, probably amassed before his enclosure during zoo hours – which in summer 1969, for example, were 9 a.m. to 7 p.m.[94] The building's designers had taken into account the potentially harmful impact of the crowds on the apes, and had installed a separating pane of thick double-glazed glass to soundproof the captives and protect them from anthroponoses, inappropriate feeding, and "teasing."[95] However, visitors certainly attempted to attract Gust's attention in other ways, for example by banging on the glass. As the Dutch writer Siegfried Emanuel van Praag noted in 1961 regarding the ape building, zoo-goers tried their utmost to make the gorillas and orangutans react to their presence by any means possible, even if the apes preferred to focus upon themselves.[96] It is more than likely that Gust, who "kept shifting his gaze to the people watching him,"[97] suffered from their continual presence, particularly as his chance to physically retreat was reduced. Several ethological studies show that "high visitor density" and "large active groups of visitors" increases stress, intragroup aggression, and stereotypies (see below on these latter behaviours).[98] But it also seems that visitors gave Gust a specific type of enrichment: zoo managers report that Gust imitated the spectators, looking at people the same way they looked at him and scratching his head if someone in the crowd did so.[99]

At the end of the day, before his day cage was cleaned, Gust had to go into his night cage. This schedule was controlled by zoo staff and, like the other gorillas in the building, Gust would wait in front of the upper door for his evening meal, which comprised the main part of his daily ration. He then spent the hours until morning in the night quarter which, invisible to the public, was two metres long, one metre deep, and two metres high, near an "ante-chamber" of two by three metres. Devoid of any enrichment, it was furnished with "beds made from a heap of hay placed on a solid shelf."[100]

Experiencing Captivity

Gust lived in the Antwerp Zoo ape building for almost thirty years, until his death in 1988. Beyond the mere description of infrastructures and typical days, several sources as well as primatology research allow us to shed some light on his experience of captivity. His life, of which most aspects were managed by zoo staff, prevented him from displaying most species-typical behaviours. He could not live in a group, choose his social conspecifics, or emigrate at will as regularly occurs in the wild.[101] Gust's food and food processing differed from what would be common in the wild, as free-living Western gorillas select and process certain fruit, leaves, stems, pith, roots, shoots, or bark from an estimated 148 or more plant species, with seasonal variations, and range several kilometres each day in search of food.[102] His captive environment was furthermore devoid, among other things, of "access to sun, shade, wind, rain, seasonal changes, natural photoperiod, undulating topography, large spaces, visual barriers, living and fallen trees."[103] Even this very evocation of the experienced environment of free-living gorillas cannot itself avoid reproducing a kind of impoverishment, as the abundance of natural surroundings and, even more so, of the animal uses of them cannot be easily caught and described.

Gust adapted by exploiting the few possibilities left to him. In 1953, ten days after his arrival, he was seen eating basswood leaves, apparently looking for edible plants. He seized every opportunity to find other activities, for example eating the putty in his cage (1958) or in the ape building after the glass had been renewed (1962).[104] In 1975, Van den Bergh noted that the gorillas ate the straw provided as bedding material if it was "not completely [cut up] by [an] automatic packer, looking for grains,"[105] thereby responding to the environmental poverty, lack of plant materials, and poor enrichment in the night cage.

In her study on the history of American circus elephants, historian Susan Nance demonstrates that "elephants had agency but no real power ... they had no effective way to challenge circus life broadly, and many circus people certainly believed they would if they had the means." Nance, in particular, emphasizes the development of a vicious circle: the more elephants resisted human control, the more humans strengthened their constraints.[106] Similarly, the zoo managers, themselves constrained by the zoo's very structure, did not seem to be in favour of gorillas with more agency. Several of Gust's behaviours provoked unease in staff. For example, at least at age ten, Gust began to charge at and pound the glass of his enclosure in an aggressive manner,[107] which frightened the public and provoked Kora's flight.[108] In 1964, the zoo managers decided to add bars in the front of his cage. Van den Bergh denied the possibility of an escape and argued, unconvincingly, that the bars had been installed for "psychological" reasons since visitors backed away when Gust charged.[109] During the following years, zoo staff continued to address the common issue of charging by increasing the constraints on the animals rather than by changing their environment. At the end of the 1960s and in the early 1970s, they worked with the firm Splintex to try to find a way to electrify the glass partitions,[110] though sources do not indicate if such a system was implemented (apparently not).

The inertness and coercion of this environment, in contrast to the animals' evolutionary needs and inclinations, explains why, along with a significant proportion of captive gorillas, Gust expressed "disturbed behavior," or stereotypies.[111] In August 1963, a zoo-goer wrote to the director: "I was distressed at the plight of your Lowland Gorillas, who seemed to be very unhappy. The larger one [i.e., Gust] ... vomited on the floor, and then in what I presume was an endeavor to keep his living quarters clean, re-ate his food. This seemed to amuse or embarrass the people watching him and they laughed. It made me ashamed of being a human."[112] After internal discussions at the zoo, Van den Bergh composed an answer that justified this behaviour: "The gorilla has the habit to vomit, and [pick out only] the things it likes best. In captivity a gorilla has nothing to do once feeding is over. That's why the animal is re-eating the food it [threw] up; this is repeated a second and even third time."[113] This exchange highlights the discomfort of both visitors and staff, and their awareness that something about the gorilla's behaviour, related to its captivity, was wrong. Beyond this intuitive knowledge, from the 1980s onwards, several ethological studies were conducted in zoos around the world in order to determine experimentally what variable of captivity was involved in the etiology of "regurgitation/reingestion,"[114] particularly related to "stress and boredom."[115] It seems that much of Gust's lifetime was affected by such behaviour. In 1973, Van den Bergh noted that all of Antwerp Zoo's adult gorillas manifested regurgitation and reingestion, among them "mostly" Gust and Kisubi, while Kora and Pega exhibited the behaviour around eight times a day.[116] Gust, like other captive gorillas including Kora, also suffered from fur-plucking; the staff noted on 22 November 1986 that he tore the hair off his arms and ate it from time to time, and on 9 December that his arms were becoming bald.[117]

Gust's Death

The older Gust becomes, the more difficult it is to find information about him. The zoo magazine in the late 1970s and early 1980s still related gorilla anecdotes but focused on the Eastern gorilla pairs due to their potential reproduction. Rare and short articles about Gust, produced after his death, mentioned either his youth or his adult habit of banging on the glass. One article indicated that, in the late 1980s, "Kora had become dominant."[118] It is as if Gust's monotonous life prevented any further coverage.

In 1986, zoo managers began to renovate the ape building, arguing that transformation, notably improved layout of enclosures and expansion of available space to encourage the formation of social groups, was necessary to keep up with advancing knowledge about the behaviour and psychology of free-living apes.[119] Work began in 1987,[120] and Gust, like the other adult gorillas, was left in the building during construction;[121] while its effects on his life are not documented, he surely had to endure the clamor of workers and tumult of machinery. In early 1988, he suffered from breathing difficulties and stiffness in his limbs,[122] and in March and early April he became lethargic and refused to leave his night cage. Gust died on 11 April 1988; the autopsy identified the cause of death as myocardial degeneration and insufficiency – heart failure.[123]

Just like other zoo celebrities, Gust was exploited in life and in death.[124] One month after he died, students of a culinary technical college organized a fundraiser for the zoo that encouraged visitors to guess the weight of a large "chocolate Gust."[125] The zoo's 1988 annual report noted that the staff missed Gust, "known throughout Flanders."[126] For years, moulds of parts of his body (his head, one hand, and one foot) were exhibited in the ape building.

Conclusion: Beyond Symbols

About Menocchio we know many things. About this Marcato, or Marco –
and so many others like him who lived and died without leaving a trace –
we know nothing.
– Carlo Ginzburg, *The Cheese and The Worms*[127]

If Gust's life was unique in many ways, dozens of zoo animals shared several aspects of his experience. For example, surveys in the 1980s found that re-gurgitation and reingestion were estimated to occur in 62 to 69 per cent of captive gorillas, and in 84 per cent of gorillas over the age of five years old.[128] A 1992 study indicated that the behaviour "ha[d] ... been accepted as nor-mal by many keepers."[129] Gust's individual trajectory therefore sheds light on broader dynamics which the prevailing, teleological perspective masked. As I have shown, the second half of the twentieth century appears as a critical period in these narratives, as zoos began, in a decolonializing context, an eth-ical and conservationist turn. Gust's history, as well as the muted violence towards other animals such as Kobus (who was shot) and Kora (who had her toes amputated), shows that ethical concerns were not solved during this period. Furthermore, captivity could not be separated from a commodifica-tion of wildlife that appeared contradictory to conservationatist perspectives, unless "conservation" itself is a new form of reification by which animals are considered to be individuals, representatives of their species, and "reser-voirs" of genes as breeding tools. These simian experiences thereby challenge the teleological perspective. They show that zoos develop through decade-long cycles: they implement new infrastructures and management schemes; the animals, visitors, and staff challenge their relevance; and then the zoos develop new infrastructures and management policies, ad infinitum. Indeed, Antwerp Zoo's ape building, renovated in 1989, now appears outdated, and the zoo has recently opened two adjacent "broad outside enclosures" for gorillas and chimpanzees.[130]

Beyond these chronological issues, both the details and omissions of this pointillist biography force us to interrogate the essence of human-animal relationships at the zoo. There are decade-long gaps in the history of Antwerp Zoo's most famous animal, related to silence within the official sources that was a result of Gust becoming a product of his captive conditions: that is to say, a less interesting gorilla, confined with Kora in the indoor part of the ape building, regurgitating his food. These gaps can be partially filled by assembling the experience of captivity, yet the omissions can themselves reveal the extent of (dis)interest in the animals. Gust's treatment, and that of the other gorillas, was regularly accompanied by fictional constructions, built by both visitors and zoo managers. In the visitors' mirage, Gust, their favourite gorilla, was roaming his terrace. In the zoo magazine, Kaisi's chest-beating was the "joke" of a "clown" or a demonstration of "boundless virility."[131] The captive gorillas were forced to fit into a human narrative framework. When the gorillas suffered from regurgitation, the zoo journal tried to determine, by observing how the apes ate, if they could, like humans, be left- or right-handed.[132] This personification transforms the animals into symbols or emblems and resonates with dressage spectacles. While it encourages human sympathy, it diminishes the importance of the animals' interests and, far from blurring the line between humans and animals, powerfully reasserts it by decontextualizing animals, hiding the technologies of constraint in captivity, and glossing over the animals' unique biographies and idiosyncracies.[133] This sort of mute violence is deeply interlinked with the captives' treatment and conditions. When the apes' dissonance with their alleged adaptability to the zoo structures and schemes became impossible to adapt into a narrative, zoo staff prevented their behaviours by further restrictions around charging against the glass, entering the moats, or escaping, which involved further confinement and the killing of certain individuals. Following Gust and other zoo animals in a diachronic perspective forces us to guard against the temptation to neglect, marginalize, or avoid the contemplation and study of unpleasant and prevalent aspects of the zoo, such as this implicit violence involved in human narratives and constraint, stereotypic behaviours, or boredom. Looking at the things we usually dismiss underscores how impossible it is to separate symbolic dominance over other beings, even when infused with deep affection and paternalism, from marked effects on their bodies, flesh, and minds.

NOTES

1 Ginzburg, *The Cheese and the Worms*, xxvii.

2 Nance, *Entertaining Elephants*, 7.

3 My special thanks to Tracy McDonald, Daniel Vandersommers, Nigel Roth-fels, Susan Nance, Sophie Harris, and all the participants in the "Zoo Studies and a New Humanities" workshop for their comments and remarks.

4 On the naming of wild animals held in captivity as a sign of affection but also as a marketing tool, see Nance, *Entertaining Elephants*, 45.

5 Baetens, *Le chant du paradis*, 163; Van Eysendeyk and Van Bocxstaele, *De Tuin van het Leven*, 37; *Zoologie* (Brussels: Cinémathèque, 2009).

6 Pouillard, "Conservation et captures animales au Congo belge (1908–1960)."

7 Baratay and Hardouin-Fugier, *Zoo*, 216–20; Rothfels, "Touching Animals."

8 Herzfeld and Van Schuylenbergh, "Singes humanisés, humains singés," 258–60, 262.

9 Baratay, *Le point de vue animal*; Kean, "Challenges for Historians Writing," 57–72; Nance, *Entertaining Elephants*.

10 Pouillard, "En captivité"; Alberti, *The Afterlives of Animals*; Herzfeld, *Wattana*; Baratay, *Biographies animales*.

11 Ginzburg, *The Cheese and the Worms*, xxviii, 105–6.

12 Revel, "L'histoire au ras du sol," xiii.

13 Quoted in Coquery-Vidrovitch and Mesnard, *Etre esclave*.

14 Rothfels, *Savages and Beasts*; Baratay and Hardouin-Fugier, *Zoo*.

15 See Kisling Jr, *Zoo and Aquarium History*.

16 Baratay and Hardouin-Fugier, *Zoo*; Rothfels, *Savages and Beasts*; Pouillard, "En captivité."

17 Pouillard, "Vie et mort des gorilles"; Cincinnati, "Too Sullen for Survival."

18 Physical and behavioural comparisons and analogies between Africans and gorillas persisted well beyond the nineteenth century. See for example, Lavauden, "Les Gorilles," 398, 400.

19 "Le Cercle Zoologique Congolais," *Bulletin du Cercle zoologique congolais* 19, 2 (1953): 5.

20 AA, AGRI 451, Henry to Staner, 18 December 1950; Stadsarchief Antwerp (SAA), 1#2853, Van den Acker to Van den Bergh, 30 March 1950.

21 Gijzen and Tijskens, "Growth in Weight of the Lowland Gorilla," 185.

22 "Juvenile" is the period from three to six years of age, "subadult" from six to eight years. Other age categories include: adult female (over eight years),

blackback male (eight to twelve years), and silverback (over twelve years). Robbins et al., "Social Structure and Life-History Patterns," 50.

23 Ibid.; Fossey, "Development of the Mountain Gorilla."

24 Pouillard, "Vie et mort"; Cincinnati, "Too Sullen," 172–3; Geddes, *Gorilla*, 16, 65, with one exception, 191.

25 Fossey, "Development," 177–8.

26 Herzfeld, *Petite histoire des grands singes.*

27 SAA, 1#1972, Deheyn to Van den Bergh, 16 May 1953.

28 Pouillard, "Vie et mort"; Cousins, "Diseases and Injuries."

29 Cousins, "Diseases and Injuries," 212; AA, GG 16840, de Medina, *Rapport (...) au 30 juin 1949*, 6–7.

30 AA, AGRI 187, 59 Ch., Van den Bergh to the governor general, 6 June 1953; Pouillard, "Conservation et captures."

31 Gorilla "infancy" has been defined as zero to three years of age. This part of the article refers to a specific chapter in Gust's life that also encompasses when he was a juvenile (see n22 supra).

32 AA, AGRI 187, 59 ch., Van den Bergh to the governor general, 6 June 1953.

33 Antwerp Zoo (AZ), Gust card.

34 SAA, 1#2843, Van den Bergh to Cordier, 13 November 1958; quoted in M. Palmans, "Scènes de la vie privée de Gust," *Zoo*, 9–15: 10; Gijzen, "Liste des mammifères ...," *Bulletins de la Société royale de Zoologie d'Anvers* 16 (1960): 11; Pouillard, "Vie et mort."

35 AZ, Gust card.

36 SAA, 1#1972, Van den Bergh to Deheyn, 30 July 1953.

37 Palmans, "Offert par le Gouverneur-général du Congo-Belge," 30; AZ, Gust card; Cousins, "Diseases and Injuries," 213.

38 Palmans, "Offert par le Gouverneur-général du Congo-Belge," 30.

39 Ibid., 31; AZ, Gust card, 11 July 1953.

40 The international studbook has identified forty-eight gorillas that arrived in zoos from 1945 to 1954, among whom three (6.25 per cent) did not reach age three and three more did not reach age six. T. Wilms et al., *International Studbook for the Western Lowland Gorilla* Gorilla g. gorilla *Savage & Wyman, 1847* (Frankfurt: Frankfurt Zoo, 2011). Some gorillas who had died at an early age could have been omitted from this census.

41 Fossey, "Development," 147.

42 *Gust*, directed by Paul Favresse, 1953–4, in *Zoologie*; Palmans, "Offert par le Gouverneur-général du Congo-Belge," 31; Palmans, "Scènes"; Fossey, "Development," 147–51; "Beeldbank, Antwerp Zoo," Antwerp Zoo, http://media.kmda.org/Site/HistorischeBeeldbank?_ga=1.51252393.1622578040.1476869849.

43 "Travaux dans le Jardin," *Zoo* 21, 3 (1956): 73. The zoo magazine also mentions a young female gorilla named Isabelle, but she could be the same animal as she does not appear in the studbook. Gijzen, "Nos collections zoologiques," 118–19.

44 Gijzen, "Nos collections zoologiques," 85; Pouillard, "En captivité."

45 Among them Akeley, *In Brightest Africa*.

46 Baetens, *Le chant du paradis*, 258.

47 *Gust*, directed by P. Favresse; Palmans, "Offert par le Gouverneur-général," 31; Deckers, "Aventures avec des animaux," 101; quotation from Fossey, "Development, " 151; "Beeldbank, Antwerp Zoo."

48 Gijzen and Tijskens, "Growth," 184.

49 Palmans, "Scènes," 10.

50 Gijzen and Tijskens, "Growth," 184; Baratay and Hardouin-Fugier, *Zoo*; Pouillard, "En captivité."

51 AZ, Gust card; Palmans, "Scènes," 10.

52 Gijzen and Tijskens, "Growth," 184.

53 Gijzen, "Nos collections zoologiques," 84–5.

54 Ruch, *Diseases of Laboratory Primates*, 428–30.

55 Zook, Sauer, and Garner, "Lead Poisoning in Captive Wild Animals"; Fisher, "Lead Poisoning in a Gorilla," 478–9.

56 Gijzen, "Nos collections zoologiques," 84–5.

57 Deckers, "Aventures," 100.

58 Gijzen, "Nos collections zoologiques," 85; Gijzen, "Chronique des Gorilles," 51; quotation from Deckers, "Aventures," 101.

59 SAA 1#1868, Van den Bergh to Brassard, 27 June 1957; A. Gijzen and J. Tijskens, "Growth," 187.

60 "Gust est décédé," *Zoo* 54, 1 (1988): 41.

61 SAA, 1#1870, Van den Bergh to Terasawa, 29 August 1969; Van den Bergh, "The New Ape House," 8–9; Van den Bergh, "Les réalisations 1958 au Zoo," 4.

62 Van den Bergh, "The New Ape House," 10.

63 Van den Bergh, "Les réalisations 1958," 4; Van den Bergh, "The New Ape House," 11.

64 Ibid.

65 See, on the causes of colds, SAA, 1#1869, Van den Bergh to Sasaki, 3 May 1963.

66 Van den Bergh, "The New Ape House," 11.

67 Six and Gijzen, "Kaisi amuse son public," 100–1.

68 De Waal, *Sommes-nous trop "bêtes,"* 72.

69 Brown, Dunlap, and Maple, "Notes on Water-Contact," 243–9.

70 Van Puijenbroeck, "Bâtiment des anthropoïdes," 30–1.

71 Ibid., 31; Van den Bergh, "The New Ape House," 8–9.

72 Van den Bergh, "The New Ape House," 10.

73 Van Puijenbroeck, "Bâtiment des anthropoïdes," 31.

74 Van den Bergh, "The New Ape House," 11.

75 Van Puijenbroeck, "Bâtiment des anthropoïdes," 31.

76 On 4 April 1985, the staff noted on both Gust's and Kora's cards that "komt niet drinken wegens promenade," maybe with reference to a walk on the terrace. There is furthermore at least one picture of Kora, without any date, on the outside terrace: Van Puijenbroeck, "Nos gorilles," 93.

77 See notably, Six and Gijzen, "Kaisi," 100–1.

78 Van den Bergh, "The New Ape House," 9.

79 Gijzen, "Chronique," 51.

80 AZ, Gust card.

81 Van den Bergh, "The New Ape House," 9.

82 SAA, 1#1872, Van den Bergh to Jones, 29 January 1975.

83 "Introduction: New Developments in the Keeping of Great Apes in Captivity," *International Zoo Yearbook* (1960): 2; Pouillard, "Vie et mort."

84 Mortelmans, Vercruysse, and Thienpont, "Accidents et amputations," 77.

85 Deckers, "Aventures," 101.

86 Gijzen and Tijskens, "Growth," 184.

87 Mortelmans, Vercruysse, and Thienpont, "Accidents et amputations," 77.

88 AZ, Gust card, Kora card.

89 Van Puijenbroeck, "Evénements," 70. See also, Van Puijenbroeck, "Bâtiment," 31.

90 Quoted in Meder, "Effects of Hand-Rearing," 367–8, 371–2; Burks et al.,
    "Managing the Socialization," 347–58.

91 SAA, 1#1872, Van den Bergh to Jones, 29 January 1975.

92 Vercruysse and Mortelmans, "Régimes alimentaires," 103–4; Pouillard,
    "En captivité."

93 Quoted in Van den Bergh, "A nos membres," Zoo 36, 4 (1971): 15;
    Deckers, "Aventures," 101.

94 SAA, 1#1870, Van den Bergh to Terasawa, 29 August 1969.

95 Van den Bergh, "The New Ape House," 9.

96 Van Praag, "À propos de Singes et leur beauté," 93.

97 SAA, 1#2725, Carter to the director, 13 August 1963.

98 Quoted in Wells, "A Note on the Influence," 3–7; quoted in Hosey, "How
    Does the Zoo Environment," 112.

99 Van Eysendeyk and Van Bocxstaele, De Tuin van het Leven, 37.

100 SAA, 1#1870, Van den Bergh to Terasawa, 29 August 1969, 1#1872, Van
    den Bergh to Jones, 29 January 1975; quoted in Van den Bergh, "The New
    Ape House," 9; Gijzen, "Où il est à nouveau question de gorilles," 58.

101 Harcourt, "Behaviour of Wild Gorillas," 250, 253; Robbins et al., "Social
    Structure," 145–59.

102 Remis, "Western Lowland Gorillas (Gorilla gorilla gorilla) as Seasonal
    Frugivores," 87–109; Rogers, "Western Gorilla Diet: A Synthesis from
    Six Sites," 173–92.

103 Bruner and Meller, "Convergent Evolution," 216.

104 AZ, Gust card.

105 SAA, 1#1872, Van den Bergh to Jones, 29 January 1975.

106 Nance, Entertaining Elephants, 97.

107 Meder, "Effects of Hand-Rearing," 67.

108 Gijzen, "Chronique," 51.

109 Van den Bergh, "A nos membres," 4.

110 Ibid., 159.

111 Cousins, "Diseases and Injuries," 215; Ruempler, "The Cologne Zoo Diet,"
    225.

112 SAA, 1#2725, Carter to the director, 13 August 1963.

113 SAA, 1#2725, draft of letter, 14 August 1963, Van den Bergh to Carter,
    20 August 1963.

114 See Ruempler, "The Cologne Zoo Diet," 225; Gould and Bres, "Regurgitation and Reingestion," 241–50; Lukas, "A Review of Nutritional and Motivational Factors," 237–49.

115 Akers and Schildkraut, "Regurgitation/Reingestion and Coprophagy," 106.

116 SAA, 1#1872, Van den Bergh to Curtis, 4 October 1973.

117 AZ, Gust card, Kora card (21 May 1960, 6 July 1960, 18 November 1980, 20 January 1985); D. Cousins, "Diseases and Injuries," 215.

118 "Calendrier-Zoo," *Zoo* 54, 1 (1988): 41; quoted in "Rapport annuel de 1988," *Zoo* 55, 1 (1989): 23.

119 Daman, "Le 'Nouveau' Pavillon," 13–14. This knowledge had been expanded upon since Schaller's fieldwork, *The Mountain Gorilla*.

120 "Zoo-News," *Zoo* 53, 2 (1987): 4.

121 Demoor and Fornoville, "La Construction de Longement," 21.

122 "Calendrier-Zoo," 41.

123 AZ, Gust card, Van Puyenbroeck, "Evénements," 26.

124 Alberti, "Maharajah the Elephant's Journey," 47.

125 "Calendrier-Zoo," 45.

126 "Rapport annuel de 1988," 23.

127 Ginzburg, *Cheese and the Worms*, 121.

128 Gould and Bres, "Regurgitation and Reingestion," 248.

129 Ruempler, "The Cologne Zoo Diet," 225.

130 "Découvrez un nouveau zoo," Antwerp Zoo, http://www.zooantwerpen.be/fr/nouveautes/decouvrez-un-nouveau-zoo-danvers; "Wandelen tussen gorilla's en chimpansees," Antwerp Zoo, https://www.zooantwerpen.be/nl/mensapenvallei/.

131 Six and Gijzen, "Kaisi," 101. On the sexualization of captive animals' bodies, see Acampora, "Zoos and Eyes," 69–88; Barua, "Circulating Elephants," 3.

132 Gijzen, "Bonnes manières à table chez les anthropoïdes en captivité," *Zoo* 38, 1 (1972): 15–20.

133 See Malamud in this volume; Nance, *Entertaining Elephants*; Servais, "La visite au zoo," 157–84; Flack, *The Wild Within*, 160–1. On the use of animals as symbols, see Ritvo, *The Animal Estate*.

CHAPTER EIGHT

CHILD STARS AT THE ZOO: THE RISE AND FALL OF POLAR BEAR KNUT

Guro Flinterud

"Massive Uproar over Berlin Polar Bear Cub: Will Cute Knut Be Put to Death?" The red and white headline covered most of *Bild*'s front page and greeted people at German newsstands on 19 March 2007. Knut was a hand-raised, four-month-old cub, and the headline referred to an interview with animal rights activist Frank Albrecht, who claimed that the Berlin Zoo would have to kill their famous young polar bear. Albrecht intended to use Knut's fame to shed light on the practice of breeding and culling that is common in many zoos. Little Knut had already become a media celebrity across Germany, and Albrecht wanted to make it clear that the nation's new pet might have a grim, and typical, fate waiting for him. But instead of attracting attention to his cause, German media misinterpreted his statement as a death threat against Knut, and news that activists wanted to kill a cute polar bear cub went viral. In this chapter, I will investigate how the media defined Knut's narrative during his first two years of life as he moved from local zoo celebrity to global child star.

Knut's story began in late autumn, 2006. At the Berlin Zoo, the former circus bear Tosca was expecting. It was her third pregnancy, and her previous cubs had all died soon after birth. In the wild, polar bears give birth during winter in closed dens of snow, rearing their newborn in a silent, almost sterile environment. In zoos, these conditions are impossible to re-create, and environmental stress often makes it difficult for polar bear mothers to nurse their cubs after birth. Because of Toscas's history, zoo staff monitored her closely as her due date drew close. On 5 December 2006, Tosca gave birth to two cubs. After several hours of trying to nurse, she retreated, exhausted, to her den. Zoo staff hoisted the cubs out of the enclosure with a long landing net and placed them in an incubator made for parrots. One cub died, but the other was reared behind the scenes. When the story of the hand-reared polar bear cub named Knut reached the media in February 2007, he was already three months old and looked like a living plush toy.[1]

The way the media represented Knut existed on the border between (animal) zoo baby and (human) child star. From the very beginning, he was pictured transgressing nature as he grew up among humans, almost like a Mowgli in reverse. As a cub, Knut was thoroughly under human control: he drank from a bottle, bathed in a tub, was rubbed with baby oil, and was weighed every day. He received balls and stuffed toys with which to play and a rubber mat on which he learned to walk. When he was presented to the public at the end of March 2007, he appeared in specific time slots dubbed "The Knut Show," where he could be seen playing with his keepers in an enclosure. This closeness to humans that defined his initial celebrity was an important element in interpreting his subsequent development into a "deviant," as growing into an adult polar bear inevitably meant the separation of Knut and his human companions.

Knut was a product of what historian Harriet Ritvo calls a system of starring in zoos.[2] Ritvo shows that this system goes back as far as the early nineteenth century – almost as long as the history of the modern zoo itself. As zoological gardens appeared as public places of recreation for the middle class, and gradually the working class as well, they came to depend on visitors and entrance fees. In order to attract crowds and encourage return visits, the animal star was born. The earliest such celebrity at the London Zoo, for example, was its first hippopotamus, Obaysch: in being given a name, the audience could relate to him as an individual.[3] Today, the system of starring is most often geared towards animal babies.

However, Knut was not only a zoo star, but also an international media celebrity. Here I argue that Knut's story illuminates the intersection of the child star system in popular culture and the system of starring in zoological gardens. In Western popular culture, child stars are praised while they are young and talented, often dismissed when they become awkward and rebellious teenagers, and then replaced with new child stars – despite their expected trajectory. Similarly, zoos produce animal babies but struggle to accommodate them in adulthood. This is also the case with many animals in the movie industry. Film studies scholar Claire Molloy writes about how the chimpanzees in Hollywood during the 1940s and 1950s were sent away as soon as they reached adolescence and became more difficult.[4] I argue that the move from local zoo baby to international media celebrity prepared the ground for a narrative that interpreted Knut's development by referring to the myth of the cursed human child star rather than the lived reality of the zoo baby star. This shift obscured the fact that Knut was a product of a star system that created superfluous animals in zoos.

Zoo animals are frequently mentioned in German media. Yet Knut became an international phenomenon. Media technologies, especially the Internet and its immediacy of information, were clearly part of this transition. The transition from local to global is similar to what happened with the advent of silent film. Historian Diana Serra Cary describes this shift with regards to the child star phenomenon: "With the release of *The Kid* (a Charlie Chaplin-film about an orphan child who is brought up by a homeless man), the durable myth of the redemptive child was once more let loose upon the public. But this time, because the screen was larger than life and silent films were exported to and understood in every corner of the world, the phenomenon was no longer merely an American one."[5] With the Internet and digital media, the local zoo baby could potentially become an international child star.

The Appeal of Cuteness

The most important concept in the celebritization of Knut, as a cub and as a child star, was "cuteness." Both the media and zoo-goers had the clear sense that cuteness was the force behind the representation of Knut as celebrity. The concept of cuteness does not refer, however, to Knut's lived reality as a polar bear cub; instead, it is a culturally invested concept that only makes sense for the human who ascribes the trait. It could be argued that the popularity of cute animals was the very reason why the zoo bred polar bears in the first place. Yet the decision to hand-raise Knut after his mother abandoned him was made not because of cuteness, but out of a feeling of responsibility for a living creature, and perhaps because breeding polar bears would sell tickets and give the zoo a good reputation. Marianna Szczygielska in this

volume holds a similar discussion on cuteness and pandas, as she argues
that pandas are presented as "innocent cuteness ambassadors," covering
up the racialized normativity that their representations reinforce. In addition, Takashi Ito in this volume discusses the "cult of the cute," or *kawaii*,
in Japan.

The concept of *Kindchenschema* (baby schema), developed by the founder
of modern ethology, Konrad Lorenz, appeared in German media reports on
Knut soon after his first public appearance. *Der Tagesspiegel* reported on the
global interest in Knut on 26 March, quoting Berlin Zoo biologist Heiner
Klös saying that the *Kindchenschema* "opens the heart. The round head, the
large eyes – the baby-effect that makes anyone who watches an infant
glow."[6] *Stern, Die Welt*, and *Süddeutsche Zeitung* all quoted psychologist
Peter Walschburger saying that it is natural that the *Kindchenschema* played
a major part in Knut's popularity: "The little ears, button eyes, the contrast
between the black snout and the white fur, along with the soft, rounded body
always release positive emotions in humans. It awakens the protection instinct."[7] These traits point to neoteny, a term used to describe characteristics
similar to those of human babies that make human adults react with protective feelings.

While the *Kindchenschema* explains why adults react so strongly to Knut,
the media treated this point as the most surprising feature of "knutmania"
and therefore the most worthy of attention (children's interest in Knut was
considered self-explanatory). Psychologists Arnulf Baring and Gabriele Baring wrote a comment in German tabloid *BZ* mentioning their daughter, who
compared Knut to her teddy bear.[8] The girl was nineteen years old, making
her statements even more interesting: "Mom, he's just as cute as my teddy!"[9]
When asked why she thought so, she answered: "My teddy is always there.
He always comforts me. Always loves me. He always listens to me. He
warms me."[10] This girl represents youth, between child and adult, and provides an additional element that challenges the *Kindchenschema*: she does
not want to protect Knut, but wants Knut to comfort her. Knut's cuteness reminds her of her childhood, just like her teddy that she still turns to when
she needs comfort. This sentiment is also discovered through a survey conducted by Carmen Rosa Caldas-Coulthard and Theo van Leeuwen, which
became the foundation of their semiotic analysis of the teddy bear in the
United Kingdom. The adult respondents to their questionnaire all recalled

their childhood teddy bears with fondness, and many still kept them around for comfort.[11]

Historically, the teddy bear is a recent toy, invented in 1902 in the United States by Russian immigrant Morris Michton.[12] Michton owned a toyshop in New York and, inspired by the story of how President Theodore Roosevelt refused to shoot a bear while on a hunting trip, he created a stuffed bear and obtained the rights to call it Teddy. The bear's success was immediate and soon became too much for the Michtons to handle. They sold the rights to Ideal Toy Company, which began to mass produce teddy bears in 1904. Simultaneously in Germany, Margarete Steiff, paralyzed from polio but intent on making a living, was becoming known for her homemade felt toys.[13] Her nephew Richard joined her business in 1902, and created a toy bear out of mohair plush. The bear was presented at the Leipzig Toy Fair in 1903, where an American wholesaler, familiar with Michton's success, ordered three thousand. Such were the origins of the Steiff Company, soon synonymous with teddy bears in Europe and, a century later, the owner of the rights to stuffed Knut-bears. As cultural historian Michel Pastoreau points out, it seems that "the stuffed bear was in the air in the early twentieth century."[14]

Yet the teddy bear has undergone many changes in its short existence. Although popular from the start, it has evolved from "a long-nosed, long-limbed bear to a cute, snub-nosed, baby-like creature."[15] Psychologists Paul Morris, Vasu Reddy, and R. Bunting ask in their paper "The Survival of the Cutest" why this development has occurred, and hypothesize that it followed consumer preferences that speak more to adults than to children.[16] They tested three groups of children aged four, six, and eight, and found that the four-year-olds preferred teddy bears that looked adult, but the six- and eight-year-olds preferred those with baby-like features. The older children also expressed a greater desire to cuddle with the bears, while the youngest children preferred to play. All this leads to the conclusion that a change might take place between ages four and six, especially because all of these children had been exposed to baby-like teddy bears all their lives. Morris et al. conclude that "teddy bears are now better at being bought by adults, not better at being cuddled by the young children they are usually bought for."[17]

Biologist Stephen Jay Gould maps the same development in the evolution of Disney's Mickey Mouse, who over the course of fifty years evolved shorter and thicker legs, a larger head with a bulging forehead, larger eyes, and a thicker snout.[18] Historian Elizabeth Lawrence looks at the cultural implications of Mickey's neotenization and suggests that Mickey is not only popular because he is pleasing to children, but also because he allows adults an escape into childhood.[19] From a business perspective, it would make perfect sense to combine marketing towards children with marketing towards parents, as it is parents who ultimately buy toys, pick which movies to see, and decide where to go on holiday.

As I have shown, the German press explained Knut's fame as grounded in biology. Yet the biological reaction to neoteny has been increasingly emphasized in Western culture since the 1950s. Hence, Knut's fame was obviously also a cultural phenomenon, embedded in the increasing focus on youth and cuteness in contemporary Western culture.

Cute Knut, or Cursed Child Star?

The myth of the cursed child star, as it prevails in Western culture, first appeared after the public downfalls of some of the most famous Hollywood child stars of the 1920s and 1930s, a period often referred to as the child star era. During this time, child actors such as Judy Garland and Jackie Coogan were launched as miracle kids and framed as the happiest children on earth. Later, they succumbed to drug abuse and self-destruction: Writer Joal Ryan suggests that the popular cursed child star myth was cemented in 1976, when the first headline to read "child star found dead" appeared in a newspaper.[20] The use of "child star" rather than "celebrity" or "actor" indicates the increasing interest in the child star myth in popular culture. Furthermore, the myth gained currency as once-famous children were increasingly portrayed as "former child stars" in adulthood.

The cursed child star myth is relevant in two important ways. First, the media depicted Knut as a child as much as an animal. Indeed, he was an animal child, and the anticipation that he would grow into an "ugly" predator already lurked in the background of media reports during his initial celebration. At Knut's initial presentation to the public, *Guardian* journalist Kate Connolly mentioned that although cute now, he would not be cute for long.[21] Second, more generally, the relation between child star and zoo baby is in itself interesting because they are both celebrities who do not actively choose to strive for stardom, evoking the idea that they are being exploited.

This myth provided the tabloids with a narrative to describe what happened when Knut suddenly started to look less like a teddy bear and more like a polar bear. As with the initial controversy, *Der Spiegel* was the first to mention his transformation. On 30 April 2007, its English-language online version featured the headline "The End of an Era Nearing: Knut Steadily Growing Less Cute." The introduction read: "It's a tragic fact of life. Celebrity polar bear cub Knut, now almost five months old, is gradually mutating from a fluffy porridge-lapping cub into a heavy bruiser with a penchant for meat off the bone."[22] The use of the word "mutating," in addition to hyperbolic descriptions of what Knut has been and will become, indicates that this is a comment on the perceived development of the media discourse and not on the development of the actual polar bear Knut. The article further notes that "Knut's days of extreme cuteness are numbered now that he has acquired a markedly longer snout and weighs a chubby 17 kilograms (37 pounds), twice as much as when he first appeared before an adoring public five weeks ago," thus claiming neotenous features as the only desirable ones.[23] All of these descriptions allude to common notions of the awkward adolescent: weight gain, disproportionate bodily features, losing interest in playing, and pulling away from social situations. Although the article points out that visitors are still flocking to the zoo, the tone clearly foreshadows the downfall that awaits Knut when he is no longer cute.

In mid-June, premonitions such as "Polar Bear Knut More and More Dangerous" and "Cute Will Soon Be Over" started to appear in the headlines, paired with photos of Knut apparently snapping at a keeper's head during play.[24] Connolly picked up the story, reporting that "[Thomas Dörflein's] cuts and bruises are testimony to Knut's adolescent aggression."[25] In these reports, the photographic evidence presented by *Der Spiegel* of a visibly longer snout precedes images of visibly sharper teeth and a willingness to use them. One popular photograph depicts Knut and his keeper in the water. Knut faces the back of the keeper's head, mouth open as if ready to take a bite. The keeper turns away, presses his eyes shut, bares his teeth, and puts a hand on Knut's throat as if struggling to get away from the attacking bear. The familiar reference to a play-fighting pet made when Knut was a tiny cub is now "adolescent aggression." Comparing images and video clips, it seems that his behaviour at play has not changed much, yet the danger that he might injure someone is attributed not to his increasing size and strength, but to his increasing aggression.

This discrepancy between the idea of Knut as a fun playmate and the experience of his intense power in actual play correlates to what Derek Bousé in his analysis of wildlife films calls "false intimacy."[26] Bousé writes: "If it is true that we (a) interpret facial close-ups on the basis of images juxtaposed with them through editing (not to mention narration) and (b) that we project human expressions onto non-human things, including animals, then there is little to argue that facial close-ups in wildlife films cannot be used to ascribe to animals almost whatever feelings and emotions the film-maker wishes to assign them according to the requirements of the storyline at that moment."[27] Video clips and photographs of Knut were experienced within the context of the media-constructed "cute Knut" narrative. Quickly, public interest made it advantageous for the zoo to present Knut in a controlled environment dubbed "The Knut Show," which further contextualized the narrative about the playful cub and his humans. Bousé argues that a consequence of false intimacy is the circumvention of the real dangers of wild animals, a point that became apparent as images that show Knut as quite obviously a predator emerged. False intimacy is arguably also an important element in the cursed child star myth, as it explains why people become so offended when cute, talented, and compliant children develop into adolescents who assert their individuality.

The best known "evidence" of Knut's perceived deviance entered circulation in February 2008: a photograph that shows a small boy leaning towards the glass wall of Knut's enclosure with Knut jumping out of the water on the other side, teeth bared, inches from the child's head. *Berliner Morgenpost* pointed out the image's similarity to the well-known promotional poster for the movie *Jaws*, in which the jaws of an enormous shark fill most of the frame as the predator heads up towards a tiny woman.[28] However, the caption to the photo points out that the little boy seems quite unmoved by the seemingly intimidating situation. The rest of the article discusses how humans pose a much more severe threat to polar bears than polar bears do to humans. *Berliner Morgenpost* thus applied the photography as a contrast to the message conveyed in the article.

Most other newspapers presented the image as one not of a predator following its developing instincts, but of a child star finally gone bad. *Bild* asked, "Is Knut turning into a wild beast?" as if he had not always been a polar bear, and indeed to reveal that as far as the paper was concerned, he had not been.[29] *Bild* poetically describes the incident: "The boy squatted, peered down into the moat behind the window and knocked on the unbreakable glass with his tiny hand: 'Hello Knut! It's me, Adrian!' Knut appeared to have heard him. Suddenly he shot out of the water, tore his jaws open and smashed his snout against the glass. A whisper went through the crowd, zoo guests were terrified – but not Adrian. Fearless, he stayed by the glass."[30] In just a few lines, the journalist manages to depict the transition from mascot to wild beast. The first section depicts the past: the young boy innocently addresses Knut as a friend. The middle section is the transition: Knut's behaviour is depicted as violent through the use of the verbs "shot out," "tore ... open," and "smashed." The last sentence represents the new reality, rejection: the crowd's bustle is lowered to a whisper; people are terrified. Yet at the same time there is still hope, represented by little Adrian, who sits fearlessly on the other side of the glass.

BZ was less concerned with the connection to the little boy and wrote in its introduction, "With wide open jaws, our polar bear has lately taken to jumping towards the window of his enclosure. Only play, or has Knut meanwhile become dangerous?"[31] *BZ* made it clear that Knut was still "*our* polar bear," but that this status might be about to change. The question is nonsensical, as it is obvious that a one-year-old polar bear is dangerous to humans even if he is "only playing." Half of the subsequent text is dedicated to Knut's teeth, clearly emphasizing danger. Still, veterinarian André Schüle had the last say, claiming that Knut's jumping was a form of play and not an aggressive reaction to the audience.[32] Despite Schüle's attempt to correct people's perceptions, the constructed link between aggression and danger had a lasting impact, underscoring the force of the anthropomorphism that the photograph invited.

The saying "a picture is worth a thousand words" is, however, a fitting description of the photograph's global reception. The British *Daily Mail* printed the photograph along with the headline "Still Think I'm Cute? One Year on, Cuddly Knut Has Turned into a 22 [stone] Killing Machine," finding it newsworthy that the "teddy bear" actually grew into a polar bear.[33]

The contrast between "cuddly Knut" and "killing machine" indicates a move from passive to active. Where "cuddly Knut" inspires active humans snuggling a passive Knut, "killing machine" depicts an active Knut harming passive humans, automatically and indiscriminately. Knut is suddenly perceived as in control of the situation, which simultaneously indicates that he is out of control, or rather, out of human control. In the *Daily Mail*, the child in the photograph is interpreted as "startled," unlike the *Bild* article in which he is "fearless."

The farther the picture travelled, the more elaborate the narrative of Knut's deviance became. In an interview after the release of the book *On Thin Ice: The Changing World of the Polar Bear* in January 2010, the marine biologist Richard Ellis commented on the Knut phenomenon and noted, "His keepers describe him as psychotic. They had to put him behind glass because he was lunging at visitors."[34] The incident to which he refers is obviously the one depicted in the photo, but its interpretation is now completely altered. The comment "they had to put him behind glass" in particular seems strange; it is quite obvious that a polar bear in a zoo is kept behind glass, as much for the protection of the polar bear as for the protection of the visitors. In light of this fact, it seems that Ellis is playing into the myth about the fallen polar bear child star in order to tap into some of the emotions that were connected to the Knut case. That an American author used Knut in this way three years after the initial hype testifies to the prevailing global interest in him. More importantly, it gives a sense of the force of both Knut's celebrity and the child star myth through which it was interpreted.

Ellis discusses several other polar bears on display in circuses and zoos in addition to Knut. Yet when dealing with Knut, he reproduces the cursed child star myth. He quotes an ABC News piece in which an anonymous zookeeper states that Knut was acting in a psychotic manner, without any reference to how a nonpsychotic polar bear would behave. It also appears that Ellis was selective with his references; elsewhere in the article, zoo veterinarian André Schüle said that Knut was not acting deviant and was developing normally for a zoo polar bear of his age.[35]

The shift in the media from cute to dangerous was marked by a shift in authority. As Knut grew, zoo staff who had initially been described as "experts" were suddenly merely keepers and veterinarians. Animal rights activists, previously presented as villains for their critical voices, were now described as experts, and their statements not opinions but knowledge. This shift happened because their statements tapped into the cursed child star myth. Animal rights activists had continuously criticized the Knut phenomenon, but as Knut grew their statements began to match the media's narrative about "cute Knut"'s disintegration. The story of a happy polar bear's descent into madness followed a narrative structure familiar to Western media consumers because of its similarity to stories of human child stars, and anyone not particularly interested in digging into Knut's background would easily accept the story as the truth.

The Problem of Child Stars at the Zoo

Knut's inevitable descent from angel to predator was a backdrop in the media throughout the first months of hype. The reports from his first public appearance contain several mentions of how, in just one year, Knut would become too big and strong for his keeper to play with him. The zoo also said from the start that Knut would have to be moved to another zoo because of the difficulties of having two male polar bears in the same enclosure. Offspring management is a challenge for all zoos and is particularly urgent when it comes to large male predators. It is a question not just of male predators being rendered superfluous because they are no longer cute and cuddly, but of the immense problems in finding them a suitable living space because they often cannot be kept together. The problem of redundant male mammals in zoos is regularly criticized by animal rights groups. Yet in Knut's media representation, the issue was individualized, and depicted more as a standalone problem of where Knut should live than a structural problem that applies to most zoo-born male mammals.

Initially, the problem of a suitable living space existed only in the background. The mantra of Knut's early public appearances was that one day he would have to be moved somewhere else, but just look at how adorable he is now! The dissonance between the happy present and the less happy future is also found in the constant reproduction of child stars. New children are celebrated while former child stars are demonized. This tendency is also seen in the tabloids in Knut's case, as his tentative successors were presented even during the height of his fame in 2007: on 10 May, *Bild* announced a jaguar cub with the headline "The new Star in the Zoo"; on 16 June, *Bild* covered newborn pygmy hippopotamus Paul and asked, "How Much Knut Is Hidden in Paul?"; and on 8 August, BZ reported that "The Zoo Has Got a Donkey-Knut!"[36] The hottest contestant was a sun bear named Ernst, born shortly after Knut and mentioned by Connolly in her report from Knut's first public appearance as the potential next superstar. As summer reached Berlin in 2007, *Frankfurter Allgemeine Zeitung* called for the replacement of the polar bear with the sun bear.[37]

The media hype surrounding Knut also brought to light stories of previously famous polar bear cubs. An obvious parallel to Knut was Brumas, the first polar bear cub to be bred in captivity. On 25 March 1950, *Picture Post* informed its readers that Brumas was the twenty-third polar bear cub to be born at the London Zoo, but the first one to survive beyond two days: "Brumas is a milestone in Zoo history. That's why she's famous, but it isn't why she's popular."[38] The reason why she was popular was, of course, her "quintessential cuddliness."[39] Noteworthy here is the reporter's distinction between fame and popularity: Brumas was famous because she was the first polar bear cub to survive beyond infancy – an achievement for the zoo. But she was popular because she was cute – an ascribed, superficial trait that easily lured the masses. There is a sense that, while Brumas deserved fame, the audience came to see her for the wrong reason. Before its opening in 1828, the London Zoo had made a similar statement; that animals were to be brought "from every quarter of the globe and applied to some useful purpose in connection with scientific research, not merely exposed to the ignorant admiration of the individual."[40] In 1950, reporting on Brumas, the *Observer* quoted the London Zoo, and labelled the hysteria around Brumas the "ignorant admiration" of her cuteness. Fifty years later, Knut's reception paralleled the sentiment.

The tension between scientific knowledge and ignorant admiration is the fundamental contradiction upon which zoological gardens are built. Although created as institutions for science and education, they are also institutions for the display of animals. As such, they depend on visitors who come to be entertained, moved, and amused – a contradiction of which zoos became increasingly aware as the twentieth century unfolded.[41] What is constantly changing, however, are their star animals. Initially, exotic species never before seen were the zoos' main attractions. As the public became acquainted with the diversity of the world's animals, baby animals gradually started to take the spotlight. The value of being rare and "the first" has by no means disappeared, but is now connected to being the first born rather than the first displayed. In this way, the idea of "new" is also inextricably connected to cuteness.

These days, many zoos have an information board at the entrance to tell visitors where they can look for newborn offspring. This practice is connected to the problem of redundancy, as breeding is often undertaken without regard for whether or not the zoo can accommodate the offspring once they are grown.[42] Historian Elizabeth Hanson points out that the myth that only healthy and happy animals procreate has, historically, been a driver of zoo breeding, as if an abundance of offspring serves as living proof of a well-run zoo.[43] Thus, Knut fits into part of a long tradition of animal babies as crowd pleasers, which explains the recurring media reports that present new offspring as "taking over." However, Knut's popularity among his little group of local fans did not wane over time, even if his reputation as a media celebrity changed from good to bad. Knut grew up in the public eye, more like a human child star than an animal zoo baby but represented as both and doubly doomed.

Yet the most important problem with the media narrative that wrote Knut into the child star myth was that it undermined real problems caused by the focus on zoo babies. Most of the tabloid stories about Knut's fall are, upon closer scrutiny, easily dismissed as hyperbolic and silly. The superficiality of these stories not only obscured real problems that Knut was facing, but also masked the fact that he was only one example of the significant structural problem of redundancy. A massive public protest made sure that Knut was neither euthanized nor relocated, but thousands of other juvenile zoo animals were moved or killed without anyone noticing. Thus, as the media narrative depicted Knut as a child star rather than a zoo baby, it framed him as representing problems connected to show business, like being addicted to attention and exploited for financial gain, rather than problems connected to the system of zoo celebrity.

A Question of Exploitation

Accusations of exploitation are central in criticism of the production of both child stars and zoo babies. Knut was no exception, as the zoo's attendance and income spiked dramatically during his first year. The zoo established a special Knut souvenir stand, which sold a variety of Knut-related merchandise as well as general polar bear souvenirs from stuffed polar bears to key chains and pencils. The stand was brought out every summer season of Knut's life, remaining for years after the media had announced the end of his celebrity.

The Berlin Zoological Garden annual report for 2007 states that the year was "characterized by the surprisingly large and enduring worldwide interest by visitors and media in the upbringing of the polar bear baby Knut that led to an enormous media presence in the zoo and opened up new challenges and opportunities for the company."[44] There was an increase of 52 per cent in total income from the previous year. The estimated increase without the "Knut factor" was 15 per cent. The zoo also secured the copyright for Knut as a brand, and *Bild* reported in April that the zoo's value on the stock exchange had increased by 130 per cent, illustrated by a spectacular yet simplified red graph showing the first three months of 2007 with a steep ascension towards the end of March.[45] The fact that *Bild* found the report on stock exchange values relevant testifies to the perceived public interest not only in Knut as a fluffy symbol, but also in the economic value of the Knut phenomenon. As in the child star myth, the realization that someone else is making money from the star (and hence potentially exploiting them) lurked behind these optimistic reports.

The broadsheet *Süddeutsche Zeitung* brought a more sober perspective on financial gain on 27 March 2007. It quotes the zoo's then-business director Gerald Uhlich saying, "In actual fact, I am not in favor of the marketing of animals."[46] But Knut was an exception. "The demand by the visitors for merchandise is enormous," Uhlich said, claiming that Knut was "the ideal messenger for our core concerns, such as protection of species or the fight against climate change."[47] Thus, it would follow that it was sensible to use the Knut brand for all it was worth.[48] This view turned out to be Uhlich's alone: the annual report for 2007 noted that he was "released from his duties at the zoo from 31 December 2007." The *Frankfurter Rundschau* on 12 December 2007 reported that the reason for his departure was irreconcilable differences concerning marketing.[49] In an interview, the director Bernhard Blaszkiewitz said that Uhlich only cared about money and that he was glad to see him go.[50] In a 2011 documentary on animals' living conditions in German zoos, Uhlich maintained his views on Knut's marketing.[51] Interestingly, the Knut souvenir stand continued to reappear by Knut's enclosure during summer seasons even after Uhlich's departure.

The internal strife at the zoo did not generate headlines beyond Uhlich's resignation. Even though the media in large part created and maintained Knut's celebrity, this construction also entailed criticizing the zoo for exploiting Knut. On 14 April, in *die Tageszeitung*, journalist and biologist Cord Riechelmann discussed why people find the business element of the Knut case so disturbing. Building on philosopher Jean Baudrillard's analysis of how humans have become alienated from nature since the Industrial Revolution, Reichelmann argues that we now meet animals either on television, as toys, or through news reports of animal-borne diseases and the resulting mass death that reminds us of the disastrous consequences of industrialized animal production.

Knut as a celebrity bridged the gap between extremes, as he was the fluffy teddy bear who was also used for financial gain as part of a capitalist system. In fact, this very system saved him from death. Reichelmann argues that the mechanisms that arouse compassion for Knut are the very mechanisms that enable indifference to keeping animals in terrible conditions; both are made possible by the removal of animals from humans' daily lives. Reichelmann's analysis is perhaps the most sophisticated media analysis on Knut's marketing, as he places Knut's case and the reactions to it in a larger system of animal exploitation.

The bulk of the tabloid reports, however, did not echo Reichelmann's perspective, but continued to play into the all-too-pervasive child star myth. In a 30 March headline, *Bild* asked: "Who Makes a Profit on Knut?" listing several entities in addition to the zoo who, in one way or another, made money from the cub. The article concludes in capitals: "EVERYONE MAKES A PROFIT ON KNUT, JUST NOT THE LITTLE POLAR BEAR HIMSELF," emphasizing the associations to an exploited child who is not allowed to experience the benefits of the money he is making.[52] "Knut" even experienced his own share of legal strife when Neumünster Zoo, which owned Knut's father

Lars, drew attention to a clause in the lending agreement that stated it was entitled to Lars's first offspring. After a year of negotiations, the Berlin Zoo agreed in July 2009 to pay €430,000 for the sole rights to Knut – most likely the largest sum ever paid for a polar bear, yet considerably less than Neumünster's initial demand of €1.5 million.[53] The BBC reported the story as a "Custody Battle over Polar Bear Knut," emphasized that the conflict was more about money than care, and underscored the potential for profit by interviewing visitors who had come all the way from England to see Knut.[54] The angle of these media reports echoes the trials from 1930s Hollywood in which child actor Jackie Coogan sued his mother for spending his earnings. These trials resulted in what is known as the "Coogan law," which requires an employer to set aside 15 per cent of the child's earnings in a blocked trust account to prevent parents from squandering them.[55] Although one has to assume both zoos were interested in the money for improving the lives of their resident animals, there was a sense in the media reports that they were driven by greed.

Conclusion

A disturbing element of the success of popular sentiment and myth in Knut's story is the naïve relation to polar bears that it discloses. While several actors involved surely conceived of Knut as a polar bear, his media representation reveals little effort to represent him as such. Rather, Knut's behaviour is described with reference to human – not polar bear – behaviour. Words like "psychopath" and "psychosis" are employed without any discussion of what these conditions might imply for an animal in general or this polar bear in particular. There are repeated references to behavioural disorders, without a mention of what normal young zoo polar bear behaviour looks like. Thus, the anthropomorphism inherent in Knut's media representation as a fallen child star does not provide an understanding of Knut as animal, but rather actualizes cultural fears about human interference in nature. Instead of using knowledge about the biology of polar bears, the media explained Knut's development as that of a monster.

The convenient concurrence between Knut's bodily development and the child star myth firmly grounded Knut in celebrity culture – but not as polar bear. Indeed, the narrative that dictated the demise of "polar bear Knut" stands out as a desperate grappling with a body out of human control. A closer look at the media coverage shows that it was not the animal body, but its narrative construction, that was getting out of hand. Knut's story is not a tale of a psychopathic polar bear as much as it is a desperate attempt to make sense of a nonhuman animal body that started to escape its tidy human categorization. There were two generic accounts competing for the power to define Knut: on the one hand, the media-constructed child star; on the other, the zoo's insistence that he was a normal zoo polar bear. Yet under scrutiny, both narratives must be modified. In real life, he was no deviant child star. He was, though, a very special zoo animal, connecting with the audience in an unusual way because of his special upbringing. Knut's story is thus an example of how animals are individuals who constantly resist our generalizations.

The anthropomorphism that drove Knut's story is not only part of media culture, but also part of the constant production of zoo babies. Knut's media fame gave him a broader frame of reference in human culture, but he also showed how zoo animals are interpreted into a framework based on knowledge of the human species rather than the specific species in question. The tension that arises between Knut's media narrative and the generalized zoo baby is a tension between killable and not killable. In this context, his story serves to cover up a general problem rather than shed light on it. Knut's fame made him not killable, but the attention he received served to take attention away from the fates of other, less individualized zoo babies.

NOTES

1 Knut lived at the Berlin Zoo until his death at four years old, in April 2011. He died of drowning after suffering a seizure caused by a rare autoimmune disease previously found only in humans.

2 Ritvo, *The Animal Estate*.

3 Ibid., 217.

4 Molloy, "Being a Known Animal," 37.

5 Cary, *Hollywood's Children*, 60.

6 Christian van Lessen, "Animal Superstar," *Der Tagesspiegel*, 26 March 2007, http://www.tagesspiegel.de/weltspiegel/animal-superstar/827030.html.

7 "Kindchenschema: Warum macht ein Eisbär alle verrückt?," *sued-deutsche.de*, 10 April 2007, http://www.sueddeutsche.de/panorama/kindchenschema-warum-macht-ein-eisbaer-alle-verrueckt-1.663580; "Knut: Warum lieben alle Knut?," *Welt Online*, 6 April 2007, http://www.welt.de/vermischtes/article796257/Warum_lieben_alle_Knut.html; "'Knutmania': Können diese Augen lügen?," *Stern.de*, 3 April 2007, http://www.stern.de/wissen/mensch/knutmania-koennen-diese-augen-luegen-586218.html.

8 Arnulf Baring and Gabriele Baring, "Warum ein kleiner Eisbär unsere Herzen erwärmt," BZ, 24 March 2007.

9 Ibid.

10 Ibid.

11 Caldas-Coulthard and van Leeuwen, "Teddy Bear Stories," 5–27.

12 Pastoureau, *The Bear*, 248.

13 "History of Steiff Teddy Bears and Steiff Animals," accessed 10 November 2011, http://www.steiffteddybears.co.uk/more-things-steiff/history-of-steiff-bears.php.

14 Pastoureau, *The Bear*, 249.

15 Morris, Reddy, and Bunting, "The Survival of the Cutest," 1697.

16 Hinde and Barden, "The Evolution of the Teddy Bear," 1371–3.

17 Morris, Reddy, and Bunting, "The Survival of the Cutest," 1699.

18 Gould, *The Panda's Thumb*.

19 Lawrence, "In the Mick of Time," 65–72.

20 Ryan, *Former Child Star*, 58.

21 "Kate Connolly Meets Knut the Polar Bear," *Guardian*, 23 March 2007, http://www.guardian.co.uk/news/audio/2007/mar/23/0323kate.connolly.meets.knut.the.polar.bear.

22 "End of an Era Nearing: Knut Steadily Getting Less Cute," *Spiegel Online*, 30 April 2007, http://www.spiegel.de/international/zeitgeist/0,1518,480321,00.html.

23 Ibid.

24 "Bald ist schluss mit niedlich," *Altmark Zeitung*, 15 June 2007; "Eisbär Knut immer gefährlicher," *Berliner Kurier*, 15 June 2007.

25 "Kate Connolly on Knut the Polar Bear," *Guardian*, 11 July 2007, http://www.guardian.co.uk/world/2007/jul/11/germany.conservation.

26 Bousé, "False Intimacy," 123–32.

27 Ibid., 128.

28 "Knut – der weiße bär," *Berliner Morgenpost*, 23 February 2008.

29 D.-E. Jacob and C. Vejr, "Wird Knut zur wilden Bestie?," *Bild*, 23 February 2008.

30 Ibid.

31 Lea Grote, "Knut, du Großmaul," *BZ*, 23 February 2008.

32 Ibid.

33 Allan Hall, "Still Think I'm Cute? One Year on, Cuddly Knut Has Turned into a 22st Killing Machine," *Daily Mail Online*, 2 March 2008, http://www.dailymail.co.uk/news/article-524382/Still-think-Im-cute-One-year-cuddly-Knut-turned-22st-killing-machine.html.

34 "Psychotic Polar Bear, Sarah Palin Spell Arctic Doom: Interview," *Bloomberg*, 28 January 2010, http://www.bloomberg.com/apps/news?pid=206 01088&sid=aSEEa_iSCC7Y.

35 "Keeper Calls Knut the Bear a 'Psycho,'" ABC News, 26 March 2008, http://abcnews.go.com/International/story?id=4528271; Ellis, *On Thin Ice*, 253.

36 "Der neue Star im Zoo," *Bild*, 10 May 2007; Robin Hartmann, "Wie viel Knut steckt in Paul?," *Bild*, 16 June 2007; "So Süß! Zoo hat einen Esel-Knut," *BZ*, 8 August 2007.

37 "Nun is' gut, Knut: Wir machen Ernst!," *Frankfurter Allgemeine*, 13 April 2007, http://www.faz.net/aktuell/gesellschaft/nun-is-gut-knut-wir-machen-ernst-1437045.html.

38 Brian Dowling, "The Polar Bear's Child," *Picture Post*, 25 March 1950, 36–7.

39 Ibid., 37.

40 "Profile-London Zoo," *Observer*, 9 April 1950.

41 Mullan and Marvin, *Zoo Culture*.

42 There are two strategies for breeding in zoos. The first is to prevent pregnancies using contraception or keeping sexes apart. The second, called a breed-and-cull program, is to allow animals to breed freely and later cull surplus animals. The rationale behind this is that it allows the adult animals to go through the full range of their instinctual behaviour. Hosey et al. write that euthanasia is illegal in some countries, and laments that public perceptions and negative media coverage "puts pressure on zoos to avoid using this measure, despite its many associated benefits for animals." Hosey, Melfi, and Pankhurst, *Zoo Animals*, 338.

43 Hanson, *Animal Attractions*, 169.

44 "Zoo Berlin AG Jahresabschluss 2007," 1, http://www.zoo-
    berlin.de/uploads/media/Zoo_Berlin_AG_Jahresabschluss_2007.pdf.

45 "Knut tut Zoo gut: Aktienkurs 130% rauf!," *Bild*, 4 April 2007.

46 Angelika Slavik, "Kohle mit Kuschel-Knut," *Süddeutsche Zeitung*, 27
    March 2007.

47 Ibid.

48 Ibid.

49 "Zoo Berlin AG Jahresabschluss 2007," 4; "Knut entzweit Zoo-Chefs,"
    Frankfurter Rundschau, 12 December 2007.

50 Interview at the Berlin Zoo, 24 January 2012.

51 "Zoogeschichten: Was passiert wirklich mit Eisbär, Elefant & Co.?" WDR
    Fernsehen, 8 June 2011,
    http://www.wdr.de/tv/diestory/sendungsbeitraege/2011/0606/zoo.jsp.

52 Colmenares and Stenzel, "Wer Verdient an Knut?," *Bild*, 30 March 2007.

53 Kögel, "Zoo stottert Knut ab," *Der Tagesspiegel*, 9 July 2009.

54 "Custody Battle over Knut the Bear," BBC, 21 December 2008, http://news.
    bbc.co.uk/2/hi/science/nature/7794292.stm.

55 "Coogan Law, Screen Actors Guild," accessed 27 July 2012,
    http://www.sag.org/content/coogan-law.

CHAPTER NINE

PANDAS AND THE REPRODUCTION OF RACE AND HETEROSEXUALITY IN THE ZOO

Marianna Szczygielska

"Brace yourself for a little Canadian Panda-monium," states a 2012 *Toronto Sun* news report from Beijing, officially announcing the long-awaited agreement between China and Canada to lend a breeding pair of giant pandas to the Toronto and Calgary zoos.[1] The "panda pact" was the highlight of Canadian prime minister Stephen Harper's visit to China in February 2012, which resulted in trade deals totalling $3 billion, and which secured Canada's access to the Chinese market, promoted energy cooperation, and sealed eighteen years of negotiations on a foreign investment protection agreement.[2] A photo of Harper and his wife Laureen holding a panda cub during their visit to the Chongqing Zoo in Western China, where the official Giant Panda Cooperation Agreement had been signed, was one of the most publicized images of this primarily economic trip (figure 9.1). In 2013, two carefully selected adult panda bears named Er Shun and Da Mao arrived at the Toronto Zoo with a mission to reproduce for their species' survival. As part of an international agreement, the breeding pair will reside in Canada for ten years. In March 2016, a photograph of Harper's successor, Justin Trudeau, holding a pair of panda cubs in the Toronto Zoo, outshined the previous "panda publicity." The new prime minister was photographed with the first giant pandas born in Canada – a huge success of the zoo's elaborate breeding program.

In this chapter, I will focus on the giant panda exhibition in the Toronto Zoo. I will analyze the ways in which this animal display not only evokes reproductive hopes (with breeding the focal point of the pandas' residency)

Figure 9.1 Stephen and Laureen Harper with a panda cub.

and naturalizes heterosexuality as national, public, and precarious; but also racializes the nonhuman animals as powerful symbols of Canadian-Chinese friendship. Drawing on cultural theorist Mel Y. Chen's *Animacies*, I will show how the public display of institutionalized panda intimacy in the zoo is deeply entangled with the symbolic economies of race, class, and gender, as well as with international diplomacy, global capitalism, and neoliberal politics.[3] I will trace the multidirectional flows of human and nonhuman animals, capital, economic values, natural resources, and cultural meanings attached to the Giant Panda Experience Exhibition at the Toronto Zoo, which I visited in September 2014 and December 2016.

I follow Er Shun and Da Mao's journey to Canada and situate it within the historical context of human migration and trade agreements between China and Canada in order to interrogate the parallel processes of the construction of race and sexuality that transform the giant panda into a powerful naturalizing symbol. Even though the giant panda is a species on the brink of extinction and is extremely difficult to breed in captivity, it is fetishized as a symbol of wildlife protection. Given this context, the exhibition of heterosexual desire, as part of the zoo's pronatalist efforts realized through the fixation on the animals' successful reproduction, faces many difficulties that may paradoxically result in a parody of normative sexuality.

While most analyses of "panda diplomacy" focus on China's soft-power strategy realized via the international panda loan system, I shift attention towards the mechanisms at play on the Western end of this commercial and political agreement. There is a vanishing point between Chinese political gains and Canadian commercial use of pandas that becomes apparent through the structurally bound reproductive aspect of the giant panda conservation plan. I argue that, within the context of Western zoo exhibitions, pandas function not only as political ambassadors of their country of origin, but also as symbolic refugees of a racial fantasy that is critically tied to issues of gender and sexuality. While Lisa Uddin, in her analysis of the Smithsonian's National Zoological Park's panda exhibition, argues that, within the historical context of the United States, pandas epitomized a naturalized American heterosexuality, I relocate this sexual transposition onto a racial identity attached to the nonhuman animals, rather than to their audience in the place of display.[4] In other words, what is on display is a reimagined Asian American sexuality – one that is strictly controlled with modern reproductive technologies. In this sense, the sexualized aspect of the panda breeding plan constitutes the visible economy of race implied by China's nonhuman symbolic and material property. As the intersectional theorist Zakiyyah Iman Jackson suggests, race is constructed as "a structural position, as an ontology rather than an identity or sociological experience."[5] I argue that, as such, race is a highly structured power category that can function across the species boundaries and be exercised on nonhuman bodies.

While this volume's Randy Malamud casts "the zoo as a venue for symbolically playing out issues of human sexuality – straightforwardly or ironically,"[6] I suggest switching the attention from humans to the control of the nonhuman animals' sex lives and their impact on human visitors. I do so to show how these public establishments mutually produce gender, sexuality, and race through the construction of nature. Contemporary zoos no longer serve as simple collections, menageries of species frozen in their taxonomic moments, but rather as spaces of intense chronopolitics, materialized in Species Survival Plans or the Frozen Zoo™, designed to alleviate the trauma of extinction and, with the tools of modern technoscience, secure "a better future." More importantly in the case of the Toronto Zoo pandas, public interest in breeding is shaped by the reproductive imperative the zoo's regulatory regime employs, which incites curiosity about the animals' sex lives. In this sense, human reproductive hopes construct the panda as an ideal "immigrant," uninterested in reproduction. The assisted reproductive technologies not only mediate this process, but also ensure its (illusionary) control.

Panda Pact

Historically, zoos have been key sites for colonial traffic in animals. Explorers brought animals as trophies, curiosities from foreign lands, and exotic gifts from newly acquired colonies. The Australian studies scholars Nancy Cushing and Kevin Markwell note that some animals gained special cultural status because they "were generally highly prized in their homeland for their physical appearance, fierceness or rarity and were often procured as ceremonial gifts, tributes signaling submission or alliance, bribes or reparations from local rulers."[7] They point out that the crucial element of animal diplomacy is the animals' direct and exclusive association with their country of origin. Pandas are perfect examples of a distinctive charismatic megafauna that naturally occur only in portions of six isolated mountain ranges in central China, specifically in the provinces of Sichuan, Gansu, and Shanxi. In other words, pandas can become exclusively synonymous with China.

The practice of using giant pandas as tools for diplomacy has a long history in China that dates to the seventh century, when the Empress Wu Zetian sent a pair of these rare animals to the Japanese emperor. This panda diplomacy serves as a "soft" way to foster relationships with other countries.[8] Most studies claim that panda diplomacy went through at least three crucial stages, starting with the transformation of all giant pandas into legal property of the state in the 1930s when the Chinese government recognized the great public interest and enthusiasm the bears fostered in the West.[9]

Pandas played an important role in the Cold War political game, when the People's Republic of China started to give them as diplomatic gifts to strategically selected countries as part of their foreign policy plan. In 1972, China offered pandas as a diplomatic gift to a Western political power for the first time when it sent a pair (Hsing-Hsing and Ling-Ling) to the United States following Richard Nixon's visit. This marked a clear sign of warming Sino-US relations. Between 1957 and 1983, China gifted twenty-four pandas to nine nations to strengthen its geopolitical power.[10]

The second stage of panda diplomacy commenced in 1984 when China loaned two pandas to the Los Angeles Zoo for the Olympic Games. In these closing years of the Cold War, as China began to introduce market principals to the socialist state, "free" panda gifts were replaced by rent-a-panda programs. Following a capitalist lease model, the precious animals were leased for $50,000 per month to zoos in countries seen as important allies for a Chinese economy that was opening up to foreign investments.[11] Most importantly, this shift in panda diplomacy coincided with the classification of the giant panda as an endangered species by the United States Fish and Wildlife Service in 1984 and its placement on the Red List of Threatened Species by the International Union for Conservation of Nature in 1986.[12] Zoos had always cherished pandas for their rarity, but their classification as an endangered species significantly increased their value within a zoo industry focused on conservation.

China entered the third stage of panda diplomacy with the 1996 ban on the import and export of endangered species for commercial purposes under the Convention on International Trade in Endangered Species of Wild Fauna and Flora (CITES). In consultation with the government of China, CITES issued a special permission on the giant panda loans in cases that generate positive conservation benefits to the species.[13] Breeding programs are presented as the crux of giant panda conservation and stand as a major justification for their global travels.

While the giant pandas are supposed to be protected against commercial exploitation by international laws like CITES, it is clear that, at the time of writing, the Toronto Zoo hopes for a major increase in visitors and merchandise income. Chinese friendship, expressed by an agreement to host the precious panda ambassadors, is costly – Er Shun and Da Mao are on loan to

Canada for $1 million per year. This money is devoted to conservation proj-
ects in China. Additional costs include $14.5 million to build panda facilities
at the Toronto Zoo, approximately $200,000 per year to supply the pandas
with fresh bamboo, and twelve years of intense logistical preparation by the
zoo's Giant Panda Task Force.[14] According to the loan contract between
Canadian zoos and the Chinese Association of Zoological Gardens, the zoo
must also pay another $100,000 for each cub born in captivity, while China
claims property rights over the offspring of any loaned pandas.[15] The commercial character of the pandas' visit is obvious and points to the expected
revenue increase generated by greater attendance.

Panda diplomacy could be explained in terms of the classic gift-exchange
economy that ethnographer Marcel Mauss describes: "Exchanges and contracts take place in the form of presents; in theory these are voluntary, in
reality they are given and reciprocated obligatorily."[16] Several authors point
out that the Canadian panda pact prioritizes economic gains on both sides
of the agreement that reach far beyond the moral and biological values of
wildlife conservation.[17] Geographer Rosemary-Claire Collard links the panda
loan directly to Chinese access to Canadian oil.[18] Media and communication
scholar Falk Hartig also positions it as a diplomatic-commercial gesture within the framework of Canadian energetic security, recognizing the 2013 panda
loan as a shift towards Canadian-Chinese political relations and away from
dependency on American markets.[19]

There is no doubt that the return of the giant pandas to the Toronto Zoo
after a twenty-eight-year absence was a high-profile event. The last time giant
pandas were at the Toronto Zoo was in 1985, when Qing Qing and Quan
Quan visited for one hundred days. The zoo chairman Ron Barbro, inter-
viewed by the CBC's the *Journal* just hours after the pandas arrived, stated:
"To have the rarest, most loved animal in the world on exhibit in your place
for a while, it's like the art gallery having the Mona Lisa. It's a marvelous
feeling."[20] When Er Shun and Da Mao arrived in Canada on 25 March 2013,
they were welcomed at Pearson International Airport by Harper and Hu Jintao, the president of the People's Republic of China. According to the Toronto Zoo's press release, the pandas' arrival drew more media attention than
the queen's visit.[21] Ontario's minister of tourism, culture and sport, Michael
Chan, commented: "People from the West are gifted a treasure from the East,

creating a lasting legacy."[22] But what makes giant pandas so effective in me-
diating such powerful international relations?

From Cuteness Combat to Subtle Racialization

Among other national animals such as the mythological Chinese dragon, the
red-crowned crane, or the Imperial guardian lions, pandas hold a special
place thanks to their unique diplomatic value. As a cultural icon, these cuddly, clumsy bears are primed to serve as goodwill ambassadors of friendship
and peace – their cute appearance evokes empathy, they are given "cute
names" (for example, Er Shun translates into "double smoothness"),[23] and
they are "vegetarians." Moreover, with their upright posture and "panda
thumb"– an elongation of the wrist bone that enables them to grasp bamboo
– they are easy to anthropomorphize. In their book *Men and Pandas*, Ramona and Desmond Morris, popular human sociobiology writers, point to
other similarities between the bears and humans, like a flat face, small tail,
and even lack of visible sexual organs, as characteristics that prime them to
be innocent cuteness ambassadors.[24] Those characteristics of pandas can also
be described as neotenous due to their juvenile-like appearance (a topic that
Guro Flinterud in this volume discusses in regards to Knut, a famous zoo
polar bear).

The Toronto Zoo capitalizes on these unique traits to boost public attention for the giant pandas' new exhibition. From highly visible media
events, such as the Inaugural Black and White Gala Fundraiser, the VIP
panda exhibition opening, or the ceremonial planting of a maple and bamboo tree (botanical symbols of friendship between the two nations), to the
celebration of panda birthdays, the launch of the Giant Panda Awards, and
the distribution of videos from panda cams, these bears are fetishized as
living mascots of the Chinese-Canadian friendship. Cuteness serves as a common denominator for these publicity events. At the announcement of the
Moon Festival Gala, held as part of the celebration of the Toronto Zoo's
fortieth anniversary, Mr Fang Li, consul general of the People's Republic
of China in Toronto, said: "The pandas have brought the people of China
and the people of Canada together again. We continue the celebration of

close cultural ties between the two countries symbolized in the pandas."[25] "Cuteness combat" (as one of the headlines on the zoo's website framed the marketing-generated competition between views of Er Shun and Da Mao's webcams) ensues in the name of international friendship based on economic revenues and wildlife conservation efforts to save a species so lethargic in reproducing itself, with or without human intervention.

While the economic significance of the panda loan system transformed these bears into "animal capital,"[26] they acquired another layer of meaning when assembled as cultural and political trademarks of China – namely, as subtle references to racial citizenship. Consider, for example, a 1972 illustration of Smokey the Bear, the symbol of American forest fire prevention between the 1950s and 1970s, and his family welcoming Hsing-Hsing and Ling-Ling to the National Zoo in Washington, DC (figure 9.2).[27] Wearing his iconic US National Park Service campaign hat, Smokey and his anthropomorphized family represent the American public welcoming the two Asian newcomers. In the illustration, Smokey's wife holds a bamboo cake with frosting that reads, "Welcome neighbor." Both her attire – an apron and scarf patterned with the slogan "prevent forest fires"– and the recipe for the bamboo delicacy tucked under her arm suggest that, like her husband, she is an icon: one of postwar women's domesticity. In contrast to this American bear family, the two almost-identical pandas who approach with their suitcases, covered with air travel stamps, show few gender-specific characteristics. This trope of uniformity ties together two levels of this animal metaphor: it draws on the species-specific low sexual dimorphism of the giant pandas, and it racializes them by implying the "all Asians look alike" stereotype.

The depiction of this fictional meeting of two "bear cultures" bears some significant material traits. On the one hand, the characters in this illustration each have living equivalents. The original Smokey was an American black bear who was rescued from a wildfire in Lincoln National Forest as a cub and who later resided in the National Zoo from 1950 to 1976. In 1962 another orphaned bear joined him – a female named Goldie. The two never mated, but they had an "adopted" son.[28] The real Hsing-Hsing and Ling-Ling were officially presented to the Smithsonian's National Zoological Park on 20 April 1972.[29] On the other hand, this comical and seemingly innocent anthropomorphization of two iconic species of the same family (*Ursidae*) is a clear reference to racial citizenship. While Smokey and his family are pre-

Figure 9.2 Illustration of Smokey Bear and family welcoming the pandas to the National Zoo, 1972.

sented as almost stereotypically American, Hsing-Hsing and Ling-Ling are supposed to represent their Chinese neighbours.

This racialization of the pandas rests upon a long tradition of making them synonymous with their country of origin. The complex blend of the pandas' role in the global politics of nature conservation, the focus on their reproduction (partially induced by the international animal trade laws designed to restrict their commercial use), and their unique status as one of

China's key cultural icons make these nonhumans into rich material-semiotic (and context-specific) referents to national belonging, and specifically to the category of race. The human idea of race can be articulated through non-human animality.[30] Particularly those traits that make the giant pandas anthropomorphizable also usher those nonhumans into a kind of "panda orientalism." The media scholar Cynthia Chris, in her analysis of wildlife documentaries about pandas, notes that the representations of pandas "are infused with a kind of textbook Orientalism, always mediated through exoticizing and controlling gazes."[31] Stemming from that, I ask: What exactly is the relationship between zoo exhibition, colonialism, and the production of race?

Sojourner Pandas

The coercive power of the zoo exhibition creates a controlled environment for producing desired cultural meanings and, in the case of Er Shun and Da Mao, frames panda bodies as desired migrants whose reproduction is technologically controlled under the watchful eyes of scientists and of the general public. In this section, I show how, in the context of migration from China to Canada, pandas became a material-symbolic expression of diasporic citizenship. To trace this traffic in meanings, which mirrors the colonial animalization of migrant bodies, I turn to late-nineteenth- and early-twentieth-century racial relations in Canada, when the pioneer industrial economy depended firmly on foreign labour, yet the building of strong national belonging subsequently excluded Chinese migrants from the ideal of the white Canadian nation.

To complete my depiction of racial signification in animal symbolism, I first arrange a meeting of two species that serve as strong national symbols in the context of the Canadian panda loan, and juxtapose the panda as China's animal trademark and national treasure with Canada's deployment of the beaver as a figurative brand of organic national identity. In *Animal Capital*, cultural theorist Nicole Shukin traces the fetishistic use of the beaver as a seemingly "innocent" symbol of national identity to the modernist project of building Canadian national unity in a colonial setting, which exploits an organic/animal metaphor to construct and naturalize the indigenous authenticity of a settler nation. For her, the Canadian beaver's symbolism is also reminiscent of the colonialism that travels from the material/bodily currency of the fur trade to the literal kind of capital minted on coins.[32] Shukin locates animal capital mobilized with the beaver within the dominantly white Euro-Canadian discourse of national culture, demystifying the apparent racial, ethnic, linguistic, gender neutrality, and universality of this animal symbolism.

My interpretation of the Giant Panda Experience Exhibition in the Toronto Zoo considers the symbolic labour in making pandas synonymous with China (as well as with its political and economic interests) and, therefore, recognizes the crosscutting discourses of race, sexuality, gender, and class that pervade this animal fetish. In order to unpack the many layers of signification and racial references projected onto the panda exhibition in Toronto, I analyze the intimate interweaving of animality and racialization in the figure of "John Chinaman," prominent in late-nineteenth- and early-twentieth-century Canada. As much as the beaver naturalizes and legitimates white settler colonialism, the panda builds another narrative of harmonious multiculturalism, where the history of Canadian Sinophobia is being conveniently unremembered.

John Chinaman was a common representation of Chinese immigrants in the nineteenth and twentieth centuries in North America. Among many other derogatory names, the menacing John Chinaman was a cluster of racial stereotypes derived both from superficial knowledge about China (based on the accounts of travellers, diplomats, and missionaries) and from home-grown anti-immigrant sentiments.[33] The first accounts of Chinese migration to Canada date back to the late eighteenth century. Early Chinese migrants concentrated mostly in the Pacific Northwest, with the largest settlements in Victoria and Vancouver. This migration was predominantly work related. In British Columbia, contractors needed a cheap workforce to realize the grand dream of uniting the Canadian provinces and eagerly hired Chinese labourers to construct the Canadian Pacific Railway. According to John Gray, who was appointed in 1884 to report on the "the social and moral objections taken to the influx of the Chinese people into Canada," out of 9,870 adult male Chinese migrants, about 7,200 were engaged in railroad construction, mining, farming, and canning throughout the province.[34]

Most of the anxieties mobilized against the Chinese newcomers in British Columbia were based upon the apparent danger to the economic status of

white workmen. While the public works' contractors praised Chinese labourers' efficiency, steadiness, and aptitude for hard work by accepting lower
wages and enduring arduous working conditions, Asian workers were believed to pose a threat to their white competitors. In a statement from the
Knights of Labor from 1884, Chinese migrants were blamed for taking white
men's places in the labour market:

> They are simply parasites preying upon our resources, and draining the
> country of the natural wealth which should go to enrich it, and serve
> to still further develop it, but which all goes to their native land, from
> whence comes their chief supplies of food and clothing, and to which
> they invariably return dead or alive. They have no ties to bind them to
> this land; for they come without wives or families, and rarely make per-
> manent investments ... They live, generally, in wretched hovels, dark,
> ill-ventilated, filthy, and unwholesome, and crowded together in such
> numbers as utterly preclude all ideas of comfort, morality, or even de-
> cency, while from the total absence of all sanitary arrangements, their
> quarters are an abomination to the eyes and nostrils and a constant
> source of dander to the health and life of the community.[35]

The stick figure of John Chinaman appears here as an amalgam of racist
stereotypes, most of which stem from economic exploitation of Chinese
workers, who white entrepreneurs treated as an unending reservoir of un-
skilled, cheap labour. In the heart of a rapidly industrializing Canadian economy, Chinese labourers constituted a surplus population that could not enjoy
the political and economic privileges already limited for white workers, and
thus reveal the deeply classist and racist character of the nation-forming
processes of early capitalism.

In the eyes of many white British Columbians, the hostile image of John
Chinaman was a serious threat to public physical and moral health, spilling
out of the overcrowded quarters in Chinatowns from the fumes of opium
smoke, and lurking in the darkness of gambling dens. The key feature of the
Chinese migrant was his apparent unassimilability – an obstacle to the project of making a homogeneous Canadian society. The crude comparison to
parasites shows that, for the host community, the Chinese were undesirables
and their undesirability was strikingly represented through depicting them

as nonhuman. In *White Canada Forever*, historian W. Peter Ward argues that the stereotype of the "unassimilable Asian" was the most prominent racial characteristic in the West Coast imagination.[36]

Ward notes that the Chinese immigrants' social backgrounds played an important role in the way they were perceived by the white population in British Columbia.[37] Migration driven by economic motives brought men of working age who were not invested in the place of their work but were committed to supporting their families back in China. This specific gender composition of the migrant population fuelled many anti-Chinese sentiments concerned with racial hygiene and mysterious sexualities. According to historian Margot Canaday, during the Progressive Era, "the association between racial difference and sexual deviance was first and most clearly articulated in the case of Chinese migrants."[38] Moral depravity was believed to spread from the "improper" intimacies of male homosocial spaces and from the unruly bodies of the few Chinese women in the community who were commonly classified as sex workers by whites. An excerpt from the *Royal Report on Chinese Migration* states: "It is said these women bring with them a most virulent form of syphilis, and that in a special way they corrupt little boys."[39]

Racial hygiene was thus closely tied to the preoccupation with sexual and personal hygiene. The white Canadian public was terrified by the vision of epidemics spreading from lascivious Chinatowns. In those racist fantasies, dangerous diseases mutated into new, unrealistic forms, including a conviction that all Chinese are inherently leprous to "a certain disease introduced by them called the China-pox, distinguished from other syphilis by that name."[40] Many of those racist convictions were contradictory: on the one hand, Asian migrants were accused of not establishing any "healthy" ties in Canada, while on the other hand, their sexuality was constructed as inherently contaminated, contagious, and dangerous for the Canadian society.

Anti-immigrant sentiments are usually deeply concerned with controlling the reproductive capacities of "alien" populations. The fear of the "Yellow Peril" is an equivalent of this common xenophobic trope, but it took a different turn in Canadian settler colonialism. The source of overpopulation was not recognized as unregulated sexual reproduction, but rather as the untamed influx of new migrants from China, who "would over-run the land like grasshoppers."[41] After many attempts to legally halt this migration, the

Chinese Exclusion Act (1923) imposed an almost-complete prohibition of Chinese settlement in Canada. This racist act was repealed only in 1947. In 2006, Harper issued an official apology and offered compensation for an exclusion that was "inconsistent with the values that Canadians hold today."[42] What values became crucial for Canadian national identity at the end of the twentieth century?

With the Canadian Charter of Rights and Freedom (1982) and Canadian Multiculturalism Act (1985), multiculturalism has become an official state policy. With the investment in multiculturalism and a knowledge-based economy, the rhetoric around Chinese migrants in Canada switched from "drain to the economy" to "brain gain."[43] Chinese Canadians make up the second-largest visible minority in Canada.[44] Sociologist Peter Li asserts that "ironically, the much-celebrated multiculturalism policy of Canada that came into effect in 1971 has promoted only a superficial appreciation of minority cultures ... The result is that minority culture and arts tend to be appreciated in Canadian society less for their artistic merits than for the exotic contrast they represent to Western aesthetic traditions."[45] The Giant Panda Experience Exhibition aligns well with this critical account of the "multikulti" fascination with Oriental aesthetics, where the nonhuman animals' physical presence serves as an excuse for a spectacle of cultural appropriation.

With the ubiquitous bamboo patterns, red accents, and titles in hànzì (Chinese script), the Toronto Zoo's panda exhibition design follows a common zoo practice of envisioning animals in the human cultural context of their place of origin. The official press release from the launch of the interpretative center states: "The clean white lines of the tent's interior space have been punctuated with vibrant red accents which celebrate Chinese culture and traditions, while bold black and white structures play off the Panda's iconic appearance."[46] Vast spaces, moderate minimalism, and sanitized wilderness bring the defining features of Canadian landscape (its vastness, harshness, and wildness) into the exhibition of an exotic species and affirm the modernist approach to the exhibition design.

In his essay on the modernist architecture introduced in the London Zoo in the 1930s, geographer Pyrs Gruffudd shows how architecture used the close interweaving of human and nonhuman spaces and turned the zoo into an experiment in social engineering. According to him, in modernist zoo architecture "the cultivation of the perfect animal body in the enclosures stood not so much as a metaphor *for,* as an experiment *in,* the cultivation of the perfect human body."[47] Just as in Gruffudd's example where "penguinness" is produced through theatrical enclosure design,[48] the Giant Panda Experience Exhibition, with its hygienically controlled environment and minimalistic design, produces black and white bears as exotic ambassadors of wildlife protection, as an iconic endangered species, and, most importantly, as thoroughly recuperated Asian modern migrants. The cult of perfect panda reproductive bodies, enacted through the exhibition, turns pandas into desirable migrants.

Taking into account sociologist and ecocriticist Catriona Sandilands's argument about the nineteenth-century North American investment in urban nature spaces (such as parks, botanical gardens, and zoos) as a form of retreat from the "corrupting filth" of industrializing cities,[49] the contrast between the insistence on purity in the Toronto Zoo's panda exhibit and the racist construction of Chinatowns as an unclean source of disease can be read as a reparatory measure that introduces still racialized, gendered, and classed ideals of moral purity. Arguably, this kind of selective intervention into the fragile tissue of national memory is part of the official state multiculturalism. The zoo exhibit does the work of erasing the worst parts of the national history of migrants and instead celebrates Chinese culture through stereotypical aesthetics and animal symbolism.

My comparison between pandas and migrants is not an easy one to make, especially given the politically charged history of the animalizing language and imagery in North American anti-Orientalist discourses. As Chen describes, "animality 'sticks' indelibly to specific races,"[50] and Asian bodies have indeed been marked by racialized animality deeply concerned with aspects of gender and sexuality – from the feline emasculation of Fu Manchu[51] to the hypersexual "dragon lady." The mysterious Asian sexuality often bears traces of "primitive animality," and the mystery itself is part of the allure for Westerners.[52] In the nineteenth- and twentieth-century backlash against Chinese migration, the animalistic figurations of race took the form of an unstoppable wave of uniform, alien-like organisms. The issue of reproduction is therefore critically linked to modes of production. Along the lines of the old adage "all Orientals look alike," the Yellow Peril was envisioned either as a plague that threatened Canadian resources (grasshoppers) or as a parasite that drained the economic vitality of the healthy national body. The biggest sin in the settler-colonial logic was to refuse assimilation. Therefore, the sojourner condition of Chinese labourers was one of the most prominent reasons for the white citizenry's anti-Asian sentiments.

For example, this passage from the *Royal Report on Chinese Migration* illustrates how an anti-immigrant rant employed an animalizing racist discourse: "Just as one of the lower animals will go and remain where he is fed, so the Chinaman will go and stay for a certain time in any place where he is paid a certain wage, admittedly not high."[53] In this sentence, racial difference is coded through species hierarchy and an implied subordination of the "lower animals," one modelled on domestication. The latter presupposes another hierarchy, in which the "higher" animals and races rule over the domesticated and docile species. In this sense, the giant panda is yet again positioned as an ambiguous creature that needs to be partly domesticated to facilitate species conservation through reproduction in the zoo, while at the same time remaining wild for the purpose of this very conservation mission.

Another example strikes me as an important point of reference to a figuration of the giant pandas as sojourners of zoos around the world. In 1885, Arthur Bunster, an MP from British Columbia, reports to the royal commissioner: "I have been informed by Chinamen themselves that they give bonds, before leaving China, to Chinese companies, to work for them for a term of from five to ten years, and all that the Company have to do in order to carry out their part of the contract, is to furnish them with the bare necessities of life and their clothing, and the company have all their earnings."[54] The similarities between the Chinese migrants' five- to ten-year work contracts and the pandas' ten-year loan to Western zoos (divided between the Toronto and Calgary zoos, five years each) might be just a coincidence, but it restages both the route and time spent in Canada by Chinese migrant workers in the nineteenth and twentieth centuries. It links human and non-human bodies across history in another figuration of racialized animality. Er Shun and Da Mao are just temporary guests in Canada. They are not supposed to create any strong bonds there, except for sexual and reproductive ones between each other – their "work contract" requires them to reproduce successfully. They are made into another type of sojourner: an exotic, portentously welcomed precious resource whose political significance extends beyond the task of zoo entertainment and into diplomatic relations and international trade agreements.

Thus, the Toronto Zoo becomes a site of restaging Canadian and Chinese relations according to the rules and values of official state multiculturalism, which, on the one hand, embraces the Oriental exoticism of the zoo-goers, but, on the other, conveniently forgets the persistent exclusion and violence against Chinese migrants at the historical birth of national unity. If for Shukin "under the universal alibi of species life, proverbially innocent of political designs, the Canadian beaver subtly counter-indicates the relinquishment of white English cultural and economic privilege pronounced by official state multiculturalism,"[55] then the Chinese pandas visiting the Toronto Zoo can be read as racialized figures of ideal migrants, new sojourners in the context of the new direction of Canadian multicultural politics towards embracing the rapidly industrializing Chinese economy. This change comes at a time when Chinese Canadians are cast as a model minority, and migrants' unassimilability is no longer an obstacle for flexible capitalism, benefiting from any unfixed surplus labour in the global North.

Untangling Reproductive Desires

From the abundance of panda-themed imagery that visitors encounter on their way to the Toronto Zoo, one could conclude that this species reproduces quite well – at least through its mass merchandise representations. Panda faces peek out from subway ads and street signs that lead to the zoo. From the entrance, it is obvious that the Giant Panda Experience Exhibition is (in 2016) the zoo's main attraction. However, the thrilling moment of meeting those furry celebrities is suspended until the zoo-goers travel through the Panda Gate that leads to the interactive Panda Interpretative Centre. Geared with the latest multimedia technology, this labyrinth of panda-related facts amplifies the well-known narrative of bizarre gentle creatures under the threat of extinction. This educational facility is what this volume's Nigel Rothfels describes as an immersion exhibit: "a place where both the animal, and increasingly, its human observer appear to be 'immersed' in a natural environment."[56] Carolyn Smiths, the exhibit's senior designer, notes: "Within the Centre, visitors will be immersed in everything they need to know about this iconic, fascinating and endangered animal. Our combined aspiration is that the experience will inspire visitors to join in the conservation and efforts currently underway to help protect this and other endangered species."[57] Of course, the "naturalness" of this display is a convention, and the bamboo forest in which the viewer is supposed to be immersed is a two-dimensional wallpaper print.

Just after leaving the two-dimensional forest, visitors are invited to join the panda "mating game" (figure 9.3). This part of the exhibit builds upon another unique trait of the giant pandas – their extremely low fecundity. The information board game explains that, in the wild, pandas are solitary, yet in captivity scientists must match healthy, genetically suitable breeding partners. In this game, visitors are asked to find the "right" match for a female panda by rotating a die with four "candidates" and choosing one according to a list of the future mate's desired qualities, including sexual maturity and genetic relatedness. There is only one correct answer, marked with a heart symbol, that appears between the two "suitable" panda "lovers." The mating game is meant to educate the public about a process that actually occurs in Chinese panda breeding centres and zoos, where genetically suitable breeding pairs are preselected for each loan contract. The Toronto Zoo website states that "Er Shun and Da Mao were chosen to come to Canada because they are a good genetic match for breeding,"[58] but as I demonstrate shortly, not everything went smoothly with selecting the breeding partners.

The reason that these breeding puzzles allow the audience to choose between several males for only one female is because female pandas are monoestrous, which means that they have only one reproductive cycle per year, in which they are receptive to males for twenty-four to seventy-two hours. In the case of pandas, the reproductive window is well-represented by the "Moon Gate"– a detail of zoo architecture described by Uddin in her analysis of Ling-Ling's and Hsing-Hsing's outdoor enclosure at the National Zoo. The Moon Gate is a circular walkway or window in the garden wall typical of traditional Chinese garden architecture and usually employed by the rich upper class.[59] In the zoological garden, a simplistic ornamental window that mimics this style allowed for brief, intimate encounters between the otherwise separated female and male pandas, inscribing the idea of narrow breeding opportunity and short reproductive cycle into the zoo landscape design. Uddin notes that "the moon gate was a key prop for panda courtship, converting a delicate flavor of wildness into what exhibit architect Avery Faulkner called 'Chinese flavor.'"[60] Recreating the wild conditions for these solitary

Figure 9.3 "The Mating Game" at the Giant Panda Experience Exhibition, Toronto Zoo.

mountainous bears motivated the separation of the pandas. In this sense, the gate's function in the zoo was threefold: it was an ornamental referent to the pandas' "country of origin"; as part of the design that divided the space into "female" and "male," it allowed zoo-goers to better identify (and gender) the pandas; and it was supposed to induce the animals' courtship behaviour in captivity. Through this cultural-natural knot, the zoo exhibit becomes a space for staging national identity, gender binary, and reproductive sexuality, with the last aspect clearly highlighted at the Toronto Zoo.

The next part of the exhibit introduces the people "behind the scenes" who work with the pandas during their five-year residency. Among the experts who take care of Er Shun and Da Mao is a reproductive physiologist whose role is to "help make a baby panda." The information board titled "High-Tech Help for Pandas" features reproductive equipment used in the Toronto Zoo to realize this dream: a spectrometer to analyze hormone levels from female panda's urine, a liquid nitrogen storage container for frozen sperm samples, an insemination catcher, a microscope, an incubator, and an ultrasound machine. This modern reproductive technology is presented as the "magic bullet" that will help to realize reproductive hopes and, at the same time, interpellates the zoo as a procreative space.[61] It is noteworthy as well that this reproductive equipment collection might seem familiar to some zoo-goers because the items are the exact same ones used in human assisted reproduction. An image of a newborn panda cub in an incubator, a machine that is equally capable of holding a human baby, contributes to the pandas' anthropomorphization. The transgression between human and nonhuman reproduction is, in this sense, technologically mediated, and produces a shared space in the human-nonhuman kinship structures.

The zoo monitored Er Shun's hormone levels every day from mid-March until the end of May to establish precisely when she entered the "magical" window of estrus. The Toronto Zoo's chairman Joe Torzsok ensured: "The zoo will try its best to make that time as romantic as we can in panda terms."[62] The technologies of artificial insemination embody this "zoo romanticism." Yet not everything can be under strict surveillance in this conservation mission. And indeed, not everything went smoothly. In 2012, a giant surprise nearly thwarted the carefully designed breeding plan. Originally, Er Shun was supposed to be sent to Canada with Ji Li, another female panda. However, a genetic examination conducted at the Sichuan University and the Genetics Institute of the Chinese Academy of Sciences revealed that Er Shun was actually a female. To correct this situation, Da Mao, a male panda, replaced Ji Li in her diplomatic mission. This kind of sex misassignment is common because giant pandas are not sexually dimorphic, so it is extremely difficult to determine their sex without genetic testing from blood samples. Their external genitalia appear very similar regardless of sex. In pop-science literature, much attention is paid to the male panda's penis size, visible only during intercourse and under three inches long, which according to Morris and Morris is "ridiculously short for so large an animal."[63]

This preoccupation with the "unseen/absent" panda penis is in sync with the reproductive "failure" the species endures – sexual performance is, commonsensically, believed to depend on the sexual organs' anatomy, and humans seem to pay extra attention to the size of male genitalia. Taking into account the significance of Freudian psychoanalysis in Western culture, sexual organs are critically tied to social schemes of gender, sexuality, and race, especially through their reproductive function. If we agree that captive giant

pandas persistently serve as figurations of racialized animality, the representation of the male panda's vanishing penis also aligns with "the missing Asian
male phallus,"[64] which Chen refers to when talking about queer animality
and the materiality of the Asian body in the North American context.[65] This
point of uneasy collapse between representations of human and nonhuman
sexual embodiment is especially important given the focus on masculinity in
the construction of Asian Canadian identity as a result of the predominantly
male migration from China to Canada in the nineteenth century.[66] It also critically links gender, sexuality, race, and class.

The difficulty in sexing pandas without medical intervention was one of
many obstacles in realizing the captive reproduction mission. However, the
Toronto Zoo still insisted on reproducing a clear-cut gender difference between two almost identical bears. After leaving the Giant Panda Experience
tent, and just before seeing the two main stars of the exhibition, an outdoor
banner instructed the visitors how to tell them apart: "Da Mao (the male) is
a little bigger and has a wider face than Er Shun (the female)." The banner
describes the male against the female in terms of her lack – an unspoken rule
of zoo information plaques that tend to describe the males as bigger, more
colorful, and stronger than the females in various species, ignoring even the
lack of gender dimorphism. The personalized information banners about
each panda leave no doubt about the artificial character of sexual difference
imposed on nonhuman animals from a human naturalizing perspective: Er
Shun's character traits include being "docile, lively and affectionate towards
the zookeepers," while Da Mao is described as "lively, tender and quite a
gentleman." This gender differentiation is a necessary element of building a
credible story of a heterosexual romance between two nonhuman animals
so similar in appearance and behaviour that their sex can be only determined
in the laboratory.

Conclusion

After attempts to mate the two pandas proved unsuccessful, Er Shun was ar-
tificially inseminated with the sperm, sent from Chengdu, of two additional
panda males. In October 2015, the Toronto Zoo proudly announced the
birth of two giant panda cubs – the first born in Canada. The labour took

place between 3:31 and 3:44 a.m., but anyone could watch it online thanks to a camera installed in the maternity holding area of the Giant Panda House. The video shows Er Shun from above as she grips the cage bars and gives birth to the long-awaited twins. The surveillance-type camera zooms in and out, trying to follow the tiny pink newborn cubs while the milliseconds flicker in the frame of this panda family video.

According to Chen, "animals serve as objects of almost fetishistic recuperation, recruited as signifiers of 'nature,' or 'the real,' and used to stand in for a sometimes conflicting array of other cultural meanings (including fear, discipline, sexuality, purity, wisdom, and so on)."[67] However conflicting and complicated the cultural meanings activated in the case of giant pandas might seem, as "token Asians" they are employed to recuperate the terms and conditions of the Chinese presence in Canada and to ensure a steady flow of economic goods between the superpowers in the future. The public rituals mobilized around this visit confirm the high stakes of this animal spectacle.

Consider the giant panda cubs' naming ceremony in the Toronto Zoo held on 7 March 2016, almost a year after they were born. Important politicians, including Trudeau and Chinese Ambassador to Canada Lou Zhaohui, joined the ceremony.[68] A viral picture of the newly elected prime minister holding the twins captures this event. After official speeches, all honourable guests gathered in front of the cameras with two boards hiding the cubs' names. Those gendered pink and blue boards materialize the stakes of this breeding success and reveal more than just the names of the new zoo celebrities written in both Latin and hànzì. The name-reveal ceremony followed a public vote, and the chosen names were Jia Pampan for the male, which translates into "Canadian Hope," and Jia Yueyue for the female, which translates into "Canadian Joy." These baby pandas born in the Toronto Zoo with their hybrid names, which still suggest Canadian ownership, are the embodiment of diasporic citizenship. The haunting spectre of the past comes with another image of the officials holding a frame with panda paw-prints – a reminiscence of the border regime.

In this chapter, I grapple with neocolonial tropes interwoven into contemporary nature conservation discourses and practices, with a focus on the intertwined routes that the categories of race, gender, sexuality, and class take in travelling through such varied spatio-temporal realities as zoological exhibitions, the history of migration, nation-building narratives, and environmental politics. In my analysis, the giant pandas in the Toronto Zoo form an important figuration of American Asian identity in the context of the Canadian employment of multiculturalism as a policy to regulate and manage diversity. This "humanistic" multiculturalism is designed to sustain national unity by taming differences and neatly classifying them in an archive, a museum, or a zoo. The spectacle of pandas as "ambassadors" of China in Canada eminently links the Giant Panda Experience Exhibition at the Toronto Zoo to the history of human migration from China to Canada. Er Shun, Da Mao, and their offspring become highly medial symbols not only of Canadian-Chinese, oil-fuelled friendship, but also of a furry embodiment of a specific kind of diasporic citizenship, haunting the multicultural harmony with its settler-colonial past. Yet the pandas themselves are not as innocent as they might seem. Even though the zoo as a regulatory space attempts to consolidate and naturalize the ideals of sexual difference and heterosexual reproduction by writing the script of the panda love story, the non-compliant, non-dimorphic, under-reproductive panda bodies are a perfect example of queer distortion to the normative idea of an always re/generative nature.

NOTES

1 David Akin and National Bureau Chief, "Harper Brings Home Pandas from China," *Toronto Sun*, 9 February 2012, http://www.torontosun.com/2012/02/09/harper-brings-home-pandas-from-china.

2 "Harper's China Visit Ends with Panda Pact," CBC, 11 February 2012, http://www.cbc.ca/1.1144815.

3 Chen, *Animacies*.

4 Uddin, "Panda Gardens and Public Sex at the National Zoological Park."

5 Jackson, "Waking Nightmares," 358.

6 Malamud, "Zoo Spectatorship," 226–7.

7 Cushing and Markwell, "Platypus Diplomacy," 256.

8 Wen-Cheng, "China's Panda Diplomacy" (Taipei: Taiwan Mainland Affairs Council, 2009).

9 Cushing and Markwell, "Platypus Diplomacy," 256.

10 Schaller, *The Last Panda*.

11 Ibid.

12 Imbriaco, *The Giant Panda*.

13 "Notification to the Parties no. 932 CONCERNING: Loans of Giant Pandas," CITES, Geneva, 4 September 1996.

14 Hartig, "Panda Diplomacy."

15 Althia Raj, "What If Something Happened to These National Treasures?," *Huffington Post*, 27 March 2013, http://www.huffingtonpost.ca/2013/03/27/chinese-giant-pandas-canada_n_2961614.html.

16 Mauss, *The Gift*, 3.

17 Buckingham, Neil, David, and Jepson, "Diplomats and Refugees," 265.

18 Collard, "Panda Politics," 230.

19 Hartig, "Panda Diplomacy," 70–1.

20 Geoff Nixon, "Do You Remember the Pandas? The 1985 Toronto Visit," CBC *News*, 22 March 2013, http://www.cbc.ca/news/canada/toronto/do-you-remember-the-pandas-the-1985-toronto-visit-1.1337844.

21 "Toronto Zoo Giant Panda Retrospective 2013–2014," Toronto Zoo, 25 March 2014, http://www.torontozoo.com/Pandas/First-Year-Giant-Panda-Retrospective.pdf?b.

22 Ryan Wolstat, "Giant Pandas Settling in at Toronto Zoo," *Toronto Sun*, 16 May 2013, http://www.torontosun.com/2013/05/16/panda-preview-at-the-toronto-zoo.

23 In 1999, the San Diego Zoo celebrated the birth of the first panda born in the United States to survive to adulthood. The cub was named Hua Mei, which means "China-USA," and symbolizes friendship between two nations whose political relations had been tense.

24 Morris and Morris, *Men and Pandas*, 197–202.

25 "Moon Festival Gala in Support of Giant Panda Conservation Fund," *www.GiantPandaZoo.com*, 21 July 2014, http://www.giantpandazoo.com/panda/news/consul-general-of-china-and-toronto-zoo-board-of-management-to-co-host-moon-festival-gala-in-support-of-giant-panda-conservation-fund.

26 Shukin, *Animal Capital*.

27 Lisa Uddin briefly describes the same watercolour painting in her book analyzing the modern American zoos in the context of 1960s and 1970s urban renewal as testing grounds for homegrown white fears about the city. See her *Zoo Renewal*.

28 Alex Hawes, "Smokey Comes to Washington," *Smithsonian Zoogoer*, December 2002, https://web.archive.org/web/20090223211929/http://nationalzoo.si.edu/Publications/ZooGoer/2002/6/smokey.cfm.

29 Jennifer Wright, "Panda-monium!," *Smithsonian Institution Archives,* 16 April 2012, http://siarchives.si.edu/blog/panda-monium.

30 Haraway, *Primate Visions,* 11.

31 Chris, *Watching Wildlife,* 169–70.

32 Shukin, *Animal Capital,* 4.

33 Ward, *White Canada Forever.*

34 Immigration, Chapleau, J.A. (Joseph Adolphe), 1840–98, Gray, John Hamilton, 1814–89, Canada Royal Commission on Chinese, *Report of the Royal Commission on Chinese Immigration: Report and Evidence* (Ottawa: Printed by order of the Commission, 1885).

35 Ibid., 156.

36 Ward, *White Canada Forever,* 13.

37 Ibid., 15.

38 Canaday, *The Straight State,* 28.

39 Immigration, *Report of the Royal Commission on Chinese Immigration,* xxix.

40 Ibid., 354.

41 "Select Committee on Chinese Labor and Immigration," testimony of J.S. Thompson, MP, Journals of the House of Commons of the Dominion of Canada, Ottawa: MacLean, 14 May 1879, https://babel.hathitrust.org/cgi/pt?id=uc1.b2887979;view=1up;seq=9.

42 "Prime Minister Harper Offers Full Apology for the Chinese Head Tax," Prime Minister of Canada, 27 June 2006, http://www.pm.gc.ca/eng/news/2006/06/22/prime-minister-harper-offers-full-apology-chinese-head-tax.

43 According to a survey of Chinese millionaires by the Bank of China and Hurun Report from 2011, 37 per cent of the richest Chinese have chosen Canada as their migration destination. See Jeremy Page, "Many Rich Chinese Consider Leaving," *Wall Street Journal,* 2 November 2011, https://www.wsj.com/articles/SB10001424052970204394804577011760523331438.

44 Colin Lindsay, "Profiles of Ethnic Communities in Canada," in *The Chinese Community in Canada, 2001* (Statistics Canada, Social and Aboriginal Statistics Division, 2007).

45 Li, *Chinese in Canada,* 155–8.

46 "Reich+Petch Designs Highly Anticipated Panda Interpretive Centre at the Toronto Zoo," Toronto Zoo,,http://www.torontozoo.com/Pandas/pdfs/Reich%20and%20Petch%20Pandas%20Press%20Release_FINAL.pdf.

47 Gruffudd, "Biological Cultivation," 238.

48 Ibid., 230.

49 Mortimer-Sandilands, "Unnatural Passions?," 6.

50 Chen, *Animacies*, 115.

51 Chan, *Chinese American Masculinities*.

52 Lee, *Orientals*.

53 Immigration, *Report of the Royal Commission on Chinese Immigration*, xcv.

54 Ibid., xxv.

55 Shukin, *Animal Capital*, 4–5.

56 Rothfels, "Immersed with Animals," 199.

57 "Reich+Petch Designs Highly Anticipated Panda Interpretive Centre at the Toronto Zoo."

58 "Toronto Zoo Giant Pandas," Toronto Zoo, accessed 2 November 2016, http://www.torontozoo.com/pandas/.

59 See Henderson, *The Gardens of Suzhou*.

60 Uddin, "Panda Gardens and Public Sex at the National Zoological Park," 87.

61 See Friese, *Cloning Wild Life*.

62 Jenny Yuen and Toronto Sun, "Panda Love Is in the Air at the Toronto Zoo," *Toronto Sun*, 12 April 2014, http://www.torontosun.com/2014/04/12/panda-love-is-in-the-air-at-the-toronto-zoo.

63 Morris and Morris, *Men and Pandas*, 187.

64 Chen, *Animacies*, 121; Fung, "Looking for My Penis."

65 See also Eng, *Racial Castration*.

66 Ward, *White Canada Forever*, 109.

67 Chen, *Animacies*, 100.

68 "Toronto Zoo Giant Panda Cubs," Toronto Zoo, accessed 4 November 2016, http://www.torontozoo.com/GiantPandaCubs/?pg=Reveal.

CHAPTER TEN

FLYING PENGUINS IN JAPAN'S NORTHERNMOST ZOO

Takashi Ito

In May 2015, Takasakiyama Natural Zoological Garden in southern Japan sparked a public debate about the naming of a newborn Japanese macaque, "Charlotte," a name chosen by public vote that reflected the popularity of the British royal family, the celebratory mood surrounding Princess Charlotte's birth, and the cult of the cute (kawaii) in Japanese consumer culture.[1] Upon the announcement of the monkey's name, however, Takasakiyama received many letters and phone calls of complaint. The critics held that naming the monkey Charlotte was disrespectful to the British monarch and urged zoo officials to imagine how people in Japan might feel if a British zoo were to name a monkey after a Japanese princess. When the zoo decided to revoke the name, the public relations official for the British royal family replied, though not officially, that they were not offended at all. In January 2016, Charlotte became "Queen Monkey" of Takasakiyama, after another popularity vote, this time dubbed a "general election."[2]

The reason that one provincial zoo attracted nationwide attention was related not only to the political correctness of naming zoo animals, but also to the general revival of zoological parks in Japan, which began in the late 1990s at Asahiyama Zoo on the island of Hokkaido. In his study of the Tokyo Ueno Zoo, *The Nature of the Beasts*, historian Ian Miller contemplates Japan's "ecological modernity" through the lens of the Japanese imperial landmark from the time of its birth to the postwar period. Miller uses this term to highlight his claim that "when the Ueno Zoo made caged animals into representatives of pristine 'nature' it instituted a separation between people and the natural world, introducing a break between humanity and animality that recast Japanese – together with Westerners – as the rational masters of a new natural history based on Linnaean nomenclature and the tenets of evolutionary theory."[3] I begin this chapter where Miller's book ends, by addressing "ecological postmodernity" from the standpoint of another provincial zoo, this time located in Japan's northernmost periphery.

By adding the prefix "post-," I intend to encourage critical thinking about modernity from an ecological perspective, a popular trend in Japanese intellectual and popular culture in the 1980 and 1990s. Interestingly, this rise in popularity was contemporaneous with the nationwide decline of zoos, as people became increasingly skeptical about the type of conception of nature that modern zoos presented for mass consumption, with some even rejecting the institution as an anthropocentric delusion. Indeed, Miller's statements that "people are always embedded in the natural world" and that "modernization meant, not the physical separation of nature from society, but their increasingly rapid interpenetration" can be identified alongside a critical evaluation of "ecological modernity."[4] In philosophy, the concept of "becoming-animal" articulated by Gilles Deleuze and Felix Guattari, the French postmodernist thinkers, resonates with the intellectual movement that rethinks the position of humans in the natural world as well as the boundary between humanity and animality.[5] In the realm of Japanese popular culture, Studio Ghibli has projected criticism of "ecological modernity" onto animation films such as the very successful 1997 film Princess Mononoke.[6] In this chapter, I aim to explore how this sociocultural environment has framed, or has been projected onto, one particular expression of "ecological postmodernity" – an allegedly unique form of animal exhibit that appeared in Japan's northernmost zoo.

Before an analysis of the type of nature that Asahiyama Zoo has recreated, however, in this chapter I outline the historical background against which the zoo emerged into the public spotlight. I then consider the zoo's exhibition philosophy by focusing on its two most representative animal exhibits: the Penguin House and the Seal House. Finally, I analyze the cult of the cute as a key component of the emotions that zoo visitors feel towards the animals on display. The blurring of the human-animal boundary and the transcendence thereof constitute a central theme for this analysis, as a step towards the comprehension of Japan's ecological postmodernity.

Historical Background

There were two developments in the history of modern zoos in Japan. As Miller discusses, the first was related to the beginning of the "Westernization" of the late nineteenth century.[7] After the Meiji Restoration in 1868, the Japanese government dispatched several groups of leading statesmen and scholars to the West. As one of these groups, the Iwakura Mission (embassy) travelled to Europe and the United States from 1871 to 1873, visiting a variety of political, economic, and cultural institutions that altogether were thought to exemplify the wealth and strength of Western civilization.[8] On this tour, the Japanese delegates visited the London Zoo and were quite impressed with the scale of its collection. For them, zoos represented the combination of naval power, commercial wealth, and scientific knowledge that sustained Western hegemony of the world. As Kume Kunitake, official journal keeper of the Iwakura Mission, recorded:

At every step one paused; at every turn one raised one's head. There was not enough time to gaze at everything. In the midst of this landscape, enclosures had been created with various different structures, and in them were kept birds and animals which had been sought and trapped all over the world ... Most of the unusual animals kept in these gardens come from South America, Africa, India and the islands of the South Seas, and to buy them requires the expenditure of a great deal of money. If they are not kept in conditions appropriate to their natures, then even if they do not die they will waste away and will not be worth seeing. By that alone can be seen the degree to which the care of animals has progressed as a science in this country. Members of the monkey family are born in the tropics. In a cold climate their lungs are affected and they die, so they must always be kept in a heated house ... We saw nothing in Europe to compare with the richness of this zoo.[9]

Kume recognized that it was wealth and political power that enabled Britain to collect such a wide variety of living animals, but also that it was scientific expertise that allowed the zoo to maintain its collection. What was important for the Japanese recorder was not only the zoo itself but what it represented, and in his view the zoo embodied the essence of Western civilization.

The Iwakura Mission returned with the idea of establishing a zoo in Japan. After twists and turns, the Tokyo Ueno Zoo opened in 1882 as an associate institution of the Ministry of Agriculture and Commerce. As the process of nation-state building advanced, government-funded zoos were established in other major cities, including Kyoto (1903), Osaka (1904), and Nagoya (1906).[10] The science of biology was also imported and studied as an academic discipline at Tokyo Imperial University.[11] Charles Darwin's evolutionary theory and Herbert Spencer's social Darwinism were much discussed among those who obtained access to Western-style higher education, and the development of both the Tokyo Ueno Zoo and biological science reflected Japan's ambition to govern the wild nature of its newly acquired colonies. Zoos and botanic gardens were constructed in Taiwan and Korea as subordinate institutions to the zoological community in Tokyo, and scientific explorations were carried out in Southeast Asia. By the early twentieth century, the Japanese empire had followed in the steps of its European predecessors to produce a system of knowledge that aimed to control the natural resources of its colonial possessions.[12]

Western science also influenced the Japanese conceptualization of "nature" itself. The very term "shizen" (nature) came about through attempts to translate and adopt the Western notion of nature. It is often said that the influence of Western science, as epitomized by Cartesian dualism, has deprived Japanese people of the feeling of oneness with nature, and has manipulated them into an eternal longing for what has been lost forever.[13] At the same time, there is still a cliché that their perception of nature is still not quite the same as that of Western civilization. In the popular, conventional discourse, this reminiscence of "something unchanging" in the Japanese physical experience of nature is often sought after in the periphery of "westernized Japan," where the influence of modernization remains marginal both geographically and ideologically. Japan's northernmost zoo serves as a perfect window into zoo history, because it reveals how the ideology of modernity, which zoological gardens had originally espoused in a civil society in nineteenth-century Europe and North America, was appropriated into a supposedly postmodern reconfiguration of the construct of nature.

The second development in Japanese zoo history was the emergence of profit-oriented zoos at the beginning of the twentieth century. These zoos, which did not receive state or municipal subsidies, were established at the same historical moment that private companies were developing railway networks. As zoo designer and historian Kenji Wako demonstrates, these corporations competed to offer train commutes between work places in city centres and residential areas in suburbs. Among the strategies implemented to increase the number of passengers who regularly used their trains were amusement parks established along the railway lines. For example, Hanshin Railway, one of the largest private companies in Greater Osaka, established Koroen Park in 1905, two years after the company had launched its railway business. The park not only had a small zoo, but also housed other recreational facilities including a museum, a concert hall, a playground, and a hotel. The idea of establishing a zoo to attract the urban population arose from other successful examples of government-funded zoos, but this second type included those located in relatively smaller prefectural capitals and provincial towns such as Kagoshima (1928), Kumamoto (1929), Kokura (1933).[14]

These two developments converged in the making of zoological parks in postwar Hokkaido. The island's first zoo, Maruyama Zoo, evolved from the travelling exhibition of the Tokyo Ueno Zoo and opened in its capital city Sapporo in 1951.[15] Another zoo appeared in Obihiro in 1963 and, in the following year, Asahikawa's city government decided to found its own zoo on the gentle slope of Asahiyama Mountain on the east side of the city. At that time, trams ran between the city centre and the proposed site for the zoo and, in 1967, Asahiyama Zoo opened with 505 individuals of seventy-five species, including 200 carp specimens. Annual attendance is shown in figure 10.1. In its first year, the zoo had a recorded attendance of around 460,000, a number that rose steadily alongside the population of Asahikawa until the early 1980s. Like other provincial zoos, Asahiyama Zoo was primarily designed as a place of family recreation, with amusement attractions such as a roller coaster, a Ferris wheel, and a mini-train. These attractions certainly helped to boost attendance, but their effect did not last long. As existing attractions became outdated, the criticism that they were irrelevant to the zoo's original mission began to resound.

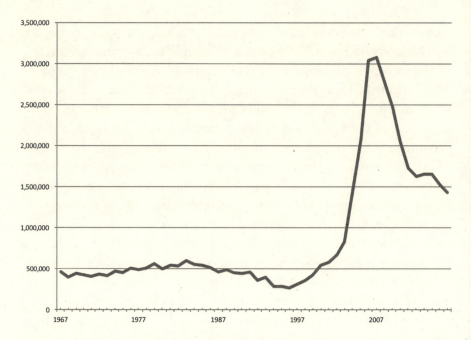

Figure 10.1 Annual attendance at Asahiyama Zoo, 1967–2014.

By the late 1980s, Asahiyama Zoo had begun to dwindle; a situation made worse in 1994, when the death of a gorilla and a fox by echinococcosis, a parasitic disease infectious to humans as well, caused zoophobia in the local community.[16] After a temporary closure that lasted several months, however, a turning point occurred: the city elected a new mayor, Kohichi Sugawara, who during his election campaign had pledged to establish an amusement park to boost the local economy. Since there were no extra financial resources in the municipal budget, Sugawara considered reforming Asahiyama Zoo with lower operating costs, and commissioned this task to the recently appointed director, Masao Kosuge, who had previously been opposed to the zoo's commercial orientation.[17] Kosuge took this opportunity to carry out the plan to renew animal houses under his unique exhibition policy, discussed below. In 1997, the Children's Stock Farm and an extensive aviary called the Forest of Birds opened; almost every year since then, the zoo has created new exhibitions and facilities, including the Forest of Ezo Deer, the Forest of Chimpanzees, the Enclosure of Spi-Capy (mixed exhibit of spider monkeys and capybaras), the New Giraffe House, the Penguin House, and the Seal House.[18]

As the local and national media frequently reported, these renovations attracted a dramatically increasing number of visitors. In 2006, attendance was recorded at over three million, and as far as the summer months were concerned, Asahiyama managed to outdraw the Tokyo Ueno Zoo. Numbers have fallen in recent years, but in financial terms gate receipts are still large enough for the zoo to continue renovations. As of July 2017, admission fees are as low as 820 yen (approximately ten Canadian dollars) and the annual pass costs only 1,000 yen. Certainly, and perhaps surprisingly, Asahiyama Zoo has been the most successful zoo in Japan in the last two decades, despite its peripheral location in Hokkaido, the northernmost island of the Japanese archipelago.

Animals in Action

One of the zoo's main exhibits is the enclosure of the indigenous Ezo deer; meanwhile, Ezo venison cutlet is served in the zoo's cafeteria. In fact, until some time ago there was a handwritten notice at the enclosure that aimed to promote the consumption of Ezo venison:

Hello Madam, we would like to suggest an extra dish! Ezo venison is highly valued in European cuisine. Low in fat, it is a healthy food. The Hokkaido Government is trying to stop the damage to agriculture and forestry caused by the increasing population of Ezo deer, and to establish distribution channels for its meat in the food market. I have had sashimi and steak of Ezo venison myself, though it might be unwise to make this confession as keeper of Ezo deer – of course, the venison I ate was not the product of Asahiyama Zoo!! If you have not tried Ezo venison yet, why not this time? It tastes very good. If you come from the mainland, take one as a gift to your friends and families.[19]

This statement is an unintended reminder of the fact that human-animal relationships are multifaceted: animals can be and are food, materials, labour force, experimental subjects, companions, and vermin. In general, however, the ways in which humans deal with different animals for different purposes tend to be compartmentalized in the modern world. In zoos, we are encouraged to develop respect for animal life, not an appetite for exotic animals or wild game. Still, many zoos have cafes and restaurants that offer meat. In the Berlin Zoo, for example, Currywurst, the local specialty, can be found at a self-serve cafeteria, while visitors to the Prague Zoo or the Budapest Zoo may watch a variety of ungulates and then eat goulash. In these and many other zoos, the two activities – respecting animal life and eating animal meat – are not seen to be related to one another. In general, zoo-goers may not recognize the linkage, and even if they do they can almost unconsciously deceive themselves as if the link did not exist at all. In Asahiyama Zoo, however, the signage about the deer venison intentionally reveals the seemingly contradictory attitudes towards animals.

What is also interesting about this statement is that it unintentionally problematizes the unique status of Hokkaido in the history of Japan's nation-state building. Hokkaido, an island formerly called Ezo or Yezo, was integrated into Japan's official territory only after the Meiji Restoration. In 1869, the colonization of Hokkaido began with many immigrants who were sent from the mainland to pioneer the sparsely inhabited area. Towards the end of the century, these mainlanders came to constitute the majority of the Hokkaido population, while the indigenous Ainu people faced marginalization and discrimination. For the central government, Hokkaido was the hinterland to be westernized for the Japanese nation-state: it should be neither obstacle nor disgrace to the invention of "modern Japan."[20] Meanwhile, its alleged backwardness was considered to have its own merit, as the Ainu and their deep reverence for nature offered a rich source for ethnological and archeological studies.[21] The international scholarly attention to the Ainu and their culture made Yoshikiyo Koganei (1859–1944), professor of anatomy at Tokyo Imperial University, very famous for his anatomical studies of over one hundred Ainu skulls, which he had surreptitiously exhumed in Hokkaido.[22] This example is one of many that illustrate the relationship between Japan's mainland and Ezo/Hokkaido as that of the colonizing and the colonized. No explicit element of Hokkaido's colonial history is, however, displayed in Asahiyama Zoo. Indeed, despite its garrulity, the handwritten notice about the Ezo deer leads the viewers to stay focused on the animals in front of them and the related and identified contemporary issues.

Nevertheless, the Ezo deer is a species that witnessed the twofold process of Hokkaido colonization from an ecological perspective. Wild herds of Ezo deer were common in the nineteenth century, but, as the colonization by the mainlanders progressed, they were overhunted to the brink of extinction. A ban on deer hunting was implemented in the early twentieth century and in turn caused a rapid increase in the deer population, because its natural enemy, the Ezo wolf, had been declared a pest and exterminated by the turn of the century.[23] Consequently, the deer population has grown so dramatically that "urgent" culling has taken place for the last several years.[24] In short, this indigenous species not only testifies to the continuous human intervention into nature, but also signifies Hokkaido's colonial history.

Furthermore, there is firm evidence of the zoo's colonial connection on a broader geographical scale. As Yasuhiro Inuzuka points out, Asahiyama Zoo's first director, Mitsushi Nakamata, was the director of the Xinjing Zoological and Botanical Gardens until the end of World War II.[25] Constructed, but not completed, in the capital of "Manchuko" (a puppet state created in 1932 under the influence of the Japanese Kwantung Army), the Xinjing Zoo was designed to become the largest zoo in the Japanese empire. The central theme of this colonial enterprise was "acclimatization": to bring a variety of foreign animals and to adapt them to the cold climate of northeast China. Nakamata stated that the new zoo would prove that Manchuko was a safe and pleasant country and would encourage many Japanese to immigrate to this colonial land, an objective that supported the population policies of the Japanese government. Since the United States had restricted immigration of many nationalities, including the Japanese, by the Immigration Act of 1924, the Japanese government tried to send surplus population to Manchuko. World War II ended before construction was completed, and in the aftermath of the war Nakamata was appointed director of the Maruyama Zoo, Hokkaido's first, in 1951. He was then invited to a municipal committee of Asahiyama to plan the construction of Asahiyama Zoo, and became its first director in 1967. As Inuzuka argues, it is reasonable to think that Nakamata's career at the Xinjing Zoo preconditioned him for zoos in the snowy, cold region.[26]

Figure 10.2 Giraffes standing in the snow.

Asahiyama Zoo seems to have taken over the mission of acclimatization from the Xinjing Zoo. The sight of giraffes standing in the snow in figure 10.2 is a good reminder of this mission. Yet, as far as I can tell, any textual information provided at the zoo – including that which encourages consumption of Ezo venison – does not refer to the historical origin of Asahiyama Zoo. Indeed, the elements of colonial history are overshadowed by the exhibition policy that regenerated Asahiyama Zoo in the late 1990s. It is therefore important to contemplate that policy, as it reveals how the zoo bypassed its history to create an ideal form of nature in a postmodern society.

Asahiyama Zoo self-styled its exhibition policy as the "animals-in-action exhibit" (kōdō tenji). It is defined in contrast to the "ecological exhibit" (seitai tenji) or the "immersion exhibit," the international standard for zoo animal exhibits that spread from the United States to many other countries including Japan. According to Kosuge, while the immersion exhibit aims to recreate a naturalistic environment in which zoo visitors feel as if they are walking in the habitats of exhibited animals, the animals-in-action exhibit is intended to encourage animals to reveal their own characteristics in proximity to observers. He claims that the animals-in-action exhibit is the invention of Asahiyama Zoo, with the implication that the immersion exhibit is an import, and not necessarily an ideal one, from the West.[27] The characterization of animals-in-action exhibits vis-a-viz immersion exhibits, as well as the higher evaluation of the former over the latter, might be easier to comprehend when explained in Japanese, due to the contrasting phonetic implications of the two terms: kōdō as dynamic, and seitai as static. Kosuge believes that by observing lively animals in the closest possible proximity the viewer could better appreciate their beauty and vitality.

The Penguin House and the Seal House are the two examples that best illustrate the essence of an animals-in-action exhibit. No wild penguins inhabit Hokkaido, and the seals displayed in the zoo are not the species indigenous to the island, but there is nonetheless a climatic association between Hokkaido's severe winter cold and the sea animals of polar regions. Both exhibits are officially named "museum" in English, although it is appropriate to describe them as "house" in terms of the buildings' scale and size. The intention behind "museum" rather than "house" lies in the pedagogical justification of zoos as a site of environmental education. Visitors are guided not only to watch penguins and seals swimming in the aquariums, but also to learn about their habits and habitats from the texts and visuals shown on the interior walls.

Although the idea of exhibiting living animals as a gateway to environmental education is common in contemporary zoos, the Penguin and Seal Houses have unique characteristics that warrant further analysis. One of the conventions that has started at this site, and has gained currency in other zoos, is the way in which information about displayed animals is communicated: the keepers handwrite textual and visual information. While this habit was originally meant to reduce expenses on designing and printing posters, it has had an important psychological effect on visitors. Partly because of Japanese ideography and calligraphy, handwriting is perceived as "natural and organic," as opposed to "mechanical and lifeless" printed letters. Similarly, handwritten descriptions of the displayed animals help to represent them (even lions and tigers) as cute and winsome, and so approachable, and this strategy is more highly valued than photographic realism. In what follows, these characteristics are explicated with reference to the Penguin House and the Seal House.

The Penguin House

The Penguin House entrance is hidden slightly behind a wall of concrete, a typical building material for modernist architecture (see figure 10.3). The cold, lifeless impression that the industrial material might produce in the front is neutralized by the colourful sign board printed in a handwritten font. The unusual choice of hiragana, rather than katakana, which has been conventionally used to denote nomenclature, helps visitors to feel at ease and comfortable. Behind the entrance gate, visitors are led through an underwater tunnel. The first part of the tunnel uses transparent acrylic flooring so that visitors can watch the penguins swim in all directions, invited to imagine that penguins are flying like birds under water (figure 10.4). At the end of the tunnel, a handwritten note attached to the wall asks why penguins do not need to close their eyes under water. It then explains the role of their nictitating membrane, or third eyelid, in a language understandable to primary school children. Indeed, this question is of some interest to young children who might struggle to keep their eyes open under water in their swimming class at school (primary schools have their own swimming pools and swimming is part of the mandatory school curriculum in Japan).

The end of the tunnel is connected to the basement floor of a dome with a mural of flying penguins (figure 10.5), created by a zookeeper, Hiroshi Abe, who later resigned and became an author of picture books. The passage leads to a staircase to an upper level, filled with a series of handwritten illustrations, each of which depict a different penguin species in real size. Moreover, a large mobile of swimming penguins hangs from the ceiling, confirming the design concept of the penguin exhibit: penguins do fly (figure 10.6). At the exit of the building, visitors emerge into an outside enclosure with a swimming pool, where a variety of penguin species are displayed. At this point, they realize that the underwater tunnel they have just walked through is part

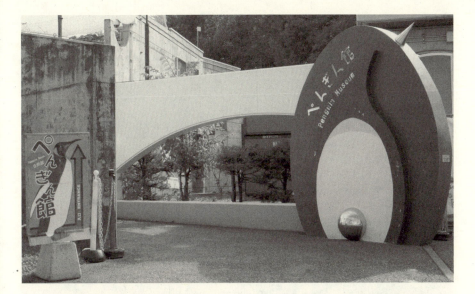

Figure 10.3 *Top* The front of the Penguin House.

Figure 10.4 *Bottom* The underwater tunnel of the Penguin Aquarium.

Figure 10.5 *Top* Mural painting of flying penguins in the Penguin House.

Figure 10.6 *Bottom* Mobiles of flying penguins in the Penguin House.

Figure 10.7 *Opposite* The penguin walk on the snow-covered promenade.

of this large-scale aquarium. On the other side of the aquarium, a dozen penguin figures are lined up horizontally above the lawn, which again highlights the conceptual image of penguins as flying birds.

In winter months, the "penguin walk" exhibit takes place outside the building. Penguins parade on the snow-covered promenade prepared by the zoo staff, and almost all the visitors line the promenade to watch and photograph them (see figure 10.7). As there are no fences, the penguins pass by only a metre away from the observers. By attracting an unprecedentedly large number of tourists, this exhibit helped to rescue the zoo from bankruptcy. Meanwhile, the penguin walk has invited the criticism that this and other "attractions" in Asahiyama Zoo are not so different from the shows of performing animals. Kosuge, however, contends that penguins were neither forced to go out of the enclosure nor enticed by food rewards to walk the walk. According to the zoo, in winter months when food is in short supply, penguins tend to travel long distances in search of sustenance; the sight of the snow-covered ground activates this biological instinct.[28]

The Seal House

The same justification underpins the design of the Seal House. On its lawn, about fifteen real-size models of different seal species are displayed. Each model is labelled with its name and body length in handwriting. The entrance signpost of the museum avoids using the kind of typeface that is used in text-books (figure 10.8). These unstably shaped letters might give the impression of being "unscientific" and "unprofessional," but they feel "natural," "approachable," and "warm-hearted." Like the entrance post to the Penguin House, this calligraphic design counterbalances the lifeless facade of the modernist building.

Once inside the building, visitors realize that they are in the basement level of a large aquarium (figure 10.9). Their attention is easily drawn to the acrylic column at the centre of the floor, through which one of the seals swims vertically. As this column highlights the dynamism of swimming motions, crowds of visitors tend to gather around it, many of them waiting for the best timing to photograph the sea mammal. The building has the nearly same structure as the Penguin House: the way out of the basement floor leads to a slightly curved aisle with a wall painted with swimming seals. At the end of the aisle, a staircase leads to the ground level, where visitors can observe seals from above the aquarium.

One might doubt that these exhibits truly benefit seals and penguins, but Kosuge believes that the animals-in-action exhibits enhance zoo animals' physical and mental life. According to him, the structure of the penguins' aquarium allegedly lowers their stress levels by enabling them to swim more freely. The same argument holds with the Seal House. Often asked how the seals are led to swim into the acrylic column, Kosuge replies that they try to approach humans, out of curiosity, and when bored, they swim away to different zones in the aquarium. He explains that when appropriately controlled, the visibility of the human observers is a source of entertainment, not physiological stress, for the animals.[29]

His confidence in the animals-in-action exhibit is based upon his long career as the veterinarian of Asahiyama Zoo. In a TV documentary by NHK, Kosuge explains that each zookeeper develops a "personal" relationship with an animal of which they take care every day, and can thus "think" in the same way as the attended animal does.[30] Zookeepers sense that different

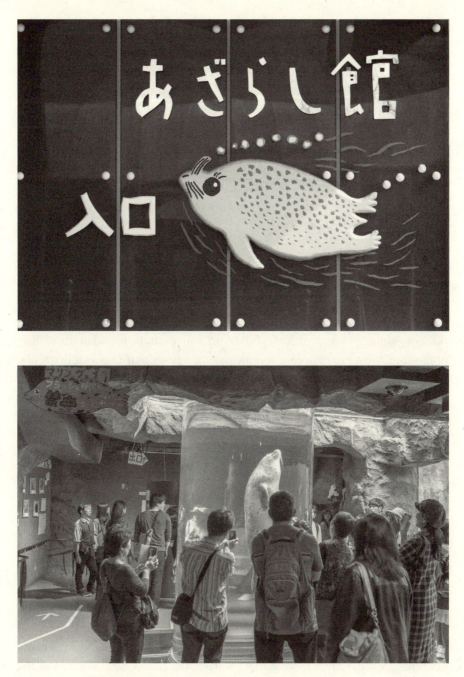

Figure 10.8 *Top* Panel at the entrance of the Seal Museum.

Figure 10.9 *Bottom* A spotted seal swimming in the Column Aquarium.

animals have their own forms and behaviours that constitute the intrinsic part of what they are. For zoo-goers, however, the animals' real natures are hidden behind the scenes. Therefore, the keepers' task is to contemplate how to best encourage the animal to demonstrate its real nature to the public, sometimes by trying to think in the same way as a penguin or seal. The Penguin House and the Seal House were designed around this idea, and Kosuge argues that animals will not fail to reveal their real natures, just like "treasure at your feet." In his view, the acrylic tunnel is an apparatus with which to unfold nature's treasure.

The Cult of the Cute

Kosuge's justification of his exhibition philosophy might sound anachronistic, as a similar (if not identical) kind of discourse can be found in the history of modern zoos. For example, as cultural studies scholar Lisa Uddin argues, London Zoo's Penguin Pool, a representative of modernist architecture in the 1930s, was once acclaimed for its aesthetic minimalism and transparency in which people optimistically hoped animate nature would reveal itself.[31] Kosuge might appear to be a revived traditionalist of this kind, but in fact his exhibition philosophy differs significantly from the modernist approach.

An analysis of the underwater tunnel calls attention to this difference. Kosuge explains that his intention in creating the acrylic tunnel was not merely for visitors to observe penguins. Rather, it was to let them imagine that they were just like them. In his view, while watching penguins under their feet, humans can imagine themselves as penguins, flying in the azure sky rather than swimming in the blue water. This belief is, Kosuge notes, the fulfilment of humankind's eternal desire to fly with wings wide open.[32] The concept of flying penguins is also captured in a snow globe, sold at the zoo's gift shop, which commodifies this anthropocentric fantasy of avian freedom (figure 10.10). The posture of the miniature penguin is arranged diagonally upwards as if the animal were metamorphosed into a bird, soaring in the snowy sky. The vision of becoming a penguin can therefore be reimagined, memorized, and shared at home.

This experience does not necessarily represent the animals' "otherness" as opposed to the human "self." Neither does the transparency of the acrylic

Figure 10.10 Snow globe of a flying penguin.

tunnel constitute the boundary between this (human) and the other (animal) side of the world. On the contrary, a penguin object to gaze upon is a subject of possession: the human observer's mind transcends into the penguin's body. This process of becoming a penguin is zoomorphism, the adoption of animal characteristics by a human. It should be noted, however, that the experiential context within which this zoomorphism takes place is different from that of the Enlightenment-model zoo. It is undeniable that the essence of modern zoos has remained unchanged: it has lain in collecting animals and displaying them in captivity since the age of Enlightenment, or even as early as the Antiquity. Asahiyama Zoo is no exception in this regard. Nevertheless, in the realm of fantasy, humans enchanted by an animal doing what we ourselves are incapable of doing can subscribe to the dream of becoming an animal. It is an irrational dream that the Enlightenment-model zoo would despise, but one that can be fulfilled in Asahiyama Zoo by imagining the animal transcending into one's body. In the underwater tunnel, young children are often excited by the sight of a swimming penguin and open their arms to imitate their swimming/flying posture. This spontaneous response testifies to the penetration of the dream into physical reality.

The implications that zoomorphism has for the Deluzian concept of "becoming-animal" is open to philosophical inquiry. There is also room for debate about the moral and ethical evaluation of the animals-in-action exhibit. Instead of developing the philosophical or ethical investigation, however, I hope to discuss the affective structure of this particular genre of zoomorphism, because it is a key to understanding how the process of becoming, or being possessed, occurs at a level of an intersubjective reality.

Kawaii, or the cult of the cute, provides an important emotional component for zoomorphism. "Cuteness" is an aesthetic and affective category that has recently attracted scholarly inquiry. Collected essays on *The Aesthetics and Affects of Cuteness* suggests understanding cuteness as "an appeal – intentional or unconscious, made by an animal- or human-like entity – that seeks to trigger a particular affective response."[33] Meanwhile, partly because "cute" is not a perfect translation of "kawaii" and partly because kawaii seems to be omnipresent in today's Japanese consumer society (while being arguably embedded in its history back to the Edo period), it is difficult to give a comprehensive account of the term and its related cultural phenomenon.[34] What is important here is the fact that animals or their anthropomorphic figures, such as Hello Kitty, have been one of the main sources of the proliferation of kawaii objects and have created a niche in popular culture. Against this backdrop, zoo animals are ready to be used as a motif for the imaginary creation of hybrid creatures, just like fictional species in Pokémon.[35] Indeed, Pokémon Go, a mobile gaming application that uses augmented reality, encourages its players to visit a zoo, where they can hunt a creature that "spawns" at a specific site within the zoo's space. Meanwhile, nearly all mammal species exhibited in zoos, from elephant to lion to capybara, can be described as kawaii, and it is the most common word that people speak upon catching the sight of their favorite animal in the zoo. When the zoo turns into the hunting field for zoo-goers to search for "cute-ified" animals, the boundary between an animal that is real and an animal that is fictional does not matter as much as the difference between an animal that is kawaii and an animal that is not. In this augmented reality, the real and the imagined are multilayered and interpenetrated.

Furthermore, the blurring of the boundary takes place between the experiencing subject and the experienced object and can be explained within a more general cognitive framework of cuteness. As the cute studies scholar Joshua Paul Dale and others discuss in relation to the aesthetic theorist Sianne Ngai's study of the cuteness of the avant-garde: "The power differential at the heart of the relationship between subject and (cute) object that results in Ngai's 'cute-ified' subject also involves a partial dismantling of the subject, in which the intimacy offered by the cute object serves to blur the boundaries between that object and the 'cute-ified,' baby-talking subject."[36] By considering its emotional effects, the cognitive process and meaning of zoomorphism via kawaii animals can be identified more specifically. My hypothesis is that to say an animal is kawaii is not simply to praise and admire, but to figuratively possess the described body by perceiving it as an extension of oneself. In other words, what is kawaii is not the animal itself, but the one who has just found and appreciated the aesthetics of kawaii latent in that animal. Without this self-referential metaphorical transformation, the display of flying penguins would not be able to ignite the human desire to fly. Zoomorphism would remain incomplete.

The other hypothesis regarding the imaginary transcendence of oneself into an animal body is related to the antonym of cute. As Dale and others suggest, cuteness has "a significant degree of malleability, allowing for the attachment of antagonistic categories while still retaining the capacity to precipitate an affective response in some (though not all) observers."[37] In Japanese subculture, kimo-kawaii (ugly-cute) composes the most important subcategory of cuteness that testifies to the ambidexterity of this affective label. As the perception of ugliness is not always excluded from the appreciation of cuteness and, on the contrary, could even constitute the intrinsic component of cute-ifying and/or cute-ified experience, it would be incorrect to treat these two concepts as mutually exclusive.[38]

While kawaii and kimoi can be the opposite sides of the same coin, I would suggest that the antonym of kawaii is not ugly, but kawaiso (piteous). Kawaiso is an expression of compassion that generally comes out of an emotional attachment to living beings in distress and suffering. In common usage of the word, one would say kawaiso in watching an animal confined in a small cage or farmed chickens limping in battery cages. The best-known anecdote of such piteous animals in the Japanese zoo history has been told with regard to the elephants of the Tokyo Ueno Zoo killed during World War II.[39] As Ushio Hasegawa and, more recently, Miller discuss, the popularized children's story of the event, which distorted the historical facts concerning the time of the American air raid and the person responsible for the "elephant massacre," narrated the sacrifice of "innocent" Japanese nationals by projecting their suffering onto the body of "innocent" animal victims.[40] The criticism of this story is that it only addresses the disastrous effects of war on Japanese nationals and evades the question of their agency with regard to the war at large. At best, the readers would perceive the sacrifice of elephants as if it were their own and would take a vow of nonviolence and pacifism. Meanwhile, they are "freed" from the question of why the war was waged, who was responsible for it, and how it involved and affected people outside Japan. After all, the story does not clarify whether it is the massacred elephants or the readers themselves to whom the feelings of kawaiso is and ought to be attributed.

The ambiguity of agency is entangled with the exhibition philosophy of Asahiyama Zoo. When an animal dies in the zoo, the portrait of the deceased animal is often displayed in their cage, with an official handwritten notice: "amidst mourning."[41] It is a custom for many Japanese people to exchange new-year greeting cards with friends and colleagues, ideally with a handwritten message, and they are posted to be delivered in the morning of New Year's Day. When a close relative dies, a notice of amidst mourning is sent off to those with whom the greeting cards are exchanged every year, well in advance of the posting weeks, as a polite decline of the card exchange for the ensuing year. Asahiyama Zoo appropriated this convention to create animals' individuality, as if registering their names, dates of birth and death, and "personality" into a public memory would confirm that the zoo is not a timeless space, with its past and present constituted by many animals who deserve agency and are therefore qualified to die their own deaths. This agency does not occur, however, in a way that animal rights theorists would advocate: it appears only within the experiential frame of intersubjectivity. The functioning of this frame is explicit in the very absence of the definable subjective agency in the zoo's mourning message. The original phrase – "amidst mourning" – can be interpreted as saying that the zoo staff, other animals, or anonymous visitors are in a mourning period. Indeed, it can be reasonably understood that all of them *should* mourn the animal's death and share the feelings of condolence.

In short, the affective dynamics of kawaiso are linked to that of kawaii. It is the feeling evoked by looking at others in distress and suffering, but at the same time it hurts those who hold this very painful emotion. As with the case of feeling kawaii, the boundary between the person who feels ka-waiso and the living beings to whom that feeling is attributed is eroded so profoundly that it seems nonexistent from the beginning. If kawaii is on the positive end of the spectrum of emotional attitudes towards animals, kawaiso is on the negative end of the same spectrum. Both emotions are nonetheless equal in that they blur the human-animal boundary rather than clarify it.[42]

The question remains to what extent the intersubjectivity of the affective experience of kawaii and kawaiso is intrinsically embedded in Japanese lan-guage and culture, and thus found in other Japanese zoos and similar sites of human-animal interactions. It is not reasonable to say that it is all gener-ated solely by Asahiyama Zoo, but its exhibition philosophy certainly aims to enhance and navigate the transcendent experience of kawaii and kawaiso. The zoo's motto, which appears omnipresent in its space, is "to communicate [the importance of] life." Like the mourning message discussed above, this expression does not specify who shows the importance of life to whom. One reading is that the zoo curators communicate the importance of life by means of animal exhibit, while another is that animals on exhibit demon-strate the importance of life to zoo-goers. Or, it might be that the zoo ex-emplifies how valuable a life is to those who work and visit there. This hermeneutical versatility underpins the affective architecture of the whole experience at Asahiyama Zoo.

NOTES

1   Earlier versions of this chapter were presented at the workshop Zoo Studies and a New Humanities, Hamilton, 2–3 December 2016; in the panel session "Zoos and Global Histories" at the Annual Meeting of the American Histor-ical Association, Denver, 6 January 2017; and at the workshop Rethinking

the Center/Periphery Model in European History at Tokyo University of Foreign Studies, Tokyo, 4 February 2017. I would like to express my gratitude to the participants in these research meetings and the anonymous reader for their valuable comments and suggestions. Special thanks to Alice Kuzniar for encouraging me to discuss the concept of zoomorphism, and to Yūmin Mori for drawing my attention to an important historical origin of Asahiyama Zoo. I am deeply grateful to Tracy McDonald and Dan Vandersommers for reading and editing my work closely and thoroughly. Research for this chapter was supported by JSPS KAKENHI (grant number 16K03108) and JSPS Program for Advancing Strategic International Networks to Accelerate the Circulation of Talented Researchers (reference number J2601).

2   "Japan: Zoo Sorry for Naming Monkey after New Princess," BBC News, http://www.bbc.com/news/blogs-news-from-elsewhere-32608553; "Takasakiyama no saru sousenkyo," Asahi Shimbun, http://www.asahi.com/articles/ASK1T4GTQK1TTPJB00R.html.

3   Miller, *The Nature of the Beast*, 2–3.

4   Ibid., 3.

5   Bruns, "Becoming-Animal."

6   *Mononoke Hime* (Princess Mononoke), directed by Hayao Miyazaki (Tokyo: Tōhō, 1997).

7   Miller, *The Nature of the Beasts*, 42–5.

8   Yamamoto, "A Reappraisal of Kunitake Kume," 95–110.

9   Kume, *Japan Rising*, 124–5.

10 Wako, *Dōbutsuen kakumei*, 2–68.

11 Setoguchi, "Darwin Commemorations," 532.

12 Miller, *Nature of the Beasts*, 81–9.

13 Yanabu, *Honyakugo seiritsu jijō*, 127–48.

14 Wako, *Dōbutsuen kakumei*, 26–8.

15 "History of Maruyama Zoo," http://www.city.sapporo.jp/zoo/info/shokai/history/history.html.

16 Kosuge and Iwano, *Tatakau dōbutsuen*, 96–9.

17 Ibid., 116–21.

18 "Asahiyama Zoo History," http://www.city.asahikawa.hokkaido.jp/asahiyamazoo/2200/p008757.html.

19 Kosuge, *Asahiyama dōbutsuen kakumei*, 35.

20 Toyoko Kozai, "Ainu wa naze 'yama ni nigeta' ka: Bakumatsu ezochi ni

okeru 'wagakuni saisho no kyōsei shutō' no okuyuki," *Shisō* 1017 (2009): 78–101.

21 Hudson, Lewallen, and Watson, eds., *Beyond Ainu Studies*.

22 Ueki, *Gakumon no bōryoku*, 46–69.

23 The Ezo wolf is akin to the Japanese wolf, but in taxonomical terms they are identified as different subspecies of the grey wolf (*Canis lupus*). The Japanese wolf also went extinct at the beginning of the twentieth century. Walker, *The Lost Wolves of Japan*; Hishikawa, *Ōkami no minzokugaku*.

24 "Ezo Deer Section," http://www.pref.hokkaido.lg.jp/ks/est/.

25 Inuzuka, "Shinkyo dōshokubutsuen kō," 18–25.

26 Ibid., 21.

27 Kosuge, *Asahiyama dōbutsuen kakumei*, 18–19.

28 Kosuge and Iwano, *Tatakau dōbutsuen*, 53–4.

29 Kosuge, *Asahiyama dōbutsuen kakumei*, 51–3.

30 "Asahiyama dōbutsuen pengin sora wo tobu," *Project X*, NHK, 15 November 2004.

31 Uddin, *Zoo Renewal*, 46–8.

32 Kosuge and Iwano, *Tatakau dōbutsuen*, 27–31.

33 Dale, Goggin, Leyda, Mcintyre, and Negra, eds., *The Aesthetics and Affects of Cuteness*, 4.

34 Yomota, *Kawaii ron*.

35 Ibid., 16, 175–8; Kato, "Goodbye Godzilla, Hello Kitty," 72–9.

36 Dale et al., *Aesthetics and Affects of Cuteness*, 5; Ngai, "The Cuteness of the Avant-Garde."

37 Dale et al., *Aesthetics and Affects of Cuteness*, 4.

38 Yomota, *Kawaii ron*, 77–81.

39 Akiyama, *Kawaisō na zō*.

40 Hasegawa, "Zō mo kawaisō, 8–30; Miller, *Nature of the Beasts*, 152–62; see also Itoh, *Japanese Wartime Zoo Policy*, 46–7, 50–2. For more general discussions of animals and war, see Hediger, *Animals and War*, in which John M. Kinder writes a chapter on "Zoo Animals and Modern War" based largely on European and America cases. Itoh's book also has chapters on European and American zoos in wartime.

41 Kosuge, *Asahiyama dōbutsuen kakumei*, 36–7; Harako, *Asahiyama dōbutsuen no tsukurikata*, 158–9.

42 Maeda, *Nihongogen daijiten*, 374; Masui, *Nihongogen kōjien*, 242–3.

CHAPTER ELEVEN

AL GORE, *BLACKFISH*, AND ME: ECO-ACTIVIST PROGRESS AND PROSPECTS FOR THE FUTURE

Randy Malamud

I begin this chapter with appreciative invocations – perhaps even verging on adulation – of two radical and unexpectedly popular documentary films from the last decade: Al Gore's *An Inconvenient Truth* (directed by David Guggenheim, 2006) and Gabriela Cowperthwaite's *Blackfish* (2013). They are among the most prominent, most watched, and most acclaimed nature documentaries of the twenty-first century.[1] Both of these films present their stories and arguments in ways that were resoundingly successful for mass audiences, who are often presumed to have limited attention spans for depressingly accurate accounts of our ecological behaviour and the likely consequences of our living habits.

Gore's film took a larger ecological scope, while Cowperthwaite's film focused more tightly on one animal's story. But mass and social media took great interest in both documentaries in the wake of their success. Audiences, critics, and writers "telescoped out" from the implications of *Blackfish*, and "microscoped in" on many of the ramifications of *An Inconvenient Truth*. The story of one exploited, troubled, captive orca prompted far-reaching extrapolations about how we view and value nonhuman animals in a range of settings and, even more broadly, about how we determine what counts (and what does not count) as authentic engagement with animals. The telling of one macrocosmic truth prompted audiences to discover their own local truths, and spurred popular interest in recycling, biking, green/clean homes, teach-ins, and a range of other small-scope, grass-roots sustainability initiatives.

The films suggested profound, fundamental changes to how we live on the earth among and amid other life forms. At the same time, their styles, their voices, seemed strikingly and appealingly less radical than I think they actually were, as evidenced by the fact that they have proven palatable, winning their rhetorical challenges in ways that radical discourse usually does not. We might regard these films as Trojan horses, delivering unthreatening and comprehensible messages about environmental realities, ethics, ideals, and necessary future remedies without unsettling audiences unduly, but planting the seeds of a much larger garden in which environmental advocates may disseminate and recirculate the issues raised in both films along with a host of other reforms that intertwine with Gore's and Cowperthwaite's visions.

I am interested in these mainstream popular phenomena because they were so rhetorically clever and, more simply, because they were true. Aspirationally and, I hope, not narcissistically, I fold in my own scholarly and writerly experiences and consider my own personal portfolio as a representative example for the community of people who write about zoos, animal rights, and larger ecological concerns. While I cannot deny that I have occasionally dreamt about the acceptance speeches I would deliver as the cinematic version of my 1998 book *Reading Zoos* sweeps the Golden Globes, Oscars, and Critics' Choice award ceremonies, I am generally resigned to the fact that my scholarly monograph is just one among countless voices who have, over the last generation, taken up the cause of ecocriticism; ecofeminism; animal rights; animal welfare; critical animal studies; and the places these engage with components of larger theoretical communities, including queer theory (queering anthropocentrism), deconstruction (with a hat tip to Derrida's cat), postcolonialism, Marxism, and others whose adherents advance the agenda of making the world a better place for animals of all stripes (and feathers and fins and antennae).[2] As much as I would love to see my star on Hollywood Boulevard, I am not expecting that call to come.

But I would nonetheless like to insert myself into the Gore-Cowperthwaite flow of discourse and co-opt the self-assured and valuable tenor that their films embody. And I invite my fellow scholars in this volume and in the larger field of critical animal studies to position ourselves, out and proud, on some continuum as activists and ecological ethicists with the potential to reach significant audiences full of citizens who are prone and poised to move forwards along the paths that we stake out.

Zoos and zoo studies have been, in my experience and perspective, the keystone in the fascinatingly important, complex, fraught business of environmentalist activism and advocacy. Zoos are big business and, I maintain, zoos are bad business. They teach us the wrong things. Americans and other prosperous Westerners urgently need environmental education, but zoos miseducate their customers, the overconsuming and undersustaining citizens of the twenty-first century. We need to feel uncomfortable, worried, haunted by our track record and our ecological trajectory, but zoos palliate us: they suggest that we are doing just fine, that we are like Noah building the ark to take care of everything just as God commanded.

Zoos may warn (somewhere, in small print, on a sign that likely does not get read or understood[3]) of extinctions and habitat desecrations, but zoo-goers generally perceive such concerns as distant, theoretical, and possible but unlikely. Instead, at the zoo, evidence of an exquisitely exotic multi-species prosperity is in our faces (and our ears, and nostrils). Furry-slimy-scaly-leathery animals surround us, high and low, hither and yon, spread out as far as we can walk in the hour or two that a zoo visit lasts. In such a well-populated spectacle, what could possibly be wrong with the balance of life? Why worry about, say, the disappearance of pandas? Pandas are indeed excessively cute, and so are obviously worthy of the intensive ecological life support Marianna Szczygielska describes in her chapter of this volume. Zoo Atlanta seems to have ensured an endless supply of these bears for the millions of zoo-goers who demand to see them, and if Atlanta runs out, San Diego and Washington have plenty – and zoos can always rent more from China.

Zoo-goers, I suggest, are indeed extremely interested in the prosperity of pandas, and a handful of other charismatic megafauna, but they are not concerned or educated about those animals in ways that are remotely appropriate to ecological science. Their fears about losing species, too, are misguided, narcissistic. I want giraffes, the zoo-gooer thinks: they amuse me on my zoo outings. I want them to be here, always, for me to see. That is the purpose of a giraffe, in my life: to be seen at a zoo. We should do everything we can to ensure that there will always be giraffes in zoos.

If we take the story of Noah as a template (as zoos very commonly do), the narrative implies that we are in a troubled time and the waters of destruction will rise, but they will recede soon afterwards, and then we can go back to business as usual. God shines his favour upon those who build these modern-day arks, so once we weather this ecological hiccup, we can return to our old ways and find ourselves back in the driver's seat, oozing hubris, knowing incontrovertibly that we have and deserve dominion just as promised in Genesis 1:26. The supreme power trusts us to use nature and the environment as we see fit, for our own benefit and betterment. All is right in the world.

What is so impressive about *An Inconvenient Truth* is how wide-ranging it is in its implication. Ecology itself, is, of course, interconnected. Gore's ideas are big ideas, presented in the discourses of science, politics, business, geography, climatology, statistics, morality, and personal choice, as the film describes and connects the phenomena of global warming, greenhouse gases, glacial transformations, and the extensive chain of ecosystemic consequences. "This changes everything," I felt, along with millions of other fans, anticipating a phrase Naomi Klein uses in her best-selling book *This Changes Everything: Capitalism vs. the Climate.*

Gore and Guggenheim's film is not, and does not claim to be, encyclopedic or absolute. "This is not everything you need to know about global warming: that's the point," writes A.O. Scott in his *New York Times* review. "But it is a good place to start, and to continue, a process of education that could hardly be more urgent."[4] Indeed, that process of education has continued broadly. As Jeff Skoll, executive producer of *An Inconvenient Truth*, wrote in 2016, "I am proud of the progress we have made. Solutions are now within reach. But more than ever, there is no time to waste. We must bring these solutions to every corner of the globe."[5] Takepart.com marked this anniversary with a rich and popular web presence, and bid visitors: "Share your truth on the 10-year anniversary of *An Inconvenient Truth*." Dozens of journalists, scientists, teachers and students, businesspeople, activists, and politicians testified that the film had opened their eyes, changed their lives, and inspired them to continue to press on with the challenges that it embodied.

What did Gore really discover, and what did he simply package? Is it all just rhetoric? Perhaps it is – in which case, I would celebrate none the less ecstatically that we have a rhetoric, and that it is working. To be sure, there is a counter-rhetoric out there, which disseminates the lie that climate change (a term that tests as slightly less unsettling than global warming[6]) is not human-made, and by the way the earth is flat and dinosaurs existed on the ark.[7] But without ignoring the disturbing persistence of such balderdash (for we must not become complacent about recent advances in the public understanding of the ecological crisis), we can be sure that the Louisiana (2005) and North Carolina (2016) floods, the annual California wildfires (especially those of autumn 2017 and 2018), the intensifying hurricanes, the arctic melting, the droughts and record highs, and the so many more troubling new weather and climate events that are happening frequently and strikingly will guarantee that people realize global warming is real, and dangerous. As individuals, as communities, and as geopolitical actors, we have begun to learn what it means, why it happens, and what we need to do to reverse it.

The bandwagon has grown so large that the truths of Gore's movie now seem more mainstream than inconvenient. In a 2007 Nielsen/Oxford University survey, 66 per cent of respondents who said they had seen *An Inconvenient Truth* stated that it had "changed their mind" about global warming; 89 per cent said that it had made them more aware of the problem; and 75 per cent said it had changed some of their habits.[8]

Gore's truths were right, and while I am not aware of any direct influence that his film had on Cowperthwaite's *Blackfish*, it seems impossible that she was not aware of his rightness when she made her own low-budget documentary on a topic that seemed to go against the grain of American culture and that also turned out to be right in its accusations of malfeasance and dysfunctional nature-tourism.

In *Blackfish*, the sleeper hit documentary about a tragedy at Orlando's SeaWorld, audiences are tempted to empathize with Tilikum, the orca who killed his trainer Dawn Brancheau during a 2010 performance. The whale had been abused for decades in the service of mindless entertainment masquerading as environmental education. "SeaWorld artfully combines education and entertainment in a way that connects people to the sea and sea life like nowhere else," the company's webpage once boasted.[9] Susan G. Davis describes how SeaWorld co-opts audiences' ecological concerns in *Spectacular Nature: Corporate Culture and the SeaWorld Experience*: "Customers want to see the amazing, performing killer whale ... but they also hope to feel agency, that is, that however indirectly, a visit to the theme park is an act of caring ... American business has worked hard to define consumption as a form of concern, political action, and participation ... As one of the killer whale show scripts puts it, 'Just by being here, you're showing that you care!'"[10]

I felt a kind of justice in Tilikum's eventual revolt against his handler, who must have epitomized, for him, the humiliating captive animal displays in which he had the misfortune to spend his life. (Tilikum died in captivity after a year-long illness in 2017, as I was completing this chapter.) In his *Death at SeaWorld: Shamu and the Dark Side of Killer Whales in Captivity*, the activist David Kirby examines Brancheau's death as the inevitable culmination of a long history of violence at SeaWorld and other marine theme parks: an accident waiting to happen, as many scientists had vociferously argued to no avail.[11]

In nature, orcas are not inherently threatening to people. They are curious, playful, clever, highly social, keenly emotional, and profusely communicative animals. Indeed, their complex social structures and bonds make it all the more debilitating for them to be removed from their natural habitats and communities, to be cooped up – as Tilikum was – in small, dark, steel aquarium tanks, where they are deprived of their freedom and their roaming and grouping habits. In this claustrophobic imprisonment, orcas become extremely disturbed, and consequently violent, because they cannot conduct their lives as they would choose to do. If they attack humans under these circumstances, it is because humans have driven them mad.

"Killer whale," a loaded human label that reveals more about the namer than the named, constructs a human narrative that reflects a human perspective. The implication lurking in the denomination of orcas as killer whales suggests the violence that we fear, imagine, or construct in these big, "dangerous" creatures. The name comes from Spanish sailors, who saw orcas attack larger cetaceans and called them *ballena asesina* (assassin whale). Orcas are neither killers nor whales – they are dolphins – though they have become both in the popular imagination. This gruesome designation serves to drum up publicity at a place like SeaWorld, where people capture, constrain, dominate, and exploit these "killers" to show how much more powerful we are than they. In the words of *Blackfish*, SeaWorld's mission was "to turn killer whales into killer profits."[12]

What audiences do to these animals by kidnapping and transforming them into crowd-pleasing clowns suggests that, paradoxically, people simultaneously both admire and scorn their natural force. Spectators act as if they admire that force, finding it exhilarating to bask in its energy. At the same time, they scheme to take it away from the animal and commodify it, for themselves, as if they believe that the essence of life is zero-sum, and so if they want to experience the cornucopia of nature, they must harvest or colonize it. People must take it from other animals. Apparently, SeaWorld audiences can appreciate a majestic, dynamic, powerful whale only by depriving him of everything that it means to be a whale. His overseers cram him into a cage in Orlando because audiences cannot see him easily in the ocean: he will not be on show whenever people come by to look for him. For audiences' construction (reconstruction, or really, falsification) of his whaleness, he must be there for audiences to witness day after day, year after year.

People (SeaWorld administrators, trainers, audiences) demand that he submit himself to their greater power, and they decide how he will manifest this phony, cheesy whaleness that is on display multiple times a day. Instead of his natural behaviour, they would like him to swim in circles, wave to the crowd, and prance and canoodle with the trainers. Audiences pay (a lot) to see him doing what they would like him to do rather than what he would like to do. The circus barkers are in control, calling the shots. When they say jump, we expect orcas like Tilikum to say, "How high?"[13]

I am not a violent person, and I do not endorse violence. But it is hard for me to avoid feeling that there is something that we might have expected (if we thought more sensibly about our relationship to the other animals with whom we share this planet) when Tilikum attacked Brancheau. I have had the same feeling when Montecore attacked Roy Horn (of Siegfried and Roy) on the Las Vegas strip; when Tatiana, a Siberian tiger (who had been made to reside in San Francisco instead of Siberia), attacked Carlos Eduardo Sousa Jr, who tried to climb into her cage; and when Travis, a "pet chimpanzee" (not a good idea) tore off the face of Charla Nash, who stopped by to visit him in the Stamford, Connecticut, home where he was kept. These incidents are not limited by institutionalization, either. At the Denver Zoo, a black rhinoceros bit off a woman's finger. The woman was participating in an innovative program, now "indefinitely suspended," in which zoo-goers could feed and touch a caged rhino for $60.[14] Other zoos have similar programs; for instance, at Zoo Miami's Rhino Encounter Station, patrons can not only touch but also brush and smell a rhino.[15]

Of course, as with Tilikum and Brancheau, what could be read as justice through animal eyes should also be read as tragedy through human eyes, for though all of these attacks are different and for complex reasons, they occur only because the human and animal victims have found themselves in a society that fetishizes dominion over nature instead of valuing respect, empathy, or even just commonsense. Google "when animals attack"; it happens all the time. YouTube is filled with compilation videos like "Top 15 Animal Attacks," "25 Worst Animal Attacks," "Crazy Animals Attack!" These animals are not crazy; we are. Just move away from the wild animals, please, people. Let them be.

I will transgress the anthropomorphic fallacy (the pronouncement that it is impossible to attribute human emotions to nonhuman creatures) and suggest that what goes around comes around. Choose your cliché – there are lots of them, and they all fit. Sometimes you eat the bear, and sometimes, well, the bear eats you (*The Big Lebowski*). In Werner Herzog's *Grizzly Man* (2005), Timothy Treadwell got too close to the bears and, indeed, got eaten. Robinson Devor's 2007 documentary *Zoo* tells of how Kenneth Pinyan, who enjoyed sex with horses, was anally penetrated to death. And *The Crocodile Hunter*: When I heard of Steve Irwin's death, my first thought was, what did you expect, messing around with poisonous giant stingrays? All of these tragedies reflect different kinds of encounters and a range of varying triggers on the animals' part, but they all reveal the potential hazards of crossing a line (and flaunting it) as we try to engage with other animals in ways that are laden with danger: immediate, literal, physical danger, as well as more systemic ecological dangers. There are safe and unsafe, proper and improper, venues for interspecies interaction.

These kinds of incidents should be teachable moments: moments when we are painfully, irrefutably shown that we do not understand other animals very well. We do not understand what they are like, or what they need, or how we can most honestly and equally relate to them. We do not appreciate them. We do not respect them. We see them as fodder for our amusement.

I walked out of *Blackfish* thinking that the film's lesson – that captive animal display is a shameful and cruel desecration – applied not just to the ridiculous shows at SeaWorld, but to those at all zoos and aquariums. (Full disclosure: I walked into the film thinking that already, but Cowperthwaite's documentary struck me as a vital, incisive, universal argument against animal captivity.) All three SeaWorlds – in Orlando, San Antonio, and San Diego – belong to the Association of Zoos and Aquariums, an entity that presents itself as the authority in maintaining the highest standards of zoo practices and as the "leader in the protection of endangered species." What is wrong with SeaWorld is that it is a microcosm of what is wrong with the institution of animal display everywhere.

Numerous effective animal rights campaigns have begun to chip away at the unremitting exploitation of animals that is consequent upon our intrusive voyeurism. Various zoos (including Chicago's Lincoln Park Zoo, the Bronx Zoo, the Detroit Zoo, and, as of 2009, every zoo and circus in India) have phased out elephant exhibits. Elephants were perceived as especially unsuitable inmates in zoos: They suffer high rates of death and injury resulting from their captivity, including chronic foot problems caused by standing on hard surfaces and musculoskeletal disorders from inactivity that results from their being constantly penned or chained instead of able to roam freely and widely as they would like to do. The Georgia Aquarium, where many Beluga whales have already died, was in 2015 denied permission to import more of them from Russia (some of whom would have gone into tanks in Atlanta, and others of whom would have been franchised out to the circus that is SeaWorld).

Cutting back on the captivity of elephants and whales is a good first step. I applaud the dawning awareness that certain animals are obviously unhappy in zoos and unfit to be locked up in cramped, inadequate cages. Finally, three centuries after René Descartes pronounced that animals are merely automata, machines to which human beings could have no moral obligations, a backlash is growing.

But it is no worse, ethically, to kidnap and ruin the life of an elephant or an orca than it is to do so to a smaller animal – a capuchin monkey, a Chinese alligator, an East African crowned crane, a meerkat, a reindeer, a rattlesnake. Each of these animals has an array of needs and desires that cannot be met in captivity. The zoo deprives them of a free range of movement; of a certain climate, and temperature, and light; and of proximity to members of their species and interaction with members of other species. An environment that the animal desires and needs, comprised of certain plants and waterways and topographies and ecologies, is rendered inaccessible. It may be a more obvious case to free the whales than it is to free the alligators, and it is fine to start with the more obvious cases, but please: keep it going.

There are myriad arguments against zoos; the one that *Blackfish* amplifies most emphatically is: how can we appreciate wild animals by humiliating them, by showing them in a decontextualized, painful condition of constraint and alienation from nature, when captivity has tormented them physically and psychologically? Hordes of people come to gawk at this? In the seventeenth century, paying audiences by the hundreds massed for visiting day at London's Bethlem Royal Hospital – commonly known as Bedlam – to gape at the human "Lunatickes" and sometimes poke them with sticks; have we become any more enlightened since?

We are told (by those who profit from the prosperity of these corporations) that we demonstrate good ecological citizenship by visiting zoos, aquariums, and SeaWorlds to connect with and befriend other species. Those animals must be thinking: with friends like these, who needs enemies? Again, please excuse the anthropomorphic fallacy, which I like to think of as the "anthropomorphic-fallacy fallacy," the pretense that we cannot understand what animals are thinking. We might like to think we are unable to imagine their hopes and fears, because that makes them comfortably "other" and exculpates us from guilt about how they suffer at our hands and for our amusement, but this is just a convenient self-deception.

In fact, we can easily imagine exactly how captive animals feel about being in cages or tanks: not very appreciative; crazed. We have constructed the human-animal contact zone as a degrading spectacle. The physical retribution that Brancheau, Irwin, Horn, and others have suffered from animals who could no longer endure the ridiculous sideshows to which we relegate them stands as an ominous metaphor for the catastrophic ecological blowback that awaits us if we continue to treat our earthmates like slaves, freaks, and fools.

I have painted Gore's and Cowperthwaite's achievements as major victories, clever rhetorical, political, ecological, and cinematographic strategies. They are. But they are also, simply, just *right*. I do not claim to have invented this rightness, but I got there, and I have stayed there, and I recognized it as right, and I did whatever I could to add my voice, my two cents, my thinking and my writing, to help amplify that rightness. Whether or not I ever get my Oscar moment, I stand as a collaborator and as a colleague with these filmmakers as I work to learn, disseminate, act on, and inspire others to act on the truth.

As my title indicates, this chapter, to a significant extent, seems to be about me. I am not so egocentric as to assume that I alone can solve the problem of anthropocentric deafness to other animals' thoughts and needs and ideas and suffering and survival. Rather, my point is to encourage all readers, all ecologically attuned citizens in our network of life, to find their own perspective and inspiration for branching out beyond our constrained little boxes, beyond our cone of silence, and enthusiastically into the polyglot world, the overwhelming symphonic chorus, of voices and expressions and desires and habits – into the very life-force of our ecosystem – with a newly developed awareness of how many new and important conversations we can have if we train ourselves to listen to other animals and other agentic realms of life (think of Aldo Leopold's "Thinking Like a Mountain"). These other voices, I feel certain, will generally confirm what I am saying here.

After listening to other animals, we may begin, tentatively, like collaborators rather than imperialists, to speak for them: to say the things that they cannot say (or, more accurately, the things that most other people cannot hear them say) about their worlds, their habitats, their air (our air), their water (our water), their biodiversity and sustainability (etc.). And after listening to and speaking for, finally the ideal culmination of this process would be speaking with these other animals. We must merge our voices with theirs, learn how much common cause we share and how strong a coalition we can comprise by joining ranks and learning to speak our truths in concert with the other living creatures who know and express so much less than we do about some of the problems and hazards in our world and, at the same time, know and express so much more about other aspects of the ecocide that threatens to take us all out, community by community, species by species.

As the editors write in the introduction to this volume (and as every contributor affirms in one form or another), "Until we listen to what animals have to say themselves, the reflection we see upon their surfaces will always be marred by our own chimeras." I suggest that we try to listen to and speak with our cohabitants in order to most effectively crowdsource the ongoing battle to survive the anthropocene. A famous human, Ben Franklin, once said: We must all hang together, or we shall all hang separately.

Many more filmmakers, writers, and activists feature in my hall of fame – Carol Adams (*The Sexual Politics of Meat*), Louis Psihoyos (*The Cove*), and Naomi Klein – and have followed, like me, in the tradition of Paul Ehrlich, Aldo Leopold, Barry Commoner, Rachel Carson, and other prophets who put the pieces together and spoke the truth. Inspired by their success, their demonstrated truths, I add my own. I condemn zoos as placebos, distractions. They are places of inauthenticity, untruth. They allow their communities to pretend that zoo-goers are connecting with other animals and that they are learning something about and appreciating them. But all that happens when people go to zoos is that animals are sucked into human "frames." People frame everything. We draw a boundary around what we are looking at, and we ignore everything outside of it.

When someone puts a rhinoceros in the zoo, the frame is the enclosure. When a shark is relegated to an aquarium, the frame is the tank. Audiences and zookeepers fetishize what is inside the frame, commodify those exhibits, and hold contests to come up with funny "names" like Starlet O'Hara for an elephant at Zoo Atlanta, Winnie the Roo for a kangaroo in the Los Angeles Zoo, and Stubbley for a tiger cub in the Virginia Zoo. Included within the zoo-frame, of course, is merchandise. There is an extra level of cybersurveillance – panda cams, penguin cams – beyond the in-person Foucauldian voyeurism of the zoo visit. But these animals' habitats, their ecosystems, and their real lives are all beyond the frame. How can zoos help visitors connect with other animals and grapple with their existential crises when the main point they demonstrate is that animals (along with human viewers of animals) do not need their habitats?

German playwright Bertolt Brecht thought that his shows were failures if, at the end of the evening, the audience did not go out in the street and riot. The same should hold true for zoo studies. People should read our work and then go out and close down zoos, or make films like *Blackfish*, or lobby to ban circus elephants and Beluga imports, or protest any of the other ridiculous things that happen to other animals inside zoos (to Dinah in New York, to Gust in Antwerp, to Knut in Berlin, to Harambe in Cincinnati) and outside zoos (the killing of Cecil). People do nasty and inhumane things to animals in the fog of our anthropocentric fantasies. We deny them rights, we deny them justice. We must do better or we are all doomed. In the words of another environmental pioneer, Barry Commoner, "Everything is connected to everything else." Preach.

NOTES

1 *March of the Penguins* (directed by Luc Jacquet, 2005) ranks higher than these films in box office receipts, as do several of the Buena Vista-produced films (*Earth*, 2007; *Oceans*, 2009) developed from the *Planet Earth* television documentary series. While these are worthy and informative documentaries, they lack the tenor of advocacy that Gore's and Cowperthwaite's films present at centre stage. Box office receipts are furthermore an inexact measure of the success of *Blackfish*, as one of its most prominent viewing venues was a CNN broadcast; 1.3 million viewers watched the 2013 television premiere, and CNN rebroadcast the film several times later that year and in 2014.

2 See, for example, Despret's *What Would Animals Say*; Iovino and Oppermann, *Material Ecocriticism*; Huggan and Tiffin, *Postcolonial Ecocriticism*; Hurn, *Humans and Other Animals*; Morton, *Hyperobjects*.

3 Kellert's research demonstrated that zoo-goers do not read signs, though they claim they do. See his "Perceptions of Animals in America."

4 A.O. Scott, "Warning of Calamities and Hoping for a Change in 'An Inconvenient Truth,'" *New York Times*, 24 May 2006, http://www.nytimes.com/2006/05/24/movies/24trut.html.

5 Rachel Kraus, "An Inconvenient Truth: Letter to the Community," 21 May 2016, http://skoll.org/2016/05/21/an-inconvenient-truth-letter-to-the-community.

6 Tim Hrincher, "Climate Change vs. Global Warming: How Politics Created a New Term," *Newsmax.com*, 14 November 2014, http://www.newsmax.com/FastFeatures/climate-change-vs-global-warming-politics/2014/11/14/id/607457/.

7 Alan Burdick, "Looking for Life on a Flat Earth," *New Yorker*, 30 May 2018, https://www.newyorker.com/science/elements/looking-for-life-on-a-flat-earth.

8 Nielsen news release, "Global Consumers Vote Al Gore, Oprah Winfrey and Kofi Annan Most Influential to Champion Global Warming Cause: Nielsen Survey," 2 July 2007, http://www.nielsen.com/content/dam/nielsen/en_us/documents/pdf/Press%20Releases/2007/July/Global%20Consumers%20Vote%20Al%20Gore,%20Oprah%20Winfrey%20and%20Kofi%20Annan%20Most%20Influential%20to%20Champion%20Global%20Warming%20Cause%20Nielsen%20Survey.pdf.

9 SeaWorld, landing page, accessed 18 September 2013, https://seaworld parks.com. This material has long since been removed; on 14 October 2016, the webpage announced, apologetically and strategically, "See how we are changing."

10 Davis, *Spectacular Nature*, 39.

11 Kirby, *Death at SeaWorld*.

12 "Blackfish" is how indigenous communities refer to what the SeaWorld crowd calls "killer whales," and unsurprisingly, their relations towards these animals are much less adversarial and exploitative. The Tlingit view the blackfish as a protector of humankind, and many other tribal communities honour the blackfish as their emblematic clan animal, respecting their need to have a wide berth rather than trying to capture, own, and contain them. Native Americans enact their awe for the animals from afar, rather than demanding, as SeaWorld's audiences do, the proximity that necessitates the whales' painful dislocation from ocean to tank, from wild to captive, and from authenticity to a demeaning parody of their natural existence.

13 We humans are not actually in control; the world is in a pretty tenuous state. We are destroying animal habitats on an exponentially increasing scale and extinctions are spiking as a consequence. Toxicities of every kind are rampant as never before in the history of existence. In a perversely fascinating lesson about the marvelous, far-reaching complexities of ecosystemic stability and decline, we are only beginning to see the multitudinous ways in which our global warming will afflict every species of animal, including us – the tip of the iceberg, if you will, though the iceberg is quickly melting. But the people whose job it is to monetize orcas are keenly aware that this tableau of ecological crisis is not a very cheery spectacle: better to watch prancing whales and sustain the implicit illusion that we have everything well in hand.

14 Associated Press, "Black Rhino at Denver Zoo Bites Woman's Finger," *Denver Post*, 28 August 2013, http://www.denverpost.com/2013/08/28/black-rhino-at-denver-zoo-bites-womans-finger/.

15 Zoo Miami, "Zoo Camps: Rhino Encounter," http://www.zoomiami.org/kaziranga-camp-rhino-encounter.

CHAPTER TWELVE

REORIENTING THE SPACE OF CONTAINMENT, OR FROM ZOOSPHERE TO NOÖSPHERE AND BEYOND

Ron Broglio

What are the limits of consciousness? We experience some persistent boundaries around the self with ego's fear of death and loss of identity into something else, a more expansive terrain of mind. Speculatively, what is the dawn of consciousness not only for humans, but also for nonhumans? What foundational roots can be tapped for a broader and more substantive perspective? The dawn of consciousness for humans, beyond reason, is entwined with nonhumans and with nonhuman sentience. Shamans, human-animal hybrids in art and legend, and animistic sensibilities are a few clues to this state of being. What if animals point us elsewhere? What if our metaphysical verticality and judgment has it wrong? What if our comportment of animals and their adaptation around our technologies is a way of speaking, one that tells us that there is another future that is not in line with our techno-capitalist teleology? With their voices and bodies, nonhumans signal (to themselves and to us) the existence of nonhuman spheres of being in the world we share. Why, then, are there bars in zoos? As an inheritance of the Enlightenment, zoo barriers provide us with an all too safe and insistent boundary by which to delimit the range of valid sentience and consciousness. The bars keep our boundaries of self, ego, and sense safely walled in.

Something is knocking from the basement of human dwelling. Something is pounding on the floorboards from the stories beneath where we thought ourselves scaffold-high above the fray. The sides of our house begin to show wear of something chipping away at the walls. We can lift the floorboards, or we can wait. The results will be the same – a paw, a claw, a viscous ooze

– some thing or things will emerge and intrude upon this small domicile of civil space we call home. Using zoos as the object of contemplation, in this chapter I will demarcate human striated space and show how animal being creates, even amid our dwelling, lines of flight and otherly architectured smooth spaces.

Uprightness

Historian of religion Mircea Eliade begins his three-volume *A History of Religious Ideas* with a simple and foundational claim: things changed when humans stood upright. From paleoanthropologist André Leroi-Gourhan in *Gesture and Speech*, we know that verticality enabled a different comportment of body that over time became a physiological shift: "The situation of the human, in the broadest sense, thus appears to be conditioned by erect posture. The phenomenon would seem incomprehensible were it not one of the solutions to a biological problem as old as the vertebrates themselves, that of the relationship between the face as bearer of the organs of nourishment and the forelimb as an organ not only of locomotion but also of prehension."[1] The vertical stance freed the hands, which changed tool use and eating habits, and which together allowed several major physiological transformations: the jaw structure became less protruded, opening the throat and mouth for speech; through an increase in food intake (particularly protein and lipids that foster encephalization), the skull enlarged to make room for an expanding cerebral cortex; and verticality favoured sight over the other senses.

For Eliade, the beginnings of religious meaning starts with this very early physical transformation towards becoming human, which coincides with Leroi-Gourhan's work:

It is sufficient to recall that the vertical posture already marks a transcending of the condition typical of the primates. Uprightness cannot be maintained except in a state of wakefulness. It is because of man's vertical posture that space is organized in a structure inaccessible to the prehominians … It is from this original and originating experience – feeling oneself "thrown" into the middle of an apparently limitless, unknown, and threatening extension – that the different methods of *orientation* are developed; for it is impossible to survive for any length of time in the vertigo brought on by disorientation. This experience of space oriented around a "center" explains the importance of the paradigmatic divisions and distributions of territories, agglomerations, and habitations and their cosmological symbolism.[2]

Verticality and wakefulness coincide in Eliade's origin story. To be upright is to be alert and aware. It is also a "threatening extension," to be exposed. It is a disorientation that demands we reorient by marking out new axes of movement. Jonathan Osborn's contribution to this volume reveals some of these axes of movement, challenging verticality and embracing disorientation, and re-orientation.

At a different register, that of philosophy, the story of verticality is a mark of metaphysics. We have been building upwards, story upon story, and scaffolding a transcendental reach for the skies. This origin story can begin with Plato, who advocated leaving the cave and looking up to the sun, the good, the true forms of which all else is a copy and by which all else is judged. From Plato onwards philosophy builds upwards, such that somewhere up there we are constructing – a work in progress – a divining rod, a differentiator that in its values and valuations mark the true from the false pretenders, the clean from the unclean, and the human from the nonhuman throng. And like Eliade's verticality as wakefulness, reason (marked by Aristotle's *Prior Analytics* through the Enlightenment's privileging of reason) is a singular insomniac eye. It is singular in that it does not admit the need for bodily form and our bioptic vision. It is insomniac in that it cannot rest, lest it lose the authoritative position of height. From on high the cycloptic, insomniac eye of reason marks and demarcates like a surveyor's apparatus with Masonic precision, creating striations for building, dwelling, and thinking. And as Heidegger deftly shows, the way we think determines the way we build and dwell, which then anticipates further reinforcement of thought, which in turn projects further like-minded building and dwelling. In each iterative process we create striations, marks of signification; we forge meaning into our world. The stories of verticality become no longer a myth but instead physically realized within our world. Alphabetic bricks for the house of language and numbered plots make and mark objects-as-possessions. Epistemological matrices of tables and branching trees are referenced and cross-referenced so that the lines and stories close in on themselves to complete the hermeneutics as weather strips the seams against the frost or heat or dampness of a nonhuman outside, an outside not on our terms.

Of course, it does not have to be that way. There are other stories we could tell that would align with Philippe Pignarre and Isabelle Stengers's cry in *Capitalist Sorcery*: "Another world is possible."[3] Other worlds are already actual. Humans and animals share the same earth but live each in their own different worldings. To say that another world is possible is to affirm nonhuman comportment upon the earth. Yet it is also to hold the possibility that another world is possible for us humans, the "we of 'we.'"[4] Can we imagine a world of "being-with" nonhumans differently than how we comport ourselves today? Can we imagine a being-with that is not domestication or domination but cohabitation, what Donna Haraway calls "mess mates"?[5] For this possibility, consider the aptly named *Cave of Forgotten Dreams* by Werner Herzog, where he films the archeological exploration of the Chauvet Cave in France with its paintings made some thirty-two thousand years ago.[6]

Forgotten Dreams

As the *New Yorker* writer Judith Thurman explains in her essay "First Impressions":

Some of the most remarkable art ever conceived was etched or painted on the walls of caves in southern France and northern Spain. After a visit to Lascaux, in the Dordogne, which was discovered in 1940, Picasso reportedly said to his guide, "They've invented everything." What those first artists invented was a language of signs for which there will never be a Rosetta stone; perspective, a technique that was not rediscovered until the Athenian Golden Age; and a bestiary of such vitality and finesse that, by the flicker of torchlight, the animals seem to surge from the walls, and move across them like figures in a magic lantern show.[7]

What we find here is a different set of relations to animals; it is a forgotten dream in which another world is possible. It is a different thinking that made for different building and dwelling and for a different comportment upon the earth. Layers of horses stacked upon one another seem to gallop, their motion caught by repetition of line and pattern as they push from folds in the stone. Herzog calls this a proto-animation. Indeed, an anima or spirit seems to be infused within these paintings.[8]

By way of cave painting one sees a heightened intensity of relation to the environment. It is worth noting that this Paleolithic art was created by hunter-gatherer communities, that is to say, before human domestication of animals such as cattle, horses, and sheep. Throughout the cave paintings of the period, bison, auroch, and horses are depicted, along with some deer and ibex. Felines, rhinos, bears, and mammoths appear occasionally. Dangerous animals occur with even less frequency, but often with a noted importance in their depiction. Some cave images show animals in specific comportments, a "young female who appears to be waiting" or "an old male ready to attack."[9] Others, but by no means a majority of the images, depict hunting or the sympathetic marks of willing a good hunt. But these are not technical manuals of hunting, nor do they depict animals as stock or as standing reserves that lie in wait for human use. (One could say that zoos are the offshoot of conceiving animals as standing reserves waiting for, and reduced in meaning to, use.) What we find in these paintings are sets of relations without domestication or mastery. They capture a liminal moment of trying to make a space within culture for a-other, for animal others. It is not that these hunter-gatherers are immune to naming and categorizing the animal. Rather, animals' cultural spaces and meanings are large enough to accommodate animal agency and mark a space for the animals' unknowability – their animality beyond culture.[10] Alongside animals are imprints of human hands, humans marking a space, or spacing a space, of relation to their environment. This taxonomic matrix is a very different set of spacing from that of Linnaeus and the Enlightenment tradition of knowledge. Rather than a taxonomic system that objectifies animals, these paintings, along with markings of human hands, display relation and mutual vulnerability.

In *Cave of Forgotten Dreams*, Herzog leaves one of the most haunting discoveries for near the end of his film. In the far recesses of the cave, in the End

Chamber, a well-wrought bison looks singularly into the distance. Just past it, in the Sacristy, hangs a stalactite formation with a curious image. On the back side of the protruding rock, "wrapped around, or, as it appears, straddling, the phallus is the bottom half of a woman's body, with heavy thighs and bent knees that taper at the ankle. Her vulva is darkly shaded, and she has no feet. Hovering above her is a creature with a bison's head and hump, and an aroused, white eye. But a line branching from its neck looks like a human arm with fingers. The woman's posture suggests that she may be squatting in childbirth, and the animals, on a level with her loins, seem to be streaming away from her."[11] Here we enter a world far from alphabetic bricks and the insomniac eye of reason.

It is a world of shamans and hallucinations and hunter-gatherers who dwell upon the land. The interest here is in the type of relations that formed between humans and nonhumans, how these formations are represented, and what other worlds might be possible. While below I outline a shamanism related to these cave paintings, there is a range of interesting recent work on contemporary shamanism including anthropologist Eduardo Kohn's *How Forests Think: Toward an Anthropology beyond the Human*, anthropologist Homayun Sidky's *Haunted by the Archaic Shaman: Himalayan Jhakris and the Discourse on Shamanism*, and philosopher and cultural ecologist David Abram's *Becoming Animal: An Earthly Cosmology*.

In *The Shamans of Prehistory*, archaeologists Jean Clottes and David Lewis-Williams connect cave painting to spiritual cultural meaning. They focus on the shaman, who goes into a trance – either frenzied or passive – in order to heal the sick, change weather, foretell futures, control animals, or talk with sprits and spirit animals. These authors claim that there are, neurologically, three stages of trance with distinct features that coincide with different images in cave art. In brief, these altered states of consciousness range from a first state of more mild hallucination with abstract marks – such as waves, dots, and cross-hatchings – to a second stage where these marks become figures – such as a wave becoming a snake or dots becoming a bowl or stars – and finally, through a dramatic dark tunnel transition, one reaches a stage of human-animal transformations and combinations, as well as objects becoming animated. In this final stage, so critical to shamanism, monsters, people, and settings become intensely real. In many cases, the shaman is a gateway between worlds – both existent and not readily visible. Returning from these altered states, the shaman is able to convey to the community the state of affairs beyond the visible.

Shamans' experiences revise the vertical structure of human comportment that Eliade describes. A typical example is a southern African Sans rock art image that depicts an antelope-human, wherein a shaman takes on horns and stoops down, losing human uprightness to enter another world and set of re-lations. In contrast to Eliade's claim that "uprightness cannot be maintained except in a state of wakefulness," the shaman enters a different state of con-sciousness where the privileged wakefulness of verticality is challenged by the vertical-gone-horizontal of trance awareness. Eliade claims that from up-rightness, "this original and originating experience," comes "the different methods of *orientation* ... developed [for humans]"; in contrast, the shaman, through vertical-gone-horizontal decomportments, reconfigures spatial ori-entation between human and nonhuman being.[12] As Kohn describes this way of seeing: "like a shaman, one can be simultaneously aware of both view-points as well as how they are connected by something greater that, like a trap springing shut, suddenly encompasses them ... such moments of aware-ness is a signature of ... multinatural perspectivalism."[13] It is not enough to be either vertical or horizontal as a dialectical comportment. The shaman's path is not a synthesis of the dialectic but a whole other field and ecology that is possible.

In a fundamental way, the shamanistic experience and the complex relat-edness in cave art show a different way of thinking about human relation-ships to the world. As Wendy Wheeler explains in her ongoing work in biosemiotics, it is a Batesonian mind-as-ecology or mind-as-relatedness that works over and against mind as a singular system within a body:

Where in the world is meaning? ... The conventional modern scientific account of subjectivity is that meaning and knowledge are "*in*" people's minds, and that minds are somehow "in" people's brains. Since brains are essentially neurochemical meat, this materially "additive" account of meaning (as both experience and interpretation) is that it must, in the end, be causally reducible *in its entirety* to neurochemical activity – if not, as experienced mind and will, an illusion entirely. This latter is the position taken by "eliminative materialists" such as Patricia and Paul Churchland and Daniel Dennett. However, mind, as we know, is always "intentional" – i.e. the experience of self in relation. The colours, tones and feelings of these are nowhere to be found in meat.[14]

In other words, mind is not caged by brain or by body. It is "the result of sensuous body-plus-environment-plus-memory relations," a thrownness in the world that is calibrated and oriented, recalibrated and reoriented, according to experience within a milieu. Wheeler's work on biosemiotics takes up Bateson's revision of Darwinian evolution. Following natural history and Malthusian figuring of populations, Darwin constructed natural selection and evolution along species and family lines. Species and family were the units of survival. But as Bateson asserts, "the unit of survival is organism plus environment." He goes on to say that "we are learning by bitter experience that the organism which destroys its environment destroys itself. If, now, we correct the Darwinian unit of survival to include the environment and the interaction between organism and environment, a very strange and surprising identity emerges: *the unit of evolutionary survival turns out to be identical with mind.*"[15] Bateson here draws from a "continuously connected" model of biology, devised by geoscientist Vladimir Ivanovich Vernadsky, where "man is elementally indivisible from the biosphere. And this inseparability is only now beginning to become precisely clear to us. In reality, no living organism exists in a free state on Earth. All of these organisms are inseparably and continuously connected – first and foremost by feeding and breathing – with their material-energetic environment."[16] Perhaps what shamans have been pointing to all along is the broader field of evolutionary survival where organism plus environment becomes mind. The dissolution of the hominoid ego barriers of consciousness in the shaman's journey becomes an open plane, a smooth space, of mind as, and with, environment.

In his *Darwin's Pharmacy: Sex, Plants, and the Evolution of the Noösphere*, English and sts scholar Richard Doyle explores how altered consciousness – primarily through plants – opens a window into the "continuously connected" model of biology. Doyle's work reveals the bars of the Enlightenment human subject, the matrix of Linnaean species nomenclature, and Darwinian units of survival as they give way to a more expansive universe.

To the noösphere and beyond! Doyle considers the challenge of expressing this more expansive mind using the alphabetic blocks of language, the syntax that favours autonomy, and the insomniac eye of reason: "If the Upanishads instruct that 'Tat Tvam Asi,' 'You are that,' and they do, 'that' is an ecosystem subject to sudden volatility and massive extinctions even as it is increasingly interconnected with an otherwise dynamic, even lively, cosmos. It is therefore a rhetorical challenge to make this perception available to those humans who so violently cling to visions of autonomy even as they are forced to adapt."[17] Doyle develops an alternative subjectivity and epistemology, an "ecosystem subject," by threading together religious and philosophical nondominant, minor histories of consciousness. The logic of division between self and other dissolves in the claim, "You are that." Basic Aristotelian logic dissolves as an ecological thinking claims that not-you is also you, or there is neither you nor not-you but only an "are," a being and residing. *Darwin's Pharmacy* makes evident how psychedelics (derived from "manifest" and "mind") can dissolve the bars and barriers to a broader ecology of mind. To experience such an ecology is to change one's cultural comportment. And it is here that we can rethink what a zoo can be: from zoosphere to noösphere and beyond.

The manifest mind, where "You are that," corresponds with the dissolution of self as described by Judith Thurman in her experience of the Chauvet Cave:

> Every encounter with a cave animal takes it and you by surprise. Your light has to rouse it, and your eye has to recognize it, because you tend to see creatures that aren't there, while missing ones that are. Halfway home to the mortal world, I asked Alard if we could pause and turn off our torches. The acoustics magnify every sound, and it takes the brain a few minutes to accept the totality of the darkness – your sight keeps grasping for a hold. Whatever the art means, you understand, at that moment, that its vessel is both a womb and a sepulcher.[18]

As sepulchre there is a death to the ego boundaries. Like a sensory deprivation tank, here in the darkness Thurman struggles to get a hold, to find a grasping point by which to orient verticality and self. This is the "nightwatch" in phenomenologist Alphonso Lingis's *The Imperative* (to which this chapter will return later), where "twilight dissolves the surfaces" and "things lose their separateness." He explains that the darkness and loss of optical orientation "depersonalizes." "The night affects the identity we had." We feel a dark lure as "night itself summons us" and the self dissolves.[19] It is in and through this sepulchre that one is born to something new; it is both tomb and womb, as Thurman describes it. The cave is a site for rituals and initiations. Can we be born into a larger mind-world? And how would this dissolve the zoosphere?

Striated to Smooth

By way of example, consider this sympathetic biopolitical uprising converging around Sami, the chimpanzee who fashioned a line of flight from Belgrade Zoo (a zoo whose logo invokes the verticality of transcendence – a chimp hand stretches out towards a human hand modelled after Michelangelo's Sistine Chapel God creating Adam). Arriving in 1988, Sami's residence was "a small, drab cage, whose grid was reinforced in order to resist the strength of an adult chimpanzee."[20] Sami escaped twice and both times headed for the city centre. The first was around 8:00 p.m. on 21 February 1988. He roamed from the Balkan cinema towards a city tunnel, then to Kalemegdan Park (or Belgrade Fortress), and was eventually accompanied by some dozen police cars. Finally, the one person he trusted, zoo director Vuk Bojovic, had a long talk with the chimp. Bojovic got Sami into his car and drove him back to the zoo. It was the second zoo break that became a sympathetic biopolitical uprising. Just a few days later, he once again overcame a number of zoo and city obstacles. Sami walked past confused and frightened zoo handlers, through open doorways, over fences, and past dense city traffic to the courtyard of number 33 Cara Dusana Street, where he rested first on a tree then later on the roof of the garage. Word got around of his escape and news media covered the event minute by minute. Over four thousand citizens of Belgrade watched Sami on the roof. Some carried signs that read, "You are not alone. We are with you!," "Do not come down," and "Do not give up!" Sami transformed from a potentially harmful animal to a figure of freedom. People cheered Sami and did not want him apprehended. Again, Bojovic was able to convince Sami to return. Newspapers called him Belgrade's favourite dissident, the Dorćolska refugee.[21] Sami is remembered today with a bronze statue at his burial site across from the zoo's new and improved residence for chimpanzees.

The signs of solidarity at Sami's escape are reverberations of humans caught unhappily in the communist system in then-Yugoslavia, which was under the shadow of the Soviet Union and still haunted by the specter of its first revolutionary leader and president for life Josip Tito. Sami's escape invoked fellow feeling among humans who identified with his confinement. His escape became a momentary rupture in the social fabric. The animal was not complying with its prescribed place in the social system, and this line of flight ignited desires just below the surface of Belgrade's citizens. Had Sami been a human, those who aligned with him could have faced arrest, but as a liminal figure on the edge of the social circle, as an animal, Sami could be cheered by the crowd with impunity. In cathartic voices and presence, they connected their concerns with his. The biopolitics that confined the chimp to a realm outside the human in turn aided the humans confined within Yugoslavian communism. Together with Sami, the people of Belgrade could imagine that another world was possible. Humans and chimp together, for a moment, levelled the geopolitical ecology. It is for this that there is a memorial statue to him today. And perhaps it reminds us that we, too, are caught within an ideology that limits the biopolitical and ecological implications of a "continuously connected" model of biology. It reminds us of the Upanishads dictum, "You are that."

In his film *Underground* (1995), the Serbian director Emir Kusturica uses the World War II bombing of Belgrade for similar ends.[22] The plight of citizens in the bombing is echoed by the animals' cries of pain and confusion. Then, after the bombing and with zoo barriers demolished, exotic animals roam freely across the city and provide a surreal aura to scenes in the film. Eventually, through a series of twists, some characters move underground for safety and, even after the war has ended, are told by leaders that the war continues and that they must stay underground and work for the good of the country. This charade continues for some twenty years until the zookeeper's pet monkey, Soni (sounding similar to Sami), climbs into an underground tank and fires a round of ammunition from its large-caliber cannon into a wall, creating a hole for the underground dwellers to slowly venture into the above-ground world. Soni is Sami with weapons to reconfigure the field of play within the film. The deluded biopolitical captives kept underground receive a new ecological terrain from an animal revolutionary. The film continues with mazes and enclosures for Belgrade's citizens, but this nod to Sami shows the potency of animals dissolving barriers. In such a line of flight there is a disorientation of identities and comportments such that another world is possible.

In thinking of animal rebellion, George Orwell had it wrong; *Animal Farm* was still too human. In the preface to the Ukrainian edition, Orwell explains the origin of his novel: "I saw a little boy, perhaps ten years old, driving a huge carthorse along a narrow path, whipping it whenever it tried to turn. It struck me that if only such animals became aware of their strength we should have no power over them, and that men exploit animals in much the same way as the rich exploit the proletariat."[23] Such repressive conditions are ripe for revolution. Orwell goes on to tell the allegorical tale of animals rebelling against their human overlords. As the quotation from the preface indicates, Orwell uses animals as an allegory in which our power over them figures "in much the same way" as that of the rich over the proletariat. But what happened to the actual animal – the carthorse Orwell saw being whipped?[24] It drops out of the story or, at most, serves as a figure for power relations among humans. Orwell is not alone in using actual incidents of animal suffering to describe such contested relations. When will the animals have their revolution in which animal life (using bioethicist and posthumanist Cary Wolfe's words) "burst[s] through power's systematic operation in ways that are more and more difficult to anticipate"?[25] Is it possible to think of lives and bodies as other than those which "[have] to be redeemed by its radical subordination to a 'genuinely political' project for which it [animality] is merely the vehicle"?[26] In other words, it is not that Sami or Soni or the carthorse that begot *Animal Farm* are simply figures in human political allegory. Rather, something is pounding below the floorboards of the vertical and increasingly unstable human dwelling. Something is pecking through the walls, and seeping in from the cracks of the hermeneutic circle. The animals are smoothing our striated spaces. Following Soni, they are blowing out a wall using our own technologies against our homestead. Following the shaman, they are leveling the upright and proper barriers of an Enlightenment notion of self-contained subjectivity and enclosed mind. Channelling Bateson, and smoothing these striations, the body becomes connected to environment as a continuously connected mind.

In yet another tale of escape, J.J. Grandville's *The Public and Private Lives of Animals* imagines animals of all sorts uniting in a revolution and breaking free from the human constraints upon them. As John Berger relates, the end of part two of Grandville's story addresses the reader with some haunting news: "Goodnight then, dear reader. Go home, lock your cage well, sleep tight and have pleasant dreams. Until tomorrow."[27] Perhaps we are all in cages and only simulating freedom. This follows Jean Baudrillard, writing in *Simulation and Simulacra*: "Disneyland is there to conceal the fact that it is the 'real' country, all of 'real' America, which is Disneyland (just as prisons are there to conceal the fact that it is the social in its entirety, in its banal omnipresence, which is carceral)."[28] The Disneyland-esque entertainment of zoos and the carceral nature of zoos both obscure the fact that we live in a simulacra of the real world. So, while zoo escapes are important to document, every escape from our current state of affairs is a zoo escape from our cages. As Daniel Vandersommers writes, "most zoogoers remained blind to the politics that encapsulated them within the zoo, the same politics that tethered the zoo itself to the ontology of capital underwriting the socio-psychological demand for the peculiar institution in the first place."[29] We are interpolated into that system of capital and sociopsychological demands. In yet another moment in Grandville's text, a wild jay explains to a caged song bird, "You cannot form just impressions of objects seen through the bars of a cage, they must appear distorted and confused … All this renders it impossible for you to give an intelligent account of things of which you know absolutely nothing."[30] We must reconfigure our comportment and way of seeing to escape the simulacra and the distortions from the bars of our cages.

Responding to the Imperative

Such self-abandonment and reorientation is the project of Lingis's *The Imperative*. For Lingis, the imperative is a call from outside, a call from the environment, which asks us to respond. Our response is not an objectification of nature, but rather a fittedness between the human body and the entities that call to us. Lingis pushes phenomenology to its limits and then beyond by claiming that the ordering of perception is not found in mind but rather in entities in the world that offer an imperative. We cannot see the world's full coherence, but we can catch onto it through adjustment of the self as fitted to entities and their call. The form and scheme of objects is abandoned for a sensual immersion and being-with other entities: "The primary ego is not that of a body positing or positioning itself, it is the exclamation of a body in abandon exposing itself ... This nakedness is not lived as vulnerability and in timidity and precautions, but, beneath its garb and its armor, as sensuality of life exposing itself to the elements, enjoying its exposure."[31] Here is an opening up of body and environment as expanded mind, through a felt relatedness. Throughout *The Imperative*, Lingis carefully crafts a relatedness that does not create a subject-object dualism. Sensation is not simply a reaction by the nervous system. Rather, it is a force outside ourselves that reminds us that we are involved within a sensible field.[32] For Lingis, we do not actively apprehend or consciously comprehend sensation. There is not the prehension or grasping with opposable thumb; rather, we are "infolded" (in Lingis's terminology) within it:

The sensibility for the elements is not apprehension which makes contract with the contours of a substance, nor comprehension which takes hold of something consistent and coherent. It is not a movement that casts our synergic forces toward some object-objective present across a distance. Sensuality is not intentionality, is not a movement aiming at something exterior, transcendent, a movement that objectifies ... Sensuality is a movement of involution in a medium. One finds the light by immersion, one is in atmosphere, in sonority, in redolence or in stench, in warmth or in cold.[33]

Sensation interrupts our routines and habits to call us elsewhere. Sensations and the sensual world function in the "interrogative mode," meaning they relate and ask for relation and response.[34] As such, they induce in us a "postural integration," a shift in comportment and orientation by which we respond to the interrogative mode.[35] One can think of the shaman's vertical-gone-horizontal of trance awareness as such a shift.

Such a mode of thinking is far from the taxonomic structures of a Linnaean system. Entities are not objects to be comprehended or apprehended and placed within categories and zoo architectures. Again, to return to the field of sensation as an open questioning, Lingis explains: "It is because we find ourselves despite our own stock of concepts and our taxonomies, continually implicated in things that are trying out their reality in indecisive and inconclusive appearances, their opaque colors and bulk and resonances besetting the space they occupy with the gravity of a question beset by questions to follow their essence consistent and coherent evidence that elude formulation."[36] Sensation acts as open questions that prevent intellectual comprehension by eluding formulation. As the 1960s psychedelic band Ultimate Spinach says in the acid classic "Mind Flowers," "Sacrifice! Of your ego! Sacrifice, sacrifice, let it go! Let it go! Let it go!"[37] It shatters and smooths psychic space, disorients in order to reorient outside of ego towards what the song calls the "myriad conscience of tomorrow's mind." It is a tomorrow not already demarcated by habits of the past, but responding to our involution in a medium.

What if this medium is a massive environment, or sets of environments, in which we are on an earth with other animals? What if this earth is a distributed network of porous enclosures? In other words, what if we are infolded within a global plane that one could call a zoo, or better still a zoesphere (not a zoo of containment, but *zoe* from the Greek for biological life)? And what if this zoesphere is an output of sensible forces which ask for a response – a call to the noösphere and beyond? Our human-architectured zoos – built with blunt alphabetic bricks and numbered plots – are a mere decoy and distraction from a larger field of global sensation. Ideally, a collection of essays on zoos – a collection such as the one of which this chapter is a part – is more than a caged discourse that reinforces the fundamental premises of zoos, that maintains the boundaries but shifts the furniture of the container. Instead, by minute particulars the stories and histories of zoos can dispel the Enlightenment foundations and premises that authorize zoos and instead suggest other pathways.

Timothy Pachirat opens *Every Twelve Seconds: Industrialized Slaughter and the Politics of Sight* with an event in Omaha, Nebraska, in 2004.[38] Six bovine escaped a slaughterhouse. One ambled down the main street and was easily apprehended. Another escaped only to cross the road to another slaughter facility. But four cattle made a line of flight to a parking lot – not any parking lot but a church parking lot, and not any church but the Church of St Francis of Assisi, the patron saint of animals. Yet because we do not accept that cattle understand allegory, and because we do not allow cattle to have miracles, the animals were gathered up and taken to their death. A decade later, on 26 January 2014, Pope Francis released two doves. Doves, of course, are symbols of peace derived from the hope and possibility that a dove offered to Noah after the flood. The dove was the second bird Noah used, after the first – a raven he released to find dry land – refused to return: "it kept flying back and forth until the water had dried up from the earth."[39] So, Pope Francis released two doves to ascend skywards as a symbol of peace and hope and a promise between God and humans. The doves were immediately attacked by a seagull and a black raven (perhaps, echoing Poe, crying "nevermore"). Flying from human hands, the doves entered a space of animality where the Church's transcendental signification and symbolism held no meaning. If humans allot no miracles for animals, then why should we expect superior treatment for ourselves and the animals we use as symbols?

Animals will continue to remind us of a space outside of human stratifications and markings, and they will continue to remind us that we are infolded within a global zoesphere. On 15 January 2009, US Airways Flight 1549 was hit in mid-air. The plane lost thrust on both engines and was forced to land on the Hudson River. The movie *Sully* soon followed. The culprit was a skein of Canadian geese asserting their right to airspace. What if we took the cattle, the seagull, the raven, and the Canadian geese more seriously? What if they are showing us a space outside of our techno-capitalist future and pointing us to the "myriad conscience of tomorrow's mind"? Animality appears to us in what Jean-François Lyotard would call an event: "The event, that is, happens in excess of the referential frame within which it might be understood, disrupting or displacing that frame."[40] As Bill Readings summarizes Lyotard on this point, the event "disrupts any pre-existing referential frame within which it might be represented or understood. The eventhood of the event is the radical *singularity* of happening."[41] These animal events, as Soni in a tank, blow a hole through the walls of human stratification.

If zoos are evidence of the way we think with animals – a way inherited from Enlightenment epistemology – then the challenge is to think otherwise. In this chapter, I reveal the possibilities of radically other modalities of thought and other ways to build and dwell. I reject the cultural histories of zoos, which normalize the current state of affairs by tracing a standard history of zoological gardens as sites of science and recreation and then follow this by explaining contemporary models of zoos as sensitive to animal ecologies and as arks in the blundering spaceship earth. Instead, consider speculative futures and other ways to build with animals. There are other cultural histories with animals that work on a fundamentally different (meta)physical and mental architecture. Another world is possible and with it another way to infold in the world.

NOTES

1   Leroi-Gourhan, *Gesture and Speech*, 19.
2   Eliade, *A History of Religious Ideas*, 3.
3   Pignarre and Stengers, *Capitalist Sorcery*, 4.
4   Snæbjörnsdóttir and Wilson, "The We of 'We,'" 125–30.
5   Haraway, *When Species Meet*.
6   Herzog, *Cave of Forgotten Dreams*.
7   Thurman, "First Impressions."
8   For the caves as a sound space of voicing with the nonhuman, see Hendy, *Noise*.
9   Clottes and Lewis-Williams, *The Shamans of Prehistory*, 49.
10 This aligns with work by Despret, *What Would Animals Say*.
11 Thurman, "First Impressions."
12 Eliade, *A History of Religious Ideas*, 3.
13 Kohn, *How Forests Think*, 97.
14 Wheeler, "Biosemiotics."
15 Bateson, *Steps toward an Ecology of Mind*, 491 (emphasis original). Cited in ibid.
16 Doyle, *Darwin's Pharmacy*, 7.
17 Ibid., 7–8.
18 Thurman, "First Impressions."
19 Lingis, *The Imperative*.
20 Belgrade Zoological Gardens, http://www.beozoovrt.rs/sami-chimp.
21 Sami is one of several zoo celebreties discussed in the chapters of this collection.
22 Kusturica, *Underground*.
23 Orwell, *The Collected Essays*, 3:458–9.

24 For other examples of the placeholder role of animals, see Tyler, *Ciferae*; Young, "Animality," 9–21.

25 Wolfe, *Before the Law*, 32–3.

26 Ibid. Wolfe elaborates, "But what is fascinating in all these examples is the almost hysterical condemnation and disavowal of embodied life as something that always already has to be redeemed by its radical subordination to a 'genuinely political' project for which it is merely the vehicle, merely the gateway to 'the immortal' or 'the infinite.' And so one has to wonder if the problem here is not with *ethics* but with politics conceived as the realm of 'Good versus Evil' … Are we not witnessing here (as even the most sophomoric psychoanalytic analysis would surely note) a nearly stereotypical disavowal of the fact of our embodied existence that links us fatefully to mortality, and thus to a domain of contingency over which we finally have less than complete control?"

27 Berger, *About Looking*, 19.

28 Baudrillard, *Simulation and Simulacra*, 12.

29 Vandersommers, "The Sectionalism of the National Zoo."

30 Grandville, *The Public and Private Lives of Animals*, 331–2.

31 Lingis, *Imperative*, 18.

32 Sparrow, "Bodies in Transit," 105. See also Wheeler, "Alphonso Lingis," in *Kantian Imperatives*.

33 Lingis, *Imperative*, 15.

34 Ibid., 29.

35 Ibid., 65.

36 Ibid., 64.

37 Ultimate Spinach, "Mind Flowers."

38 Pachirat, *Every Twelve Seconds*, 1–2.

39 Genesis 8:7.

40 Readings, *Introducing Lyotard*, 57.

41 Ibid., xxxi. See also Readings, "Postmodernity and Narrative," 233.

CHAPTER THIRTEEN

ZOOMORPHIC BODIES: MOVING AND BEING MOVED BY ANIMALS

Jonathan Osborn

The conscious visual and sensorial presence of each of the three hundred and sixty animals is the only entryway into the execution of ARK, an entryway that has profoundly changed my way of thinking about movement creation, execution, and communication. The use of visualization, essential during the learning phase and with each execution of the piece, is profound on two levels. With each passing movement I recall the memory of a close focus, one that is situated directly on the part, texture, colour, body, or actions of the animal I am drawing from. Second, though nearly simultaneous, is a wider lens through which is seen the organization of the zoo that we visited and the geographical placement of the animal. These impressions are made visceral in movement. This use of visualization gives me combined sensations of inner and outer territory that are new and allow me to engage in a deeply somatic experience that is also replicable and strongly connected to form and specificity. I did not know this was possible. This particular balance is also what allows me to bypass strong movement patterns that exist in my body from years of training and performing, making new physical coordinations, sensations, and nuances possible. The moment the animals slip away from my consciousness is the moment my physicality resorts to habit.

– Danielle Baskerville, ARK performer

In this chapter, I am concerned with ARK, a dance-based, research-as-creation work initiated in 2015, which accompanies this collection as an online video/text resource.[1] An eighteen-minute choreographic work created in collaboration with Canadian performer Danielle Baskerville, ARK imagines the Toronto Zoo as an anthropomorphically designed space for animals in which the human body has the potential to become zoomorphically affected through kinaesthetic exchange with living nonhuman bodies. Although conceived of prior to, and independently from, my dissertation research focused on expanding on the work of scholars such as Jane Desmond who explore the performative resonances of the artificial staging of human and animal bodies, ARK has been a quiet companion to my academic work and has persistently whispered insights about the choreographic nature of environments, the embodied relations between different species, and the often-overlooked phenomenological nature of academic research. In this chapter, I will outline the work's domain, conceptualization, research process, and methodological practices, and their resonant effects on choreographic structure and movement vocabulary. Then, I will reflect on how an aesthetic practice grounded in movement, kinaesthetic empathy, and embodied memory can produce novel critical insights into the decentring of the humanist subject as well as alternative ways to relate to zoos and their inhabitants.

A procession of specifically nonhuman gestures that unfold within the specifically human topography of the Toronto Zoo is the conceptual basis for ARK's creation and performance, and the work actively situates animals' bodies as vectors for nonhuman movement transmission. In collusion with this idea, the work acknowledges the zoo as a forum of modernity in which animals are simultaneously subject and resistant to our monolithic ideological mediation of their bodies and identities through the undeniable presence of their perceptive forms, forms which in most cases are visibly ill-suited for the spaces we design for them. ARK does not actively dispute academic critiques descended from John Berger's iconic refutation of the zoo as a natural space in *Why Look at Animals?*,[2] but it does propose different ways to see animals by insisting that those in zoos are always already more than emblems of human culture.[3] Within the work, there is continual tension between the animal body that teaches us about unimagined possibilities of human movement and the animal body that teaches about human failure – a tension made palatable through attention to the specifics of animal bodies and the delib-erate truncation of the unfolding of their movement within space.

Although the subject of movement is not entirely absent from academic discussions about the zoo – researchers routinely refer to the animals' lack of movement, stereotypic movement, and prescribed modes of bodily train-ing[4] – tacit relations between human and animal bodies in such institutions have been less studiously examined.[5] Consequently, the bodies of animals at the zoo are often seen as only prisoners; failed avatars; pale shadows of their wild brethren; or denatured forms warped by cultural constructions, commerce, and politics. By approaching the zoological garden as a living space through the lens of dance, I have found it to be a place of discovery that overflows with real bodies, complex movement, and negotiated multi-species relations. I have seen a myriad of unique articulations, rhythms, and exchanges, a breathing collection of wildly different ways to inhabit, navi-gate, and experience the world.

My kinaesthetic zoological observations are not unique. In her memoir *Blood Memory*, modern dance pioneer Martha Graham discusses a pacing lion at the Central Park Zoo as vital to the development of her revolutionary approach towards movement: "I would watch this lion for hours as he'd take those great padding steps four times back and across the cage. Finally, I learned to walk that way. I learned from the lion the inevitability of return, the shifting of one's body. The shift of the weight is one key aspect of that technique, that manner of movement."[6] Although the repetitive steps of Gra-ham's lion might be now recognized as symptomatic of the animal's discon-tent (and ironically Graham might have unknowingly integrated the duress, rather than any wild "essence" of an animal, into her work), the zoo's rela-tionship to this critical aspect of her technique is incontestable. Similarly, Merce Cunningham, another American dance icon, had a lifelong interest in movement research conducted at zoos.[7] Credited with having "altered the audience's very perception of what constitutes a dance performance and [having] explored previously inconceivable methods of putting movement together,"[8] Cunningham's studies of zoo animals and their movement pro-vided material for specific dances, such as *Solo* and *Boy Who Wanted to Be a Bird*, as well as for innovative choreographic material throughout his ca-reer.[9] Carol Teitelbaum, a former Cunningham company member, stated that it was an "offset rhythmic effect" used to create "kinetic texture" that characterized his nature-based works.[10]

In "Dancing the Animal to Open the Human: For a New Poetics of Locomotion," dance scholar Gabriele Brandstetter reflects on the theoretical importance of the figure of the animal to dance in light of Giorgio Agamben's statement: "Man is the animal that must recognize itself as human to be human."[11] Brandstetter asserts that the "boundary between man and animal runs through man,"[12] a situation highlighted by the paradoxical means through which a dancer "adopts the movements of an animal, dissimulating his 'human' nature by presenting himself as 'animal' for *cultural* reasons. And by so doing, by becoming an animal, he underlines his continuing existence as a man."[13] Brandstetter explores the resonances of this idea through reference to theatrical and social dances that evoke the figure of the animal, including Nijinsky's *Rite of Spring*, Fokine's *Dying Swan*, ragtime dances, Merce Cunningham's *Beach Birds*, Jan Fabre's *Vervalsing zoals ze is, onvervalst*, Wim Vandekeybus's *It*, and William Forsythe's *Decreation*. Reflecting on these works, she recognizes that "the physical reflection of the 'animal' and 'animal locomotion' in dance also implies the possibility of giving movement expression to the fleetingness, the vulnerability, the aliveness of the 'Other.'"[14] Appropriating the term "decreation" from Forsythe, Brandstetter postulates that the opportunity the animal body provides to the dancer is the opportunity to decreate themselves as conventionally human.

The potential for animals to affect human bodies and practices has also been examined outside of dance studies and is a persistent theme in the work of phenomenologist Alphonso Lingis. Here, the living animal body and its motion are positioned as a tonic to counter the stagnating hegemonic forces of cultural habit, injecting difference into human lives while prompting awareness about the tacit links human bodies share with other lifeforms. In "Animal Body, Inhuman Face," Lingis examines ways that kinaesthetic relations with animals and their bodies provide points of entry for humans to understand and interpret themselves and relate to others. Reflecting on how "our legs plod with elephantine torpor; decked out fashionably we catwalk; our hands swing with penguin veracity; our fingers drum with nuthatch insistence,"[15] Lingis poetically situates animals as bodies that disrupt, enhance, and elaborate "human" experience and kinaesthetic means to ornament, decorate, and perhaps decreate social existence. Lingis's brief yet lush and visceral essay is significantly influenced by Deleuze and Guattari's ideas on "becoming animal," developed in A Thousand Plateaus. In a work that brims with vivid and moving passages, the image of the human body as an assemblage of bodies, operating in concert with other "natural" and "cultural" assemblages, stands out: "Our bodies are coral reefs teeming with polyps, sponges, gorgonians, and free-swimming macrophages continually stirred by monsoon climates of moist air, blood, and bile. Movements do not get launched by an agent against masses of inertia; we move in an environment of air currents, rustling trees, and animate bodies. Our movements are stirred by the coursing of blood, the pulse of the wind, the reedy rhythms of the cicadas in the autumn trees, the whir of passing cars, the bounding of squirrels and the tense, poised pause of deer."[16]

The creation of ARK is particularly indebted to this conceptual framework for thinking about and relating to other bodies. Consequently, the work attempts to approach the Toronto Zoo simultaneously as a space in which human and animal bodies produce meaning together despite their unequal terms; a human-animal interface saturated by, yet somehow oblivious to, difference; and a curated and bounded assemblage of bodies with diverse modes of inhabiting the world with the potential to induce new configurations, new relations, and new trajectories for humans and nonhumans. Consequently, I see parallels between my artistic work and both Ron Broglio's observations in this volume about animals reminding "us of a space outside of human stratifications and markings" and Takashi Ito's focus on dynamic exhibits designed around salient kinaesthetic aspects of animal bodies (and the lived human-animal relations that inform these designs).

I proposed ARK as an experimental project to a longtime dance colleague, Danielle Baskerville, during the summer of 2015. While visiting Toronto Island, a large city park located a short ferry ride away from downtown Toronto, I pitched the project as a choreographic study of an underexamined urban space that could create a detailed choreography and would integrate visualization and interpretive approaches to performance. Sitting in lush parkland as shorebirds soared freely overhead, Danielle was unsurprisingly skeptical that a zoo could yield any insights beyond the predictable thematics of animal confinement and human domination. Prepared for her response, I immediately produced maps of the zoo space (see figure 13.1), images of the many animal species that reside there, and a copy of "Animal Body, Inhuman Face." I credit Lingis's stirring yet morally ambiguous observations with affecting Danielle and coaxing her to commit to this project despite her ethical reservations.

Our first zoo visit together occurred in the early autumn of 2015 and lasted approximately five hours. Although Danielle was visibly hesitant when we approached the zoo entrance, she became less so when we were confronted by a zoo employee with a bald eagle perched on his arm. Barely an arm's length away from the majestic bird, who repeatedly stretched out its great wings, Danielle remarked on its sheer size, the specific articulations of its head, and its strong talons grasping the employee's arm. As curiosity gradually replaced her discomfort, we ventured through the different "zoogeographic"[17] regions. Moving counterclockwise through the zoo, as represented on the visitors' map, we passed through the exhibits in the following order: Kids Zoo, Eurasia Wilds, Australasia, Tundra Trek, the Americas, the Canadian Domain, the African Savanna, the African Rainforest, Indo-Malaya, and the Malayan Woods. We stopped at each exhibit to examine its inhabitants, and discussed various aspects of the zoo, including confinement, breeding programs, cooperative initiatives between zoos, the animals' unique features and physical gestures, and the design of both the entire zoo as well as specific regions and enclosures.

We experienced the zoo as a space full of diverse bodies and contradictions. We recognized that a zoo space collapses dichotomies about personal experience and mediated engagement, culture and nature, care and domination, and freedom and confinement. We agreed that our artistic work should attempt to embody, rather than displace, as many of these contradictions as possible. We discussed the establishment of certain "rules" that we would rigorously apply to our composition in order to embed aspects of our critical observations within it. These rules were:

1 We would use our route as a means to determine the work's general spatial composition. This (re)presentation would reference the manufactured zoo topography and simultaneously create spatial pathways that reference both our experience as zoo-goers and our continual engagement with the zoo's mediation of itself.

2 We would creatively engage with every species or breed of animal that

Figure 13.1 Map of the Toronto Zoo, 2018.

was exhibited at the zoo once, rather than make preferential choices about which animals deserved attention, recognition, or could be the focus of an aesthetic work. We would not focus on individual members of the collection when there were numerous specimens present, due to our awareness that we might not have the skills to identify them during subsequent visits.

3 We would choreographically enact each animal in relation to the topographical space of the zoo and one another. Simply put, we would reference each animal in the order they appeared to us and recreate the zoo's own classification of its animal bodies so as to not ignore the physical and architectural reality that assembled this collection of creatures. Corre-

spondingly, the rate at which we referenced animals would increase in areas of high animal density (such as within specific buildings).

4 We would generate detailed movements and kinaesthetic visualizations from our observations of animal bodies, animal actions, animal rhythms, and the lived relations between animals without the need for the viewer to recognize any specific animal as such. We would prioritize our specific experience of the animal over the replication of persistent cultural tropes about specific species.

5 We would not aim to create a perfect correspondence between the actual size of animals and the size of movements that referenced them, or a perfect correspondence between an animal body and analogous parts of our body. We would instead focus on how the animal body affected us and encouraged us to think about our body and movement differently so that we would not demonstrate an anthropomorphic preference for one animal over another.

6 We would try to reference the actual animal's body and movement and avoid the temptation to anthropomorphically alter animal movement so that it became grandiose, spectacular, symmetric, geometric, whole, or "beautiful" by the conventions of Western dance aesthetics.

7 We would attempt to keep each animal movement phrase distinct through specific qualitative differences. We would welcome the rupture of movement and avoid the depiction of any extended lyrical moments of kinaesthetic freedom or flow so that the choreography would physically embody the very real physical barriers present at the zoo that separate animals from one another, from people, and from the general environment.

After we settled on these rules, I returned to the zoo five more times to create a comprehensive document that would become the organizational schematic or choreographic "score" for the dance.[18] Updated periodically in response to new observations, we eventually finalized the score with 360 individual entries, each one representing one kind (either species or breed) of mammal, bird, reptile, amphibian, fish, or invertebrate. Breaking down the score into discrete sections that referenced specific exhibition areas, the specific numbers for each area were as follows: Kids Zoo had ten species as well as two breeds of domestic goat; Eurasia Wilds had fourteen species; Australasia had fifty-six species; Tundra Trek had five species; the Americas had seventy-five species; the Canadian Domain had twenty-five species; the African Savanna had twenty species plus one breed of domestic cattle; the African Rainforest had fifty-six species; Indo-Malaya had forty-eight species); and the Malayan Woods had forty-eight species. A complete list of all animal species, in the order they are referenced in ARK, is available online through accessing the choreographic score. All animals are listed with specific choreographic notes made during the working period.

With the score and resource document completed, we could begin to create choreographic material. However, before we entered the studio, we returned to the zoo together to examine the animals and their bodies, take detailed notes, and align our observations with our rules. Our first action in the studio in the spring of 2016 was to walk the space of the zoo in the space of the studio and decide where the choreography would begin, unfold, and end. Through repeated reference to the zoo map and discussions about the landscape, we transferred aspects of the zoo topography onto the studio floor, and gradually gained a sense of where each section existed in relation to the studio space. We decided that the upstage centre of the space would be the entrance (and exit) to the zoo and organized the spatial relations of the other sections accordingly. After deliberation, we decided that we would not represent the architecture of the inside spaces of the zoo with any exact verisimilitude due to their complex layout, but we would show the animals in order in relation to each other.

With the mapping of the space complete we began to generate choreographic material (or movement phrases) from our memory of the animals, a process that we repeatedly augmented with discussion and viewing of the supplementary videos. Work in the studio proceeded linearly, and we compsed the choreography slowly over a period of months, working without music, one animal at a time. We did not use one specific method to generate choreography, but developed gradually a set of zoomorphic visualization strategies that could be applied in response to our observations. These visualization tools aimed to pair a specific movement or set of movements with a sensorial image of the animal body, part of the animal body, or a group of animals. Once completed, Danielle recorded a personal description of the movement into the score for future reference. Individual movement phrases were linked to one another in a procedural linear process that used the end of one movement phrase as a starting place for the next. Qualitative aspects of movement were not retained between phrases. A new movement phrase would match a new gesture or action with an equally new visualization generated from observation of the species, which maintained the spatial relation established between the animal and its general topographical location. Through this process, movements sequenced from one another not through gradual transformation and flow, but through kinaesthetic ruptures. These ruptures prevent the creation of a visual or kinetic sense of unbounded space or specific grand narrative within the choreography. A detailed examination of one short section of ARK will illuminate aspects of this process.

ARK's Tundra Trek section is one of its briefest and contains the fewest number of animal species. In the online video, it begins at 4:14 and ends at 4:58, occurs slightly upstage of the centre of stage right, and is organized around the geometry of the loop along which zoo-goers travel. Although the region can be accessed in a clockwise or counterclockwise fashion, during our visit we travelled counterclockwise and encountered, in order, polar bears, snowy owls, reindeer, snow geese, and arctic wolves. The spatial pathway that Danielle follows during this section corresponds to this experience; it is a loop, with the reindeer and snow geese enacted at the most downstage parts of this section, the snowy owl enacted in the centre, and the polar bears and arctic wolves enacted on the opposite sides of the most upstage portions. Our original documents only contained the name of the animal followed by shorthand score notes. To illuminate our creative process, I have qualitatively elaborated on the basic score in order to explain details that are kept in mind during the execution of the dance. I have also indicated the timeframes within which specific actions occur so readers may observe these visualizations unfolding.

TUNDRA TREK (4:56–5:37)

Polar Bear (4:56–5:06)
Danielle's Score Note: Slow heavy sink to knees and elbows, focus turns away upstage right.
Detailed Explanation of Note: The body is imagined to take on the dimensions and mass of a polar bear sitting upright under the water, which we observed through the exhibit's viewing tank. The body slowly

yet decidedly sinks onto all fours, submerged under the water. The water supports the massive body, and waves of undulating thick, white hair flow around the body.

Snowy Owl (5:07–5:16)
Danielle's Score Note: Come up onto hands, ripple contraction into release, send the body over the right knee/thigh. Rising halfway through clavicle wings, then come up with windy feather foot, still focus.

Detailed Explanation of Note: Placing the image of the owl's long wings into the torso, the body unfurls as though into flight. These same wings move into the collarbones, suspended in flight, while the left foot reflects the action of the wind ruffling the owl's feathers.

Reindeer (5:17–5:27)
Danielle's Score Note: Kick grab with right foot then left.

Detailed Explanation of Note: Rising onto all fours the body creeps forward and the feet are imagined as tiny hoofs which attentively dig into the snow in order to uncover hidden vegetation. The use of this image results in an action that disrupts prescriptive uses of the foot and leg which stress a particular coordination between the hip, knee, and ankle joints.

Snow Goose (5:28–5:30)
Danielle's Score Note: Breastbone/scapula wing action ~ small.

Detailed Explanation of the Note: The body turns quickly and transfers from a four-legged position to kneeling position with the upper body hinged back. The quick action of wings beating is transferred into the semi-mobile area between the scapula and the breastbone and results in a rapid pulsing action.

Arctic Wolf (5:31–5:37)
Danielle's Score Note: 1. Wolf head as whole body, 2. Japanese "kabuki" wolves (elbows and knees).

Detailed Explanation of the Note: 1. Beginning in a kneeling position, the body is imagined as the neck and head of a wolf stretching up into a high vertical position. The crown of the head is imagined to be where the nose/nostrils are located. Using this image, the body is shifted into position for part 2 of the movement. 2. The knees and elbows are imagined to be individual members of a pack of wolves first moving independently and then, after an event which draws their attention, collectively as a pack. Both images reference behaviour seen during observation of the wolves at the zoo.

With regards to the entire work, specific beginning and ending times for other sections of ARK are: Kids Zoo at 0:11–0:43, Eurasia Wilds at 0:44–1:58, Australasia at 1:59–4:55, the Americas at 5:38–8:44, the Canadian Domain at 8:45–9:50, African Savannah at 9:51–11:29, African Rainforest at 11:30–13:02, Indo-Malaya at 13:03–15:34, and Malayan Woods at 15:35–16:53.

ARK's basic structure and choreography was completed in the summer of 2016, and the work was shown a number of times in the studio to transition it from a movement research study to a performance piece. Initial showings were private and attended by Patricia Beatty, an artistic mentor and icon of Canadian modern dance. Beatty has a noted interest in formal aspects of modern dance and a history of creating works that reference the natural world.[19] Rarely hesitating to offer praise, voice objections, or propose solutions to issues she perceived in the work (such as its decidedly undramatic performance quality, unorthodox use of space, and its multiple kinetic ruptures), Beatty's presence was passionate yet removed. Invested in ideas regarding composition drawn from primarily modernist dance icons and humanist artists,[20] many of her ideas conflicted with the basic concepts that informed the work, especially those that were not invested in an anthropomorphic rendering of nature. Nevertheless, we did attempt to integrate, in discrete ways, some of her lucid compositional strategies through slight shifts in Danielle's location or trajectory, and through the magnification of certain phrases or gestures in order to create more tacit contrast. For example, in a part of the Eurasia section, the spatial pathway that Danielle describes is considerably larger than our original "to scale" choreography (see 0:30 to 1:25). Although we disagreed on many fundamental ideas related to dance composition, Beatty's participation in this process was of tremendous benefit through her emphatic confirmation that many aspects of the work were in conflict with a (her) conception of dance centred around humanistic conceptions of the body, space, and aesthetics that veered towards universalizing the specific and yielded pronouncements about "human nature."

A public showing was held at the Toronto Dance Theatre, attended by professional dancers, choreographers, dance educators, graduate students, academics, and children. Since an original musical compositional had not been acquired, ARK was set to Monolake's "Alpenrausch" and Autechre's "Drane 2" in order to establish a general mood and to create cohesion for an audience watching a dance work comprised of fragments.[21] In written correspondence, one viewer remarked: "Building on both animal movement patterns and physical/geographical locations, you seemed able to create and develop physical material that transformed a research 'study' into dance performance. The individual movements and the movement patterns generated were unusual, 'authentic,' non-derivative; essentially a 'language.' I think your work spoke with a unique physical voice."[22] Another viewer conferred her impression of "beautiful bodies with nowhere to move."[23] Other viewers referred to Danielle's performance quality as "single-mindedly attentive to the task at hand" and noted that her "investment in the research deterred her from bringing any preconceived, personal performance behaviours and interpretation preferences to the work."[24] Oral feedback from the group regarding music, movement vocabulary, performance quality, and structure was overwhelmingly positive and provided a concrete direction for the finalization of the choreography and future collaborative efforts towards procuring an original musical score and a costume.

For the finished choreography, we contacted sound artist Benjamin Boles and textile artist Alicia Zwicewicz individually. Both visited the zoo and attended a showing of the work. They were introduced to its theory and process and were given free rein to interpret our ideas. Zwicewicz initially wished to incorporate the physical features of many different animals into her design, but eventually chose to invoke an abstracted interpretation of the animal at the zoo with whom I had the most direct physical contact: a red-tailed black cockatoo. The beautiful bird had landed on me while Danielle and I were in the Australasia aviary, surreptitiously displayed its vibrant and detailed plumage, removed a button from my jacket, and then paced up and down my arm until a zoo employee removed it. Boles chose a different approach for his electronic composition and, as he wrote to me in an email:

focused primarily on shifting textures and percussion arrangements, constructed using found sounds recorded around Toronto. Those samples were then manipulated and processed until they began to vaguely evoke environmental noise and animal sounds, with care taken to avoid any overtly literal references to "natural" soundscapes. Analog synthesis and multiple hardware sequencers were also used to create layered rhythmic arrangements that could move in and out of phase with each other in fluid and unpredictable ways. Rather than arrange the work in a computer, I recorded a series of live electronic performances, manipulating the various elements in real time. I presented an early rough version to Jonathan, and had further discussions about how to develop it to fit better with the choreography. We decided to stretch out the melodic theme over a longer duration, in order to give the performer more space to work within. Aspects of the rhythmic ideas were reworked to avoid unintentional references to popular music forms, and many of the sounds were processed further into abstraction.

A performance of the finished work occurred on 5 May 2017 at the Canadian Contemporary Dance Theatre in Toronto. The online video that accompanies this collection is a record of that performance. Although filmed in a studio rather than a theatre, future ARK performances will retain aspects of the studio environment including the relatively large use of space, the minimal use of theatrical lighting, and the absence of set pieces or spatial decorations in order to draw attention to the "real" bodies and "real" space to which the dance continuously refers.

Reflection

The animal bodies at the zoo invariably become subject to human choreographies, but human trainers, architects, caretakers, and visitors also become subjected to animal choreographies. Despite its prescriptive and theatrical staging, which organizes, frames, and contains animal bodies, the animal bodies at the zoo are neither wholly subservient to human design nor mere reflections of our cultural imagination; unlike objects at a museum, the bodies at the zoo can and do resist our constructions, desires, and expectations.

The slumbering body, the semi-concealed body, the reticent body, and the seemingly despondent body hold as much information about our supposed understanding of the natural world as the gregariously active body. After witnessing the staggering multitude of bodies at the Toronto Zoo, I sometimes suspect that zoo detractors are most offended by the continual display of human failure that the zoo embodies – a vivid challenge to the conceit of humanist progress and reminder of the limits of our understanding of other beings. The animals of documentary films can be edited and transformed by our narratives, and the virtual animals of animated films can be generated to suit our fancy, but our urban menageries often denude our epic visions with a less spectacular kinetic candour.

The denuding of a nostalgic utopian vision of the world in which animals and humans can coexist peacefully and independently might be painful for some to contemplate, but seems more appropriately tuned to the ecological reality of an era designated the Anthropocene. This does not necessarily mean that we need to abandon the dream of a human-animal utopia, but rather that we must discard a particular conceptualization of how it could and should manifest itself in the world in response to the almost inevitable prospects of an "artefactual" planet overlaid by human designs.[25] To look at the space of the zoo without wonder and see only multiplied instances of homogeneous relations with animals requires a special kind of blindness. There is gross evidence of the exact opposite in terms of the enactment of differently designed spaces and regimens, which point to the developing awareness of the living animal both as belonging to a species with specific histories and proclivities and as an individual with certain desires and preferences. The observation that animals are specifically ill-suited for life in captivity is beyond asinine in a world increasing ill-suited for anything specific, where it seems more prudent to speak of degrees of captivity rather than the romantic fantasy of wild nature.

In *Staging Tourism: Bodies on Display from Waikiki to Sea World*, Jane C. Desmond refers to the zoological garden as the "kinaesthetic embodiment of an imperialist eye,"[26] a site that gives visitors the opportunity to "consume radical body difference."[27] Her detailed study of the performative aspects of zoos and their deliberate staging of animal bodies offers an astute glimpse into the historical and contemporary manufacturing of digestible visions of animals for capitalist consumers. In the introduction to the second part of

the work, Desmond qualifies her use of the word "consumption" and explains that it signifies more than simple ties to a market system through the
implication of "a physicality and a merging."[28] As a choreographer, artist,
and researcher, I am intrigued by the opportunity for our somatic experiences
of phenomena – our different embodied consumption of the things to be con-
ceptualized, regardless of its context. The ingestion, absorption, assimilation,
and production of new material offers the chance to become intimate with
things from beyond our specific physical or social bodies and to literally
begin to constitute new and different bodies. Is it possible to imagine that the
kinaesthetic relations at the zoo create conditions that also propel understanding through the embodied recognition and subsequent negotiation of
"radical body difference"? If so, the lessons learned from zoological failures and successes will be invaluable to the bodies who move in the human-
animal choreographies of the future.

NOTES

1 A recording of ARK is available at https://vimeo.com/255658524. A video of
   the dance before completion is available for viewing at https://vimeo.com/
   210992178. ARK was created with the generous support of the Toronto
   Arts Council and the Ontario Arts Council.
2 Berger, "Why Look at Animals?"
3 This is a reference to John Berger and Mike Dibb's 1972 *Ways of Seeing* tel-
   evised documentary series, which was subsequently adapted into a book of
   the same name. Both examined ideological ideas embedded within historical
   and contemporary visual culture.
4 In Berger's "Why Look at Animals?," Malamud's *Reading Zoos*, and
   Mullan and Marvin's *Zoo Culture*, animals' lack of movement, stereotypic
   movement, or unnatural behaviour are referred to as indicators of the false
   nature of the zoo environment. Similarly, critiques of zoos in newspapers
   and magazines also routinely refer to the obvious limits on animal movement.
5 In *Zooland*, Irus Braverman discusses the zoo environment in light of Foucault's concept of pastoral power and refers to humans' bodily training of
   animals for the purposes of multispecies care. In Warkenstin and Fawcett's
   chapter "Whale and Human Agency," the authors discuss choreographic

modes of interaction between populations of captive and "wild" cetaceans and humans. Present in the same collection are Bulbeck's "Respectful Stewardship of Hybrid Nature" and Lulka's "Boring a Wormhole in the Zoological Ark," both of which examine the zoo as space with kinaesthetic components that extend beyond the visual.

6 Graham, *Blood Memory*, 103–4.

7 Anna Kisselgoff, "Merce Cunningham the Maverick of Modern Dance," *New York Times*, 20 March 1982, http://www.nytimes.com/1982/03/21/magazine/merce-cunningham-the-maverick-of-modern-dance.html.

8 Ibid.

9 Alastair Macaulay, "Merce Cunningham's Multifaceted Mirror, Held up to Nature," *New York Times*, 6 January 2017, https://www.nytimes.com/2017/01/06/arts/dance/merce-cunninghams-multifaceted-mirror-held-up-to-nature.html.

10 Ibid.

11 Agamben, *The Open*, 26.

12 Brandstetter, "Dancing the Animal," 6.

13 Ibid., 5.

14 Ibid.

15 Lingis, "Animal Body, Inhuman Face," 114.

16 Ibid.

17 Toronto Zoo, "Toronto Zoo: Facts & Figures," http://www.torontozoo.com/EducationAndCamps/Elementary/InformationBooklets/Toronto%20Zoo-%20Facts%20and%20Figures.pdf.

18 I repeatedly retraced our initial route and made a detailed list of all inhabitants of the zoo's exhibit areas in the order I encountered them. I checked my lists against zoo signage and with information available on the Toronto Zoo's website. Predictably, this information often did not align with my list (i.e., my list contained more species than the zoo's virtual catalogue of animals, yet still fell short of the zoo's advertised claim to house over 460 species). Realizing that I would have to make some concessions to the reality of studying an ever-shifting institution that displayed live bodies, I synthesized my personal observations and the official zoo information. This choice addressed the reality that not all animals were on display (or in the same area) each time that I visited due to the vicissitudes of health, curatorial choices, and seasonal conditions. Recognizing that there were animals I

had seen that Danielle had not, I supplemented the score with video footage of these animals. This footage was embedded into another document sourced from YouTube that would serve as a memory aid and an imperfect solution to the problem of an ever-shifting zoo population. Preference was given to virtual footage of animals at the Toronto Zoo, and when this footage was unavailable concerted efforts were made to avoid spectacular or dramatized documentary footage that depicted animal behaviour absent from the zoo environment.

19 Patricia Beatty's dance work with environmental themes includes *Gaia* (1990), *Seastill* (1979), and *Skyling* (1980).

20 Beatty made repeated reference to choreographers and artists she considers to be iconic, including Jose Limon, Martha Graham, Pearl Lang, and Bertram Ross, who are routinely associated with American modern dance and were heavily invested in humanist subjects and values.

21 Alpennraush" appears on Monolake's album *Cinemascope* (2001); "Drane 2" appears on Autechre's album *LP5* (1998).

22 Fraser, Patricia, email to the author.

23 Anonymous comments from audience members received after initial artistic showing.

24 Fraser, Patricia, email to the author.

25 Lee, *Zoos*.

26 Desmond, *Staging Tourism*, 145.

27 Ibid., 146.

28 Ibid.

BIBLIOGRAPHY

Acampora, Ralph, ed. *Metamorphoses of the Zoo: Animal Encounter after Noah.* Lanham: Lexington Books, 2010.

– "Zoos and Eyes: Contesting Captivity and Seeking Successor Practices." *Society and Animals* 13, 1 (2005): 69–88.

Adams, Carol J. *The Sexual Politics of Meat: A Feminist-Vegetarian Critical Theory.* New York: Continuum, 1990.

Agamben, Giorgio. *The Open: Man and Animal.* Translated by Kevin Attell. Stanford: Stanford University Press, 2004.

Akeley, Carl. *In Brightest Africa.* New York: Doubleday, Page & Co, 1923.

Akers, Jean S., and Deborah S. Schildkraut. "Regurgitation/Reingestion and Coprophagy in Captive Gorillas." *Zoo Biology* 4 (1985): 99–109.

Akiyama, Chieko. *Kawaisō na zō.* Tokyo: Kinnohoshisha, 1970.

Alberti, Samuel J.M.M., ed. *The Afterlives of Animals: A Museum Menagerie.* Charlottesville: University of Virginia Press, 2011.

– "Maharajah the Elephant's Journey: From Nature to Culture." In Alberti, *The Afterlives of Animals,* 37–57.

Ames, Eric. *Carl Hagenbeck's Empire of Entertainments.* Seattle: University of Washington Press, 2009.

Anderson, John D. *Inventing Flight: The Wright Brothers and Their Predecessors.* Baltimore: Johns Hopkins University Press, 2004.

Autechre. "Drane 2." *LP5,* Warp Records, July 1998.

Baetens, Roland. *Le chant du paradis: Le Zoo d'Anvers a 150 ans.* Tielt: Lannoo, 1993.

Bak, Meredith A. "Democracy and Discipline: Object Lessons and the Stereoscope in American Education, 1870–1920." *Early Popular Visual Culture* 10,
2 (2012): 147–67.

Baker, Frank. "The Ascent of Man." *American Anthropologist* 3, 4 (October
1890): 297–320.

Bantjes, Rod. "Reading Stereoviews: The Aesthetics of Monstrous Space."
History of Photography 39, 1 (2015): 33–55.

Baratay, Eric. *Biographies animales, retrouver des vies.* Paris: Seuil, 2017.

– *Le point de vue animal: Une autre version de l'histoire.* Paris: Seuil, 2012.

Baratay, Eric, and Elizabeth Hardouin-Fugier. *Zoo: A History of Zoological
Gardens in the West.* London: Reaktion Books, 2002.

– *Zoos: Histoire des jardins zoologiques en occident, XVIe–XXe siècle.* Paris:
La Découverte, 1998.

Barrington-Johnson, J. *The Story of London Zoo.* London: Robert and Hale,
2005.

Barthes, Roland. *Camera Lucida: Reflections on Photography.* New York: Hill
and Wang, 2010.

Barua, Maan. "Circulating Elephants: Unpacking the Geographies of a Cosmopolitan Animal." *Transactions of the Institute of British Geographers* 39, 4
(2014): 1–16.

Bateson, Gregory. *Steps toward an Ecology of Mind.* Northvale, NJ: Jason
Aronson Inc, 1972.

Bender, Daniel E. *The Animal Game: Searching for Wildness at the American
Zoo.* Cambridge: Harvard University Press, 2016.

Bentley, Amy. *Eating for Victory: Food Rationing and the Politics of Domesticity.*
Urbana: University of Illinois Press, 1998.

Berger, John. "Why Look at Animals?" In *About Looking,* edited by John Berger,
1–26. New York: Pantheon, 1980.

Berger, Robert. *In the Garden of the Sun King: Studies on the Park of Versailles
under Louis XIV.* Washington: Dumbarton Oaks, 1985.

Bierlein, John, and Staff of HistoryLink. *Woodland: The Story of the Animals and
People of Woodland Park Zoo.* Seattle: University of Washington Press, 2017.

Blanchard, Pascal, Nicolas Bancel, Gilles Boëtsch, Eric Deroo, Sandrine Lemaire,
and Charles Forsdick, eds. *Human Zoos: Science and Spectacle in the Age of
Empire.* Liverpool: Liverpool University Press, 2008.

Blanchard, Pascal, Gilles Boëtsch, and Nanette Jacomijn Snoep, eds. *Human
Zoos: The Invention of the Savage.* Paris: Musée du Quai Branly, 2011.

Blau, Dick, and Nigel Rothfels. *Elephant House*. University Park, PA: Penn State University Press, 2015.

Blunt, Wilfrid. *The Ark in the Park: The Zoo in the Nineteenth Century*. London: Hamish Hamilton, 1976.

Boëtsch, Gilles, Nanette Snoep, and Paul Blanchard. *Human Zoos: The Invention of the Savage*. Paris: Actes Sud, 2012.

Bostock, Stephen St C. *Zoos and Animal Rights: The Ethics of Keeping Animals*. New York: Routledge, 1993.

Bousé, Derek. "False Intimacy: Close-ups and Viewer Involvement in Wildlife Films." *Visual Studies* 18, 2 (2003): 123–32.

Brandstetter, Gabriele. "Dancing the Animal to Open the Human: For a New Poetics of Locomotion." *Dance Research Journal* 42, 1 (Summer 2010): 3–11.

Braverman, Irus. *Wild Life: The Institution of Nature*. Redwood City: Stanford University Press, 2015.

– *Zooland: The Institution of Captivity*. Stanford: Stanford Law Books, 2012.

Brewster, Sir David. *The Stereoscope: Its History, Theory, and Construction*. London: John Murray, 1856.

Bridges, William. *Gathering of Animals: An Unconventional History of the New York Zoological Society*. New York: Harper & Row, 1974.

Broglio, Ron. "Thinking with Surfaces: Animals and Contemporary Art." In *Animals and the Human Imagination*, edited by Aaron Gross and Anne Vallely, 238–58. Columbia University Press, 2012.

Brokaw, Tom. *The Greatest Generation*. New York: Random House, 1998.

Brown, Susan G., William P. Dunlap, and Terry L. Maple. "Notes on Water-Contact by a Captive Male Lowland Gorilla." *Zoo Biology* 1 (1982): 243–9.

Bruce, Gary. *Through the Lion Gate: A History of the Berlin Zoo*. Oxford: Oxford University Press, 2017.

Bruner, Gail, and Lorraine Meller. "Convergent Evolution in Design Philosophy of Gorilla Habitats." *International Zoo Yearbook* 31 (1992): 213–21.

Bruns, Gerald L. "Becoming-Animal (Some Simple Ways)." *New Literary History* 38 (2007): 703–20.

Buckingham, Kathleen Carmel, Jonathan Neil William David, and Paul Jepson. "Diplomats and Refugees: Panda Diplomacy, Soft 'Cuddly' Power, and the New Trajectory in Panda Conservation." *Environmental Practice*, Environmental Reviews and Case Studies 15, 3 (2013): 262–70.

Bulbeck, Chilla. "Respectful Stewardship of Hybrid Nature: The Role of Concrete Encounters." In Acampora, *Metamorphosis of the Zoo*, 83–102.

Burkhardt, Richard W. "Le comportement animal et l'idéologie de domestication chez Buffon et chez les éthologues modernes." In *Buffon 88: Actes du Colloque international pour le bicentenaire de la mort de Buffon*, edited by Jean Gayon, 573. Paris: Vrin, 1992.

Burks, Kyle D., et al. "Managing the Socialization of an Adult Male Gorilla (*Gorilla gorilla gorilla*) with a History of Social Deprivation." *Zoo Biology* 20 (2001): 347–58.

Caldas-Coulthard, Carmen Rosa, and Theo van Leeuwen. "Teddy Bear Stories." *Social Semiotics* 13, 1 (2003): 5–27.

Canaday, Margot. *The Straight State: Sexuality and Citizenship in Twentieth-Century America*. Politics and Society in Twentieth-Century America. Princeton: Princeton University Press, 2009.

Cary, Diana Serra. *Hollywood's Children: An Inside Account of the Child Star Era*. Boston: Houghton Mifflin, 1979.

Chan, Jachinson. *Chinese American Masculinities: From Fu Manchu to Bruce Lee*. New York: Routledge, 2001.

Chen, Mel Y. *Animacies: Biopolitics, Racial Mattering, and Queer Affect*. Durham: Duke University Press, 2012.

Cheyne-Stout, Captain R. *At the Zoo: The Stereo-Book of Animals*. New York: Farrar and Rinehart, 1937.

Chris, Cynthia. *Watching Wildlife*. Minneapolis: University of Minnesota Press, 2006.

Chrulew, Matthew. "Animals as Biopolitical Subjects." In *Foucault and Animals*, edited by Matthew Chrulew and Dinesh Joseph Wadiwel, 222–38. Leiden: Brill, 2016.

– "'An Art of Both Caring and Locking Up': Biopolitical Thresholds in the Zoological Garden." *SubStance* 43, 2 (2014): 124–47.

Cincinnati, N. "Too Sullen for Survival: Historicizing Gorilla Extinction, 1900–1930." In Nance, *The Historical Animal*, 166–83.

Clottes, Jean, and Lewis-Williams, David. *The Shamans of Prehistory*. New York: Harry N. Abrams Publishers, 1998.

Collard, Rosemary-Claire. "Panda Politics." *The Canadian Geographer / Le Géographe Canadien* 57, 2 (1 June 2013): 226–32.

Collingham, Lizzie. *The Taste of War: World War II and the Battle for Food*. New York: Penguin Books, 2011.

Coquery Vidrovitch, Catherine, and Eric Mesnard. *Etre esclave: AfriqueAmériques, XVe–XIXe siècle*. Paris: La Découverte, 2013.

Cousins, Don. "Diseases and Injuries in Wild and Captive Gorillas." *International Zoo Book* (1972): 211–18.

Cowperthwaite, Gabriela. *Blackfish*. US: Manny O. Productions, 2013.

Crary, Jonathan. *Techniques of the Observer: On Vision and Modernity in the Nineteenth Century*. Cambridge, MA: MIT Press, 1990.

Crissey, S. "Nutrition." In *Encyclopedia of the World's Zoos*, vol. 2, edited by C.E. Bell, 890–3. Chicago/London: Fitzroy Dearborn Publishers, 2001.

Crist, Eileen. *Images of Animals: Anthropomorphism and Animal Mind*. Philadelphia: Temple University Press, 1999.

Croke, Vicki. *The Modern Ark: The Story of Zoos, Past, Present and Future*. New York: Scribner, 1997.

Crouch, Tom D. *A Dream of Wings: Americans and the Airplane*. New York: W.W. Norton, 2002.

Cushing, Nancy, and Kevin Markwell. "Platypus Diplomacy: Animal Gifts in International Relations." *Journal of Australian Studies* (1 January 2009): 255–71.

Dale, Joshua P., Joyce Goggin, Julia Leyda, Anthony P. Mcintyre, and Diane Negra, eds. *The Aesthetics and Affects of Cuteness*. New York: Routledge, 2017.

Daman, Frederic J. "Le 'Nouveau' Pavillon des Anthropoïdes." *Zoo* 52, 2 (1986): 13–18.

Davis, Susan. *Spectacular Nature: Corporate Culture and the SeaWorld Experience*. Berkeley: University of California Press, 1997.

Deckers, L. "Aventures avec des animaux." *Zoo* 40, 3 (1975): 100–3.

Deleuze, Gilles, and Felix Guattari,. *A Thousand Plateaus: Capitalism and Schizophrenia*. Translated by Brian Massumi. Minneapolis: University of Minnesota Press, 2007.

DeMello, Margo. *Animals and Society: An Introduction to Human-Animal Studies*. New York: Columbia University Press, 2012.

Demoor, Guy, and Luc Fornoville. "La Construction de Logement pour Groupe de Primates." *Zoo* 54, 4 (1989): 19–21.

Denisenko, E.E. *Ot zverintsev k zooparku: Istoriia Leningradskogo zooparka*. SaintPetersburg: Iskusstvo-SPb, 2003.

Derrida, Jacques. *The Animal That Therefore I Am*. Edited by Marie-Louise Mallet. Translated by David Wills. New York: Fordham University Press, 2008.

Desmond, Jane C. *Staging Tourism: Bodies on Display from Waikiki to SeaWorld*. Chicago: University of Chicago Press, 1999.

Despret, Vinciane. *What Would Animals Say If We Asked the Right Questions?* Minneapolis: University of Minnesota Press, 2016.

Deuchler, Douglas, and Carla W. Owens. *Brookfield Zoo and the Chicago Zoological Society*. Mount Pleasant: Arcadia Publishing, 2002.

De Waal, Frans. *Sommesnous trop "bêtes" pour comprendre l'intelligence des animaux?* Paris: Les liens qui libèrent, 2016.

Donahue, Jesse, ed. *Increasing Legal Rights for Zoo Animals: Justice on the Ark*. Lanham: Lexington Books, 2017.

Donahue, Jesse C. *Political Animals: Public Art in American Zoos and Aquariums*. Lanham: Lexington Books, 2007.

– *The Politics of Zoos: Exotic Animals and Their Protectors*. DeKalb: Northern Illinois University Press, 2006.

Donahue, Jesse C., and Erik K. Trump. *American Zoos during the Depression: A New Deal for Animals*. Jefferson, NC: McFarland, 2010.

Donaldson, Sue, and Will Kymlicka. *Zoopolis: A Political Theory of Animal Rights*. Oxford: Oxford University Press, 2011.

Doyle, Richard M. *Darwin's Pharmacy: Sex, Plants, and the Evolution of the Noosphere*. Seattle: University of Washington Press, 2011.

Egorovoi, L.V. *Moskovskii zoologicheskii park: K 140-letiiu so dnia osnovaniia. Strannitsy istorii*. Moscow: Ellis Lak, 2000, 2004.

Ehrenreich, Nancy, and Beth Lyon. "The Global Politics of Food: A Critical Overview." *University of Miami Inter-American Law Review* 43, 1 (Fall 2011): 1–2, http://repository.law.miami.edu/umialr/vol43/iss1/3.

Ehrlinger, David. *The Cincinnati Zoo and Botanical Garden: From Past to Present*. Cincinnati: Cincinnati Zoo and Botanical Garden, 1993.

Eliade, Mirceal. *A History of Religious Ideas*. Vol. 1. Chicago: University of Chicago Press, 1982.

Ellenberger, Henri. "The Mental Hospital and the Zoological Garden." In *Animals and Man in Historical Perspective*, edited by Joseph and Barrie Klaits. New York: Harper and Row, 1974.

Ellis, Richard. *On Thin Ice: The Changing World of the Polar Bear*. New York: Knopf, 2009.

Eng, David L. *Racial Castration: Managing Masculinity in Asian America*. Durham: Duke University Press, 2001.

Etter, Carolyn, and Don Etter. *The Denver Zoo: A Centennial History*. Boulder, CO: Denver Zoological Foundation/Roberts Rinehart Publishers, 1995.

Few, Martha, and Zeb Tortorici, eds. *Centering Animals in Latin American History*. Durham: Duke University Press, 2013.

Fisher, James. *Zoos of the World*. London: Aldus Books, 1966.

Fisher, L.E. "Lead Poisoning in a Gorilla." *Journal of the American Veterinary Medical Association* 125, 933 (1954): 478–9.

Flack, Andrew. *The Wild Within: Histories of a Landmark British Zoo*. Charlottesville: University of Virginia Press, 2018.

Fossey, Dian. "Development of the Mountain Gorilla (*Gorilla gorilla beringei*): The First Thirty-Six Months." In *The Great Apes*, edited by David A. Hamburg and Elizabeth R. McCown, 138–84. Menlo Park: Benjamin/Cummings Publishing Co, 1979.

Foucault, Michel. *Discipline and Punish: The Birth of the Prison*. Translated by Alan Sheridan. New York: Knopf, 1970.

– "Omnes et Singulatim: Towards a Criticism of 'Political Reason.'" 1979. http://tannerlectures.utah.edu/_documents/a-to-z/f/foucault81.pdf.

Fowles, Jib. "Stereography and the Standardization of Vision." *Journal of American Culture* 17, 2 (1994): 89–94.

Franklin, Alfred. *La Vie Privée d'autrefois*. Vols. 21 and 22. Paris: Plon, 1897.

Friese, Carrie. *Cloning Wild Life: Zoos, Captivity, and the Future of Endangered Animals*. New York: New York University Press, 2013.

Fung, Richard. "Looking for My Penis: The Eroticized Asian in Gay Video Porn." In *The Columbia Reader on Lesbians and Gay Men in Media, Society, and Politics*, edited by Larry P. Gross and James D. Woods. New York: Columbia University Press, 1999.

Garner, R.L. *Apes and Monkeys*. Boston: Ginn and Company's the Athenaeum Press, 1900.

– *The Speech of Monkeys*. London: William Heinemann, 1892.

Geddes, Henry. *Gorilla*. London: Andrew Melrose, 1955.

Gijzen, A. "Bonnes manières à table chez les anthropoïdes en captivité." *Zoo* 3, 1 (1972): 15–20.

– "Chronique des Gorilles." *Zoo* 29, 2 (1963): 50–1.

– "Nos collections zoologiques." *Zoo* 21, 4 (1956): 118–21.

– "Nos collections zoologiques." *Zoo* 22, 3 (1957): 84–7.

– "Où il est à nouveau question de gorilles." *Zoo* 31, 4 (1966): 157–60.

Gijzen, A., and J. Tijskens. "Growth in Weight of the Lowland Gorilla *Gorilla g. gorilla* and of the Mountain Gorilla *Gorilla g. beringei*." *International Zoo Yearbook* (1971): 183–93.

Ginzburg, Carlo. *The Cheese and The Worms: The Cosmos of a Sixteenth-Century Miller*. Translated by John and Anne Tedeschi. Baltimore: Johns Hopkins University Press, 2013 [1980].

Gordon Cumming, Roualeyn. *Five Years of a Hunters Life in the Far Interior of South Africa*. 2 Vols. London: John Murray, 1850.

Gott, Ted, and Kathryn Weir. *Gorilla*. London: Reaktion, 2013.

Gould, Edwin, and Mimi Bres. "Regurgitation and Reingestion in Captive Gorillas: Description and Intervention." *Zoo Biology* 5 (1986): 241–50.

Gould, Stephen Jay. *The Panda's Thumb: More Reflections in Natural History*. New York: Norton, 1980.

Graham, Martha. *Blood Memory*. New York: Doubleday, 1991.

Grazian, David. *American Zoo: A Sociological Safari*. Princeton: Princeton University Press, 2015.

Griffin, Donald. *Animal Minds: Beyond Cognition to Consciousness*. Chicago: University of Chicago Press, 2001.

Gruen, Lori, ed. *Critical Terms for Animal Studies*. Chicago: University of Chicago Press, 2018.

– ed. *The Ethics of Captivity*. New York: Oxford University Press, 2014.

Gruffudd, Pyrs. "Biological Cultivation Lubetkin's Modernism at London Zoo in the 1930s." In *Animal Spaces, Beastly Places*, edited by Chris Philo and Chris Wilbert, 222–42. London: Routledge, 2000.

Guerrini, Anita. *The Courtiers' Anatomists: Animals and Humans in Louis XIV's Paris*. Chicago: University of Chicago Press, 2015.

Guggenheim, Davis. *An Inconvenient Truth*. US: Lawrence Bender Productions, 2006.

Guillery, Peter. *The Buildings of London Zoo*. London: Royal Commission on the Historical Monuments of England, 1993.

Hagenbeck, Lorenz. *Animals Are My Life*. Translated by Alec Brown. London: Bodley Head, 1956.

Hahn, Emily. *Animal Gardens*. Garden City: Doubleday & Company, 1969.

Hallions, Richard P. *Taking Flight: Inventing the Aerial Age, from Antiquity through the First World War*. New York: Oxford University Press, 2003.

Hancocks, David. *A Different Nature: The Paradoxical World of Zoos and Their Uncertain Future*. Berkeley: University of California Press, 2001.

Hankins, Thomas L., and Robert J. Silverman. *Instruments and the Imagination*. Princeton: Princeton University Press, 1995.

Hanson, Elizabeth. *Animal Attractions: Nature on Display in American Zoos*. Princeton: Princeton University Press, 2002.

Harako, Yuzuru. *Asahiyama dōbutsuen no tsukurikata*. Tokyo: Bungeishunjū, 2006.

Haraway, Donna. *Primate Visions: Gender, Race, and Nature in the World of Modern Science*. New York: Routledge, 1989.

– "Primatology Is Politics by Other Means." *PSA: Proceedings of the Biennial Meeting of the Philosophy of Science Association*. Vol. 2, 1984.

– *When Species Meet*. Minneapolis: University of Minnesota Press, 2008.

Harris, William Cornwallis. *Narrative of an Expedition into Southern Africa during the Years 1836 and 1837*. Bombay: American Mission Press, 1838.

– "On a New Species of Antelope." *Proceedings of the Zoological Society of London*, part 6 (9 January 1838): 1–3.

– *The Wild Sports of Southern Africa*. London: John Murray, 1839.

Hartig, Falk. "Panda Diplomacy: The Cutest Part of China's Public Diplomacy." *The Hague Journal of Diplomacy* 8, 1 (1 January 2013): 49–78.

Harvey, Eli. *The Autobiography of Eli Harvey: Quaker Sculptor from Ohio*. Edited by Dorothy Z. Bicker, Jane Z. Vail, and Vernon G. Wills. Clinton Country Historical Society: Wilmington, 1966.

Hasegawa, Ushio. "Zō mo kawaisō: Mōjū gyakusatsu shinwa hihan." *Sensōbungaku wa shinjitsu wo tsutaetekitaka*. Tokyo: Nashinokisya, 2000.

Hediger, Ryan. *Animals and War*. Leiden: Brill, 2009.

Heise, Ursula K. *Imagining Extinction: The Cultural Meanings of Endangered Species*. Chicago: University of Chicago Press, 2016.

Henderson, Ron. *The Gardens of Suzhou*. Philadelphia: University of Pennsylvania Press, 2012.

Hendy, David. *Noise: A Human History of Sound and Listening*. New York: Ecco, 2013.

Herzfeld, Chris. *Petite histoire des grands singes*. Paris: Seuil, 2012.

– *Wattana: Un orang-outan à Paris*. Paris: Payot, 2012.

Herzfeld, Chris, and Patricia Van Schuylenbergh. "Singes humanisés, humains singés: Dérive des identités à la lumière des représentations occidentales." *Social Science Information* 50 (2011): 251–74.

Herzog, Werner. *Cave of Forgotten Dreams*. New York: IFC Films, 2010.

Hinde, Robert A., and L.A. Barden. "The Evolution of the Teddy Bear." *Animal Behaviour* 33, 4 (1985): 1371–3.

Hishikawa, Akiko. *Ōkami no minzokugaku: Jinjyū kōshōshi no kenkyu*. Tokyo: University of Tokyo Press, 2009.

Hoage, R.J., and William Deiss. *New Worlds, New Animals: From Ménagerie to Zoological Park in the Nineteenth Century*. Baltimore: Johns Hopkins University Press, 1996.

Holmes, Oliver Wendell. "The Stereoscope and the Stereograph." *Atlantic Monthly*, June 1859.

Hornaday, William T. *The Minds and Manners of Wild Animals: A Book of Personal Observations*. New York: Charles Scribner's Sons, 1922.

Horowitz, Helen L. "Animal and Man in the New York Zoological Park." *New York History* 56 (October 1975): 426–55.

– "The National Zoological Park: 'City of Refuge' or Zoo?" *Records of the Columbia Historical Society* 49 (1973–4): 405–29.

– "Seeing Ourselves through the Bars: A Historical Tour of American Zoos." *Landscape* 25, 2 (1981): 12–19.

Hosey, Geoffrey R. "How Does the Zoo Environment Affect the Behaviour of Captive Primates?" *Applied Animal Behaviour Science* 90 (2005): 107–29.

Hosey, Geoff, Vicky Melfi, and Sheila Pankhurst. *Zoo Animals: Behaviour, Management and Welfare*. New York: Oxford University Press, 2009.

Hribal, Jason. *Fear of the Animal Planet: The Hidden History of Animal Resistance*. Petrolia, CA: AK Press, 2010.

Hudson, Mark J., Ann-Elise Lewallen, and Mark K. Watson, eds. *Beyond Ainu Studies: Changing Academic and Public Perspectives*. Honolulu: University of Hawai'i Press, 2014.

Huggan, Graham, and Helen Tiffin. *Postcolonial Ecocriticism*. New York: Routledge, 2015.

Hurn, Samantha. *Humans and Other Animals: Cross-Cultural Perspectives on Human-Animal Interactions*. London: Pluto Press, 2012.

Hyson, Jeffrey Nugent. "Jungles of Eden: The Design of American Zoos." In *Environmentalism in Landscape Architecture*. Edited by Michel Conan, 23–44. Washington, DC: Dumbarton Oaks Research Library and Collection, 2000.

– "Urban Jungles: Zoos and American Society." PhD dissertation, Cornell University, 1999.

Iovino, Serenella and Oppermann, Serpil. *Material Ecocriticism*. Bloomington: Indiana University Press, 2014.

Inuzuka, Yasuhiro. "Shinkyo dōshokubutsuen kō." *Chiba daigaku Jinbunsyakaikagaku kenkyu, Journal of Studies on Humanities and Public Affairs of Chiba University* 18 (2009): 18–25.

Ireye, Masumi. "Le Vau's Ménagerie and the Rise of the Animalier: Enclosing, Dissecting, and Representing the Animal in Early Modern France." PhD dissertation, University of Michigan, 1994.

Ito, Takashi. *London Zoo and the Victorians, 1828–1859*. Suffolk: Boydell & Brewer, 2014.

Itoh, Mayumi. *Japanese Wartime Zoo Policy: The Silent Victims of World War*. New York: Palgrave Macmillan, 2010.

Jackson, Zakiyyah Iman. "Waking Nightmares – on David Marriott." *GLQ: A Journal of Lesbian and Gay Studies* 17, 2–3 (1 January 2011): 357–63.

Jahn, Ilse. "Zoologische Gärten in Stadtkultur und Wissenschaft im 19. Jahrhundert." *Berichte zur Wissenschaftsgeschichte* 15 (December 1992): 213–25.

Jamieson, Dale. "Against Zoos." In *In Defense of Animals*, edited by Peter Singer, 132–43. New York: Blackwell, 1985.

– "Zoos Revisited." In Norton et al., *Ethics on the Ark*, 52–66.

Jenkins, Virginia Scott. *Bananas: An American History*. Washington, DC: Smithsonian Institution Press, 2000.

Kato, Norihiko. "Goodbye Godzilla, Hello Kitty: The Origins and Meaning of Japanese Cuteness." *The American Interest* (Autumn 2006): 72–9.

Kean, Hilda. "Challenges for Historians Writing Animal-Human History: What Is Really Enough?" *Anthrozoos* 25, 1 (2012): 57–72.

Kellert, Stephen. "Perceptions of Animals in America." In *Perceptions of Animals in American Culture*, edited by R.J. Hoage, 5–24. Washington, DC: Smithsonian Institution Press, 1989.

Keystone View Company and the Educational Department. *Visual Education: Teacher's Guide to Keystone "600 Set."* Meadville, PA: Keystone View Company, 1922.

Kiley-Worthington, Marthe. *Animals in Circuses and Zoos: Chiron's World?* London: Little Eco-Farms Publishing, 1990.

Kinder, John M. "Militarizing the Menagerie: American Zoos from World War II to the Early Cold War." In *The Martial Imagination: Cultural Aspects of American Warfare*, edited by Jimmy L. Bryan Jr, 15–35. College Station: A&M University Press, 2013.

– "Zoo Animals and Modern War: Captive Casualties, Patriotic Citizens, and Good Soldiers." In Ryan, *Animals and War*, 45–75.

Kirby, David. *Death at SeaWorld: Shamu and the Dark Side of Killer Whales in Captivity*. New York: St Martin's, 2013.

Kisling, Vernon N., Jr. *Zoo and Aquarium History: Ancient Animal Collections to Zoological Gardens*. New York: CRC Press, 2000.

– *Zoo and Aquarium History: Ancient Animal Collections to Zoological Gardens*. Boca Raton: CRC Press, 2001.

Klein, Naomi. *This Changes Everything: Capitalism vs. the Climate*. New York: Simon & Schuster, 2014.

Kohn, Eduardo. *How Forests Think: Toward an Anthropology beyond the Human*. Berkeley: University of California Press, 2013.

Kosuge, Masao. *Asahiyama dōbutsuen kakumei: Yume wo jitsugenshita project*. Tokyo: Kadokawashoten, 2006.

Kosuge, Masao, and Toshiro Iwano. *Tatakau dōbutsuen: Asahiyama dōbutsuen to itōzunomorikōen no monogatari*. Edited by Taizo Shima. Tokyo: Chūōkōronshinsha, 2006.

Kume, Kunitake. *Japan Rising: The Iwakura Embassy to the USA and Europe*. Edited by Chushichi Tsuzuki and R. Jules Young. Cambridge: Cambridge University Press, 2009.

Kusturica, Emir. *Underground*. Paris: CiBy 2000, 1995.

Lambert, George William. *A Trip through the Union Stock Yards and Slaughter Houses*. Chicago: Hamblin Printing Co, 1893.

Latour, Bruno. *Reassembling the Social: An Introduction to Actor-Network-Theory*. Oxford: Oxford University Press, 2005.

– *We Have Never Been Modern*. Translated by Catherine Porter. Cambridge: Harvard University Press, 1993.

Lavauden, Louis. "Les Gorilles." *La Terre et la Vie* 7 (1932): 395–403.

Lawrence, Elizabeth A. "In the Mick of Time: Reflections on Disney's Ageless Mouse." *The Journal of Popular Culture* 20, 2 (1986): 65–72.

Lee, Keekok. *Zoos: A Philosophical Tour*. Hound Mills: Palgrave Macmillan, 2005.

Lee, Robert G. *Orientals: Asian Americans in Popular Culture*. Philadelphia: Temple University Press, 1999.

Leroi-Gourhan, André. *Gesture and Speech*. Cambridge: MIT Press, 1993.

Li, Peter. *Chinese in Canada*. Toronto: Oxford University Press, 1998.

Lingis, Alphonso. "Animal Body, Inhuman Face." *Social Semiotics* 7, 2 (1997): 113–26.

– *The Imperative*. Bloomington: Indiana University Press, 1998.

Litten, Freddy. "Adieu Hippo – The Nearly Forgotten Victims of the Ueno Zoo during the Second World War." *Der Zoologische Garten* 84 (2015): 35–44.

Loisel, Gustave. *Histoire des Ménageries de l'Antiquité à nos jours*. 3 vols. Paris: Doin, 1912.

Lukas, Kristen E. "A Review of Nutritional and Motivational Factors Contributing to the Performance of Regurgitation and Reingestion in Captive Lowland

Gorillas (*Gorilla gorilla gorilla*)." *Applied Animal Behaviour Science* 63 (1999): 237–49.

Lulka, David. "Boring a Wormhole in the Zoological Ark." In Acampora, *Metamorphosis of the Zoo*, 123–50.

Lydekker, Richard. "Antelope." In *Encyclopedia Britannica*, vol. 2, Andros to Austria, 11th ed., 89–92. Cambridge: Cambridge University Press, 1910.

– "Review of *The Book of Antelopes*, by P.L. Sclater and O. Thomas." *Nature* 63, 1639 (March 1901): 509–10.

Mabille, Gérard. "La Ménagerie de Versailles." *Gazette des Beaux-Arts* 116 (1974): 5–36.

Maeda, Tomiyoshi. *Nihongogen daijiten*. Tokyo: Shōgakukan, 2005.

Malamud, Randy. *An Introduction to Animals and Visual Culture*. New York: Palgrave MacMillan, 2012.

– *Reading Zoos: Representations of Animals and Captivity*. New York: New York University Press, 1998.

– "Zoo Spectatorship." In *The Animals Reader: The Essential Classic and Contemporary Writings*, edited by Linda Kalof and Amy J. Fitzgerald. Oxford: Berg, 2007.

Malin, Brenton J. *Feeling Mediated: A History of Media Technology and Emotion in America*. New York: NYU Press, 2014.

– "Looking White and Middle-Class: Stereoscopic Imagery and Technology in the Early Twentieth-Century United States." *Quarterly Journal of Speech* 93, 4 (2007): 403–24.

Marie, Alfred. *Naissance de Versailles*. Paris: Vincent, Fréal, 1968.

Marie, Alfred, and Jeanne Marie. *Versailles au temps de Louis XIV*. Paris: Imprimerie Nationale, 1976.

Masui, Kanenori. *Nihongogen kōjien*. Tokyo: Minerva Shobō, 2010.

Mauss, Marcel. *The Gift: The Form and Reason for Exchange in Archaic Societies*. London: Routledge, 1989.

Mazur, Nicole A. *After the Ark? Environmental Policy Making and the Zoo*. Melbourne University Press, 2001.

McArthur, Jo-Anne. *Captive*. Brooklyn: Lantern Books, 2017.

Meder, Angela. "Effects of Hand-Rearing on the Behavioral Development of Infant and Juvenile Gorillas (*Gorilla g. gorilla*)." *Developmental Psychobiology* 22 (1989): 357–76.

Millais, John Guille. *Life of Frederick Courtenay Selous, D.S.O., Capt. 25th Royal Fusiliers*. New York: Longmans, 1919.

Miller, Ian Jared. *The Nature of the Beasts: Empire and Exhibition at the Tokyo Imperial Zoo.* Berkeley: University of California Press, 2013.

Minteer, Ben A., Jane Maienschein, and James P. Collins, eds. *The Ark and Beyond: The Evolution of Zoo and Aquarium Conservation.* Chicago: University of Chicago Press, 2018.

Mitman, Gregg. "When Nature *Is* the Zoo: Vision and Power in the Art and Science of Natural History." *Osiris* 11 (1996): 117–43.

Molloy, Claire. "Being a Known Animal." In *Beyond Human: From Animality to Transhumanism*, edited by Charlie Blake, Claire Molloy, and Steven Shakespeare, 31–49. London: Continuum, 2012.

Monolake. "Alpenrausch." Cinemascope. Imbalance Computer Music, 2001.

Montgomery, Georgina M. "Place, Practice and Primatology: Clarence Ray Carpenter, Primate Communication and the Development of Field Methodology, 1931–1945." *Journal of the History of Biology* 38, 3 (Autumn 2005): 495–533.

Morin, Karen M. *Carceral Space, Prisoners and Animals.* New York: Routledge, 2018.

Morris, P.H., V. Reddy, and R.C. Bunting. "The Survival of the Cutest: Who's Responsible for the Evolution of the Teddy Bear?" *Animal Behaviour* 50, 6 (1995): 1697–700.

Morris, Ramona, and Desmond Morris. *Men and Pandas.* 1st ed. London: Hutchinson & Co, 1966.

Mortelmans, J., J. Vercruysse, and D. Thienpont, "Accidents et amputations." *Zoo* 32, 2 (1966): 76–9.

Mortimer-Sandilands, Catriona. "Unnatural Passions? Notes toward a Queer Ecology." 2005, https://urresearch.rochester.edu/institutionalPublicationPublicView.action?institutionalItemId=3431.

Morton, Timothy. *Humankind: Solidarity with Nonhuman People.* Brooklyn: Verso Books, 2017.

– *Hyperobjects: Philosophy and Ecology after the End of the World.* Minneapolis: University of Minnesota Press, 2013.

Mouillard, Louis Pierre. *L'empire de l'air: Essai d'ornithologie appliquée a l'aviation.* Paris: Ulan Press, 2012.

Mullan, Bob, and Garry Marvin. *Zoo Culture.* Urbana: University of Illinois Press, 1999.

Myers, Douglas G., with Lynda Rutledge Stephenson. *Mister Zoo: The Life and*

Legacy of Dr Charles Schroeder, the World-Famous San Diego Zoo and Wild Animal Park's Legendary Director. San Diego: The Zoological Society of San Diego, 1999.

Nance, Susan. *Animal Modernity: Jumbo the Elephant and the Human Dilemma*. Basingstoke: Palgrave Macmillan, 2015.

– *Entertaining Elephants: Animal Agency and the Business of the American Circus*. Baltimore: Johns Hopkins University Press, 2013.

– ed. *The Historical Animal*. Syracuse: Syracuse University Press, 2015.

Newkirk, Pamela. *Spectacle: The Astonishing Life of Ota Benga*. New York: Harper Collins, 2015.

Newman, Kathleen M. *Radio Active: Advertising and Consumer Activism, 1935–1947*. Berkeley: University of California Press, 2004.

Ngai, Sienna. "The Cuteness of the Avant-Garde." *Critical Inquiry* 31 (2005): 811–47.

Norton, Bryan G., Michael Hutchins, Elizabeth F. Stevens, and Terry L. Maple, eds. *Ethics on the Ark: Zoos, Animal Welfare, and Wildlife Conservation*. Washington, DC: Smithsonian Institution Press, 1995.

Nyhart, Lynn K. *Modern Nature: The Rise of the Biological Perspective in Germany*. Chicago: University of Chicago Press, 2009.

Ogle, Maureen. *In Meat We Trust: An Unexpected History of Carnivore America*. Boston: Houghton Mifflin, 2013.

Orwell, George. *The Collected Essays, Journalism and Letters of George Orwell*, vol. 3. New York: Harcourt Brace Jovanovich, 1968.

Pachirat, Timothy. *Every Twelve Seconds: Industrialized Slaughter and the Politics of Sight*. New Haven: Yale University Press, 2011.

Palmans, M. "Offert par le Gouverneur-général du Congo-Belge." *Zoo* (1953): 30–1.

Pastoureau, Michel. *The Bear: History of a Fallen King*. Cambridge, MA: Belknap Press of Harvard University Press, 2011.

Pietrobruno, Sheenagh. "The Stereoscope and the Miniature." *Early Popular Visual Culture* 9, 3 (2011): 171–90.

Pignarre, Philippe, and Isabelle Stengers. *Capitalist Sorcery: Breaking the Spell*. New York: Palgrave, 2011.

Plato. *Statesman, The Dialogues of* Plato. Translated by Benjamin Jowett. 5 vols. Oxford: Oxford University Press, 1924.

Pouillard, Violette. "Conservation et captures animales au Congo belge (1908–1960): Vers une histoire de la matérialité des politiques de gestion de la faune." *Revue historique* 679 (2016): 577–604.

"En captivité: Politiques humaines et vies animales dans les jardins zoologiques du XIXe siècle à nos jours (Ménagerie du Jardin des Plantes, zoos de Londres et Anvers)." PhD dissertation, Free University of Brussels and University of Lyon, 2015.

– "Vie et mort des gorilles de l'Est (*Gorilla beringei*) en captivité (1923–2012)." *Revue de synthèse* 136 (2015): 375–402.

Radick, Gregory. "Primate Language and the Playback Experiment, in 1890 and 1980." *Journal of the History of Biology* 38, 3 (Autumn 2005): 461–93.

Readings, Bill. *Introducing Lyotard: Art and Politics.* New York: Routledge Press, 1991.

– "Postmodernity and Narrative." In *Jean François Lyotard: Aesthetics*, edited by Victor E. Taylor and Gregg Lambert. London: Taylor and Francis, 2006.

Rees, Amanda. "Reflections on the Field: Primatology, Popular Science and the Politics of Personhood." *Social Studies of Science* 37, 6 (December 2007): 881–907.

Remis, Melissa J. "Western Lowland Gorillas (*Gorilla gorilla gorilla*) as Seasonal Frugivores: Use of Variable Resources." *American Journal of Primatology* 43 (1997): 87–109.

Revel, Jacques. "L'histoire au ras du sol." Introduction to Giovanni Levi, *Le pouvoir au village: Histoire d'un exorciste dans le Piémont du XVIIe siècle*, i–xxxiii. Translated by Monique Aymard. Paris: Gallimard, 1989.

Rich, Jeremy. *Missing Links: The African and American Worlds of R.L. Garner, Primate Collector.* Athens: University of Georgia Press, 2012.

Ritvo, Harriet. *The Animal Estate: The English and Other Creatures in the Victorian Age.* Cambridge: Harvard University Press, 1987.

Robbins, Louise. *Elephant Slaves and Pampered Parrots: Exotic Animals in Eighteenth-Century Paris.* Baltimore: Johns Hopkins University Press, 2002.

Robbins, Martha M., et al. "Social Structure and Life History Patterns in Western Gorillas (*Gorilla gorilla gorilla*)." *American Journal of Primatology* 64 (2004): 145–59.

Robinson, Philip T. *Life at the Zoo: Behind the Scenes with the Animal Doctors.* New York: Columbia University Press, 2004.

Rogers, M. Elizabet. "Western Gorilla Diet: A Synthesis from Six Sites." *American Journal of Primatology* 64 (2004): 173–92.

Roscher, Mieke, and Andre Krebber, eds. *Animal Biography: Re-framing Animal Lives*. London: Palgrave Macmillan, 2018.

Rosenthal, Mark, Carol Tauber, and Edward Uhler. *The Ark in the Park: The Story of the Lincoln Park Zoo*. Urbana: University of Illinois Press, 2003.

Ross, Andrea Friederici. *Let the Lions Roar! The Evolution of Brookfield Zoo*. Brookfield: Chicago Zoological Society, 1997.

Rothfels, Nigel. "Immersed with Animals." In *Representing Animals*, edited by Nigel Rothfels, 199–223. Theories of Contemporary Culture, vol. 26. Bloomington: Indiana University Press, 2002.

– *Savages and Beasts: The Birth of the Modern Zoo*. Baltimore: Johns Hopkins University Press, 2002.

– "Touching Animals: The Search for a Deeper Understanding of Animals." In *Beastly Natures: Animals, Humans, and the Study of History*, edited by Dorothee Brant, 38–58. Charlottesville: University of Virginia Press, 2010.

Ruch, Theodore C. *Diseases of Laboratory Primates*. London: W.B. Saunders Company, 1959.

Ruempler, Uta. "The Cologne Zoo Diet for Lowland Gorillas *Gorilla gorilla gorilla* to Eliminate Regurgitation and Reingestion." *International Zoo Yearbook* 31 (1992): 225–9.

Ryan, Joal. *Former Child Star: The Story of America's Least Wanted*. Toronto: ECW Press, 2000.

Sahlins, Peter. "The Royal Menageries of Louis XIV and the Civilizing Process Revisited." *French Historical Studies* 35 (2010): 237–67.

Schaller, George B. *The Last Panda*. Chicago: University of Chicago Press, 1994.

– *The Mountain Gorilla: Ecology and Behavior*. Chicago: University of Chicago Press, 1963.

Sclater, Philip Lutley, and Oldfield Thomas. *The Book of Antelopes*. 4 vols. London: Porter, 1894–1900.

Senior, Matthew. ed. *A Cultural History of Animals in the Age of Enlightenment*. Oxford: Berg, 2007.

– "The Ménagerie and the Labyrinthe: Animals at Versailles, 1662–1792." In *Renaissance Beasts: Of Animals, Humans and Other Wonderful Creatures in the Early Modern Period*, edited by Erica Fudge, 208–32. Chicago: University of Illinois Press, 2004.

– "Seeing the Versailles Ménagerie." *Papers on French Seventeenth-Century Literature* 30, 59 (2003): 351–63.

Servais, Véronique. "La visite au zoo et l'apprentissage de la distinction humaine." *Revue d'anthropologie des connaissances* 6, 3 (March 2012): 157–84.

Setoguchi, Akihisa. "Darwin Commemorations and Three Generations of Historians of Biology." *East Asian Science, Technology and Society* 3 (2009): 531–7.

Shukin, Nicole. *Animal Capital: Rendering Life in Biopolitical Times.* Minneapolis: University of Minnesota Press, 2009.

Silverman, Robert J. "The Stereoscope and Photographic Depiction in the 19th Century." *Technology and Culture* 34, 4 (1993): 729–56.

Six, Victor, and Agatha Gijzen. "Kaisi amuse son public." *Zoo* 35, 3 (1970): 100–1.

Sloterdijk, Peter. "Rules for the Human Zoo: A Response to the Letter on Humanism." In *Nicht gerettet: Versuche nach Heidegger*, translated by Mary Varney Rorty, 302–33. Suhrkamp, 2001. *Environment and Planning D: Society and Space.* 27 (2009).

Snæbjörnsdóttir, Bryndis, and Wilson, Mark. "The We of 'We': Re-thinking back to the Garden." In *Late Harvest*, edited by Northrup, 125–30. Chicago: Hirmer Publishers, 2014.

Sparrow, T. "Bodies in Transit: The Plastic Subject of Alphonso Lingis." *Janus Head*, 10 1 (2007): 99–122.

Stakelon, Pauline. "Travel through the Stereoscope: Movement and Narrative in Topological Stereoview Collections of Europe." *Media History* 16, 4 (2010): 407–22.

Stott, R. Jeffrey. "The American Idea of a Zoological Park: An Intellectual History." PhD dissertation, University of California-Santa Barbara, 1981.

– "The Historical Origins of the Zoological Park in American Thought." *Environmental Review* 5 (Fall 1981): 52–65.

Sutcliffe, Anthony. *Paris: An Architectural History.* New Haven: Yale University Press, 1993.

Tennent, James Emerson. *Sketches of the Natural History of Ceylon.* London: Longmans, 1861.

Thompson, E.P. *The Making of the English Working Class.* London: Victor Gollancz Ltd, 1980.

Thurman, Judith. "First Impressions: What Does the World's Oldest Art Say about Us?" *New Yorker*, 23 June 2008.

Tobin, James. *To Conquer the Air: The Wright Brothers and the Great Race for Flight.* New York: Free Press, 2004.

Traisnel, Antoine. *Capture: Early American Pursuits and the Making of a New Animal Condition* (forthcoming).

Tsing, Anna Lowenhaupt. *The Mushroom at the End of the World: On the Possibility of Life in Capitalist Ruins*. Princeton: Princeton University Press, 2017.

Tyler, Tom. *Ciferae: A Bestiary in Five Fingers*. Minneapolis: University of Minnesota Press, 2012.

Uddin, Lisa. "Panda Gardens and Public Sex at the National Zoological Park." *Public 0*, 41 (11 November 2013): 81–92.

– *Zoo Renewal: White Flight and the Animal Ghetto*. Minneapolis: University of Minnesota Press, 2015.

Ueki, Tetsuya. *Gakumon no bōryoku: Ainu bochi ha naze abakaretaka*. Yokohama: Shumpūsha, 2017.

Van den Bergh, Walter. "A nos membres." *Zoo* 30, 1 (1964): 1–7.

– "A nos membres." *Zoo* 36, 4 (1971): 157–67.

– "Les réalisations 1958 au Zoo." *Zoo* 24, 1 (1958): 4–5.

– "A nos membres." *Zoo* 44, 1 (1978): 1–22.

– "The New Ape House at Antwerp Zoo." *International Zoo Yearbook* (1960): 7–11.

Van Praag, Siegfried E. "À propos de Singes et leur beauté." *Zoo* 26, 3 (1961): 86–93.

Vandersommers, Daniel. "Narrating Animal History from the Crags: A Turn-of-the-Century Tale about Mountain Sheep, Resistance, and a Nation." *Journal of American Studies* 51, 3 (2017): 751–77.

Van Eysendeyk, Rudy, and Roland Van Bocxstaele. *De Tuin van het Leven: Achter de Schermen van de Antwerpse Zoo en Dierenpark Planckendael*. Gent: Ludion, 2003.

Van Puyenbroeck, B. "Bâtiment des anthropoïdes, réouverture printemps 1989." *Zoo* 54, 4 (1989): 30–4.

– "Evénements récents chez les mammifères." *Zoo* 54, 2 (1988): 19–26.

– "Nos gorilles." *Zoo* 42, 3 (1977): 89–93.

Vercruysse, J., and Mortelmans, J. "Régimes alimentaires pour animaux exotiques." *Zoo* 39, 3 (1974): 103–9.

Vessier, Maximilien. *La Pitié-Salpêtrière: Quatre siècles d'histoire et d'histoires*. Paris: Hôpital de la Pitié-Salpêtrière, 1999.

Wako, Kenji. *Dōbutsuen kakumei*. Tokyo: Iwanamishoten, 2010.

Walcott, Charles Doolittle. *Biographical Memoir of Samuel Pierpont Langley, 1834–1906*. City of Washington: National Academy of Science, 1912.

Walker, Brett. *The Lost Wolves of Japan*. Washington: University of Washington Press, 2005.

Ward, W. Peter. *White Canada Forever: Popular Attitudes and Public Policy Toward Orientals in British Columbia*. Montreal: McGill-Queen's University Press, 1990.

Warkenstin, Traci, and Fawcett, Leesa. "Whale and Human Agency in World-Making: Decolonizing Whale-Human Encounters." In Acampora, *Metamorphosis of the Zoo*, 103–22.

Wegeforth, Harry Milton, and Neil Morgan. *It Began with a Roar: The Story of San Diego's World-Famed Zoo*. San Diego: Pioneer Printers, 1953.

Wells, Deborah L. "A Note on the Influence of Visitors on the Behaviour and Welfare of Zoohoused Gorillas." *Applied Animal Behaviour Science* 93 (2005): 13–17.

Wemmer, Christen, and Catherine A. Christen. *Elephants and Ethics: Toward a Morality of Coexistence*. Johns Hopkins University Press, 2008.

West, Nancy M. "Fantasy, Photography, and the Marketplace: Oliver Wendell Holmes and the Stereoscope." *Nineteenth-Century Contexts* 19, 3 (1996): 231–58.

Wheeler, Randolph C. *Kantian Imperatives and Phenomenology's Original Force*. Washington, DC: The Council for Research in Values in Philosophy, 2008.

Wheeler, Wendy. "Biosemiotics." In *The Edinburgh Companion to Animal Studies*, edited by Lynn Turner, Undine Sellbach, and Ron Broglio. Edinburgh: Edinburgh University Press, 2018.

Wolfe, Cary. *Before the Law: Humans and Animals in a Biopolitical Frame*. Chicago: University of Chicago Press, 2013.

Yamamoto, Tetsuya. "A Reappraisal of Kunitake Kume, Who Reported the Result of Iwakura Mission." *Nīgata kenritsu hakubutukan kiyō* 13 (2012): 95–110.

Yanabu, Akira. *Honyakugo seiritsu jijō*. Tokyo: Iwanami shoten, 1982.

Yomota, Inuhiko. *Kawaii ron*. Tokyo: Chikumashobō, 2006.

Young, Fredrick. "Animality: Notes towards a Manifesto." In *Glossalalia*, edited by Julian Wolfreys, 9–21. Manchester: Edinburgh University Press, 2003.

Zook, B.C., R.M. Sauer, and F.M. Garner. "Lead Poisoning in Captive Wild Animals." *Journal of Wildlife Diseases* 8 (1972): 264–72.

Zoological Society of Philadelphia. *An Animal Garden in Fairmount Park*. Philadelphia: Zoological Society of Philadelphia, 1988.

CONTRIBUTORS

RON BROGLIO is associate professor in the Department of English at Arizona State University and senior scholar at the University's Global Institute of Sustainability. He is also a visiting research fellow at the University of Cumbria and president of the Society for Literature, Science, and the Arts. He is the author of *Beasts of Burden: Biopolitics, Labor, and Animal Life* (2017) and *Surface Encounters: Thinking with Animals and Art* (2011), among other books and collections. He is lead researcher and co-curator of *Trout Fishing in America and Other Stories* at the ASU Art Museum, in which artists Bryndís Snæbjörnsdóttir and Mark Wilson examine the cultural life of endangered species in the Grand Canyon. He also creates artwork on desert attunement and is writing an artistic and theoretical treatise called *Animal Revolution: Events to Come.*

GURO FLINTERUD is a senior researcher at the Norwegian Police University College. She received her PhD from the University of Oslo, with a dissertation on animal celebrities and zoological gardens. Her research interests include zoological gardens, environmental issues, animals in the police force, and dog breeding cultures.

TAKASHI ITO is associate professor at the Institute of Global Studies, Tokyo University of Foreign Studies, and he researches and teaches on the social and cultural history of Victorian Britain. He is the author of *London Zoo and the Victorians, 1828–1859* (2014). His current research interest lies in the comparative history of human-animal relationships in modern Britain and Japan.

JOHN M. KINDER is associate professor of history and American studies at Oklahoma State University. He is the author of *Paying with Their Bodies: American War and the Problem of the Disabled Veteran* (2015). He is currently finishing his second book, a history of zoos during World War II.

RANDY MALAMUD is regents' professor of English at Georgia State University. He is the author of nine books, including *The Importance of Elsewhere: The Globalist Humanist Tourist* (2018), *Reading Zoos: Representations of Animals and Captivity* (1998), *Poetic Animals and Animal Souls* (2003), and *An Introduction to Animals and Visual Culture* (2012).

TRACY MCDONALD is associate professor of history at McMaster University. She is the author of a number of articles and of *Face to the Village: The Riazan Countryside under Soviet Rule, 1921–1930* (2011), which won the Reginald Zelnik Book Prize in history. She was one of the three founding members of the independent documentary-film company Chemodan Films. Between 2004 and 2009, she participated in the making of four films, including *Province of Lost Film, Uprising,* and *Photographer*. She is currently working on two research projects: a gorilla biography and a study of exotic animal import-export to and from the USSR from the 1920s to the 1960s.

JONATHAN OSBORN is a PhD candidate in dance studies at York University examining human-animal choreographic relations and the staging of affective environments. An artist and choreographer, he has created over fifteen original dance works and maintains a movement practice invested in the solo form, speculative fiction, and inhuman bodies.

VIOLETTE POUILLARD received her DPhil from the Free University of Brussels and the University of Lyon (Jean Moulin-Lyon III) in 2015. Her doctoral dissertation reconsidered the history of zoos by paying attention, from the early nineteenth century to the present times, to human gestures and practices, their influences on animals, and the dynamics (or the breakage of dynamics) between humans and zoo animals. In 2015–17, she was a Wiener-Anspach postdoctoral fellow at the African Studies Centre of the University of Oxford and an academic visitor at St Antony's College. She is now a postdoctoral assistant in history at Ghent University, where she works on the (post)colonial management of wildlife in the Congo and is completing a book based on her doctoral dissertation. She is also a scientific collaborator at MMC, Free University of Brussels, and an associate researcher at LARHRA, University Jean Moulin-Lyon III.

NIGEL ROTHFELS is director of the Office of Undergraduate Research and associate professor of history at the University of Wisconsin-Milwaukee. He is the author of a study of the origin of naturalistic displays in zoological gardens, *Savages and Beasts: The Birth of the Modern Zoo* (2002), the editor of the interdisciplinary collection *Representing Animals* (2002), a co-author (with Dick Blau) of *Elephant House* (2015), and the general editor of the book series Animalibus: Of Animals and Cultures with Penn State University Press.

MATTHEW SENIOR is Ruberta T. McCandless Professor of French at Oberlin College. He has edited three collections of essays on the history and philosophy of animality: *Animots: Postanimality in French Thought* (2015), *A Cultural History of Animals in the Age of Enlightenment* (2007), and *Animal Acts: Configuring the Human in Western History from the Middle Ages to the Present* (1997). He is also author of *In the Grip of Minos: Confessional Discourse in Dante, Corneille, and Racine* (1994).

MARIANNA SZCZYGIELSKA received her PhD in comparative gender studies at the Central European University in Budapest. Her work focuses on zoos and animal collections in modernity and their critical impact on the larger structures of identity formation. Her research interests include environmental history, animal studies, queer theory, critical race studies, and feminist science and technology studies. She has published on zoos and gender; scientific research on hormones; and relations between affect, transgender, and animal studies; and has taught courses on queer ecologies and the history of science. She worked as a postdoctoral researcher at the Institute of Ethnology of the Czech Academy of Sciences and CEFRES French Research Centre in Social Sciences/CNRS in Prague in the "Bewildering Boar: Changing Cosmopolitics of the Hunt in Europe and Beyond" research project. She is now a postdoctoral fellow at the Max Planck Institute for the History of Science in Berlin.

ZEB TORTORICI received his PhD in history, and is associate professor in the Department of Spanish and Portuguese at New York University. His book *Sins against Nature: Sex and Archives in Colonial New Spain* (2018) focuses on the archiving of sodomy, bestiality, and masturbation in what is today largely Mexico, Guatemala, the American Southwest, and the Philippines between 1530 and 1821. He has edited several anthologies, including *Centering Animals in Latin American History* (2013) and *Sexuality and the Unnatural in Colonial Latin America* (2016), as well as two special issues of *Radical History Review* on "queering archives" and an issue of *TSQ: Transgender Studies Quarterly* on "trans*historicities." Zeb identifies as vegan and teaches undergraduate courses on animals, animality, and colonialism, touching on such topics as monsters, natural history, taxidermy, zoos, and bestiality in the early modern world up to the present.

DANIEL VANDERSOMMERS is a teaching assistant professor at the Indiana Academy for Science, Mathematics, and Humanities at Ball State University. Previously, he served as an NEH postdoctoral fellow at the Consortium for History of Science, Technology and Medicine and as a postdoctoral fellow in animal history at McMaster University. He has published multiple articles on zoos in history and is finishing a book about zoos and popular science between 1890 and 1920.

INDEX

Editors' note: The most lively of essences cannot be put on display, just as the most important of lessons resist categorization. In assembling this index, we realized that we were creating a kind of zoo, reducing the entanglements of writing and thinking to a neat collection, a display. The most vivid themes in this volume – life, living, death, dying, power, humans, animals, and morality – resist indexation, for they reside on every single page. The central components of a new humanities live in the spaces between the lines and pages, where they are experienced but cannot be pinned down.

abjection, 120
Abram, David, 281
Académie des Sciences, 26
Acampora, Ralph, 10
acclimatization, 30, 94–103, 172–6, 245–6
Adams, Carol, 272
aeronautics: on Aerodrome No. 5, 74–5, 83; and animality of science, 85–8; and *Experiments in Aerodynamics*, 81–2; and "The Internal Work of the Wind," 82–3; on Langley and the Great Aerodrome, 74–85; on other aerodromes, 83; and photographic towers, 84

affinity: birds and humans, 25; monkeys and humans, 72. *See also* human-animal distinction; intimacy with animals
Agamben, Giorgio, 4, 297
Ainu, 244
Alexander the Great, 26
American Asian, identity and racism. *See* racial relations in Canada
anatomy, 26, 58, 72, 80, 244
animal agency, 87, 180–1, 267–8, 271–2, 280; on animal choreographies, 307–9, 309–10n5; on animal events, 291; concerning food or gastronomic resistance, 94, 97, 146, 158–9, 162, 180; and cycles of zoo history, 183–4; and death, 258; and queer distortion, 233; on resistance and science, 85–8; runaway animals, 147, 285–6, 288, 290–1; in *Underground*, 286–7. *See also* animal biography
animal attacks, 268–9
animal biography: on the challenges and purpose of, 93–4, 114–15n2, 169–70, 183–4; of Dinah, 93–114; on the genre of, 12; of Gust, 167–84. *See also* Knut
animal combat, 26–7
animal commodities (as capital and/or resources), 61, 86, 123, 126–7, 130–3, 183, 204–7, 215–16, 218, 221, 254,

267–8, 308–9. *See also* feeding zoo
animals
animal gifts, 148, 172–3. *See also* diplomatic animals
animal history, 17n12, 170
animal individuals, 4–6, 11, 12, 22, 87, 114–15n2 170, 183, 207, 258, 285–6. *See especially* animal biography
animal labour, 130
animal painters, 33, 127
animal rights activists, 191, 200–1, 258, 263, 270
animal sculptors, 52–3, 105–7
animality: and the category of race, 220, 225, 230–1; and the Church, 291; and gender, 225; in juxtaposition to humanity, 238; and queerness, 231; of science, 85–8; underlying the human, 20; of zoos and slaughterhouses, 126–7, 131. *See also* animalization of humans
animalization of humans: on animality, 41; on madness, 39–41; on migrant, 220, 222–3, 225–6
animals and human language: concerning American Sign Language, 93. *See also* primatology
"animals in action exhibits" (kōdō tenji), 246–59
animals in movies, 193, 198
antelopes, 45–61; *The Book of Antelopes*, 57–9; discussion of eland, 54–5; discussion of hartebeest, 57; discussion of the sable, 46–50, 59; extinction, 56; fantasy of antelopes, 59; ideal form, 56
Anthropocene, 6, 272, 308
anthropological machine, 4
anthropology, 72, 171, 281. *See also* primatology
anthropomorphization and/or projection, 68–9, 97–9, 104–6, 110–13, 137, 159, 178, 184, 192, 198–200, 206–7, 217–20, 230–1, 254–9, 269, 271, 285–7, 295, 301, 305. *See especially* animal biography
Antwerp Zoo. *See* animal biography: of Gust
architectural analysis, 28–9, 33–7, 52–3, 224–5, 228–9, 248–52, 254

Aristotle, 26, 278, 284
ARK, 294–309
Arluke, Arnold, 150
Asahiyama Zoo, 237–59
assisted reproductive technology, 214
Association of Zoos and Aquariums, 269
avians and science. *See* aeronautics

Bak, Meredith, 138
Baker, Frank, 66–72, 75–80
banana trade during World War II, 149
banging on, or charging, the glass, 179, 181–2, 198–9
Baratay, Eric, 7–8, 28–30
Barbro, Ron, 216
Baring, Arnulf and Gabriele, 194
Barnes, Djuna, 104–6, 111, 117n54
Baskerville, Danielle, 294–5, 298–9. See also *ARK*
Bateson, Gregory, 282–3, 287
Baudrillard, Jean, 205, 288
Bean, Ed, and Robert, 156–7, 159
"bear bread," 154
Beatty, Patricia, 305, 311nn19–20
beavers, 220–1, 227
Belgrade Zoo, 285–7
beluga whales, 270
Benchley, Belle, 151–2, 157
Bentley, Amy, 153
Berger, John, 288, 295, 309nn2–4
Berlin Zoo, 244. *See especially* Knut
betrayal, 108
Bicêtre, 35, 39, 41
biopolitics, 19–25, 30, 285–7
biosemiotics, 282–3
Blackburne, William H., 76–80
Blackfish. See Cowperthwaite, Gabriela
Blaszkiewitz, Bernhard, 205
Blondin, Leo, 145–6, 158
Boel, Pieter, 29–32
Bojovic, Vuk, 285
Boles, Benjamin, 306
Bousé, Derek, 198
Brancheau, Dawn, 266–9
Brandstetter, Gabriele, 297
Braverman, Irus, 309n5
Brewster, David, 124–8
Bridges, William, 108

Broglio, Ron, 6
Bronx Zoo, 10, 51, 130–1, 135–7, 145,
    147, 151, 153, 154–5, 160, 270. See
    also New York Zoological Park
Brooke, Victor. See antelopes: The Book
    of Antelopes
Brookfield Zoo, 119–23, 143, 154–7, 159
Brooks, William Keith, 68
Brumas, 202
Buffon, Georges-Louis Leclerc, 31
Bunting, R., 195
business of/and zoos, 12, 147, 152, 160–
    2, 264, 266–7, 273

Caldas-Coulthard, Carmen Rosa, 194–5
Calgary Zoo, 211
Canaday, Margot, 223
captive breeding, 171, 178, 182, 191,
    193, 202–3, 209n42; technology, 227–
    32. See especially pandas
Caricuao Zoo, 161
Carson, Rachel, 272
Cary, Diana Serra, 193
cattle, 6, 133–4, 290–1
Central Park Zoo, 121–2, 157, 296
Charlotte, Princess and macaque, 237
Chauvet Cave, 279–81, 284
Chen, Mel Y., 212, 225, 230–2
Cheyne-Stout, Ronald, 124, 138–41
Chicago Zoological Society, 120
child star: in terms of animals (see Knut;
    zoo celebrity); in terms of humans,
    192–3, 196–7, 203–4, 206
chimpanzees, 71, 102–3, 108, 112, 113,
    134–7, 141–2, 158, 173–7, 193, 268,
    285–6
Chinese Association of Zoological Gar-
    dens, 216
Chongqing Zoo, 211
Chris, Cynthia, 220
Cincinnati Zoological Garden, 67
Clottes, Jean, 281
Cold War, 215
Collard, Rosemary-Claire, 216
collecting impulse, 60–1, 128–31, 174,
    240, 255
colonialism, 61, 87, 95–6, 105, 167–71,
    214, 220–7, 232–3, 240, 244–6, 268

Columbus Zoo, 178
Commoner, Barry, 272–3
communism, 286
Congolese Botanical and Zoological
    Society, 172
conservation. See zoos, contemporary:
    self-constructed identities
Convention on International Trade in
    Endangered Species of Wild Fauna and
    Flora, 215
"Coogan law," 206
Cowperthwaite, Gabriela, 262–3, 266–7,
    269–71, 274n1
Crary, Jonathan, 122
Crist, Eileen, 159
cruelty: in the Coliseum, 26; and inti-
    macy, 26–30, 205
cult of the cute (kawaii), 237, 256–9
Cumming, Roualeyn Gordon, 45–50
Cunningham, Merce, 296
Cushing, Nancy, 214
cuteness, 193–7, 202–3, 217–18, 248,
    264. See also cult of the cute (kawaii)

Da Mao. See pandas
Dale, Joshua Paul, 257
dance. See ARK
Darwin, Charles, 73, 240, 283
Davis, Susan, 9, 266
Deleuze, Gilles, and Felix Guattari, 238,
    256, 298
Denver Zoo, 268
Derrida, Jacques, 21, 42n7, 94, 114, 263
Descartes, René, 81, 86, 240, 270. See
    also aeronautics for Cartesianism "in
    action"
Desmond, Jane, 295, 308–9
Detroit Zoo, 270
diasporic citizenship, 220, 232
diplomatic animals, 172–3, 217, 232–3,
    237. See especially pandas
Dinah, 93–114
disease and illness in captivity, 102, 147,
    151, 172–3, 175, 178, 179, 242, 270
dismemberment, 123, 131, 143
Disneyland, 288
Ditmars, Raymond, 103–4, 111
Donahue, Jesse, 153

Doyle, Richard, 283–4

"ecological exhibit" (seitai tenji), 246–7
ecological postmodernity, 238–9, 246
ecological thinking, 282–6
Ehrenreich, Nancy, 161
Ehrlich, Paul, 272
elephants, 180–1, 258, 270
Eliade, Mircea, 277–8, 282
Elias, Norbert, 29
Ellenberger, Henri, 31
Ellis, Richard, 200
empathy: on the "anthropomorphic-
   fallacy fallacy," 269, 271; on cuteness
   and, 217; on the "empathy gap," 93–4;
   on kinaesthetic empathy, 295
enclosure descriptions, 119–22, 140–1,
   174–81, 224–5, 227–31, 248–54, 267,
   270, 273
endangered species. See pandas
Engelholm, Fred, 105, 109, 111
environmental enrichment, 178–9
"epistemological anthropocentrism," 8
Er Shun. See pandas
evolution: and language, 67
extinction, 56, 58–9, 128, 213–14, 245,
   264, 275n13
Ezo deer, 243–5
Ezo wolf, 245, 261n23

fake rocks, 122
feeding zoo animals, 110–11, 116n29,
   145–62, 178–80. See also acclimatization
Field, Stanley, 154
flying penguins, 254–7
food animals, 150, 243–4
Forsythe, William, 297
Foucault, Michel: on the Hôpital, 38; on
   madness, 38–40; on Statesman, 22–3;
   on Panopticon, 27–9; on voyeurism,
   273
Franklin Park Zoo, 156
Frozen Zoo™, 214

Gaillard, Aurelia, 29
Garner, Richard L.: and animality of science, 85–8; along Gabon River, 69–71,

73, 95–103; communication with Hornaday about Dinah, 94–104; concerning zoo experiments, 66–74; gaze,
   classificatory, 28, 174; gaze, courtiers',
   29; gaze, exoticizing, 220; gaze, imperialist eye, 308; gaze, panoptical, 29
gender: and Asian Canadian masculinity,
   231; assigning to pandas, 228–31; on
   bears and postwar domesticity, 218; on
   blurring lines, 100; on Dinah, Barnes,
   and early feminism, 104–5, 117n54; on
   displaying masculinity, 61, 71; and en-
   tanglement, 212, 232–3; Harvey and
   conceptions of motherhood, 106; on
   Hornaday's gendered contempt, 112–
   13; on naming animals, 96–7, 101, 232;
   and primatology, 72; on race via projection, 98–9; on "starting a family," 178;
   and stereotyping Asians and Asian
   Americans, 218–20, 225
Georgia Aquarium, 270
Giant Panda Experience Exhibition. See
   pandas
Ginzburg, Carlo, 167, 170, 183
giraffes, 54–5, 246, 264
"global politics of food," 161
Gore, Al, 262–3, 265–6, 271
gorillas: capture and traffic of, 69–70, 95,
   103, 171–2; concerning Dinah's biography, 93–114; concerning Dinah in the
   NYZP, 103–14; and extraspecific companions, 110, 174, 178; concerning
   Gust's biography, 167–84; concerning
   primatology, 69–71; on Don, 101–3; on
   ethological fieldwork, 171–2, 174; on
   Iosephine, 174; on John Daniel, 113; on
   Kaisi and Kisubi, 177, 182; on Kora,
   176, 178, 182–4; on Michael, 93; and
   moats in enclosures, 177; on Pega, 182;
   on Simba II, 172; stereoscope and, 137;
   on Tootsy, 100–1
Gould, Stephen Jay, 195–6
Graham, Martha, 296
Grandville, J.J., 288
Grant, Madison, 59
graphophone. See primatology
Griffin, Donald, 159
Gruffudd, Pyrs, 224–5

Guggenheim, David, 262, 265
Gust, 167–84

Hagenbeck, Carl: communication with
Hornaday, 53–8, 64n43, 113; historiog-
raphy of, 8; legacy of, 61; and soaring
birds, 75–6
Hancocks, David, 9–10
handwritten signage, 247–8, 258
Hanson, Elizabeth, 8, 203
Harambe, 273
Haraway, Donna, 72, 74, 93–4, 279
Hardouin-Fugier, Elisabeth, 7–8, 28–9
Harkins, Dan, 156
Harper, Laureen, 211–12
Harper, Stephen, 211–12, 216
Harris, William Cornwallis, 47–50
Hartig, Falk, 216
Harvey, Eli, 105–7, 111
Hasegawa, Ushio, 258
Heidegger, Martin: on dwelling and
thinking, 278; "house of Being," 20, 41
Hello Kitty, 256
Hershey Zoo, 152
Herzog, Werner, 279–81
Hill, Van Dyke, 138
hippopotamus, 121–2, 137, 192
history of biology in Japan, 240
Hokkaido/Ezo, 244
Holmes, Oliver Wendell, 124–5
Hôpital Général, 33, 35
Horn, Roy, 268
Hornaday, William Temple: and an-
telopes, 50–7; communication with
Garner, 94–104; communication with
Hagenbeck, 53–8, 64n43, 113; on
Dinah, 109–14, 112; and on extinction,
56–7
horseflesh, 156
Hribal, Jason, 161–2
human-animal distinction, 41, 42n7, 85–
7, 123–4, 139–43, 161, 181, 230, 238–
9, 254–9, 269, 276, 279, 286, 298
human zoos, 16n5, 25; Sloterdijk's conception of, 19–20
humanism: on the anthropocentrism of,
276–7, 287; on dance, 295, 305–6,
311n20; on disavowal, 114; on Enlight-

enment epistemology, 86, 255, 280,
283, 287, 290–1; on language, 284; on
the "philosophic mind," 109; on reason
and unreason, 278, 284 (see also madness); on Renaissance art, 285; on
Science, 65–6, 85–8, 106–8, 270; Sloterdijk on, 19–20; on taxonomy, 280, 283,
289–90; on thinking, 135; on Western
science and Nature, 240–1
humanity, 4–5, 114
hunting memoirs, 45–6; literary structure
of, 47. See also Cumming, Roualeyn
Gordon

Iman, Zakiyyah, 213
immersion exhibit, 227, 246–7
imperial ambitions. See collecting impulse
Inconvenient Truth, An. See Gore, Al
insanity. See madness
interdisciplinarity, 10–11
International Union for Conservation of
Nature, 215
intimacy with animals: Dinah and Garner,
103–4; Gust and keeper, 167–8, 174,
177, 179; gorilla-chimpanzee intimacy,
173, 175; gorilla-dog intimacy, 110;
and kawaii, 257; keepers' "personal"
relationships with animals, 252, 254;
"panda intimacy," 212; Plato's perspective on, 24; Rome and Renaissance, 26–
7; surrogacy and gorillas, 100–1,
108–9, 113, 174, 178; zoos and animal
friendship, 169
Inuzuka, Yasuhiro, 245
Irwin, Steve, 269
Iwakura Mission, 239–40

Jamieson, Dale, 10
Japanese ants, 155
Jenkins, Virginia Scott, 149
Jintao, Hu, 216

kawaii. See cult of the cute (kawaii)
kawaiso, 257–9
Kennon, Henry M., 158
Keystone View Company, 121, 128–38
Kirby, David, 267
Klein, Naomi, 265, 272

Klös, Heiner, 194
Knudson, Gus, 148
Knut, 191–207
Kodiak bears, 119–22, 143
Koganei, Yoshikiyo, 244
Kohn, Eduardo, 281–2
Kosuge, Masao, 242, 247, 252, 254
Kursaal Zoo, 151
Kusturica, Emir, 286–7

Langley, Samuel, 68, 70; on
    aeronautics/aviation, 74–85, 90n48;
    and animality of science, 85–8
Latour, Bruno, 66, 87
Lawrence, Elizabeth, 196
Lazarists. See St Vincent de Paul
Le Vau, Louis, 20, 27–8, 35–7
Lee, Keekok, 10
Leopold, Aldo, 272
Leroi-Gourhan, André, 277
Lewis-Williams, David, 281
Li, Fang, 217–18
Li, Peter, 224
"lifeworld," 159
Lincoln Park Zoo, 270
Lingis, Alphonso, 284–5, 288–90, 297–9
Loisel, Gustave, 25–7
London Zoo, 151, 155, 192, 202, 224,
    239, 254
Lorenz, Konrad, 194
Los Angeles Zoo, 215, 273
Louis XIV, 24–7
Lydekker, Richard, 58–9, 64n46
Lyon, Beth, 161
Lyotard, Jean-François, 291

madness, 38–41, 267
Malamud, Randy, 9, 123, 128, 213,
    309n4
Malin, Brenton J., 141
Mann, William, 158–9
March of the Penguins, 274n1
Markwell, Kevin, 214
Maruyama Zoo, 241, 245
Marvin, Garry, 9, 150, 309n4
Mauss, Marcel, 216
Mazur, Nicole, 10
McKay, Herbert C., 138

mealworms, German, 149
meat, 145–6, 150–2, 155–6, 243–4. See
    also feeding zoo animals; slaughter-
    houses
Meiji Restoration, 239, 244
mental hospital, 271. See especially
    Salpêtrière
Michston, Morris, 195
Mickey Mouse, 195–6
migration, 245. See especially racial rela-
    tions in Canada
Millais, John Guille, 45, 47, 50
Miller, Ian Jared, 86–7, 237–9, 258
Molloy, Claire, 193
monkey talk. See primatology
Montecore, 268
Morris, Paul, 195
Morris, Ramona and Desmond, 217, 230
Morton, Timothy, 6
Mullan, Bob, 9, 150, 309n4
multiculturalism, 224–7, 232
multispecies ethnography, 11
museums, 28, 49, 57–8, 67, 78, 174, 233,
    241, 247, 307

Nakamata, Mitsushi, 245
Nance, Susan, 167, 180–1
National Collection of Heads and Horns,
    59–61
National Zoological Park, 65–88, 154,
    213, 218
natural history, 26, 30, 49, 57–8, 60, 73,
    127–8, 238
naturalization, 130–1, 211–13
Navier, Claude-Louis, 82–3
neoteny, 194–7, 217
Neumünster Zoo, 205–6
"new humanities," 5–6, 16
New York Zoological Park: Antelope
    House, 52–6; collection of, 51–2; con-
    cerning Dinah, 93–114; primate plague,
    102. See also Hornaday, William Tem-
    ple; National Collection of Heads and
    Horns
New York Zoological Society, 50, 59,
    101, 108
Ngai, Sianne, 257
Nim, 114

Nimphius, Harry F., 157
Nixon, Richard, 215
Noah's ark, 264–5, 291
Nyhart, Lynn, 8

Obaysch, 192
Oklahoma City Zoo, 145–6, 154, 156, 158
Omaha Zoo, 152
orangutan, 142, 177, 183
orcas, 267–8, 275n12
Orwell, George, 287
Osborn, Henry Fairfield, 102

Pachirat, Timothy, 290
panda diplomacy, 213–17
"panda orientalism," 220
"panda pact," 211, 214–7
pandas, 211–33, 264; on Hsing-Hsing and Ling-Ling, 215, 218, 228; on Hua Mei, 234n23; on Ji Li, 230; on Jia Pampan and Jia Yueyue, 232; on Qing Qing and Quan Quan, 216
paradeisos, 26, 30
pastoral power, 21–5, 30, 309n5
Pastoreau, Michel, 195
patriotic animals, 145–6, 154–60, 165n68
penguins, 225, 247–51. See also flying penguins
Penny, Rupert, 113
petkeeping, 130, 137
Philadelphia Zoo, 179
photography, 127–8, 137, 138. See also stereographs and stereoscopes
Picture Book Zoos, 140
pig, 132, 137
Pignarre, Philippe, 279
Planet Earth, 274n1
Plato: on the cave, 278; on race, 42n12; Statesman, 19–24
Poe, Edgar Allan, 291
Pokémon, 256
polar bears. See Knut
Pope Francis, 291
postcolonialism, 169, 170, 263
posthumanism, 11
predators: redundant male mammals

in zoos, 201; symbolic meanings of, 196–201, 267
primatology, 66–74; and animality of science, 85–8
Psihoyos, Louis, 272
pythons and gastronomic resistance, 159

racial citizenship, 218–20
racial relations in Canada, 220–7, 232, 235n43
racialization, 212, 218–27, 230–2
racism, 69, 97–9, 137, 145; and animality, 225–6, 230–1; and the Chinese Exclusion Act, 224; and the construction of race, 212–13; and "John Chinaman," 221–3; on notions of hygiene, 223; and primatology, 72; and Western notions of sexual embodiment, 230–1. See also racialization
railroads, 221, 241
rationing: for American humans, 146, 149–50, 155–6; for American zoo animals, 145–62
Raw, William H., 121–2
Readings, Bill, 291
Reddy, Vasu, 195
redundancy, 201, 203
regurgitation and fur plucking, 181–4
Ridgeway, Robert, 78–80
Riechelmann, Cord, 205
Ringling Brothers, 113
Ritvo, Harriet, 7, 192
Roosevelt, Franklin Delano, 149
Roosevelt, Theodore, 195
Rothfels, Nigel, 8, 227

Sahlins, Peter, 29
Salpêtrière, 33–41
Samson, Aloïs, 174, 177, 179
San Diego Zoo, 151, 153–6
Sanborn Elwin R., 52, 111
Sanders, Clinton, 150
Sandilands, Catriona, 225
Schroeder, Charles, 156
Schüle, André, 200–1
science, reflections upon. See humanism
Sclater, Philip Lutley. See antelopes: The Book of Antelopes

Sea World, 266–70
seals, 247, 252–4
sexing pandas, 230–1
sexism. *See* gender
sexuality: on heterosexual desire, 212–13;
  on naturalizing heterosexuality, 227–31;
  and race, 213–14, 223, 225, 230–1;
  on reproductive "failures" of pandas,
  230–1
shamanism, 281–5, 289
shizen (nature), 240–1
Shonnard, Eugenie, 107–8, 111
Shukin, Nicole, 133, 220–1, 227
Sidky, Homayun, 281
Skoll, Jeff, 265
slaughterhouses, 123–4, 131–4, 290–1
Sloterdijk, Peter, 19–23, 31
Smiths, Carolyn, 227–8
Smithsonian Institution. *See* National
  Zoological Park
Smokey the Bear, 218
social deprivation, 174
"sociozoological scale," 150
souvenir stand, 204, 254
Species Survival Plans, 214
Spencer, Herbert, 240
St Vincent de Paul, 41
Stakelon, Pauline, 129
Steiff, Margarete, 195
Stengers, Isabelle, 279
stereo camera, 120
stereographs and stereoscopes, 119–43;
  prior development, types, and technol-
  ogy of, 124–8
stereotypies, 179, 181–2, 296
stockyards, 123–4, 131–2
Studio Ghibli, 238
surplus animals, 151
Sutcliffe, Anthony, 36

Takasakiyama Natural Zoological Garden, 237
Tatiana, 268
taxidermy, 49, 77. *See also* National Collection of Heads and Horns
teddy bear, 194–5
Terrace, Herbert, 114
theatricality, 28–30

theology and metaphysics, 38, 41, 278
Thomas, Oldfield, 58–9
Thompson, E.P., 170
Thurman, Judith, 284–5
Tierpark Hagenbeck, 155
Tilikum, 266–9
timber industry, 103
Tito, Josip, 286
Toronto Zoo. See *ARK*; pandas
trauma, 31–3
Trudeau, Justin, 211, 232
Trump, Erik, 153
Tsing, Anna, 11
tuberculosis, 102
Tyler, Tom, 9

Uddin, Lisa, 213, 228, 234n27, 254
Ueno Zoo, 240–1, 243, 258. *See also*
  Miller, Ian Jared
Uhlich, Gerald, 204–5
Ultimate Spinach, 290
Underwood & Underwood, 121, 138
United States Fish and Wildlife Service,
  215
Untermann, Ernest, 151

Van den Bergh, Walter, 176–7, 180–2
van Leeuwen, Theo, 194–5
vending machines, 154–5
Vernadsky, Vladimir Ivanovich, 283
Versailles Ménagerie, 24–33, 41
verticality, 277–9
Vincennes menagerie, 27
Virginia Zoo, 273
visuality, 124–8, 139–43

Wako, Kenji, 241
Walker, Ward R., 152
Ward, W. Peter, 223
Washington Park Zoo, 151, 154, 158
Wheatstone, Charles, 125–6
Wheeler, Wendy, 282
Wolf, Joseph, 58–9
Wolfe, Cary, 287, 293n26
Woodland Park Zoo, 148, 160

Xinjing Zoological and Botanical Gardens,
  245–6

Yerkes, Robert Mearns, 74, 89n36

Zetian, Wu, 214
Zhaohui, Lou, 232
zoesphere, 290
Zoo Atlanta, 264, 273
zoo baby, 192–4, 196–7, 203, 207, 232.
   See also Knut
zoo birds. *See* aeronautics
zoo celebrity, 82–4, 227. *See especially*
   animal biography; Knut
zoo history, 7–8, 170–1; academic literature of, 16–17; in Japan, 239–45
zoo marketing, 46
Zoo Miami, 268
zoo restaurants, 243–4
zoo studies, 7–11, 264, 273; academic literature of, 16–18

zoology, 75, 86, 127–8
zoomorphism, 255–7, 295
zoophobia, 242
zoos, contemporary: self-constructed
   identities, 51, 57, 61, 65, 138, 170,
   202–4, 215, 239–40, 247, 255, 266,
   271, 273
zoos during the Great Depression, 153,
   156, 160
zoos during war, 26–7, 147–62, 170,
   261n40; and gardening, 153–4; and
   killing animals, 150–2, 258; and mortality rates during World War II, 159–
   60; *Underground*, 286–7
Zulueta, Concepción Cortés, 93
Zwicewicz, Alicia, 306